The Story of The Great War

History of the European War from Official Sources

COMPLETE HISTORICAL RECORDS OF EVENTS TO DATE.
ILLUSTRATED WITH DRAWINGS, MAPS, *and* PHOTOGRAPHS

Prefaced by

WHAT THE WAR MEANS TO AMERICA
MAJOR GENERAL LEONARD WOOD, U. S. A.

NAVAL LESSONS OF THE WAR
REAR ADMIRAL AUSTIN M. KNIGHT, U. S. N.

THE WORLD'S WAR
FREDERICK PALMER

THEATRES OF THE WAR'S CAMPAIGNS
FRANK H. SIMONDS

THE WAR CORRESPONDENT
ARTHUR RUHL

Edited by

FRANCIS J. REYNOLDS   ALLEN L. CHURCHILL
Former Reference Librarian of Congress   *Associate Editor, The New International Encyclopedia*

FRANCIS TREVELYAN MILLER
Editor in Chief, Photographic History of the Civil War

P · F · COLLIER & SON COMPANY
NEW YORK

Generalissimo of the Armies of the Allies
MARECHAL FERDINAND FOCH

The
STORY OF THE
GREAT WAR

AMERICAN FOOD AND SHIPS
PALESTINE · ITALY| INVADED
GREAT GERMAN OFFENSIVE
AMERICANS IN PICARDY
AMERICANS ON THE MARNE
FOCH'S COUNTEROFFENSIVE

VOLUME VII

P. F. COLLIER & SON, NEW YORK

CONTENTS

PART I.—THE WESTERN FRONT

CHAPTER   PAGE

I. FRANCO-BRITISH FORCES VICTORIOUS AT YPRES—GERMANS LOSE GROUND AT LENS 9

II. FRENCH BREAK THE GERMAN LINES AT VERDUN—CANADIANS GAIN AT LENS 22

III. LENS IN RUINS—BRITISH ADVANCE NEAR YPRES 33

IV. HAIG STRIKES AGAIN AT YPRES—THE FRENCH BREAK THE GERMAN LINES ON THE AISNE 42

V. GERMAN RETREAT FROM CHEMIN-DES-DAMES—BRITISH ADVANCE TOWARD CAMBRAI 54

VI. GERMANS GAIN IN THE CAMBRAI AREA—COLD WEATHER HALTS IMPORTANT OPERATIONS 66

PART II.—THE UNITED STATES AS A BELLIGERENT

VII. THE NEW ALLY IN COUNCIL 77

VIII. ON THE LORRAINE FRONT 83

IX. POPE AND PRESIDENT 97

X. AMERICA'S WAR AIMS 102

XI. MOVING THE MILITARY MACHINE 111

XII. FLEETS IN THE MAKING 119

XIII. FOOD AS A WAR FACTOR 124

XIV. TRANSPORTATION AND FUEL 128

PART III.—REVOLUTIONARY RUSSIA

XV. THE LAST DAYS OF KERENSKY 134

XVI. THE BOLSHEVIST REVOLUTION 142

XVII. THE SIEGE OF THE WINTER PALACE 145

XVIII. THE BOLSHEVIKI AND THEIR LEADERS 147

XIX. FIRST BOLSHEVIKI PEACE MOVE 153

CONTENTS

PART III.—REVOLUTIONARY RUSSIA—*Continued*

CHAPTER   PAGE

XX. THE PEACE PARLEYS BEGIN 156
XXI. PUBLICATION OF SECRET TREATIES 158
XXII. THE PEACE NEGOTIATIONS 162
XXIII. AN ATTEMPTED COUNTER-REVOLUTION 165
XXIV. LEGISLATION BY DECREES 169

PART IV.—ITALIAN FRONT

XXV. THE CAPTURE OF MONTE SANTO 186
XXVI. THE STRUGGLE ON THE ISONZO FRONT 193
XXVII. THE AUSTRO-GERMAN OFFENSIVE IN ITALY 200
XXVIII. THE ITALIANS AT BAY ON THE PIAVE 208

PART V.—CAMPAIGNS IN PALESTINE, ARABIA MESOPOTAMIA, AND AFRICA

XXIX. THE PALESTINE CAMPAIGN 214
XXX. THE FALL OF JERUSALEM 223
XXXI. PALESTINE—ARABIA—MESOPOTAMIA 232

PART VI.—THE BALKANS

XXXII. THE BALKANS—GREECE AND MACEDONIA 245
XXXIII. RUMANIA 250

PART VII.—NAVAL AND AIR WARFARE

XXXIV. ON THE SEA 253
XXXV. THE WAR IN THE AIR 260

PART VIII.—THE WESTERN FRONT

XXXVI. PREPARING FOR THE GREAT OFFENSIVE—THE ATTACK OF MARCH 21—FIRST PHASE OF THE BATTLE 269
XXXVII. THE SECOND PHASE OF THE GREAT OFFENSIVE . . . 284
XXXVIII. THE GERMAN OFFENSIVE RENEWED—YPRES THREATENED —THE ALLIES' HEAVY LOSSES 298
XXXIX. DARK DAYS FOR THE ALLIES—THE GERMAN OFFENSIVE DECLINES—FRENCH GAIN IN THE RHEIMS REGION— BRITISH VICTORY AT HAMEL 310

CONTENTS

PART VIII.—THE WESTERN FRONT—*Continued*

CHAPTER   PAGE

XL. THE NEW GERMAN DRIVE AROUND RHEIMS—THE NEW BATTLE OF THE MARNE—THE ALLIES LAUNCH A NEW OFFENSIVE MOVEMENT 325

PART IX.—THE UNITED STATES AS A BELLIGERENT

XLI. FORCE TO THE UTMOST 339
XLII. THE AMERICAN LEGIONS 343
XLIII. RAIDING THE FOE 347
XLIV. AMERICA OVER THE TOP 351
XLV. AT SEICHEPREY AND XIVRAY 359
XLVI. ON THE CHEMIN-DES-DAMES 364
XLVII. BEFORE AMIENS 367
XLVIII. CANTIGNY 373
XLIX. AROUND CHATEAU-THIERRY 376
L. A DRIVE BY THE MARINES 381
LI. BELLEAU WOOD 387
LII. THEIR PRESENCE FELT 393
LIII. VAUX AND HAMEL 396
LIV. ACROSS THE MARNE AND BACK 400
LV. FORWARD WITH FOCH 405
LVI. FIGHTING THROUGH FORESTS 409
LVII. SERGY AND SERINGES 413

PART X.—RUSSIA

LVIII. THE PEACE WITHOUT TREATY 417
LIX. THE GERMANS RENEW HOSTILITIES WITH RUSSIA . . . 422
LX. THE PEACE TREATY THAT WAS SIGNED 426
LXI. CONTINUED GERMAN AGGRESSION 429
LXII. JAPANESE TAKE ACTION IN THE EAST 432
LXIII. GERMAN POLICY OF AGGRESSION 437
LXIV. GERMANY'S APPEAL TO CLASS HATRED 439
LXV. ASSASSINATION OF THE GERMAN AMBASSADOR 442
LXVI. THE MARCH OF THE CZECHO-SLOVAKS THROUGH SIBERIA . 444
LXVII. EXECUTION OF EX-CZAR NICHOLAS 447

CONTENTS

4

PART XI.—AUSTRO-ITALIAN CAMPAIGN

CHAPTER   PAGE

LXVIII. ITALY REVIVES 450

PART XII.—THE WAR ON THE SEA

LXIX. NAVAL WARFARE 460

PART XIII.—THE WAR IN THE AIR

LXX. BOMBING AND RECONNOISSANCE 475

PRONOUNCING VOCABULARY 489

INDEX 501

LIST OF ILLUSTRATIONS

MARSHAL FERDINAND FOCH, GENERALISSIMO OF THE ARMIES OF THE
ALLIES . . . . *Colored Frontispiece*

OPPOSITE PAGE

THE FRENCH VICTORY AT FORT MALMAISON 46
GENERAL DIAZ WITH FRENCH AND ITALIAN OFFICERS 206
THE SURRENDER OF JERUSALEM 222
MARSHAL FOCH, KING GEORGE, FIELD MARSHAL HAIG, GENERALS
PETAIN, FAYOLLE, DEBENEY, AND RAWLINSON 286
AMERICAN SOLDIERS STORMING CANTIGNY 366
CHATEAU-THIERRY WITH AMERICAN SOLDIERS ON GUARD 398
THE CRUISER "BROOKLYN" IN THE HARBOR OF VLADIVOSTOK . . . 446
THE CRUISER "VINDICTIVE" AFTER THE FIGHT AT ZEEBRUGGE . . . 462

5

LIST OF MAPS

PAGE

THE WESTERN BATTLE FIELD, SHOWING THE INTERNATIONAL FRONTIERS, THE IMPORTANT RAILWAYS, THE POSITION OF THE LINES AT THE CULMINATION OF IMPORTANT CAMPAIGNS, AND THE BATTLE FRONT AS IT EXISTED IN SEPTEMBER, 1918 . . . . *Colored Insert*

THE BATTLE FRONTS OF THE GREAT WAR—AS THE LINES WERE DRAWN IN BELGIUM, FRANCE, THE BALKANS, ITALY, PALESTINE, AND MESOPOTAMIA, SEPTEMBER, 1918. THE RUSSIAN FRONT HAD COMPLETELY DISAPPEARED . . . . *Colored Insert*

THE WESTERN FRONT FROM NANCY TO CALAIS (*Colored Map*) *Front Insert*

THE WESTERN FRONT, 1917-1918 11

THE TAKING OF MALMAISON AND CHEMIN-DES-DAMES 49

THE BATTLE OF CAMBRAI 68

AMERICAN FRONT IN FRANCE WHERE THE FIRST CLASHES BETWEEN AMERICANS AND GERMANS OCCURRED 87

THE ITALIAN ADVANCE IN ISTRIA 190

DIFFERENT STAGES OF THE ITALIAN RETREAT 205

THE CAMPAIGN IN PALESTINE 219

THE BRITISH ADVANCE IN MESOPOTAMIA AND PALESTINE 235

FIVE ZEPPELINS DESTROYED AFTER THE AIR RAID ON LONDON, OCTOBER 19-20, 1917 263

GERMAN OFFENSIVE FROM ARRAS TO THE OISE, MARCH-JUNE, 1918 . 271

RANGE OF THE GERMAN 80-MILE GUN 279

GERMAN ADVANCE BETWEEN YPRES AND ARRAS, MARCH-JUNE, 1918 . 292

GERMAN DRIVE TOWARD PARIS, WHICH BEGAN MAY 27, 1918. THIS MAP SHOWS THE FARTHEST ADVANCE 309

GERMAN THRUST SOUTH OF YPRES AND WHERE IT WAS STOPPED . . 316

WHERE FOCH DEFINITELY STOPPED THE GERMAN OFFENSIVE, JUNE 14, 1918 316

LINE-UP AT THE GREAT GERMAN OFFENSIVE, MARCH-JUNE, 1918 . . 323

ALLIED COUNTEROFFENSIVE ON THE MARNE 326

MILITARY ESTABLISHMENTS IN THE UNITED STATES 345

WHERE AMERICAN MARINES STOPPED THE GERMAN ADVANCE ON THE MARNE 383

8   LIST OF MAPS

                                                            PAGE
AUSTRIAN OFFENSIVE AND THE ITALIAN COUNTEROFFENSIVE, JUNE-
    AUGUST, 1918 453
THE "MONTELLO," WHERE THE AUSTRIAN OFFENSIVE BROKE DOWN . 457
AUSTRO-ITALIAN OPERATIONS ON THE LOWER PIAVE RIVER . . . 457
RAIDS OF GERMAN SUBMARINES ON UNITED STATES SHIPPING ON THE
    ATLANTIC COAST 465
ITALIAN NAVAL EXPLOITS 469
BRITISH NAVAL ATTACKS ON THE GERMAN BASES OF ZEEBRUGGE AND
    OSTEND 472

PART I — WESTERN FRONT

CHAPTER I

THE FRANCO-BRITISH FORCES VICTORIOUS AT YPRES — GERMANS LOSE GROUND AT LENS

ON August 1, 1917, the second day of the Franco-British offensive in Flanders, Field Marshal Haig's troops delivered a counterattack at a late hour of the night against the Germans north of Frezenberg, and close to the Ypres-Roulers railway. The assault, made through heavy rain that transformed the battle field into a morass, was a complete success, the British winning back lost ground on a front of 300 yards, which Prince Rupprecht had captured in a dashing attack a few hours before. At every point in this sector the British succeeded in driving out the enemy and completely reestablished their former lines.

In the morning and again in the afternoon of August 2, 1917, persistent and violent efforts were made by the Germans to win back lost territory to the east of Ypres. In spite of heavy losses they continued to attack at short intervals British positions from the Ypres-Roulers railway to St. Julien. Every assault was shattered by the British artillery barrage or the concentrated rifle fire of the British infantry.

Although the constant falling rain made observation difficult the British aviators continued active. When not scouting for the infantry they carried out daring attacks on the German aerodromes and on transport and infantry bodies with bombs and machine-gun fire. Few German machines ventured above the lines in the unfavorable weather. The British airmen brought down six machines and lost three.

The number of German prisoners captured in this sector had now risen to 6,122, of whom 132 were officers. The captured material included eight field guns, fifty-three machine guns and thirty-two mortars.

The territory about the Ypres salient showed the devastating character of the British fire. In many places the German dead lay in piles, and from their position it was evident that they were in the act of falling back when struck down. Many had fallen victims to their own artillery, when the German gunners in frenzied efforts to stem the onslaught of the Entente troops dropped shells among their own men.

East and southeast of Rheims the Germans attempted two surprise attacks on the French positions in the night of August 1, 1917, which were crushed. On the left bank of the Meuse there was violent artillery action, the Germans renewing their attacks at 9 o'clock in the evening in the sector of Avocourt Wood. The assaults failed, and cost the Germans heavy losses. In the same region in the Apremont Forest, southeast of St. Mihiel, attempts made to surprise the French met with disaster.

August 3, 1917, the British continued to regain ground lost to the Germans earlier in the week. They established themselves again in St. Julien. North of the Ypres-Roulers railway large bodies of Germans massing for a fresh attack were scattered by the well-directed fire of British guns and were unable to deliver the assault.

In the course of the day (August 3) the British drove out the Germans from most of the positions they had gained during the previous night east of Monchy-le-Preux, and in a determined push won considerable ground south of Hollebeke.

During the night of August 4, 1917, the Canadian troops to the southwest of Lens made a spirited dash and drove enemy patrols back 200 yards over a front of over 1,000 yards, sustaining very small losses in the operation. The majority of the Germans scurried back to Lens, but many were caught by the intense gunfire. The Canadians established themselves in the

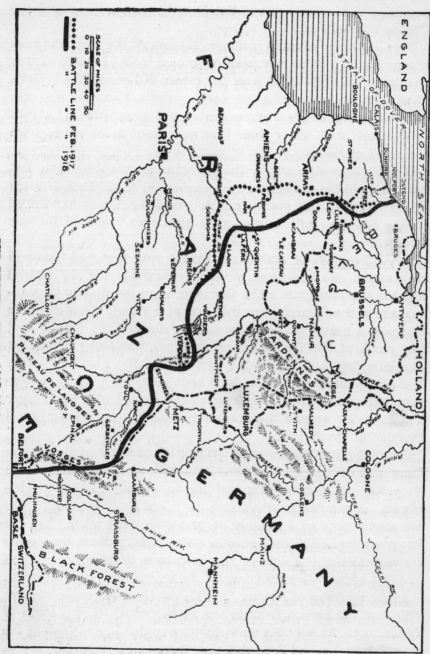

THE WESTERN FRONT, 1917–1918

buildings and ruins between the Lens-Grenay railway and the Cité du Moulin.

This dashing advance further tightened the British lines around the city. The new position gained by the Canadians was now less than 1,000 yards from the center of Lens on the western front. On the south, at Avlon and Leauvitte, Canadian outposts were now about a mile from the center, while opposite St. Laurent in the northwest sector their line was about 1,500 yards from the heart of the city.

No attempt was made by the Germans to recapture their lost positions and the Canadians were enabled to complete their work of consolidation. By morning of August 5, 1917, they had linked up the new line with barbed wire and were prepared for any emergency.

After five days of almost continuous rain that had hindered observation and hampered military operations the sky cleared and the sun shone out. The Germans were the first to take advantage of the favorable weather and at 5 o'clock in the morning launched a heavy attack against Hollebeke and the British post just north of the Ypres-Commines Canal, hoping to regain the positions they had lost in the first day of the Flanders battle. The onslaught was preceded by a tremendous fire from the German batteries to which the British guns replied with equal vigor and for miles around the ground was shaken by the continued thunder of great guns.

After shelling British positions south and north of the Ypres-Commines Canal the Germans attacked on both sides of the waterway and succeeded in gaining temporary footing in Hollebeke. A spirited counterattack launched by the British drove the enemy out and a number of prisoners were taken. On the left front the British continued to make gains, pushing their posts forward to the east side of the Steenbeek River along a front of about a mile, beginning near St. Julien and running northwest.

In the morning of August 5, 1917, the Germans made a heavy attack on the French front to the northwest of Rheims south of Juvincourt. At only one point they succeeded in penetrating the French trenches and from this they were quickly ejected. North

of the Aisne and at other points on the French front the Germans
attacked again and again, but were unable to win a foot of ground.

The Canadians, who had been closing in on Lens, made a further advance during the night of August 5, 1917, that carried
their outposts to the main line of the German defenses on the
railway embankment to the left of the city. Two battalions in
a hotly pressed attack captured a crater east of Cité du Moulin
and another to the north on the Lens-Lieven road, which runs
through the former place. These craters had been held in strong
force by the Germans from which they could work great damage
to the Canadians by rifle and grenade fire during the night. The
Canadians bombed their way forward through the ruins of
houses and fortified points and the Germans after feeble attempts
to hold fast retreated to their main positions. Having incorpo-
rated the craters in their advanced lines the Canadians rushed
forward and bombed two tunnels that were known to be occupied
by the enemy.

On the same night the British beat off two new attacks made
by Prince Rupprecht at Hollebeke southeast of Ypres and north
of Arleux.

The British lines around Lens were farther advanced on
August 6, 1917, when Canadian troops pushed forward 600 yards
over a front of about the same depth, a substantial addition to
their defenses south and west on the outskirts of the mining
center.

That the Germans were worried over the continued advance
made by the British, fearing the loss of Lens, was evidenced by
their practice of throwing a curtain of fire on the British trenches
at sunrise every day. In the morning of August 7, 1917, they
directed a heavy machine-gun barrage and artillery fire on a
crater recently captured by the Canadians. Under the protection
of this shower of shells the German infantry pushed forward
and the Canadians fighting stubbornly were forced to withdraw,
without, however, suffering any casualties.

On the Champagne front French troops during the night of
August 6, 1917, broke into the lines of the German Crown Prince
at three points, inflicting severe losses on the enemy and bringing

back prisoners. In the Verdun sector the Germans made futile attacks between Avocourt Wood and Hill 304. In Caurières Wood they gained a foothold for a time in the French first line, but were driven out by a counterattack on the following day (August 7).

The British front in Belgium to the north and east of Ypres was actively bombarded during the night of August 7, 1917. Near Lombaertzyde a British raiding party penetrated the German trenches and brought back prisoners and guns. In the early part of this same night the artillery on both sides was active over the Aisne front. Troops of the German Crown Prince attempted to reach the French lines to the east of Vauxaillon and west of the Californie Plateau but were driven back, their ranks shattered by the well-directed fire of the French guns. Other attempts at surprise attacks made by the Germans north of St. Mihiel and in upper Alsace were equally futile.

It was during the fighting at this time that the Germans introduced a curious device which they employed when withdrawing their batteries, and which would cause the opponents to believe that their guns were still in action. This was a mechanism with capsules filled with explosives which they placed on the site of the battery that had been, or was about to be, withdrawn. These capsules exploded at intervals of about half a minute, and heard at some distance would be mistaken for the reports of a field gun. Even an old campaigner would have been deceived by this device and led to believe that he was really facing artillery. By employing the mechanism the Germans were able to get their guns away unknown by their opponents, and it also prevented untimely attacks.

At an early hour in the morning of August 10, 1917, General Haig's troops by a dashing drive penetrated the German lines to a depth of several hundred yards, carrying completely the village of Westhoek and the remaining positions held by the enemy on Westhoek Ridge. Haig's successful stroke was delivered on a front of nearly two miles south of the Ypres-Roulers railway. Every forward position held by the Germans east of the town of Hooge on the fighting front between Frezenberg and the Ypres-

War St. 7—A

Menin road was won. This section had been the scene of some of the fiercest fighting on the first day of the great Flanders battle. The terrain offered many obstacles in the way of attack. The wooded sections had been strongly fortified by the Germans, and south of Westhoek the ground was broken by marshes that made military operations difficult.

Such was the spirit of the British troops on the morning of the 10th that every objective was won in a short time despite the frenzied efforts of the Germans to defend their positions. There was very heavy fighting in Glencorse Wood, where the British established themselves after inflicting heavy casualties on the Germans and taking 240 prisoners.

The British airmen during the day hovered over the scene of battle and engaged the enemy machines whenever they appeared. In every aerial engagement the British were victorious. Five German machines were destroyed and five others driven out of control. In addition two German observation balloons were brought down in flames and four others sent to earth badly damaged.

Late in the day of August 10, 1917, the German troops made no less than six desperate attacks on the British position on Westhoek Ridge, but in each offensive were driven off, their ranks shattered, and with heavy losses. The last futile attack was made at 10 o'clock at night, and after it failed the Germans began a furious bombardment of the sector above the village of Westhoek, which was continued throughout the night.

In spite of the repeated failure of their counterattacks the Germans renewed their efforts to regain the lost positions on the morning of August 11, 1917. The British, who had been exposed to heavy fire during the night in Glencorse Wood, were forced to give ground, for their position was a salient and presented an easy mark for the German guns near Polygon Wood and east of it.

About noon the British, having established their positions on Westhoek Ridge, sent a call for the guns to hold back the enemy while they strengthened their defenses. British airmen above the German lines had noted great gatherings of enemy troops in Nun's and Polygon Woods. British guns, in groups stretching miles back into the country, began to speak in thunderous tones. The Germans among the shell craters in and about Nun's Wood were moving forward when the British bombardment began. A storm of shells from the 15-inch "heavies" to the small but deadly 6-inch and 4.2s swept over them, around them, and through them. British airmen observed that as a result of this withering fire the Germans lay in heaps over the terrain and the shell craters which they had been unable to leave were full of dead and wounded. Close fighting continued during the day, but only at one point on the right could the Germans make any progress.

About 6 o'clock word came to the British gunners that German troops were gathered in the valley of Hannebeke. Two battalions had advanced some distance toward the British lines before the British guns got the range. In the storm of fire that swept through them the Germans tried to escape by flinging themselves into shell craters, but very few found safety.

The failure of their counterattacks seemed to have completely unnerved the German troops. Reserves that had been brought forward to relieve shattered battalions lost their head completely and wandered aimlessly about in the open, where they were shot down or surrendered.

The number of prisoners taken by the British since August 10, 1917, had now risen to 454, including nine officers. In the same operations six guns were captured.

During the night of August 11, 1917, French troops resumed their counterattacks against the positions which the Germans had captured during the night of August 9-10, 1917, north of St. Quentin. They were successful in recovering all the trench elements lost in the previous fighting, and also took a considerable number of prisoners. In the sector of Noissy Farm and Laffaux Mill French scouting parties penetrated the German lines at a number of points and returned with prisoners. South of Ailles German troops made a determined effort to recover trenches which the French had occupied a few days before. Two attacks were made with strong forces, the Germans displaying a reckless disregard of life, but their determined efforts came to naught and the attackers were dispersed with heavy losses. The French not only maintained their positions but in the course of the night made further progress.

During the day there was violent cannonading in Belgium and along the Aisne and in the Verdun region. The Germans also directed a scattered artillery fire all over the city of Rheims, killing two civilians and wounding another.

In the night of August 12, 1917, Lens became the center of activity on the British front. The Germans were desperately anxious to maintain their hold on this valuable city, because of its important position in the Pas de Calais coal fields.

The Canadian troops occupying strong positions in the western outskirts of the city received special attention from the German guns. They were continuously harassed too by German snipers hidden among the ruined houses to the north of the Lieven road, and early in the night of August 13, 1917, their advanced posts were pushed out over a front of 600 yards and the ruins occupied, the enemy offering only a slight resistance.

This advance brought the Canadians within 800 yards of the center of the city on the west. From houses on the other side of a belt of open ground covered with the débris of shattered buildings the Germans directed a heavy machine-gun fire on the Canadian positions. In the violent artillery duel that raged through the night the Canadian gunners had far the best of it, eight explosions being noted in German gun positions and their gun pits entirely destroyed.

Throughout the night of August 14, 1917, the British big guns were sending a stream of high-explosive shells into the German positions east and south of Loos while preparations were going forward for a big offensive movement. The attack began at 4.25 when the first light of dawn was glimmering in the east. For a short space of time the British guns were silent, but ten minutes before the Canadians, crouching in their trenches, received the order to move forward every British gun within range poured a steady stream of fire on the German positions. The battle scene was wrapped in pink-tinted clouds, shot with streaks of crimson fire. Just when the time arrived for the Canadians to strike, and when a protecting barrage was dropped before their trenches, the clouds parted and a pale-yellow moon poured its mild rays over the scene. It was by this light that the Canadians advanced to attack. They mounted the famous Hill 70, where so much blood had been spilled in days gone by, expecting that heavy fighting awaited them on the crest, which was well manned with machine guns. They were agreeably disappointed, however, for the German resistance was not strong. It was only when the Canadians gained the first houses in the outskirts that really strenuous fighting began. There was one point where the enemy was strongly intrenched in concreted cellars where a struggle of the deadliest description developed.

Lens before the war had a population of 30,000, but was now a mass of ruins. The Germans had constructed strong subterranean defenses, undermining the whole place with tunnels and dugouts reenforced with concrete. Such bits of ruined buildings that remained standing had been used for gun emplacements. It was through this stronghold that the Canadians had to force their way. The tremendous bombardment that preceded the attack had quite unnerved the Germans, and numbers were seen to desert their posts and flee to the rear, but in many parts of the outer defenses north and west of the city the garrison fought fiercely. In an hour and a half the Canadians had pushed forward 1,500 yards, having gained most of the outward bastion of Lens formed by the separate colonies, or "cités," so called, consisting of blocks of miners' cottages and works united in one big mining district.

The most important operation during the day, however, was the capture of Hill 70, which the British had taken and lost two years before, for the hill commanded a wide territory and was the last dominating position in this section that had remained in German hands.

August 16, 1917, marked another important advance for the French and British. Early in the morning the Allies, striking together on a nine-mile front east and northeast of Flanders, carried all their objectives excepting those on the right flank. French troops on the left drove the Germans from the tongue of land between the Yser Canal and the Martjevaart and won the bridgehead at Dreigrachten. Langemarck, which had been strongly held by the Germans since the Allied attack early in the month, was captured by Haig's troops, who swept forward half a mile beyond. On the right the British tried to win the high ground almost directly east of Ypres, lying north of the Menin road, but the Germans in face of appalling losses attacked in such fury that the British were forced to abandon the attempt.

More than 1,800 prisoners, including thirty-eight officers and a number of guns, were captured by the Anglo-French forces in this advance.

On the Lens battle front there was continuous fighting, the Germans making desperate efforts to recover their lost positions. The Canadians still clung tenaciously to Hill 70, having beaten off ten furious attacks directed by Prince Rupprecht. The Prussian Guard, so active in the fighting, here lost heavily. A Canadian machine-gun officer stated that his men had killed more Germans than they had ever seen together at any one time since fighting began here, having had as a target for an hour and a quarter enemy reenforcements coming up in columns of fours for use in counterattacks. The Seventh Prussian Division was completely annihilated. The fire of the Canadian guns was so intense that German ration parties refused to go to the relief of their comrades on the hill, and the hundreds of prisoners taken were in a half-famished condition, all the fighting spirit gone out of them.

It was noted in the struggle here that many of the Germans were mere children. A large number of boys, not over seventeen were in the thick of the battle, and some were even younger, belonging evidently to the 1919 class.

The attitude of the civilians who had been living in the suburbs of Lens would have puzzled a master psychologist. In the midst of terrors they remained calm and undismayed. Some had lived there since the beginning of the war, in houses that were repeatedly shelled and often wrecked. Death stalked them day and night. Yet they continued their peaceful vocations in cellars, their children being protected by gas masks going to school. When the British soldiers appeared, and while the shells were bursting a few yards away, young girls and women, for the most part neatly dressed and generally in black, were there to great with cheerful faces the welcome visitors.

On August 17, 1917, the French completed their conquest of enemy territory south of the St. Jansbeek River and the Breenbeek River by the capture of two strong German redoubts which had held out against all attacks since the beginning of the great offensive on the 16th. One redoubt, Les Lilas, was a large concrete and steel structure strongly armed with machine guns. It was impregnable against infantry attacks, and it was only when the French brought heavy guns to bear on the stronghold that the German garrison surrendered. Mondovi Farm, the other redoubt, lay in an angle formed by the St. Jansbeek and the Breenbeek Rivers. The French bombarded the redoubt during the night of the 17th, and after the concrete walls were shattered and crumbling the enemy surrendered. Attempts were made later by the Germans to shell the French out of the captured stronghold, but were not successful.

On this date the Germans counterattacked in force against the Canadian positions northwest of Lens. According to prisoners the German troops had been ordered to retake Hill 70 at any cost. In the afternoon of the 17th the first great attack was made, a fierce and determined onslaught accompanied by a storm of flaming projectiles and gas shells. The Canadians met the attack with cold steel, and the Germans were driven back in confusion with heavy losses. Another assault made in the evening against the suburb of St. Emilie and at Hugo Wood to the north failed with serious losses to the attackers.

At 1.30 in the morning of the 18th the Germans were again in action. Along the entire line north of Lens their infantry attacked, supported by a concentrated artillery fire. They fought with reckless bravery, hurling themselves again and again upon the Canadians in hand-to-hand conflicts of the fiercest description. The latter held their ground, though sorely beset by superior numbers. The Germans were loath to give ground, clinging to every foot, but were slowly forced back, their ranks shattered, leaving many dead and wounded on the field. This was the most sanguinary fighting in which the Canadians had engaged since the capture of Hill 70. Never before had they used the bayonet so freely or met the enemy in such a man-to-man grapple to the death.

During the day French and British aviators were engaged in many successful combats in the air. The British downed thirty German aeroplanes, twelve of which were known to have been destroyed. Twelve British machines were missing, two having collided during the fighting and fallen within the enemy lines. On this day, and during the night of August 17-18, 1917, French aviators shot down seven German airplanes and a captive balloon and forced down eight other machines, which, badly damaged, fell in the German lines. A bombing raid in which 111 French machines took part in various sorties dropped 13,000 kilograms (28,600 pounds) of projectiles on aviation grounds at Colmar, Friedrichshafen, and Habsheim. Aviation camps and railway stations at other points were showered with projectiles, producing fires and explosions.

British troops on the front northeast of Ypres made a further advance in an attack made in the morning of August 18, 1917, in the vicinity of the Ypres-Poelcappelle road east of Langemarck. By this operation the British advanced their lines 500 yards on a like front, winning all their objectives, including a series of strongly fortified farms. Southeast of Epihy a successful local operation was carried out by the British troops in the early morning of the following day, when German trenches in the neighborhood of Guillemont Farm were captured and a considerable number of prisoners.

It was in this the fourth year of the war that the Germans made some radical changes in their methods of defense, owing principally to the preponderance of British artillery, which reduced their front-line trenches to mere furrows of earth and made mantraps of the carefully constructed dugouts. The Germans now scattered their advanced forces over a greater depth. There was no longer an unbroken line of defenses for the British guns to shatter, but strongholds were constructed in isolated shell holes along the front, cunningly concealed from aviators. These stretched back from the first lines to a considerable depth. Along the front strong outposts were established at some distance apart, backed by fortified craters and connected by tunnels and often with dugouts.   Back of these shell-hole nests were gun emplacements commanding the openings between the shell holes. Thus when enemy attackers had forced their way through the fortified shell craters they were met with torrents of machine-gun fire.   Further back from these defenses there would be found a line of more or less connected trenches, or a series of connected fortified shell holes.   The Germans also constructed strong concrete redoubts in every farm house for their machine guns.   They built small forts of steel and concrete that were impervious to artillery fire.   Many of these strongholds were constructed underground with a steel trapdoor as the only exit, by which the Germans came out to set up their machine guns.

CHAPTER II

THE FRENCH BREAK THE GERMAN LINES AT VERDUN—CANADIANS GAIN AT LENS

NORTH of Verdun, in a region that had witnessed many of the most desperate struggles of the campaign in France during the previous year, the French won a great victory on August 20, 1917.   After three days of almost continuous shelling of the German lines the French armies attacked simultaneously on both banks of the Meuse and carried their objectives at all points.   On the west bank of the river they gained Avocourt Wood, the summit of the famous Dead Man Hill, and the Corbeaux and Cumières Woods.   The French advance reached at some points a depth of a mile and a quarter.   Over 4,000 unwounded Germans were made prisoner.

At 4.40 in the morning the French artillery preparations reached the final phase when vigorous attacks were made on Avocourt Wood and Bezonvaux.   The first objective was won by 6 o'clock and German prisoners were on their way to the rear. The three days' artillery fire had so devastated Hill 304, Dead Man Hill, and Talou Ridge that the Germans were forced to abandon their first line. The French found less opposition from the enemy than they had expected, for the well-served French guns had taken much of the fighting spirit out of their opponents. At some points, however, where the French fire had been less felt there was hard fighting. The greatest advance made was on the right bank of the river to the north of Vacherauville. They occupied Talou Ridge, Mormont Farm, and Hills 240 and 344. To the east the Germans were driven out of parts of the Fosses and Chaume Woods.

During the advance the French army was greatly aided in its operations by the brilliant and daring work of its aviators. Hovering low they showered machine-gun bullets on the enemy lines, dispersing assemblies forming for counterattacks and bombing German gunners at close quarters. In a series of combats in the air the French flyers brought down eleven German machines on the Verdun front, while two others were destroyed by antiaircraft guns.

An interesting phase of the fighting on the French front at this time was the unusually large proportion of German officers captured, 201 being taken with about 6,700 men. This seemed to show that the German officer class had deteriorated, that the best trained had been killed or made prisoners, and that the new officers who replaced them were lacking in spirit or had not become steeled to war work.

In the fighting on this front certain German army formations had been badly smashed. Three regiments which formed the Sixth Reserve Division of Brandenburgers and the kaiser's favorite troops were literally annihilated as fighting units, losing sixty-nine officers and about 2,800 men as prisoners.

On the same day that the French were advancing in the Verdun sector the Canadians around Lens were winning fresh laurels. Northwest of the city they had by desperate fighting established strong posts among the trenches and railway cuttings that formed the last line of German defense in that quarter. This was the scene of much strenuous but indecisive fighting two days before.

From their new positions the Canadians had now command of the last bit of ground from which the defenders of the city could overlook the advance from the west. They were now in a hollow all around the front which swings about Lens in a semicircular form. As every eastern exit to the city was now subjected to a continuous and harassing fire from machine guns and artillery, the work of bringing up provisions and supplies of ammunition had become extremely hazardous.

The Canadians in their continued struggle around Lens had displayed such irresistible courage and resolution that their deeds will long be remembered in the pages of history. No soldiers during the war faced more difficulties or confronted more formidable defenses. They forced their way through streets entangled with hedges of steel and houses bristling with machine guns. They penetrated tunnels too strong to be touched by shell fire. They threw themselves against fortress positions amid a fiery hail of shells and explosives. They swept through the towns of St. Laurent, St. Théodore, and St. Emilie to the north and west of Lens where sunken roads and slag heaps were strongly fortified, and so on through the apparently endless and formidable defenses to the western streets of the inner city.

The Germans never let a day pass without at least one attack on the Canadian positions, and once within twenty-four hours they launched no less than seven strong assaults. Between the attacks the men of Canada were subjected to a heavy gunfire from a wide semicircle of strong batteries.

Between August 10 and August 20, 1917, they were attacked in turn by six German divisions, each being shattered by the Canadians' dogged courage and amazing fighting power. These were the Seventh, Eighth, the Eleventh Reserve, the 220th and the First Guards Reserve Division. Besides those five divisions it was known that portions at least of the 185th Division and of the Sixth Reserve Division had also been engaged.

It was conservatively estimated by military observers of the struggle here that the German strength used at Lens was upwards of 50,000 men, and their losses were estimated at between 12,000 and 15,000 men.

At an early hour in the morning of August 20, 1917, the Canadians made a trench raid on the German front northwest of Avlon, where heavy fighting ensued. This front was strongly fortified by the Germans as protection for an important mining suburb southeast of Lens, and it was here that they had set up the guns withdrawn after the Canadian advance two days before. Here the hand-to-hand fighting was fierce and deadly, the Germans fighting with desperate courage, but the Canadians got the upper hand by slow degrees, and after inflicting heavy casualties took some prisoners and retired to their positions.

Early in the morning of the following day the forces from Canada again struck hard, attacking German trenches west and northwest of Lens. The battle raged throughout the day and far into the night. The Canadians advanced against strong opposition, using bomb and bayonet freely, winning important enemy positions to the northwest and southwest of the center of the city. It appears that the Germans had massed strong forces for a counterattack at daybreak against the newly won Canadian positions, and had already begun their forward push when they encountered the Canadians rushing across no-man's-land. Owing to a dense mist that prevailed at the time, the Germans did not see them until the foe fell upon them with bomb and bayonet.

This dramatic surprise for the Germans seemed to have had a chilling effect on their fighting spirit. They retreated in wild haste to the trenches they had left, despite the frenzied attempts of their officers to rally them. Close on their heels dashed the Canadians, and mounting the parapets showered bombs among the other troops that had gathered for the attack. As the Germans fled for the communication trenches the Canadians leaped among them, and with bomb and bayonet killed a great number.

In the Verdun region on this date the French continued to make important gains. All day long the tide of battle ebbed and flowed in waves of fire. On the left bank of the Meuse the French captured the famous Côte de l'Oie and the village of

Régneville. On the right bank of the river, sweeping through Samogneux, they seized an entire system of trenches between that village and Hill 344 which had been won on the previous day. The Germans delivered a number of strong and determined attacks on both sides of the river, but lost heavily in their attempts to check the French advance. Some idea of the French gains on the left bank of the Meuse may be gathered from the fact that when the Germans held the village of Fleury and menaced Verdun they were two and a half miles from the fortress. On August 21, 1917, when the French held the village of Samogneux, the Germans were seven miles from the fortifications.

Throughout the day's fighting the German counterattacks failed completely. The French maintained all their gains and organized captured positions. Nearly 7,000 prisoners were taken during the advance, of whom 116 were officers.

The capture of Dead Man Hill by the French troops was an especially notable achievement, for its system of underground defenses made it as nearly impregnable as human ingenuity could devise. That it could be captured in a single day was owing to the ceaseless activity of the French gunners, who had ravaged the stronghold with explosives so thoroughly that it seemed impossible that anything human could survive, however hidden underground. There were a hundred deserters to the French lines, and the Germans surrendered in squads with their noncommissioned officers. The whole garrison of Dead Man Tunnel, which included two battalion commanders, were also made prisoners. When it is considered that the Germans had 400 batteries in action back of their front lines during the two days' advance it will be understood that the French fighting man was heartened up and could look with confidence to the future.

The British resumed the offensive in the morning of August 22, 1917, east and northeast of Ypres along the Ypres-Menin road, capturing a series of fortified farms and strong points in front of their positions and gaining in the advance a third of a mile of territory.

Further to the north the British carried forward their lines about half a mile over a front of two and a half miles. Owing to the fierce character of the fighting encountered in the forward push the number of prisoners taken was out of all proportion to the total losses inflicted on the enemy. Since the offensive began in the morning of August 15, 1917, the British had taken 1,378 men, including officers. In the same period they captured thirty-one machine guns and twenty-one trench mortars.

South and southwest of Lens the Canadians continued to fight hard and to make important gains. They succeeded in getting a firm grip on a stronghold only 300 yards south of the main railway station of the town. This was a huge slag pile which had been tunneled by the Germans and was known as "Green Crassier." The odd position constituted a barrier between the Canadians and the defenses of the city proper. It was connected by tunnels with dugouts and defenses underneath Lens, and the Germans, appreciating its value, clung to it tenaciously. Preceded by a heavy bombardment the Canadians attacked at early dawn and were atop of the Germans before the latter had any warning of what was impending. The long series of counterattacks in which they had been engaged during the previous days had not entirely quenched the German fighting spirit, and the slag pile was such a network of defenses that the Canadians were from the start roughly handled, but they held on with dogged determination, though they had never faced more formidable conditions, and despite the desperate efforts of the Germans to oust them. Surrounding the slag pile or "crassier" many of the ruined buildings had been transformed into strong and most ingeniously constructed fortifications. The Canadians systematically bombed their way through these defenses and drove out the defenders, who sought refuge in the numerous tunnels under the city. Lens was crowded with German troops of the Fourth Guards Division and the First Guards Reserve. Forced to live among the dead and wounded in underground caves, their lot was hideous beyond description.

French troops operating in the Verdun sector gained an important victory on August 24, 1917. In the early morning they began a powerful offensive on the left bank of the Meuse between Avocourt Wood and Dead Man Hill. By a single charge they carried Hill 304 and Camard Wood to the west of it. All the German positions were captured and the defenders made prisoners. To make doubly secure their possession of Hill 304, the French pushed on beyond it for a distance of about a mile and a quarter. The loss of Hill 304 and Dead Man Hill, which commanded all the approaches and ravines as far as Douaumont, deprived the Germans of every observation point from which they could watch the operations of the French troops.

The Germans won some success against the British forces along the Ypres-Menin road on this date, while the Canadians were forced to retire from the crest of the "crassier," or slag-pile stronghold, and to take up positions adjoining it. The Germans had succeeded in bringing forward fresh troops against the Canadians, who were worn down but not discouraged by almost continuous fighting day and night. The enemy had the advantage of numberless underground retreats, tunnels, subterranean chambers, and a network of cellars connected by passages from which they could dash suddenly, and after striking a shrewd blow disappear mysteriously from sight. The Germans were in a precarious situation and showed a disposition to conserve their forces.

On the Verdun front the French continued their victorious progress, capturing north of Hill 304 three strongly fortified works near Bethincourt. Since the beginning of this offensive the French had taken over 8,000 prisoners. If they cherished any belief in the superiority of the Germans as fighters, they held it no longer. The German High Command had issued orders that every position must be held regardless of the cost, but except in isolated instances they had displayed no unusual fighting qualities, while the German officers often perpetrated amazing blunders.

The French renewed the offensive on August 25, 1917, when they delivered a smashing blow on the right bank of the Meuse in the Verdun sector, gaining two-thirds of a mile on a front of two and a half miles. This gave them possession of the Fosses and Beaumont Woods and brought them to the outskirts of Beaumont. Violent artillery fighting continued around Hill 304 during the day. The French continued the drive, pushing their advanced posts forward to the southern outskirts of the village of Bethincourt and Forges Brook. A violent counterattack made by the Germans from Wavrille Wood was caught by French artillery fire and driven back shattered and in disorder.

On the British front during the night of August 25, 1917, the Germans were driven out of a trench northeast of Guillemont Farm which they had captured earlier in the day. In the morning of August 26, 1917, British troops attacking east of Hargicourt on a front of over a mile won half a mile of ground, and carried by assault strong enemy positions at Cologne and Malakoff Farms. About the same hour of the morning when this advance was made the Germans under cover of a heavy bombardment attacked in the neighborhood of the Ypres-Menin road. In this assault flame projectors were freely used and they succeeded for a brief time in recovering positions in the northwest corner of Inverness Copse. Before they could organize their defenses the British rallied and in a hotly pressed counterattack drove them out and reestablished their positions.

The British did not undertake any infantry action on a large scale during the next few days, but their guns, which far outmatched the Germans', were not taking a rest. An eyewitness whose experience covered many battle fields said he had never seen so many guns great and small as on the wide stretch of country back of Ypres. For miles he walked through concentric lines of batteries and estimated that the British were able to fire a hundred shells to the Germans' one. It was probably with the hope of saving man power that the Germans now built concrete blockhouses in front-line positions capable of holding a score of men, while keeping their main forces far back for counterattacks. But notwithstanding their new methods of defense the Germans lost heavily, for the British guns in forward positions kept the enemy support lines under a constant and blasting fire.

Owing to the fine weather the German aviators were active. In the course of a number of aerial engagements the British brought down four German aeroplanes and drove three others out of control, losing two of their own machines.

It had been circulated throughout the German press that the kaiser's forces had abandoned Hill 304 to the French for strategical reasons. This was disproved by the discovery of an order signed by the German commander in this sector of the Verdun front addressed to his troops, who were urged to hold the hill at any cost and emphasized the importance of the position as a point of observation.

The new French line on the west of the Meuse, now supported by the commanding positions on Hill 304 and Dead Man Hill, ran a mile beyond these strongholds, facing Forges Brook. On the heights east of the Meuse and along the river the line of the French left was now extended at Samogneux and on Hill 344. From this point the front runs eastward down hill past Mormont Farm to the Vacherauville-Beaumont highroad, then along the ravine between the Louvemont and Beaumont Woods up to the plateau, including what remained of the larger wood of Les Fosses, and so across the north to the Chambrettes Farm.

A comparative calm reigned in the Verdun region during August 27-28, 1917. The Germans attempted a few feeble counterattacks, and there were times when their guns became vociferous, but no important operation was begun, and the French had ample time to consolidate their gains and strengthen the newly won positions.

In the midst of a driving rain British troops in Flanders launched an attack in the afternoon of August 27, 1917, along the St. Julien-Poelcappelle road. They had set out to seize some of the concrete fortifications, each of which held a score or so of Germans with machine guns and heaps of ammunition, who could sweep a wide field with fire and had caused the British many losses in men. The Steenbeke and Hannebeke Rivers had overflowed and transformed the region round into bogs. Into this marshland the men from Yorkshire and other English counties, drenched to the skin from being out all night, struggled forward to destroy the Germans' "pill boxes." There was violent fighting near the Springfield and Vancouver Farms northeast of St. Julien, which were strongly held by the Germans. The machine-gun fire was especially heavy at these places, but the British pushed forward and the Württembergers who had been sent up from Roulers to strengthen the German advance posts, were driven back. The British succeeded in capturing two of the concrete forts, making prisoners of the defenders.

On the Aisne front northwest of Hurtebise the Germans during the night of September 1, 1917, tried by desperate assaults to recover lost positions, but were driven off by gunfire. North of Hill 304, on the same date there was intermittent artillery activity, and on the heights above the river the French foiled two attempted surprise attacks.

Near Lens and La Bassée the Germans endeavored to raid British trenches, but were repulsed. Southwest of Havrincourt they achieved a temporary success, bombing their way into British advanced posts and forcing the defenders to fall back. But the British quickly rallied, and by a dashing counterattack forced out the invaders and reoccupied the posts, taking prisoners and leaving a considerable number of dead Germans on the field.

The reappearance of the sun and fair weather after days of rain made it possible to resume military operations. The Germans were the first to attack during the night of September 2, 1917, a British position southwest of Havrincourt. The assault was preceded by a heavy bombardment in which gas shells were freely used, but the British artillery and machine-gun fire was so intense that the attackers were driven back in disorder.

Southeast of Monchy on the same date the British carried out a successful raid on the German trenches that proved a complete surprise to the enemy. British troops were atop of the Germans before they could make a strong defense, but finding they were inferior in numbers the raiders, after destroying many of the enemy, withdrew with their prisoners.

At Lens, where the Canadians had been holding on with grim determination to portions of the famous "crassier," or slag pile, and among the ruins adjoining, surrounded by nests of Germans and subjected to almost continuous fire, there was renewed activity with the clearing weather. During the night of September 3, 1917, the "Kanucks" struck in upon the outer shell of Lens, gaining 250 yards on a 600-yard front. This was really an ad-

War St. 7—C

vance of importance, considering the nature of the ground fought over. For the neighborhood was packed with Germans, who had guns everywhere. This forward push brought the Canadians in some places to the north of Lens, where there was only an open space of about 300 yards between their positions and the buildings of the city proper.

Fair weather brought renewed fighting on the Champagne and Verdun fronts. No day passed without a German attack, but the French, occupying commanding positions, were successful in holding their own and slightly extended their gains.

In this first week of September the British air service carried on an extensive campaign of bombing German bases back of the lines of Belgium and northern France. Tons of bombs and explosives were dropped with good results on railway tracks at Ghent, on aerodromes near Cambrai, Courtrai, and Lille, and on billets around Douai. German air raids over the British lines one night killed thirty-seven German prisoners and wounded forty-eight.

Early in the morning of September 6, 1917, troops from British Columbia, operating on the edge of the city of Lens, captured a row of houses 300 yards long occupied by four companies of German troops. This important success served to further reduce the area within Lens that still remained in German hands.

North of Frezenberg the British carried some strong positions and dispersed a hostile counterattack launched against them later in the day. In the evening the Germans returned in strength to the attack and forced the British out.

The Canadians around Lens continued to be in the center of the storm. In the morning of September 7, 1917, the Germans counterattacked all along the front to the west of Lens. After repeated efforts of extreme violence the Canadians were bombed out of part of their positions, but in the area of the slag pile or "crassier" the men from overseas extended their holdings and the new front they established now became a serious menace to German positions along the north side of the Souchez River. This latest advance so enraged the enemy that their entire front was deluged with the heaviest shells that had ever been seen in this area, while from time to time clouds of gas were released which blotted out the scene of the battle, but not the intrepid Canadians, whose gas masks afforded perfect protection.

On the French front there was continuous activity. Every time that the German press gave notice to its public that the French military power was waning and had become a negligible factor in the war the indomitable Gauls by some dashing attack gave evidence that they were very much alive and had no thought of surrender.

For some days the French in the Verdun sector had been busy every day in beating off German attacks, but on September 8, 1917, they assumed the offensive on the right bank of the Aisne and occupied important positions on a front of a mile and a half, capturing during the advance over 800 prisoners. Assaults on the French lines east of Rheims and on the Aisne front resulted in crushing German defeats. At almost every point the French wall of defense held firm, and against it the seasoned troops of the kaiser, who lacked neither persistence nor bravery, dashed themselves in vain.

CHAPTER III

LENS IN RUINS—BRITISH ADVANCE NEAR YPRES

FRENCH positions on the right bank of the Meuse north of Verdun were attacked by strong German forces in the morning of September 9, 1917. The assault was delivered over a front of about two miles on both sides of Hill 344. In one section of the line the Germans succeeded in gaining a temporary foothold. By a vigorous counterattack made a little later the French drove them out and captured fifty prisoners. This smashing blow had cost the Germans dearly, for they left over 1,000 dead on the battle field.

On this date (September 9) the British forces carried out successful local operations southeast of Hargicourt, when Northumberland troops carried by storm 600 yards of German trenches and took fifty-two prisoners. East of Malakoff Farm the British attacked and won after heavy fighting a strip of hostile trenches which was much needed to round out their lines in that sector.

German prisoners captured around Lens spoke of the awful havoc wrought by the British gas cylinders and gas shells. The German First Guards Reserve Regiment lost twenty men when a gas shell exploded in the cellar where they lay asleep. Another company of this regiment had seventeen casualties from the same cause in one day. The failure of Germany to get a sufficient supply of rubber was a contributing cause of the gas fatalities. German masks were of poor quality and tore easily. Masks of soft leather were used by them at this time on some parts of the Lens front. The objection to masks of leather was that they could not be put on as easily as those made of rubber, a serious defect when a moment's delay might prove fatal.

Northumberland troops operating in the neighborhood of Villaret extended their gains southward 400 yards in an attack made on German trenches in the morning of September 11, 1917. During the day the Germans attempted three counterattacks with bombs on the new British positions but were driven off.

The French continued active in the Verdun region, where they had to defend themselves from frequent counterattacks. In the Champagne territory French troops struck a shrewd blow on September 11, 1917, when in successful raids they drove across the German trenches between St. Hilaire and St. Souplet and penetrated the second line. Here there was intense and deadly fighting. The German defenders were either killed or made prisoners, and the French captured large quantities of supplies.

North of Caurières Wood, northeast of Verdun, the French advanced line on a front of about 500 yards penetrated the German trenches and close fighting developed. This was the scene of continuous attacks and counterattacks for two days in which each side gained in turn a temporary ascendancy, but the result was indecisive. It was not until the night of September 14-15, 1917, that the French succeeded in ejecting the Germans

from the greater part of the trench system here and took possession. In Champagne on September 14, 1917, a surprise attack
made by the French in the region of Mont Haut was successfully
carried out. A German observatory and a number of shelters
and dugouts were destroyed and much damage wrought to the
enemy defenses.

No important operation was attempted by the British troops
around Lens for several days following, but bombardments were
incessant. The Canadians, though constantly under fire and
subjected day and night to strong attacks, firmly held their
positions. The situation of the Germans in the center of Lens
with an active enemy occupying high ground to the north and
south was not a comfortable one. When they did fight it was
with rage and despair. Prisoners taken told of the deadly effects
of the British gas projectiles which wrought awful havoc among
the troops herded in tunnels and dugouts. The constant bombardment of Lens had reduced the city to the same ruined condition as the suburbs. The subterranean caverns which the
Germans had built by the forced labor of civilians two years
and more before became death traps. Often they collapsed under
a heavy bombardment, burying alive whole companies in the
ruins. Again, as frequently happened, a shell would explode
inside the caves with fatal results to the occupants.

The Germans had every reason to wish that they had never
introduced poison gas in warfare, for as employed by the British
it had become a far deadlier destructive weapon than in their
own hands. Many times during these days the Canadians had
flooded the city with gas which soaked down into the tunnels and
dugouts and stifled men in their sleep, or they died with their
masks on if they delayed a second too long.

After days of raids and counterattacks insignificant when
considered as separate operations, but important in the aggregate, British troops under Field Marshal Haig delivered a powerful attack against the German lines east of Ypres on an eight-
mile front on September 20, 1917. According to an eyewitness,
the barrage that preceded the advance was the heaviest on
record.

The British were successful in attaining all their objectives. The German center along the Ypres-Menin road was penetrated to the depth of a mile.

Rain had fallen steadily during the night preceding the assault, but the assembling of the regiments assigned to the operation was carried through without a mishap. North Country troops carried the Inverness Copse. Australian troops stormed Glencorse Wood and Nonneboschen (Nun's Wood); Scottish and South African brigades captured Potsdam, Vampire, and Borey Farms; West Lancashire Territorials carried Iberian Farm and the strong point known as Gallipoli. After making a swift "clean-up" of these places and positions the British forces advanced on the final objectives.

Troops from the counties who drove forward on the right encountered fierce opposition in the woods north of the Ypres-Commines Canal, and in the vicinity of the Tower Hamlets, but cut through with mighty thrusts and gained the desired goal with light casualties. In the center North Country and Australian battalions pierced German positions to a depth of over a mile and won all their objectives, which included the village of Veldhoek and the western part of Polygon Wood. Zevenkote, farther north, was won and the London and Highland Territorials made a clean sweep of the second line of farms, including Rose, Quebec, and Wurst Farms, all on the line of their final objectives.

Though the Germans were prepared, the British advance worked smoothly. Some of the hardest fighting was encountered south of Langemarck to the Ypres-Roulers railway, where there were numerous strong concrete and steel redoubts. Many positions like Rose and Quebec Farms were captured by the British in the face of deadly machine-gun fire, and over a terrain of heavy mud and through pools of water.

When the advance was begun and the Australians went over the top, a heavy barrage was dropped by the Germans just back of them, but many shells fell among the advancing men and caused a number of casualties. The Australians were in an unpleasant situation, but pressed cheerfully forward without pause and gained Anzac Farm, where their standard was raised in honor of the victory.

In the course of the evening the British in local attacks northeast of Langemarck drove the Germans out of the last strong points in that region, and like operations were successfully carried out on the rest of the front, the enemy offering only slight opposition.

The Germans lost heavily at every point, especially around the Anzac Ridge, where they counterattacked six times. This ridge was one of the key positions east of Ypres and the German command appreciated its importance.

There was little change in the situation on the day following the advance, though local fights occurred, where the Germans still held on to some small defense, or redoubt, which the British needed to consolidate with their new line.

The British captured during the push over 3,000 men of all ranks. German officers paid an unwilling tribute to the British artillery and machine-gun service, which had virtually shattered every attempted counterattack.

The new German method of holding lines by small garrisons in concrete blockhouses with large reserves behind for counterattacks had broken down completely.

Massed attacks were made by the Germans on September 22, 1917, against the positions captured by the British in the recent drive, but only at one advanced point on the line did they meet with success. There was every evidence that the Germans were making desperate efforts to stem the advancing tide of British troops, regardless of the cost. In the main their attacks broke down, and where they gained a little ground it hardly compensated them for the frightful loss of life incurred. The British were forced to yield ground south of the Ypres-Menin road, where they had not as yet consolidated their positions. The Germans attacked in waves from the height, and in the hand-to-hand fighting that developed, both sides pounding away with their heaviest guns, there ensued one of the fiercest struggles of the war.

East of St. Julien the Teutons pierced the British line, but were almost immediately thrust out by a spirited counterattack. Three times the Germans assaulted the front east of Langemarck, but after heavy losses and having failed to gain the slightest advantage they drew off, greatly reduced in numbers.

During these days of heavy fighting the British airmen were continually active. The weather favored observation and scout aeroplanes and balloons performed invaluable service in finding the range for Haig's guns and in locating centers of attack where a shower of shells was needed. Over the wide battle area British aircraft swept in flocks, raining down death and destruction in their flight. Ten tons of bombs were dropped, the stations at Roulers, Menin, and Ledeghem were squarely hit, an aerodrome bombarded, while masses of German troops moving along the Ypres-Menin road were showered with explosives. These offensive operations from the air cost the British in all a dozen machines. Ten German airships were brought down and eight others were driven out of control.

Though the battle of Menin road had practically ended, the British continued to add slightly to their gains, and to strengthen their positions. North of Langemarck in Flanders they won additional German defenses in the morning of September 23, 1917, and took a number of prisoners. Since the offensive began on the 20th, the British had captured 3,243 Germans, of whom eighty were officers.

It was in the course of the fighting in Flanders that the Germans employed a new kind of frightfulness in some attacks. British troops reported that they were fired on by "flaming bullets" that set the clothing afire. It was related that men struck by these bullets had to be rolled in the mud to extinguish the flames.

During these days of busy fighting on the British front in Flanders French troops along the Aisne and the Meuse Rivers were constantly engaged in local fights with the enemy, though no important operations were attempted. The French command was exceedingly careful not to waste men unless there was some highly important advantage to be gained, contented to act on the defensive until a master stroke could be delivered. The German troops were not spared in the same way, but were constantly driven forward by their inexorable masters and lost heavily in futile attacks.

On September 24, 1917, the Teutons took the offensive at an early hour in the morning. On the right bank of the Meuse four German battalions, supported by special assaulting troops, made a drive against French trenches north of Bois le Chaume, along a front of about a mile and a half. The French "75's" broke the front of the attack, but in the center some trench elements were pierced by the Germans and violent fighting ensued. It was a short, sharp struggle at close quarters, when the French forced out the invaders and reoccupied the positions. Two other German attacks on the same front were made in the afternoon in which they gained nothing, while the French took fifty prisoners.

A more ambitious attempt was made on the same day to force the French from their positions that extended from the northwest corner of Fosses Wood to the eastern fringe of Chaume Wood, in the Verdun area. The Germans began the assault with sprays of liquid flame, which was followed by a furious grenade attack and bombardment. The intrepid French troops dashed out to meet their assailants and with bayonet and hand grenade drove them in disorder back to their trenches. There were numerous hand-to-hand struggles between the lines. The Germans made extraordinary efforts to regain lost ground around Hill 352, which offered every advantage for observation, but they were unable to break through the steel wall of French resistance. At Bezonvaux, and to the south of Beaumont, attacks were made in the hope of distracting attention from the real objective, but here the French Colonial battalions were on guard, veterans known for their dash and daring, who hurled the enemy back to his own lines, leaving heaps of dead on the field.

While the French troops, fighting against overwhelming odds, continued to hold their lines inviolate, came the painful news that their most famous aviator, Captain George Guynemer, had been killed by the enemy.

Guynemer had won world-wide fame by his daring exploits. At the time he was reported missing he had a record of having destroyed fifty-two German machines. Two years before he was a simple soldier. He entered the army as a volunteer after having been rejected five times by the medical inspectors. One of his most striking achievements was the shooting down of three German aeroplanes in less than three minutes in September, 1916. Captain Guynemer operated his aeroplane alone, serving both as pilot and gunner. He was twenty-one years old.

At daybreak on September 26, 1917, Field Marshal Haig's troops made a heavy attack against the German positions east of Ypres on a six-mile front in which they won an advance ranging from half a mile to a mile in depth. The offensive was started along the major portion of the lines reached by the British on September 20, 1917, extending from east of St. Julien to southwest of Gheluvelt. The most important points involved in the new offensive were east of the city of Ypres, between the Ypres-Roulers railway and the Ypres-Menin highway, as was the case in the previous week. Here the Germans held elevated positions on ridges and in forests, the vital points of their defenses in Belgium.

The Australian, Scotch, and English troops engaged in this new offensive had a desperately hard road to travel, forcing their way over sodden and flooded ground among steel and concrete redoubts heavily manned with machine guns. On every elevated point and in every scrap of woods the Germans had established a vast number of rapid-firing guns.

The main British attack was directed against the German front in the Zonnebeke region. The village was stormed and the Germans were thrust back nearly a mile.

To the right of this sector and north of the Menin road, there was fierce fighting throughout the day when the British drove the enemy from all positions and made secure the flank of their principal advance.

Australian troops fighting farther south swept the Germans from Polygon Wood and won a trench position to the east of it. Near Tower Hamlets an important height that had been much fought over was won by British forces, who also occupied strong field works on the eastern slope. On the left of the main attack

there was an advance of about half a mile along the road to Gravenstafel.

For days the Germans had been bringing up reenforcements in anticipation of the British offensive. The German command, appreciating the importance of the elevated positions, had given orders to their troops to hold fast at whatever loss of life. The British consequently encountered everywhere a desperate resistance, especially on the right of the offensive around Tower Hamlets Ridge west of Gheluvelt.

In the course of the afternoon and evening the Germans projected seven powerful counterattacks against positions the British had captured east of Ypres, but were unable to shake the victors' bulldog grip. Here and there the Germans were successful in capturing a redoubt, but were only able to hold it for a short time before being thrust out by a well-directed counterattack. In this offensive the British captured 1,614 Germans, of whom forty-eight were officers.

The result of this British drive was to remove almost the last cover for the Germans between their advanced line in Flanders and the Ostend-Lille railway, their principal means of communication and of supplies in this part of Belgium. Parts of this line could be clearly seen from Zonnebeke Heights and within easy reach of the British guns, six miles away.

While the British were gaining ground their naval aeroplanes were attacking this line from the sky, dropping tons of explosives on the Thourout and Roulers junctions and on the German base at Ostend. The last British advance of a mile had brought this important objective almost within reach. Its capture would result in the evacuation of Belgium as far as the Scheldt and free the French cities of Lille, Roubaix, and Tourcoing.

The Germans continued to counterattack and bombard British positions that had been won during the advance, but they were unable to score any permanent successes. The net result of the fighting in the Ypres area was the capture by the British of 5,296 prisoners, including 146 officers. They had also taken during the month eleven guns, including heavy pieces, 377 machine guns, and fifty-seven trench mortars.

On the French front during these days, particularly in the Aisne sector, there was almost continuous fighting in which the Germans displayed dogged determination and reckless bravery, but every attack broke down. On the right bank of the Meuse they were partly successful in an assault on French outposts. Here they penetrated the French center, where they held on for a time, but the French returned in force, and after a struggle of the most sanguinary description in which the opponents fought murderously at close quarters the Germans were forced out and driven back to their lines.

North of Verdun the German attacks were especially violent. Here they employed "flame throwers" freely, but were unable to overcome the French resistance or to gain any marked advantage.

Wastage of German man power was an outstanding feature of recent engagements on the French front. The combat front of Verdun was held by twelve German divisions, that along the Aisne in 1917 was held by fourteen divisions. During the same period of time from May to September, 1916 and 1917, respectively the Germans engaged along the Verdun front, twenty-five new divisions in 1916; along the Aisne thirty-five new divisions in 1917. The Allied armies had so improved their mechanical means and fighting methods that the Germans were forced to maintain a reserve of at least forty divisions for the safety of their battle line in the west.

CHAPTER IV

HAIG STRIKES AGAIN AT YPRES—THE FRENCH BREAK THE GERMAN LINES ON THE AISNE

THE greatest gun duel of the war continued to rage in the region around Ypres in the last days of September, 1917. East of the city the Germans launched six attacks during the day and night on October 1, 1917, against the British lines. Every assault was smashed by the British artillery, rifle, and machine-gun fire. Not since fighting began in this area had such hurricanes of shells and explosives been seen. The Germans gambled against great odds and lost heavily. It was only in Polygon Wood that they obtained the slightest success. Here two small posts were won, but otherwise the British line remained intact.

On October 4, 1917, Field Marshal Haig delivered another mighty blow against the German lines east of the Ypres, gaining territory at the most advanced point to a depth of about a mile and a half on a front of more than eight miles.

The ground covered by the British assault was from north of Langemarck on the Ypres-Staden railway to a point south of Tower Hamlets, a height south of the Ypres-Menin highroad. The very important system of defenses along the Passchendaele-Gheluvelt road, which the Germans had held so long, was swept over by the victorious British troops.

On the northern wing they pushed on to within a short distance of Poelcappelle and gained a footing on Gravenstafel Ridge which projects from Passchendaele Ridge on the west, and broke through Zonnebeke-Broodseinde Ridge of bloody memory. The crest of the ridge was held against counterattacks which the Germans launched again and again with desperate daring and at the cost of frightful losses.

The British had begun the attack at 6 o'clock in the morning. The day was cloudy and promised rain. A mist hung over the battle field. The advance made into the enemy country was preceded by a heavy barrage, which, breaking in a fiery flood over the German lines, created such terror that in many places the enemy rushed out in groups with raised hands in sign of surrender.

The drive forward had forestalled a German attack which was in preparation near Zonnebeke on the same morning. Three German divisions here were ordered to take the line the British had captured the previous week. As they were pushing forward they were caught in the British barrage and met with appalling disaster.

The loss of the Passchendaele-Gheluvelt Ridge was a serious one for the Germans, as it constituted a barrier between the

British and occupied Belgium. Many important positions had been torn from them during recent thrusts, and on the 4th the British by a dashing advance penetrated German lines to a depth of 2,500 yards, carrying important defenses. South of the Ypres-Roulers railway the British troops could now overlook the slopes of the main ridge, and in some places had pushed their way into the valley below. Along the Strombeek River, on the left, the advance was slow owing to the marshy condition of the ground. The troops were aided in the advance by a number of tanks which performed immense service in reducing strong redoubts and concrete "pill boxes." Poelcappelle, which the British reached by 10.30, though heavily garrisoned, did not offer very strong resistance.

Abraham Heights, near Gravenstafel, was the scene of brief cellar fighting, but a sharp struggle developed near the fort where the Germans had eight strong concrete redoubts. The fighting here was close and heavy, but in the end the German resistance broke down under rifle fire and bomb. In the course of the day's fighting the British took 4,446 prisoners, including 114 officers.

It was estimated by correspondents who visited the battle area after the fight that the Germans had lost more killed than the number of their wounded and prisoners combined. On one section of the Australian front a thousand bodies were counted. A little farther south there was another lot of over seven hundred.

The manner in which the German defense was conducted showed many flaws, and indicated faulty organization. In the attempts made to stem the advance there was a lack of cohesion among the various units that were thrown out promiscuously along the whole battle front. The German artillery work, too, was weak and showed imperfect planning. A great number of Germans were caught in British barrages, and their officers spoke of the terrifying effect of the British fire, which surpassed anything known on that front and so dazed their troops that it was difficult to get them to follow out orders.

The Germans had been punished so severely that no infantry attack was attempted by them on the following day, and the

British were free to consolidate their gains and strengthen their new positions.

In the evening of October 7, 1917, a German attack in force was made east of Polygon Wood in the vicinity of Reutel on a front of about 500 yards. For all they had made great preparations and preceded the assault by a heavy barrage, it was quickly beaten off by British artillery and machine-gun fire. During the day a heavy rainfall had turned the battle ground into a morass; every shell hole became filled to the brim, and for the time any military operation of importance must be abandoned. After the hard fighting they had been through the British troops welcomed a rest, though soaked to the skin, but it was a difficult and painful task bringing in the wounded through the deep, clinging mud.

In the early morning of October 9, 1917, British and French forces in the Ypres area launched an attack north and northwest of that city and were successful in gaining all their objectives.

The French troops, driving forward on the left of the British line north of Ypres, cut through the German positions to a depth of a mile and a quarter on a front of more than a mile and a half. The villages of St. Jean de Mangelaer and Veldhoek and a system of blockhouses were captured, and the advance reached the southern edge of Houthulst Wood, seven miles to the north of Ypres. From the south the British pushed northeast from Gravenstafel Ridge to a point about 1,000 yards southwest of the village of Passchendaele to the heights of that name. Between the Ypres-Roulers railway and the village of Broodseinde, which they occupied, the British forced the Germans down the slopes of Broodseinde Ridge on the eastern side. In these notable advances the Allied troops gained possession of most of the observation points that commanded a view of the great plain of Flanders.

A heavy rain on the day preceding the attack had transformed the battle ground into a quagmire, and many formations of the Allied troops having been without shelter during the night were drenched to the skin when the order came to attack.

The French advance was fortunately timed. The Germans in the first line were in the act of changing troops. A division newly arrived from the Russian front was about to take possession. Before they could realize the situation the French had dashed in among them, and, killing a great many, dispersed the others in every direction. After a brief pause, to allow the British on the right to advance, the French proceeded to their next objective, the village of Mangelaer, which was quickly won.

The British had gained in the forward movement to the depth of half a mile on a front of about a mile, stretching from Draeibank to Wyndendreeft.

Every point was won which they had fixed on as their objective, and more than a thousand prisoners were captured during the push. The French had gained about 1,200 yards in the two stages of their advance, taking over 300 prisoners and a large number of guns.

On the day following the British were forced to relinquish a few of their advanced posts, but in the main the positions gained in the advance were securely held.

Recent rains had transformed the battle field into a vast swamp, in which men sank to their knees, and even waists. Despite the unfavorable conditions of the terrain, Field Marshal Haig began another offensive early in the morning of October 12, 1917, along the entire front in Flanders. In less than three hours his assaulting troops had gained ground to an average depth of 800 yards, which brought them within 500 yards of the village of Passchendaele. Further operations were brought to a standstill by a heavy fall of rain, and the British command decided to make no further attempts to attain their objectives that day.

The storm did not abate until the following morning, when the appearance of the sun cheered the much-bedraggled troops. But days of fair weather must pass before the boglands that constituted the battle area could dry up and admit of any important infantry operations. The Germans indeed ventured a few counterattacks in the hope of wresting from the British positions won in the last advance, but these were smashed by artillery fire.

French soldiers are bringing German prisoners from Malmaison Fort, the dominating position on the Craonne Plateau, which was taken by the French October 26, 1917. The Germans overran the position again in their drive of May, 1918

The British carried out night raids on enemy trenches in the Flanders front on October 15, 1917, and near Rœux, east of Arras. On the Aisne front the French were successful in repulsing German assaults and carried out daring attacks on enemy trenches in the Champagne and Argonne.

For a week quiet reigned on the western front. "Quiet" meaning in a military sense that no important infantry actions were attempted. But each day, and often through the night, the guns on both sides were seldom silent, and raids, counterattacks, and patrol encounters served to keep warm the fighting spirit of the German, French, and British forces.

October 22, 1917, was a day of intense activity on the Flanders front, when, operating in conjunction with the French troops, British forces in the neighborhood of Poelcappelle carried out a successful advance in the southern part of Houthulst Forest, north of Ypres. Southeast of Poelcappelle the British stormed and occupied valuable positions, and further north, aided by French troops, a series of fortified farms and defenses south of Houthulst Farm were won. The Germans in a spirited counterattack checked the advance in the vicinity of the Ypres-Staden railway, but at other points were unable to prevent the British from pushing forward.

For more than a week the French forces in the Verdun and Champagne areas had been inactive save for sporadic raids and gun duels, but early in the morning of October 23, 1917, operating over a six-mile front, they smashed the German lines north of the Aisne and seven miles northeast of Soissons. This swift and dashing attack, one of the most brilliant of the war, resulted in a gain of ground for the French of more than two miles at one point. Over 8,000 German prisoners, of whom 160 were officers, were captured, and seventy heavy field and eighty machine guns.

The morning of the attack was misty and rainy, and it was barely light when the French sprang out of their trenches, and, with a terrific barrage fire preceding them, swept over the first German positions, driving out or destroying the defenders. The front of the French attack was from the northeast of Laffaux, n the neighborhood of Vauxaillon, to La Royère Farm.

Six German infantry divisions tried to bar their way, but these were unable to check the spirited onslaught. The various stages of the French advance, which were carried out with precision and dispatch, were as follows: In the first dash the French captured the line indicated by the quarries of Fruty and Bohéry, and somewhat later Malmaison Fort was stormed and occupied. Montparnasse quarries, which had been previously damaged by big shells, was the scene of intensely hot fighting before the Germans were finally driven out.

The French center in its advance was opposed by fresh German reserves, and the fighting became bitter around the village of Chavignon, which the Germans only yielded after a violent struggle. It was in this area that the greatest advance of the day, two and a fifth miles, was made.. On the right the French took the villages of Allemant and Vaudesson, and carried their line to the heights commanding Pargny-Filain.

Squadrons of tanks were active during the advance, while the French aviators distinguished themselves aloft by showering machine-gun bullets upon the German infantry from an altitude of not more than 100 yards.

The capture of the Malmaison plateau by the French was of the first importance, for it was the key of the ridge between the Aisne and Ailette Valleys; an unrivaled observation point commanding the Laon plain. In gaining it the French really "turned" the Chemin-des-Dames Ridge, to the northern slopes of which the Germans had clung so long.

On October 25, 1917, the French forces on the Aisne resumed the offensive, a general push being made beyond the positions reached in the last advance, extending to the Oise-Aisne Canal. The village and forest of Pinon were captured, and the hamlet of Pargny-Filain. South of Filain the fortified farms of St. Martin and La Chapelle Ste. Berthe were occupied. On the front between Mont des Singes (Monkey Mountain) and Chavignon French troops made further progress and reached Rohay Farm. The Germans counterattacked at various points on the fighting front, but were unable to make any progress. The French held securely all the new positions gained during the advance, and th

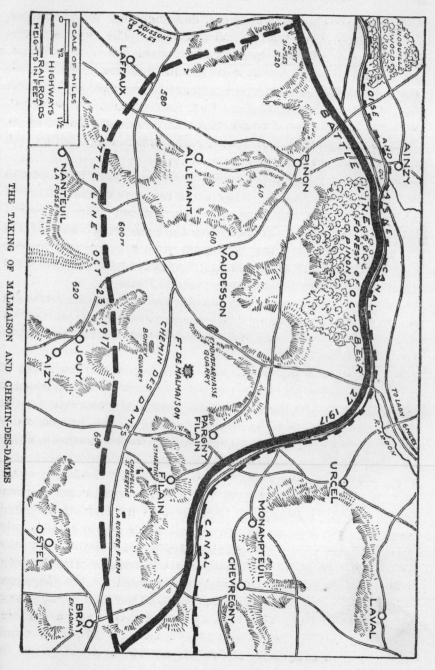

number of German prisoners had now increased to over 12,000, of whom 200 were officers. Among the spoils captured were 120 guns, many of the heaviest description.

On the British fronts in France and Flanders there were no important actions. During the night of October 24, 1917, British aviators made a successful raid on Saarbrücken. West of this place naval machines dropped three and one-half tons of explosives on the Burbach works, and other factories as well as railway communications were attacked with good results, many explosions being noted. A train proceeding from Saarbrücken received a direct hit from a big bomb and was destroyed.

On October 26, 1917, the British and French armies north, northeast, and east of Ypres renewed the offensive. The attacks began in a cold rain that had been falling for several hours. Haig's troops first advanced from a point near St. Janshoek westward through the southern fringe of Houthulst Forest to the neighborhood of Nieuemolen. The other assault was on both sides of the Ypres-Menin highway along the Gheluvelt Ridge toward the town of that name. Bellevue Spur, west of Passchendaele, was crowded with machine guns, but the British entered it an hour after the attack began. The Germans concentrated a heavy artillery fire on Bellevue, while the British were fighting arduously with rifle, bomb, and bayonet among the concrete fortifications. Through Wolf Copse, near Bellevue, that had been the scene of many sanguinary struggles, the British swept on, gaining Polderhoek Château, north of Gheluvelt, where there was close, intense fighting before the Germans were forced to yield.

On the same date the French continued their drive against the German positions along the Aisne. On the right of their attacking front they captured the village of Filain and pushed their lines forward north of Chevregny. In the Champagne area French trenches at Maisons de Champagne were heavily bombarded. Two surprise attacks attempted by the Germans were crushed. On the Flanders front, this day, the French captured the village of Draeibank, Papagoed Wood, and a number of fortified farms. Several hundred German prisoners were gathered in during these operations.

According to the reports made by French aviators scouting on the front, the Germans were preparing a retreat, for beyond the Ailette Valley fruit trees had been cut down and farms destroyed, just such destructive measures as the Germans had employed when they retired on the Somme in the spring of the year.

The French line now ran along the southern side of the Aisne-Oise Canal without a break, from westward of Vauxaillon to the town of Filain. French guns could now enfilade the German positions in three directions: northwestward of Anizey-le-Château, along the valley of Laon, and through the Ailette Valley, threatening the German lines on the Chemin-des-Dames Ridge.

German prisoners from the Empress Elizabeth's Guards Regiment captured during the recent French advance had been without food for three days and complained bitterly of their officers, who had slipped away and left them without commanders during the struggle.

The Germans had seven divisions in action during the first day's fighting here, and when it was evident that the tide of battle was running against them, fresh divisions were rushed up which had recently arrived from Galicia. The reenforcements reached the battle field only to fall under the murderous fire of French guns, or were taken prisoner, catastrophes which only added to the general confusion that seems to have reigned among the Teutonic forces.

French troops on the Flanders front began another dashing drive on October 27, 1917, capturing all the German positions on a front of two and a half miles. The advance was made on both sides of the road between Dixmude and Ypres. On the right the French gained the western outskirts of Houthulst Wood, capturing the villages of Verbrandesmis, Aschoop, Merckem, and Kippe, and also a system of strongly fortified farms. Again the French had to wade through morasses into which they sank waist deep, but there was no holding the brave "poilus" back. Soaked with mud and water they had to attack heavily defended hamlets and innumerable concrete blockhouses bristling with machine guns, but every objective was won.

West of Passchendaele the Canadians were improving the positions in this sector which they had captured in the first stages of the battle, across the neck of the Bellevue Spur. The Germans had endeavored by repeated counterattacks to force them out of this dominating height, and there were anxious moments for the Canadians, when, as the result of a struggle at close quarters, they were forced to yield ground. But they quickly rallied, and in a fierce onslaught drove out the Germans and recovered the position.

Northwest of Verdun, near Chaume Wood, the German Crown Prince's army made a strong assault on French positions on October 29, 1917. The attack was preceded by a bombardment of intense violence. The German infantry pressed forward impetuously in the face of a blasting fire from rifles and machine guns and penetrated French positions north of Courrières Wood. But they were only able to hold the ground for a short time, when the French struck back and forced them out, dispersing the invaders, who fled to their own lines.

On the Flanders front the Canadians continued to forge their way forward toward Passchendaele. In the morning of October 30, 1917, they attacked the outer defenses of that place. At Meetscheede village, a mass of ruins, there stood a number of concrete blockhouses, strongly manned, and the struggle that developed here was fierce and bloody. The place was only won by the individual cunning of the Canadians, who hid among the shell craters, dashing forward separately and in groups whenever there was a slight pause in the enemy's fire. It was slow, hard work, and costly, but they slogged away until the German guns were silent. Beyond Meetscheede stood another row of blockhouses, and more intense fighting ensued, but at length the Germans gave up and started to run, but very few were said to have escaped.

Another Canadian unit on the right, where the Passchendaele Ridge stands, was fighting its way up toward Crest Farm in the face of a heavy machine-gun fire. By dogged persistence they won the position, and quickly turning the captured German gun were enabled to smash up the counterattacks which followed quickly after the positions were occupied.

After these assaults that cost the Germans heavily the Canadians passed a quiet night in their newly won trenches only 400 yards from Passchendaele.

October 31, 1917, was warm and sunny and brought cheer to the Canadians, who had been lying out all night in the chilly air in their wet uniforms. The work of consolidating the newly won positions went forward rapidly. German gunfire, which continued during the day, was especially intense in the territory between Schaopbaillie and Poelcappelle north of the scene of the previous day's fighting. Here the Germans gained a small advantage: the British were shelled from two outposts in fortified farms.

On the French front artillery battles and local engagements were continued during October 30-31, 1917. North of the Aisne the guns thundered on the whole sector between Vauxaillon and Pinon, and along the new French positions in the region of Froidmont. German detachments, which attempted to storm French posts north of the Loivre and to the northwest of Rheims, were driven off with heavy losses. A surprise attack in the Argonne, in the region of Boureuilles, was defeated by the French after a sharp engagement in which the Germans were severely punished.

Since assuming the offensive on October 23, 1917, the French had captured over 12,000 prisoners, of whom 237 were officers. Large quantities of war material were also taken, including 180 cannon.

CHAPTER V

GERMAN RETREAT FROM CHEMIN-DES-DAMES—
THE BRITISH ADVANCE TOWARD CAMBRAI

FRENCH victories resulted in the retreat of the Germans from the Chemin-des-Dames. It began during the night of November 1, 1917, and continued the day following. The stupendous efforts made by them to hold this important rampart had cost thousands of lives and had been in vain. They were forced to retire along a fifteen-mile front to the Ailette River, the prelude, perhaps, to the fall of Laon and La Fère.

The Germans had been in control of the Chemin-des-Dames since September, 1914, when Joffre turned back the Teuton armies in the Battle of the Marne. Since then they had clung desperately to this ridge, which dominates the valley of the Aisne and the Ailette Valley. The German Crown Prince lost the best elements of his armies and the best part of their effectives in the fighting here in October, 1917. Enfiladed day and night by French guns it was impossible for the Germans to keep their front lines supplied with food and ammunition, for the carriers had to pass through a storm of fire in crossing the valley of Ailette, where they were constantly under observation from the French positions. It was in anticipation of a new offensive that the Germans decided to retire from a position that had become untenable.

Possession of the Chemin-des-Dames greatly strengthened the French lines in the Aisne sector, giving them control of the St. Gobain region northwest of the highway. St. Gobain is between Laon and La Fère and dominates both those points.

On November 2, 1917, the French forces organized the new ground conquered from the Oise Canal to Corbeny. Lively artillery actions were continued in the different sectors of the Chemin-des-Dames. In the course of the night the French made progress between these two points and reached the south bank of the Ailette River, over the entire front. The Germans retired to the north bank of the stream, destroying bridges and footbridges on the way.

The French had received timely warning of the retreat, and an hour after it began swarmed down along the whole front in pursuit. It was evident that the Germans had determined hurriedly to abandon the ridge, for the first French troops to reach the positions found tins containing soup that was still hot. The advance was made slowly and cautiously, for it was well known that the Germans left dangerous traps behind them when forced to retire. In Cerny village a German helmet was found fixed to a pole so arranged that when it was lifted off it would cause the explosion of a mine. The Germans had passed out of sight, but they were still heard from, their guns being constantly active shelling the abandoned positions.

The French discovered trenches and dugouts and two large tunnels almost intact owing perhaps to the fact that the Germans feared to destroy them lest the explosions would give the alarm. The result was that the victors had little work to do in preparing defenses, and began their tenancy under good cover.

No important actions were fought on the British front in France during the first days of November, 1917. There was fierce shelling day and night on both sides across Passchendaele Ridge.

On November 6, 1917, the indomitable Canadians began a daring drive that resulted in the capture of Passchendaele village northeast of Ypres, a key position dominating the plain of Roulers. After taking the place they pushed forward and occupied positions 800 yards farther on. The German defense was far weaker than the men from overseas anticipated, nor did the enemy launch a counterattack immediately after the town was captured. This failure to counterattack was afterward explained by one of the two German battalion commanders, who were made prisoners with their staffs when Passchendaele fell. This officer commanded a reserve battalion brought up for the express purpose of counterattacking. He had gone with his staff to consult with the battalion chief commanding in the village, and when both commanders were captured their troops were left without a responsible head. The reserve battalion waited in a state of indecision for the officer's return and never ventured forward, thus giving the Canadians time to consolidate their gains. From the village it was possible to look far over occupied Belgium, and the possibilities for artillery work from this position were wide. Its loss threatened the retention by the Germans of their defenses for many miles.

In the course of the drive the Canadians took 400 prisoners, of whom twenty-one were officers. The total would have been much higher, but a number of the enemy were killed by the fire of their own guns when they were being brought back after the taking of Passchendaele, whether by accident or design was not learned.

Two days passed, and yet the Germans made no attempt to capture the lost village, thus giving the Canadians ample time to organize their defenses and secure a firm grip on the position. The enemy's heavy gunfire had slackened too, because the Canadians had observation of his old battery positions, so he relied mainly on lighter guns.

For months little activity had been reported on the upper Alsace sector of the western front, but on November 7, 1917, the French made an attack on the German positions at Schoenholz, capturing 121 prisoners including officers, and large quantities of war material and stores.

Haig's troops began a new push early in the morning of November 10, 1917, northward along Passchendaele Ridge, on a front of one and a half miles and piercing the German lines for half a mile. It had been raining most of the night and the storm still continued when the British forces went forward at 6.05 o'clock in the morning. The Germans immediately threw a heavy barrage along the front involved, and the advance was raked by machine-gun fire from numerous strong points. The fighting was especially intense at several fortified farms strongly held by the Germans. North of Goeberg there were several concreted positions whose defenders fought with daring and tenacity. Repeatedly the British stormed and penetrated these strongholds only to be driven out a little later by counterattacks, but "dogged does it!" and by 10 o'clock they had virtually gained all their objectives.

During the morning hours of November 11, 1917, the Germans bombarded heavily the new British positions, but no counter-attack was attempted. Along the crest of Passchendaele Ridge, north of the village, the Canadians held their advanced line strongly. On the lower ground, to the west, the scene of bitter fighting on the previous day, the Germans counterattacked, and at a few points the British were forced back, though holding on to some of the newly won positions.

There were many local actions at various points on the French front, November 10-11, 1917. Surprise attacks were attempted by the Germans northwest of Rheims and north of Samogneux, which were shattered by the well-directed French artillery fire. On the front of Chaume Wood, in the Verdun sector, gun duels continued intermittently day and night.

In the Vosges the Germans after heavy artillery preparation made an attack on the French trenches at Hartmannsweilerkopf. A violent engagement developed in which the opponents fought at close quarters and the bayonet was used freely. It was a short, sharp struggle in which neither side was disposed to yield, but ultimately the Germans after gaining a foothold in the French observation line were driven off. On November 10-11, 1917, the Germans bombarded French advanced posts in the region of Ramscappelle and Pervyse as well as their trenches at Dixmude. The French guns replied with so destructive a fire that the enemy batteries were silenced. Then their "heavies" began a bombardment of German works at Woumen and positions on the outskirts of Dixmude.

After several days' intense shelling of British positions around Passchendaele the Germans made a determined effort on November 13, 1917, to recover the lost ground. They massed strong bodies of troops in the neighborhood of Westroosebeke, advancing from the cross roads north of Passchendaele under the protection of a violent barrage. The British were not caught napping and their gunners concentrated a destructive fire on the German assembly places and approaches. The first waves of the German advance were shattered by streams of bullets, and only small bodies struggled through the devastating fire to the British trenches, where after sharp fighting they were driven back.

Another section of the dominating Passchendaele Ridge was wrested by Haig's troops from the Germans during the night of November 16-17, 1917. The credit for this advance was due to the Highland, Berkshire, and Lancashire troops, who in the darkness left their shell holes and pushed forward over ground that was swept by machine-gun fire. The Germans were evidently taken by surprise, or were cowed by the impetuous dash of the British troops, for they did not attempt a strong defense. The struggle developed to the north of the ruins of Passchendaele village, and the British were easy winners. A heavily fortified redoubt known as Vocation Farm gave the attackers some trouble, but it was captured along with other strong points in the neighborhood. The Germans did not attempt an immediate counterattack, but increased their artillery fire on the sector.

On the following day the Germans made a strong raid on British lines in Flanders in the neighborhood of Guillemont Farm. At some points they were successful in piercing defenses, but the British counterattacked across the open, and after a short, sharp struggle, repulsed the invaders and took a number of prisoners. In the night of November 17-18, 1917, Lancashire and Highland troops made a successful raid on enemy trenches in the neighborhood of Monchy-le-Preux, where they killed or captured many Germans and escaped with light casualties before reserves could arrive.

These minor local actions were the prelude to a powerful offensive which Field Marshal Haig was preparing, one of the greatest operations of the war, and which broke the famous Hindenburg line. The attack was launched on November 20, 1917, and was a complete surprise to the Germans as it had not been preceded by any artillery preparations. The operation was carried out by the third army under General Sir Julian Byng, the advance being made along a thirty-two-mile front between St. Quentin and the Scarpe River. German defenses were penetrated for a distance of five miles at the deepest point, extending to the village of Cantaing, which lies less than three miles to the southwest of Cambrai.

As a substitute for the usual artillery preparation the British had secretly assembled a large number of tanks, which were sent forward under a screen of smoke, and broke down the German barbed-wire entanglements, opening the way for the infantry to make their forward rushes. The British troops were in high spirits, shouting and cheering as they pushed forward in the wake of the lumbering machines.

As the tanks rolled on, showering machine-gun bullets before them, the British guns in the rear sent hurricanes of shells screaming over the Hindenburg line. The surprise of the attack seemed to have dazed and bewildered the Germans; many of them hid in their dugouts and tunnels and then surrendered. The braver element got their machine guns in action or used their rifles to snipe the British.

The German artillery fire was feeble, their gun positions being smothered beneath the deluge of British shells. There were comparatively few batteries, and their infantry gained little help from them. It was well known to the British that they had removed many of their guns from this sector in the past few days, as this part of the battle line was considered "quiet."

During the night preceding the attack the British had massed large bodies of cavalry very close to the enemy lines, ready for a sweeping drive when the tanks had broken down the wire defenses. In hollows near the German lines were thousands of cavalry horses with their horse artillery limbered up ready for the dash forward. After the tanks had made clear the way to advance the cavalry sprang forward through the rain and mist. One squadron rode down a battery of German guns, and other bodies swept around machine-gun emplacements and through villages and captured many prisoners.

It was 6.20 in the morning when the tanks first pushed forward to break down the wire entanglements and clear the way for the advance of the British infantry. An hour later the troops were rushing through the gaps made in the German defenses. At 7.47 British troops operating west of Havrincourt had forced their way up and over the elevation known as Mount Vesuvius. It was fortunate that the movement was carried out with dispatch, for a few minutes later the knoll, which had been mined, was blown up by the Germans. Havrincourt was captured in less than an hour, the Germans evacuating the place in such haste that they had not time to inflict any serious damage. The West Riding Territorials, who captured Havrincourt, also occupied enemy trench systems to the north of the village, while Ulster battalions, covering their left flank, pressed on northward up the west bank of the Canal du Nord. La Vacquerie and the strong defenses known as Welsh Ridge were won by English rifle regiments and light infantry. In the course of the advance east, County troops took the hamlet of Bonavis and Laffaux Wood after a bitter struggle that resulted in heavy casualties to the Germans.

Later in the morning the British troops extended the advance at all points. Crossings were effected of the canal at Masnières and English, Scottish, Irish, and Welsh battalions fought together in the capture of Marcoing and Neuf Wood. East of the Canal du Nord the West Riding troops that took Havrincourt made important progress. They stormed and captured the villages of Graincourt and Anneux. In conjunction with Ulster men operating west of the canal they carried the whole German line northward to the Bapaume-Cambrai road.

Important points of the Hindenburg line were penetrated east of Epihy by the West Lancashire Territorials, while Irish troops won important sections of the line between Bullecourt and Fontaine-les-Croisilles.

In the morning of the second day of the advance the British were within three miles of Cambrai. After breaking through the German's last defense line at Anneux and Cantaing, British tanks, cavalry, and infantry were operating along a line running from west of Cambrai to the south of that town. On the left, in the region of Bullecourt, the German line had been pushed back, widening the salient which the British drove into enemy territory south and southwest of Cambrai. In the attack around Bullecourt the British took 700 prisoners.

The Germans had now recovered their fighting spirit, which suffered a decline during the first stages of the British advance, and everywhere opposed a stiff resistance. At Noyelles, Rumilly, and Bullecourt they made desperate counterattacks during the night, but were unable to overcome British resistance.

In the two days' fighting the British had captured more than 9,000 prisoners.

There was heavy fighting during the morning of November 22, 1917, near Bourlon Wood, Fontaine Wood, and the village of Fontaine Notre Dame east of it, less than three miles from Cambrai. When the British captured the last place named, they were able to release more than a hundred civilian prisoners, who hailed their rescuers with cheers and many wept for joy. At Masnières the same scene was enacted, where some hundreds of civilians were freed from the odious rule of their German oppressors. They had been kept from starving almost entirely by the American Relief Committee, and after America entered the war by the Spanish-Dutch Committee. The men had been forced by the Germans to work long hours in the fields and workshops, and the women had to sweep the roads, wash the soldiers' dirty linen, and scrub their quarters.

"For three years we lived in a nightmare," said the Mayor of Masnières, "and now we seem to be in a dream too good to be true!" One man had been living for three years in the cellar of his own house, where German officers were billeted, being fed by his wife out of the extra ration given to the baby born since the war began. Every week the house was searched and husband and wife would have been punished with death if the man had been found.

In the morning of November 23, 1917, the British drove back the Germans from an elevation known as Tadpole Copse west of Mœuvres, commanding a large section of the Canal du Nord, which runs east of that place and the village itself, still in German hands. At Fontaine Notre Dame, west of Cambrai, where the British had been pushed back, the fighting was renewed. In the eastern part of Crevecœur village the Germans had concentrated an intense machine-gun fire against the British in the western outskirts.

Heavy fighting continued throughout the day of November 23, 1917, at Bourlon Wood, and around Fontaine. The British held a line on the low ground about the southern edge of the wood, and from these positions had to charge up the slopes under the fire of many machine guns.

Assisted by the tanks the British infantry made a strong forward push, and hand-to-hand fighting ensued as soon as they had entered the forest. Every foot of the advance was fiercely contested, but the "men of the bulldog breed" were out to win, and by early afternoon had driven their way through half the wood. Later in the day they gained more ground, occupying a line through the center of the wood to the northwest of Fontaine. In hand-to-hand combats the Germans were slowly forced back toward the northern edge of the forest. A determined counterattack from the north was made by the Germans in an effort to oust the British, but they held firm. While this bloody struggle was going on in and around the wood Fontaine village, which the Germans held strongly, was the scene of fierce fighting. The place was heavily fortified, and the Germans with rifles and machine guns fired from the roofs and windows of the houses. Later in the afternoon the British tanks took a hand in the fighting here, but at the close of the day (November 23) the Germans were still in possession of the place, though sorely depleted in numbers.

The fighting was continued in the neighborhood of Bourlon during November 24-25, 1917, with varying fortunes to those engaged. The Germans about noon on the 25th succeeded in driving the British from the greater part of the village. In Bourlon Wood, where the British held strong points on the high ground, the Germans, though repeatedly attacking, failed to make any progress.

In the five days that had passed since the British began the offensive on November 20, 1917, they had captured 9,774 prisoners, including 182 officers.

The Hindenburg support line west of Mœuvres was attacked by British troops, some from London, during the night of November 25, 1917. The fighting that developed was close and sanguinary, the losses on both sides being considerable, but the British believed they had not paid too dearly for the 2,000 yards of support trenches which they won on this bitterly contested field.

At Bourlon Wood and Bourlon village the fighting still continued in one of the most bitterly contested and sanguinary struggles that had been fought up to that time on the British front in France. Bourlon Wood, to which the British clung so tenaciously, was of special value to the Germans if they were to hold their positions farther north, and for that reason they were making extraordinary efforts to regain that elevation. The British had established many guns in good working positions and were prepared to defend it.

Fighting was continued on the southern edge of Bourlon village in the night of November 26, 1917. The British broke the German line at one point and brought back a body of English troops that had been isolated for some time in the southern part of the hamlet. Having rescued their fellow soldiers they made no attempt to remain in the village, but dashed back through the gap they had made in the German lines.

At about 10 o'clock at night on the same date the Germans in a counterattack struck hard against British positions on the northeast corner of Bourlon Wood, but were driven back so decisively that they made no further attempts to recover the lost ground. The British artillery continued to pound the German lines effectively during the night, but no other infantry action was attempted by either side.

The villages of Fontaine Notre Dame and Bourlon continued to be the storm centers on the battle front. They were constantly deluged with shells by both sides, and attacks were made from time to time in which now the British and now the Germans gained some slight advantage. From their positions in Bourlon Wood the British were shelling Cambrai three and a half miles away.

On November 28, 1917, the British won a section of the ridge between Bourlon Wood and Mœuvres in the face of a heavy barrage and intense machine-gun fire from the direction of Bourlon village.

In the morning of the following day, under cover of a furious artillery fire, the Germans delivered an attack in force on the British positions between Bourlon Wood and Mœuvres on the west. In the first dash the Germans swept over the crest of the ridge west of the wood and as far as the vicinity of the Bapaume-Cambrai road north of Graincourt.

After the first shock of the assault the British organized a counterattack and fell upon the advancing Germans with such fury that the advance was checked. Fighting still continued, however, throughout the day in this region with varying fortunes to the combatants.

The Germans had been concentrating their heaviest guns in this area to replace those that had been captured by General Byng, and were using gas shells on a lavish scale.

In the morning of November 30, 1917, the Germans started an important offensive movement with the fixed purpose of driv ing the British from the territory they had won in the previou: week. Two great attacks were made early in the day, one ex-tending from Mœuvres to Bourlon Wood, the other along a 1,200 yard front southwest of Cambrai, between Vendhuile and Crevecœur.

The Germans employed strong forces, and were efficiently supported by newly concentrated guns that had been brought forward for the purpose.

Over the ridge between Mœuvres and Bourlon Wood the Germans poured in dense masses, coming under fire of the British artillery as they swept down the slope toward the Bapaume-Cambrai road. The Germans advanced in such close formation that they fell by the score under the intense fire from British rifles and machine guns. But where one fell a dozen seemed to rise up and take his place, and the hordes moved resistlessly forward like a tidal wave. British infantrymen were thrown into the battle line for a counterattack and a murderous struggle developed, but the Germans were too strong, nothing could hold them back as they pushed relentlessly on, and the rush was only checked when they reached a point in the vicinity of the Bapaume-Cambrai highway northwest of Graincourt.

Regardless of their heavy losses the Germans continued to pour over the ridge all day long in waves of massed formation, offering a splendid target for the British guns. Their ranks were torn and shattered in that storm of fiery hail, but there was hardly a pause in the advance and their numbers never seemed to diminish. Late in the day the British in counterattacks gained ground at some points, but the honors rested with the Germans, who by costly sacrifice of men won important defenses and advanced their lines. Around Bourlon Wood the British held firmly and the Germans, wearied at last of the slaughter that had decimated their ranks, gave up attacking for the day.

In the south the Germans began the attack with a force of ten divisions; six of them were on the front line. It was planned to make two turning movements on either side of the line, which were to converge toward a common point. German infantry supported by cavalry at the northern end of the line delivered an assault across the canal from Crevecœur toward Masnières. They succeeded in forcing their way into the suburbs of the last-named place, but were driven out before they could establish positions.

Farther to the south the Germans won important victories, when they broke through the British front, south of Villers-Guislain, and by an adroit turning movement to the north, surrounded Gauche Wood, Gouzeaucourt, Gonnelieu and La Vacquerie. In this operation the Germans advanced their lines at one point about 4,000 yards. This was at Gouzeaucourt, which they entered about 10 o'clock in the morning, and where fighting of the most violent description continued until the middle of the afternoon. The British had received reenforcements, but they were still heavily outnumbered. The fighting was at close quarters, a merciless hand-to-hand struggle that continued for hours without pause. The British troops, fearing the loss of their dearly bought ground, fought with desperation and about 3 in the afternoon succeeded in pushing the Germans out of the village and reoccupied it.

East of Gouzeaucourt the Germans occupied a ridge with strong forces. During the day the British repeatedly attacked, and finally forced them to withdraw from the height to the lower ground, and occupying the position, and also Gauche Wood, pushed on to the western edge of Gonnelieu.

The German line in the morning of December 1, 1917, was just west of Villers-Guislain, marking an advance of about 3,000 yards at the greatest depth. Other less important advances were won in the north and at Gonnelieu, and while the British regretted the loss of valuable territory, there was nothing in the situation to cause them uneasiness. There had been crucial periods in the fighting of the previous day, when it seemed that the Germans would win an overwhelming victory, and all the territory gained during General Byng's advance would be recovered, but British determination and dogged perseverance and unconquerable spirit prevailed, and the most ambitious plans of the enemy were frustrated.

Heavy losses had been sustained by both sides. The German attacks, made in massed formation, had caused a formidable death roll. They claimed to have taken 400 British prisoners.

CHAPTER VI

GERMANS GAIN IN THE CAMBRAI AREA—COLD
WEATHER HALTS IMPORTANT OPERATIONS

ALL day long the waves of battle rolled around Masnières on December 1, 1917. The Germans made nine strong attacks, all of which were repulsed. It was declared by eyewitnesses that the British destroyed more Germans during the fight here between dawn and dark than in any similar period since the beginning of the war. From the first German assault there was no pause in the struggle.

Late in the day south and east of Masnières the German guns heavily bombarded the town. The British line formed a sharp salient around the place, which made the position difficult to hold, as it was dominated by the high ground held by the Germans. It was therefore decided by the British command to withdraw to the southeastern outskirts of the town and there establish the line to the great benefit of the entire front.

Gonnelieu, which the British captured during the day, though the Germans still clung to portions of the ruins, was completely "cleaned up" during the night, about 300 prisoners being taken here. After the recapture of Gauche Wood the British continued to push on up to the higher ground southwest of the wood. During the assault on Gauche Wood one British tank captured fifteen machine guns from the enemy.

December 2, 1917, the Germans continued their terrific attacks on the British front south and southwest of Cambrai. With a mighty concentration of artillery, and employing great forces of infantry, they tried to pierce the British defenses in the Gonnelieu sector, but General Byng's army had been strongly reenforced and held fast.

The battle began along a front that extended from La Vacquerie southward to Vendhuile. The Germans attacked British positions at La Vacquerie at 8.45 in the morning, and penetrated the village, but only won temporary foothold, when they were forced out. As the day wore on the fighting spread northward toward Masnières, which the British had evacuated on the previous day. During the night the town was an uncomfortable place to hold, as the British continued to deluge it with shells and the Germans were forced to find refuge in tunnels and dugouts. Southwest of Bourlon village General Byng's troops won back a trench system that the Germans had captured during the push of November 30, 1917. Bourlon Wood was again in possession of the British, though a few Germans still clung to some points on the outskirts. South of Marcoing the Germans continued their powerful attacks on the British lines, but were unable to cut through the defenses.

Under cover of the darkness the British withdrew from the salient about Bourlon Wood during the night of December 4-5, 1917, to a prepared line which would be stronger and easier to hold. Not until some hours had passed did the Germans discover the retirement, when they swarmed into the vacant territory and dug themselves in. Bourlon Wood had been generally

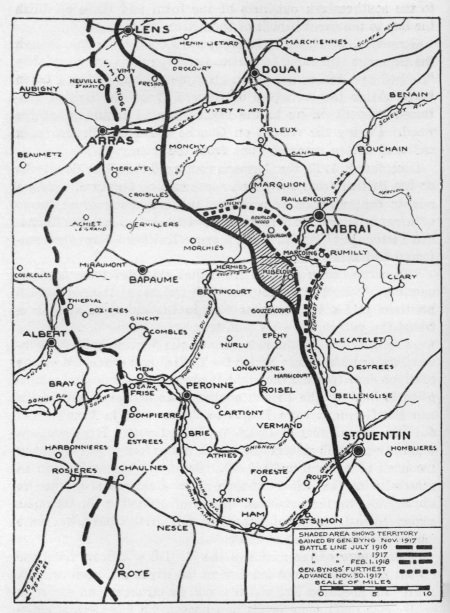

THE BATTLE OF CAMBRAI

stripped of troops; only a rear guard being left when the British retired, and they were later withdrawn. The Germans continued, however, to bombard the wood, showing that they were all in the dark concerning British movements.

The devastated area which the British had abandoned, and which included the mined towns of Graincourt, Anneux, Cantaing, Noyelles, Marcoing, and Masnières, was gradually occupied by the Germans. They had no easy task before them, for the British guns dominated this desert with tons of explosives, and hundreds of shells were hurled into their advanced ranks as they went forward to prospect for desirable positions for defense. Meanwhile the British army had found exceptional quarters in the captured Hindenburg trenches with their wonderful dugouts and network of front-line and communication trenches, all ready for occupancy.

There was continued fighting during the 6th between advanced patrols of British and Germans. North of La Vacquerie Ulster troops won some important defenses that strengthened the British line.

Artillery duels and sporadic raids were the only military events in this fighting area during the several succeeding days. The British anticipated that this lull would be followed by renewed fighting, for it was known that the Germans had been bringing forward strong reenforcements, probably from the Russian front.

The German offensive began on December 12, 1917, but was far from being as formidable as the British feared. The first attack was made at dawn against an elbow in the bend of the British line between Bullecourt and Queant, about ten miles west of Cambrai. The Germans were in strong force, the troops, principally from Bavaria, advancing in waves and close formation, and by sheer weight of numbers won about 500 yards of front-line trenches before they could be checked. Other attacks were made from the east, and the third south of Riencourt, both of which were shattered by British rifle and machine-gun fire.

The Germans were evidently trying to discover weak spots in the British lines by a process of testing, for on December 14, 1917, they made an assault on the Ypres front in Flanders. The stroke was delivered on a front of about 300 yards southeast of Polygon Wood, against British positions near Polderhoek Château. They won a section of front-line trench, but were repulsed at all other points of attack.

East of Bullecourt, in the Cambrai area, German gunfire had increased in violence. During the night the British engaged in bomb fighting that was highly successful, and enabled them to improve their lines. North of Bullecourt in the afternoon of December 15, 1917, the British carried out a successful raid in which a number of prisoners were captured and enemy dugouts and defenses were destroyed.

Snow began to fall during the night on this date, and by morning the countryside was deeply covered, and the ugly scars of battle hidden from sight. The snow lay in heavy drifts on the roads and fields. No military operation was possible, and even the sinister-looking guns were silent.

This white truce was appreciated by the British as it must have been by the soldiers of the kaiser, for both armies had been under a severe strain since General Byng's advance on Cambrai, November 20, 1917.

It was estimated by conservative military observers that the German strength on the Franco-British front at this time was 154 divisions, one less than the great force amassed here in the previous July, when the German military effort against France was at its maximum.

During these momentous days on the British battle front the French had been nibbling away at the German positions around Verdun and along the Aisne and Meuse Rivers. The capture of the entire line of lights through which runs the famous Chemin-des-Dames had given them command of the strongest positions in that region. The Germans, forced to retire across the Ailette and to abandon the whole valley to the French, were so situated that it would be taking a gambler's chance to attempt an offensive on a large scale. Nor was a direct attack on Verdun probable, for they had lost all their gains on both sides of the Meuse, while every point of vantage in this sector was in possession of the soldiers of the Republic.

The Champagne front between Rheims and Verdun offered the most favorable field for the Germans to deliver a hard blow. By a strong offensive the French positions to the east, in the Argonne Forest, might be turned, compelling the French to draw their lines back; converting into a narrow-necked wedge the Verdun lines, which would be hemmed in on nearly every side.

On the Alsace and Lorraine fronts there was little to fear of any strong action on the part of the Germans, as every movement must be made through narrow passes, conditions that rendered large operations impossible.

Meanwhile the Germans were evidently testing the French fronts for a weak spot where they might strike a shrewd blow. Around Verdun and farther east the German guns thundered unceasingly, and German trench raids were of daily and nightly occurrence throughout the month of December. For "a worn-out army," as the French troops had been called by their enemies, they fought with astonishing spirit. The Germans made slight gains from time to time, but they were unable to retain them.

On the Cambrai front the fighting was confined to raids and minor actions of slight importance. On December 30, 1917, the Germans made strong local attacks on a front of over two miles against the British position on the spur known as Welsh Ridge south of Cambrai. The attackers were forced back in the center, but on the right, toward the north of La Vacquerie, and on the left to the south of Marcoing, they penetrated and occupied two small salients in the British lines. In the morning of the following day, after a short but heavy bombardment, the Germans renewed their attack against Welsh Ridge on a front of about 1,200 yards south of Marcoing. The southern portion was assaulted by strong forces, and assisted by liquid fire they succeeded in gaining a foothold in one of the British trenches. The gain was only temporary, for the British quickly rallied, and in a fierce counterattack drove out the invaders and reoccupied the entire trench system.

German artillery thundered unceasingly throughout the day on January 1, 1918, near La Vacquerie on the Cambrai front, and in the Lens, Armentières and Ypres sectors. In the evening, under cover of a heavy bombardment, three bodies of German troops attempted to raid British positions in the vicinity of Méricourt southeast of Lens. The assaulting troops came under the concentrated fire of the British artillery and were hurled back with heavy losses before they could reach their objectives. In no-man's-land these disorganized Germans ran into a British patrol, and again lost heavily, very few escaping from the field.

The British front was now in the icy grip of winter. Snowdrifts made the roads impassable for motor cars. The Germans, however, were not deterred by unfavorable weather conditions from making sporadic raids on British positions. On January 5, 1918, they had some success at Bullecourt, where they captured a British advance post—a dearly bought operation that cost them a heavy toll in casualties. In the afternoon the British came back in force, and, after a tense, close struggle, drove out the Germans and reoccupied the position.

On the French front, where a blizzard had been raging and the heaviest snowstorm in years made military operations on any large scale impossible, the Germans continued to be active, and the French were kept busy defending their costly won positions.

On January 8, 1918, French troops carried out an extensive and successful raid which was intrusted to foreign legionaries and sharpshooters. The attack was delivered along a front of a mile and to a depth of half a mile in front of Flirey and westward toward St. Mihiel. The French completely cleaned out the German defenses, capturing 178 men and officers and numbers of machine guns and trench mortars. The Germans were so completely taken by surprise that their artillery did not get into action until the French had finished the job. The attack was carried out with such dispatch and in so thorough a manner that the French suffered not more than a dozen casualties, while the German dead lay thick about the field and the snow was streaked with ominous stains.

On the same date (January 8) the spell of silence which had brooded for some days on the British front was broken by a hostile attack made by the Germans east of Bullecourt.

In the early dawn the British lines were bombarded with high explosives and gas, and about 6.35 three parties of Bavarian troops, who had been lying concealed during the night in no-man's-land, made a quick rush for the British defenses. The front line attacked had been weakened by the recent withdrawal of troops, as an enemy attack was not expected in a sector considered "quiet."

Two of the parties of Bavarians carried flame throwers of the most approved type, which darted a jet of fire thirty feet, and literally wiped out with a touch a man's life. This engine of destruction had a terrifying effect on troops who saw it in operation for the first time, but the British soldiers defending the trenches at Bullecourt were seasoned fighters and well acquainted with every type of German frightfulness.

The Bavarians in this attack succeeded in penetrating the British line and proceeded to make themselves at home in the position and to strengthen the defenses. A swift counterattack delivered by the British killed a number of them, but the others continued to hold on through the early morning hours. Shortly before noon the snow began to fall heavily, making observation difficult. Through the storm swept a body of British troops to assault for a second time. The Bavarians were taken by surprise and driven out of the position, leaving a score of prisoners and a number of wounded in British hands. Such minor operations and small raids made on both sides were the only interruptions of the quiet that prevailed on the entire front where General Winter ruled. The troops, who were enduring every discomfort in their snow-bound trenches, longed eagerly for clearing weather, when they might find release from deadly inaction.

The British were better off than the Germans, since they had won the ridges on the front. They could keep dry, while the kaiser's troops occupied trenches that were often in a fearful condition owing to lack of natural drainage, which in bad weather transformed them into bogs. The British took prisoners in dugouts that were filled with water. The miserable occupants of these holes seemed to be glad enough to fall into the hands of their enemy.

In these days there was considerable relaxation in the iron discipline of the German army—on the British front at least. It was learned that their officers were cautious about punishing the troops too severely even for grave offenses against discipline. Deserters were not shot, but sent back to Germany, where it was said the prisons were full of such offenders. To escape service in the front-line trenches the soldiers shammed gas-poisoning and resorted to other devices to avoid duty.

On the French front during these dreary winter days the Germans continued their raiding attacks in Chaume Wood in the Verdun sector, and at other points, in which every weapon of "frightfulness," including lavish use of liquid fire, was employed. But the French troops defeated every effort made by the enemy to oust them from the important positions that had been won by costly sacrifices. These futile assaults served to keep up their fighting spirit, which otherwise might have gone down with the mercury.

During the night of January 13, 1918, Canadian troops attacked the German trenches to the north of Lens. The Germans offered only a feeble resistance, and after damaging the defenses the Canadians withdrew, bringing with them a number of prisoners. The adventure was a success, and almost unique in its way, because the raiders had not lost a man or suffered a single casualty.

On January 13-14, 1918, during the night and the day following, the guns of the French and Germans were active at various points along the Champagne front and on the right bank of the Meuse. In the region north of Louvemont the Germans had concentrated for attack, when they came under fire of the French guns and were dispersed. This discouraged any further attempts of the enemy to launch an infantry action that day.

On the Alsatian front, between the Thur and Doller Rivers, an artillery duel was fought all day on January 15, 1918. In the region of Badonviller the French carried out a successful raid that led to the capture of forty prisoners including some officers.

During these days peace reigned in a military sense on the British front in France and Flanders. There was generally, however, enough going on to keep up interest among the soldiers, even if they were not called on to do any hard fighting.

German batteries in a fitful way continued to rain a deadly fire around the outer edge of the Ypres salient from Passchendaele downward, and scattered shells lavishly among the back areas across the Menin road and the old fighting grounds of Monchy and Fampoux. The British troops holding defenses in the suburbs of Lens, Bullecourt, and Havrincourt were not spared by these destructive visitants.

The British certainly did their part in keeping the Germans at attention, doing counterbattery work with the aid of aeroplanes whenever there was an hour or two of visibility, showering tons of bombs and explosives on German working parties, trenches, and roads.

Notwithstanding the boggy condition of the ground, when it was not deep with snow, a rumor arose, though it was impossible to trace the source, that the Germans contemplated a great offensive. They possessed inventive skill and perhaps they would find means to get their cannon through the swamps of no-man's-land and the roads where heavy guns would sink wheel deep.

During the night of January 21, 1918, British aviators raided towns in the occupied parts of Belgium and German Lorraine. Two tons of bombs were dropped on the steelworks at Thionville, on railway sidings at Bernstorf, thirty miles south of Metz, and on the Arneville railway junction.

There was considerable activity on the French front on this date when German lines west of the Navrain Farm in the Champagne were successfully raided. The French cut through the enemy defense as far as the third parallel, and after destroying a trench brought away a goodly number of dispirited and bedraggled prisoners.

In Belgium during the day there was violent gunfire in the Nieuport sector. To the east of that place the Germans after a heavy bombardment made a dashing attack and succeeded in penetrating the French first-line trenches. They had hardly gained a foothold when the French rushed a counterattack and drove out the intruders, who fled to their own lines after losing a considerable number in wounded and prisoners.

On the right bank of the Meuse the artillery on both sides was active during January 23, 1918, around that much-fought-over sector, Hill 344, and the front of Chaume Wood. Following up an intense bombardment, the Germans tried to penetrate the wood, but were scattered by the French artillery fire.

On the 25th a strong assault was delivered on the French positions west of St. Gobain Forest. The enemy struck in at the western edge, and at one time seemed to be in a fair way to succeed, for the attack lacked neither daring nor persistence, but the French guns, whose fire had been withheld for a time that the Germans might advance near enough to present a better target, now poured out such death-dealing volleys that the attackers were halted and then fled back to their lines in disorder, leaving many dead on the field.

French aviators were busy on this date as long as there was visibility. Four German machines were brought down in aerial combats. Enemy defenses were successfully bombed, and tons of explosives were dropped on German establishments. Much damage was wrought to the railway stations at Thionville, and on Freiburg in Breisgau, the aniline works at Ludwigshafen and the cantonments in the Longuyon region.

Owing to the military collapse of Russia Germany was enabled to transfer thirty-eight or forty divisions from east to west, which meant that the French and British had now facing them at least 3,000,000 enemy troops. A great German offensive was in preparation on a vaster scale than any before attempted, having for its main object the capture of Paris or Calais. The Allied command expected the threatened drive might begin early in February, and had made their plans accordingly. Confident in their strength, they waited eagerly the great battle that might end the war.

PART II—THE UNITED STATES AS A BELLIGERENT

CHAPTER VII

THE NEW ALLY IN COUNCIL

THE weight of America's participation in the war did not begin to be felt until the autumn of 1917, when the aftermath of the Russian collapse, followed by the Italian disasters, made the Allies turn with more and more reliance to the new belligerent. Not alone in men, money, ships, and munitions did the Allies look for American aid, but for business counsel and administrative efficiency. The war had not been well conducted. Lloyd George frankly said so. The American mind was needed at the Allied conferences to contribute its share in remedying the defects of a division of command, from which had flowed a succession of costly errors. Hence the United States, being in the war to join hands with a unified Allied command, not to act independently, became an influential factor at the war parleys.

The presence of American representatives for the first time at an Allied war conference in Paris, which took place in November, 1917, was greeted in belligerent Europe as an event of deep significance. The United States since its belligerency had not shared in the Allied deliberations; but the need of unity—a single front, a single army, a single nation, as the French Premier, M. Painlevé, defined it—made its representation imperative. The delegation, which was headed by Colonel Edward M. House, and included Admiral Benson and General Bliss, set out on an avowed war mission while peace balloons floated in the air. As the President's reputed bosom confidant, who had been to Europe before on supposed peace missions, Colonel House was credited with bearing instructions to look over the ground for practicable peace formulas. His presence among the American representatives made this impression so general that the State Department had to deny that he was a Wilson peace envoy. He was heading a war mission pure and simple, whose aim was to weld the United States firmly as a member of the Allied powers.

The purpose of the Allied conference was to form a more complete coordination of the activities of the various nations warring against Germany. A more comprehensive understanding of their respective needs, in order that their joint efforts attained the highest war efficiency, was also sought. A prime factor to this end was to avoid any conflict of interests among the participants.

"The United States," Secretary Lansing explained, "in the employment of its man power and material resources desires to use them to the greatest advantage against Germany. It has been no easy problem to determine how they can be used most effectively, since the independent presentation of requirements by the Allied Governments have been more or less conflicting on account of each Government's appreciation of its own wants, which are naturally given greater importance than the wants of other governments.

"Though the resources of this country are vast and though there is every purpose to devote them all, if need be, to winning the war, they are not without limit. But even if they were greater they should be used to the highest advantage in attaining the supreme object for which we are fighting.

"It is the earnest wish of this Government to employ its military and naval forces and its resources and energies where they will give the greatest returns in advancing the common cause."

The American Government accordingly was represented at the conference to determine how this object could be achieved. Primarily the conferees met to create in effect a great general staff to direct the energies of the cobelligerents and so motivate military strategy that entire nations would act merely as units in the operations. They endeavored to make the whole fighting forces of the Allies into one mighty war-making machine.

The United States projected as an indispensable bulwark in this scheme by being practically the treasury and storehouse of the Allies. It had already poured out money and supplies at their call with lavish hand. Each had sent a mission to the United States to present its case and needs. The Government heard them, and the resources of the United States were freely drawn upon to meet their necessities. Each mission, however, had confined its requests largely or solely to its own requirements. Each clamored for men, ships, money, food, munitions, or whatever other war essential it wanted. A lack of coordinated plans and predetermined objectives weakened the scope of America's assistance on account of the scattered and piecemeal methods by which it was obtained. Consequently the United States, while providing for its own war necessities, determined that it must have a voice in arbitrating on the further needs of the Allied nations by weighing them side by side at the war conference, so that its resources could be distributed among them in pursuance of a coordinated plan aiming at achieving collective, not individual, advantage. Germany had pointed the way in showing the success to be obtained by combined effort. Germany and her three partners were one. The Allies were many and, so far, had been disjointed. The entry of the United States became the occasion for making an endeavor to coalesce the Allies to a closely knit *bloc* on the Teutonic method.

Great Britain, momentarily disheartened by the checks the Allied cause had sustained owing to a division of command and organization, was braced by the appearance of the American mission at the Allied conference. Said the London "Times":

"In several points, of late, things have not been going too well for the Allies, but none of their reverses or disappointments matters if only the great war power of the United States, military and economic, is rightly directed to the common end."

"The gain to the Allied cause of the alert American intellect and American freedom from convention," the "Daily Graphic" said, "should be of priceless value. Seeing that the guiding principle of the American delegates is to discover how the resources of their country can give the greatest results in bringing about the defeat of Germany, the unanimity of the conference is assured."

"Americans," remarked J. L. Garvin in the London "Observer," "have less jaded brain cells and more open minds. They are not involved in any past mistakes or shortcomings. They are uncommitted to any set theory and are relatively free from local European feelings. Their moral compass, so to speak, is less exposed to magnetic aberrations and is more likely to point true. They are in Europe only to win the war in Europe. They want to get to the bottom of the problem. They will have all conceivable data for getting to the bottom of it."

The conference found it easier to enunciate a formula than work it out practically; but at least a beginning was made in forming an organization to prevent duplication. Leaks of energy were stopped as well as waste of material. The relations of the Allies one with another were humanized by personal contact and a good feeling established which promised a guaranty against future misunderstanding. The envoys of every nation concerned met with great expectations from America. On that one subject there was a remarkable unity. All their needs were generously met, the American resources available being allocated on the basis of war needs as a whole. But the calls upon the American barrel were so great that it was tilted at an angle which revealed that it was not like the purse of Fortunatus.

As to the results of the conference, Colonel House thus reported on his return to the United States:

"Our mission was a great success. When we left Paris the efforts of all the Allies were focused. Up to the time of the Allied conferences they were not focused. They were not working together. They are working together now, and the promises are that they will continue to do so."

The principal recommendations made by the American delegation were:

"That the United States exert all their influence to secure the entire unity of effort, military, naval, and economic, between themselves and the countries associated with them in the war.

"Inasmuch as the successful termination of the war by the United States and the Allies can be greatly hastened by the extension of the United States shipping program, that the Government and the people of the United States bend every effort toward accomplishing this result by systematic coordination of resources of men and materials.

"That the fighting forces of the United States be dispatched to Europe with the least possible delay incident to training and equipment."

Much foundation work was accomplished, covering the entire field of the war organization, diplomatic, naval, military, finance, shipping, war trade, war industries and food.

An Interallied Naval Council was formed to coordinate the naval forces of the United States and those of its associates as one. Embraced in this scheme were plans for a combined prosecution of the naval war against the German submarines and keeping the American fleet informed of the operations and policy of the British Admiralty.

In the military field the extent of the operations of the American army in Europe was determined, after lengthy conference with the chiefs of the Allied armies on the western front. All military resources of the Allied belligerents were to be pooled, the contribution of each, including the United States, being specified. The pooling arrangement, according to the State Department, guaranteed that full equipment would be available to all American troops sent to Europe during the year 1918. The United States was also to participate in the deliberations of a Supreme War Council which was created. The problem of effecting the expeditious debarkation of American troops and their transport, with the needful equipment, to the military bases, called for careful survey, and new arrangements to that end, as well as for the production of military instruments and supplies, were made.

Consideration of a vital question, that of shipping tonnage, covered a study of the loss of vessels since the war began, the estimated output of new tonnage in 1918, and the framing of a program whereby the importations of all the Allies were to be restricted in order to release a maximum amount of tonnage for the transportation of American troops.

The United States plainly was not to be a silent partner in the war. In every sphere of joint action it was to have a voice and a vote. America was to be represented at a Supreme War Council to determine the conduct of military operations, at an Interallied Naval Council, at financial, shipping, and food councils. All that was to be known of the Allied war situation the American delegates ascertained. They consulted with the British Cabinet, the British Admiralty, and with all the Allied Governments; they interviewed chiefs of staff and commanders in chief, they inspected the fronts. War preparations in the United States now proceeded with the fullest cognizance of the conditions they were designed to meet.

The need of American troops in Europe was more than hinted by the agreement of the Allies to sacrifice importations so that tonnage could be available to bring the troops across the Atlantic. "Hurry your men across," Lord Derby urged. Admiral Sir David Beatty and Sir Auckland Geddes were convinced that the growing American army was destined to strike the deciding blow of the war. Germany watched the American preparations with mingled feelings, which could only find expression in simulated doubt, derision, and scorn. The projects for raising a huge army, an armada of transport and freight ships, and a fleet of airships were ridiculed by her press writers as examples of American bluff and bluster. Americans thought in exaggerations and talked in superlatives. The United States could not conduct a war in Europe on any such unexampled scale. Neither troops nor transports—supposing the latter could be built, which was doubtful—would reach their destination. German submarines would interpose. Besides, the United States never really intended to make more than a demonstration. It was merely making a flourish. The American army was weak any way and that assured its futility as a factor in the war. It was no better than Rumania's army when that country entered the war. "The

Mar..
American army,
"show a sudden inclination to square
The American call to arms suggested "advertis...
him. "The transport question would offer difficulties no. ...
than supplies," and, of course, "the German U-boats would be a
further obstacle."

The gradual on-coming of the American hosts was otherwise
seen by John St. Loe Strachey, editor of the London "Spectator,"
who drew this picture:

"I see America entering upon the field of war as does the
shadow in an eclipse. At first the orb of the moon seems barely
touched. There is only a slight irregularity perceptible on the
outline of the sphere, but gradually the inexorable shadow
spreads and spreads till the crisis of totality is reached; in the
words of the Chinese astrologers, the dragon has eaten the moon.

"What could be more soul-shaking or could bring home the
sense of a force that cannot be denied than the advance of the
shadow! Nothing can hurry it, nothing can delay it, nothing can
avert it. The process is begun; the doom will be accomplished.

"So be it, so it must be, so it will be with America and Germany in 1918."

CHAPTER VIII

ON THE LORRAINE FRONT

THE American expeditionary force in France were still in
process of being "broken in" when the war entered upon its
ourth year. They remained well behind the firing lines in their
raining camp, continuing their education in trench warfare.
he manipulation of the hand grenade, rifle, bayonet, trench
ortar, and machine gun under conditions to which the British

_____ng" in
_____ustment of masks when gas
_____on. Other companies found their way
_____British lines to drill their nerves to withstand scenes
of ruin and desolation, the whine of high-explosive shells, and the
rattle of shrapnel. All these preliminaries were directed toward
a modest aim—storming a trench line. Formerly troops were
trained for undertaking rapid marches and complicated maneuvers. In this war their endurance and fighting spirit became
restricted to a narrow field—that of penetrating enemy lines on
a front of ten kilometers, whose depth did not extend beyond one
kilometer.

The American troops did not take kindly to "digging in."
Their officers found great difficulty in impressing them with the
importance of taking cover. They were like their Canadian
brothers-in-arms, of whom it was said that they would die in the
last ditch but never dig it. They were averse to submitting to
the unheroic obligation of learning to fight in ambush; they clung
to primitive ideas of warfare and wanted to spring upon and
charge the enemy in the open. Only bitter losses finally persuaded the Canadians, French, and Australians that fighting the
Germans from a hole in the ground was the only way of fighting
them at all; but the Americans had yet to pay their toll for
yielding to their natural antipathy to fighting underground.
Their zeal for the pick and shovel, despite the war's terrible
object lessons, remained lukewarm.

"It seems a shame to curb the fine fighting spirits of our
troops," an American training officer said; "but they must be
made to understand as far as possible that impetuosity must be
subordinated to steadiness. This has become a time-clock war.
The men must advance in given time and go no further. Every
step of infantry advance must first be worked out with the
artillery, and when the plan is arranged it must be strictly
adhered to.

"We realize that it will be difficult to hold our men to this plan. If they see a battle going on, their favorite impulse will be to push on as fast as they can, and some are bound to do so, just as the Canadians did in the earlier stages. We will undoubtedly have big losses in this way, but the men who come through our first battles will be worth their weight in gold thereafter. They will learn quickly the value of steadiness and absolute discipline under fire, and they will be the steadying influence we can distribute through the newer units of our great army as they get their final preparation for trial by fire."

More to their taste was the training practice of charging dummy Germans in specially prepared trenches under the direction of an English sergeant major. At one camp three short lines of such trenches were constructed in a dip in the ground, ending at a rise some hundred yards off, with tin cans on sticks dotting them. The charge was thus undertaken:

"'Ready, gentlemen,' said the drill sergeant. 'Prepare for trench bayonet practice by half sections. You're to take these three line of trenches, lay out every boche in the lot, and then get to cover and fire six rounds at them 'ere tin 'ats. Don't waste a shot, gentlemen; every bullet a boche. Now, then, ready! Over the top and give 'em 'ell right in the stomach! Fritz likes his victuals, but not that sort. Get at 'em!'"

The men ran some ten yards and dug their bayonets savagely into dummy Germans made of sacks, which swung in the wind, and disappeared in the first trench. Their rifle butts rose and fell as they lunged desperately at the supposed foe. Then they reappeared and advanced farther, taking cover and lying spread-eagled behind a shallow trench, blazing at the cans, which fell rattling.

After some four months' training in camp, the long-looked-for tidings that American troops had taken their place beside the fighting forces of the Allies at length came from General Pershing's headquarters. On October 27, 1917, the first official announcement of war news from that source was issued in this form:

"In continuation of their training as a nucleus for instruction later, a contingent of some battalions of our first contingents, in association with veteran French battalions, are in the first-line trenches of a quiet sector on the French front. They are supported by some batteries of our artillery, in association with veteran French batteries.

"The sector remains normal. Our men have adapted themselves to actual trench conditions in the most satisfactory manner."

The "quiet sector" was occupied by helmeted infantry of the United States, without the knowledge of the enemy, by arriving at night through pouring rain and seas of mud. At six o'clock on the morning of that day, American artillery, already installed, fired the first American shot of the war at the German working party and shelled the German positions. The Germans gave shell for shell. The fusillades continued all day.

During the lull in the firing at dusk the first American machine guns appeared in a little deserted, shell-wrecked village well within hostile gun range and a few kilometers from the American trenches. The guns were hauled by Missouri mules, whose drivers were swathed in ponchos and helmeted to their eyes. The cavalcade moved in a long, silent line along a road margining a dark canal, followed by infantry rolling camp kitchens.

Other infantry followed through the cobble-paved streets. The darkness hid lines of men with packs on their backs, rifles slung on their shoulders, rain glistening on their helmets and coats, the wind whipping their coat skirts round limbs moving with machinelike precision. Only the tramp of many hobnailed boots disclosed their march through the village. They safely entered their trenches, unit by unit, and passed quickly to the places assigned them. The French welcomed them with ardor. Every American was shaken by the hand, some were hugged, and even kissed on both cheeks in the French custom. Quietness was essential, since the German trenches were not far away; but the fervor of the French troops overcame their precaution. It was too great a day for mute welcomes. The Americans had arrived!

The trenches were found to be muddy but well constructed. The troops settled down in them, and at daylight, under low-

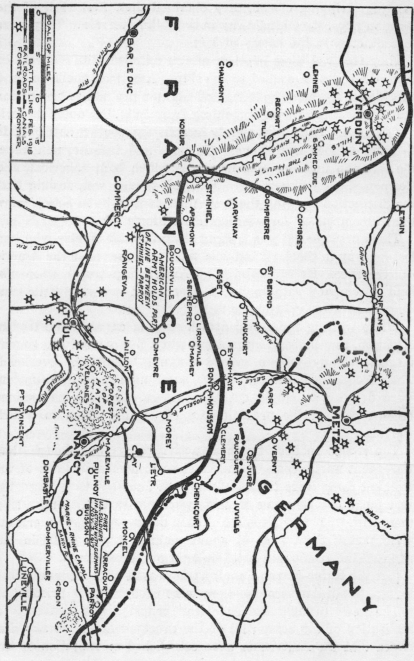

THE AMERICAN FRONT IN FRANCE WHERE THE FIRST CLASHES BETWEEN AMERICANS AND GERMANS OCCURRED

SCALE OF MILES

BATTLE LINE FEB. 1918
RAILROADS CANALS
FORTS FRONTIER

F R A N C E

G E R M A N Y

BAR LE DUC

CHAUMONT

LEHNES

VERDUN

VERDUN HILLS

RECOURT

TILTY

RIDGE OF THE MEUSE

KOEUR

SOMMEDIEUE

ST MIHIEL

COMPIERRE

COMBRES

ETAIN

APREMONT

VARVINAY

ST BENOID

COMMERCY

RANGEVAL

AMERICAN LINE OF ARMY HOLDS PART BETWEEN ST-MIHIEL - PARROY

BOUCONVILLE

SEICHEPREY

ESSEY

THIAUCOURT

DOMEVRE

LIRONVILLE

MAMEY

FEY-EN-HAYE

PONT-A-MOUSSON

CONFLANS

ORNE RIV.

METZ

TOUL

JAILLON

FOREST OF HAYE

VELAINES

MOREY

ARRY

CLEMERY

RAUCOURT

OSTURE

OVERNY

PT ST VINCENT

MOSELLE RIV.

MAXEVILLE

NANCY

LETR

CHENICOURT

JUVILLE

NSED RIV.

DOMBASLE

PT LNOY

FIRST U.S. SOLDIERS IN ACTION WITH GERMANS BUISSON CT

MONCEL

ARRACOURT

PARROY

MARNE-RHINE CANAL

SANON R.

SOMMERVILLER

CRION

LUNEVILLE

hanging, dripping clouds, they obtained their first view of the German lines, stretching away in the rolling terrain. They were in contact with the enemy at last.

They received their baptism of fire mingled with showers of mud, their clothes soaked to the skin. American shells fell and exploded in German territory, and German projectiles broke near the American positions, sprinkling fragments, but doing no serious damage. They were merely establishing contact as a prelude to more serious operations. Gunners and infantrymen alike, the latter in first-line trenches, over which both American and German shells whizzed, were satisfied, though wet, feeling that the distinction of being the first Americans to be in action more than recompensed for weather discomforts.

Their first quarry was a stray German mail carrier who had lost his way in the dark and was taken prisoner near the American trenches. He encountered an American patrol in no-man's-land in company with another German, and was shot while running away after refusing to halt.

While waiting for a real attack sniping engaged the troops' attention, especially on clear days, when German snipers sought targets. Many bullets passed singing harmlessly overhead. Their frequency called for retorts, and a number of infantrymen were detailed to single out the snipers. Sniping the sniper became part of the preliminaries of settling down to trench warfare.

The troops realized by these activities, trifling though they were, that mimic charges and class-room demonstrations of the training camp were things of the past and that they faced the real foe. The Germans in fact, were not tardy in impressing them with their new situation. They discovered that Americans were facing them and set about making a raid. Berlin announced the result in a brief bulletin on November 3.

"At the Rhine-Marne Canal, as the result of a reconnoitering thrust, North American soldiers were brought in as prisoners."

The news brought the American people a step nearer to a realization of the actualities of the great struggle. It also disclosed that the Americans were established on a section of the front defended by the German Crown Prince's army and facing Lorraine. The so-called "quiet sector" stood revealed as the only front through which war could be carried into the heart of Germany. It lay before the gap in the French barrier forts, Verdun-Toul and Epinal-Belfort, flanked by the invulnerable Verdun on the northeast and the French positions in the Alsatian Vosges on the southeast. A quiet sector it might be, but more than 40,000 German dead lie buried there, the flower of the army of the Crown Prince of Bavaria. They fell in a twenty-eight day battle in August and September, 1914, when five French army corps under General Castelnau fought seven under the Crown Prince The Germans finally retired into Lorraine after vainly attempting to cross the Moselle. Both General Pétain— who attempted an offensive there in 1916, but was checked from proceeding with it by political high commands—and General Castelnau were convinced of the vulnerability of this sector as a roadway into Germany, and prophets were not wanting who saw in the presence of the Americans there a foretoken that an American army might essay what the two French Generals had not accomplished. At any rate, after an unbroken calm of three years, the sector was no longer quiet.

The Germans had scored by drawing first blood. The Berlin press was riotously gleeful over the event, one journal, the "Lokal-Anzeiger," gloating over it in these terms:

"Three cheers for the Americans! Clever chaps they are, it cannot be denied. Scarcely have they touched the soil of this putrified Europe when they already are forcing their way into Germany.

"It is our good fortune that we are equipped to receive and entertain numerous guests and that we shall be able to provide quarters for these gentlemen. They will find comfort in the thought that they are rendering their almighty President, Mr. Wilson, valuable services, inasmuch as it is asserted he is anxious to obtain reliable information concerning conditions and sentiments in belligerent countries.

"As Americans are accustomed to travel in luxury and comfort, we assume that these advance arrivals merely represent couriers for larger numbers to come. We are sure the latter will come and be gathered in by us. At home they believe they possess the biggest and most colossal everything, but such establishments as we have here they have not seen.

"Look here, my boy, here is the big firm of Hindenburg & Co., with which you want to compete. Look at its accomplishments and consider whether it would not be better to haul down your sign and engage in some other line. Perhaps your boss, Wilson, will reconsider his newest line of business before we grab off more of his young people."

A salient of the American position occupied by a small detachment had been successfully raided by the Germans before daybreak, resulting in three Americans killed, several wounded, and a dozen captured or missing. The Teutons started a heavy barrage fire, which isolated the salient, so that help could not reach the troops, nor could they retire, and thus had the besieged men at the mercy of their superior force. The Americans fought obstinately until they were overwhelmed. They had only been in the trenches a few days and were part of the second contingent who had entered them for training under actual war conditions. They succeeded in capturing a German prisoner, and inflicting casualties; but the latter did not become known as the enemy, in fleeing the trench, took their dead and wounded with them.

After shelling the barbed-wire front of the trenches, dropping many high-explosive missiles of large caliber, the Germans directed a heavy artillery fire to cover all the adjacent territory, including the passage leading to the trenches, thereby effecting a complete barrage of the salient front and rear. Soon after the enemy, exceeding two hundred in number, rushed the breaches and wire entanglements on each side of the salient, lifting the barrage in the forefield to permit their passage.

It was an elaborate encircling bombardment to achieve a trifling object. An American platoon, numbering only nineteen men, were corraled by a heavy fire from 77's and 115's, which searched the whole line of trenches communicating with the salient where they were isolated. The French, who had only recently vacated the position to make way for the Americans, estimated that the German shells expended exceeded eight thousand.

With the raising of the frontal barrage, the German raiders advanced. They were composed of storm troops, volunteers, machine gunners, artillerymen, pioneers to destroy the wire entanglements, and stretcher bearers to carry off their casualties. They had gathered round a group of ruined farm buildings some seven hundred yards from the American trenches, armed with grenades, revolvers, trench knives, and rifles. They followed, in columns of fours, a tape across no-man's-land laid out by leaders who had previously been over the ground. Advancing across a swampy ravine toward the salient, they penetrated the gaps in the American wire entanglements, and a number reached the trenches at the rear of their barrage. The Americans were thus cut off from behind. Other raiders stayed outside the trenches to protect those who entered them and to shoot any Americans who appeared above the parapet. The trenches were stormed right and left of the salient, one party clearing them as they proceeded, the other invading the dugouts for prisoners.

The darkness of the trenches veiled what next happened. After the Germans had completed their work and retired, an American trooper, private Enright, was found with his throat cut from ear to ear on the top of the parapet. While fighting a German in front of him he appeared to have been attacked from behind by another armed with a trench knife. A second trooper, private Hay, lay dead in the trench, and outside a dugout was the body of Corporal Gresham.

In the confusion some of the American troops mistook the Germans for their own comrades, and paid for their error. Corporal Gresham, for example, was the sentry at a dugout door when three men advanced toward him. Supposing them to be Americans he shouted:

"Don't shoot! I'm an American.

"It's Americans we're looking for," answered one of the three, and shot him dead with a revolver.

It was a brief, ordinary affray, in nowise different from other happenings occurring nightly all along the front. But nineteen Americans were set upon by over 200 Germans, and it was the Americans' first taste of Teutonic warfare. They fought stoutly with pistols, knives, and bayonets until overcome, whereupon the Germans went off with an American sergeant, a corporal, and ten privates, all of whom were trapped in a dugout near the tip of the besieged salient.

The raid scarcely lasted five minutes and outside the salient no one in the American lines knew it was proceeding. The German communiqué dismissed it in three lines. From Berlin's viewpoint it was inconsequential; but to Americans it was of moment in being their first clash with the enemy. Young, inexperienced soldiers, cooped in a position they were not familiar with, encountering their baptism of fire under circumstances of surprise, uncertainty, and darkness, had acquitted themselves well against heavy odds, and prevented the enemy from penetrating beyond the first line of trenches.

The American dead were buried with due honors on French soil. The general commanding the French division in the section delivered an oration at their graves in the presence of French and American troops amid the roaring of guns and whistle of shells. His words belong to the record of America's part in the war:

"Men! These graves, first to be dug in our national soil, and but a short distance from the enemy, are as a mark of the mighty land we and our allies firmly cling to in the common task, confirming the will of the people and the army of the United States to fight with us to a finish, ready to sacrifice as long as is necessary until final victory for the most noble of causes, that of the liberty of nations, the weak as well as the mighty. Thus the deaths of these humble soldiers appear to us with extraordinary grandeur.

"We will, therefore, ask that the mortal remains of these young men be left here, left with us forever. We inscribe on the tombs, 'Here lie the first soldiers of the Republic of the United States to fall on the soil of France for liberty and justice.'

The passer-by will stop and uncover his head. Travelers and men of heart will go out of their way to come here to pay their respective tributes.

"Private Enright, Private Gresham, Private Hay! In the name of France I thank you. God receive your souls. Farewell!"

After this foray shelling became of daily occurrence. The troops continued their training under fire, the first contingent giving place to the second contingent, and the second to the third in occupying the trenches, after each had undergone a spell of patrol work, sharpshooting, and accustoming their nerves to falling shrapnel. Trench conditions enabled them to acquire a better insight of the science of war than they could learn in months of instruction in training camps. While the infantry were thus engaged in their underground finishing school, the gunners, in addition to making progress in actual firing, acquired greater facility in observation work and in locating enemy batteries by the sound method. The heavy guns on both sides engaged in duels at long range, with the lighter pieces working at targets nearer the lines. This gun activity was not without its toll. German casualties due to American marksmanship, of course, could not be ascertained, but they were probably equal to the American killed and wounded.

The troops were eager for an opportunity to retaliate on the foe for trapping their comrades in the salient, and on November 14, 1917, a patrol succeeded in exacting a partial revenge. Assisted by some French troops they planned a night ambuscade near the German lines on a shell-ruined farm. It was a dreary vigil in the mud, where they lay throughout the small hours, until their patience was rewarded by the appearance of a large German patrol, in number more than double those of the Franco-Americans. They permitted the Germans to pass, and then attacked them on their flank. The fusillade of French and American bullets from shell craters and other shelters where the sharpshooters lay concealed took the Germans by surprise. They precipitately fled, taking their fallen with them. No French or American trooper was hit by the shots the Germans fired in their hurried retreat.

More notable than such skirmishes on the American front before Lorraine was the part a number of unarmed American engineers, in company with Canadians, took in the encircling movement the Germans made on the British positions before Cambrai on November 30, 1917. For some time past American engineers had not only been of yeoman service behind the French lines in hauling tons of ammunition and other equipment to supply the French forces, but had been engaged on the railroad in the rear of the British front. They did not belong to the fighting units, and no achievements were looked for from men whose sole arms were picks and shovels. But the ramifications of the German assault on Gouzeaucourt brought these workers in the rear to the forefront of the attack, and they distinguished themselves in a manner which drew tributes from both the French and British high commands. A staid official account of the rôle they played thus describes the situation:

"Two and one-half companies of railway engineers, with a strength of eight officers and 365 men, were encamped at Fins on November 30, 1917, having completed their work in the neighborhood. At 6.30 four officers and 280 men went to Gouzeaucourt, arriving at 7 and starting to work with Canadian engineers. The entire contingent was under a Canadian major and an American captain. The area was three miles in the rear of the line and none of the troops was armed.

"At 7.15 German barrage fire moved on Gouzeaucourt after heavy shelling to the east. At 7.30 a general retirement was ordered, and it was effected with some difficulty, due to the artillery, machine-gun and airplane fire.

"A number of losses were sustained at this time, and also among the men who, cut off by the German advance, had taken refuge in dugouts. Some of these men who had been cut off succeeded in joining British combatant units and fought with them during the day."

A story of American grit and pluck lay concealed in the last sentence. The American and Canadian engineers, cut off as described, were taken prisoners by the Germans. They were fifty in number, and accompanied by a German escort marched along the road leading from Gouzeaucourt to Cambrai. As they proceeded disconsolately toward the zone of the German prison cages, they encountered a small body of British troops who had been separated from their comrades and were wandering about aimlessly. The appearance of the Germans with the prisoners produced an immediate charge toward them by the British. The Germans sought to drive their captives toward La Vacquerie before the advancing British reached them. But the prisoners, seeing rescue at hand, turned upon their guards and fought them barehanded until the British troops interposed and vanquished the Germans. The American engineers and their comrades thereupon took possession of the German rifles and with their rescuers found their way back to the British lines.

A number of American engineers were killed and injured, presumably during the German attack on Gouzeaucourt, since no mention was made of casualties in the adventure on the highroad. Their losses were largely due to their being unarmed when the Germans came, a predicament which forced them to seize the guns of dead and wounded soldiers to protect themselves. The army commands afterward ordered that all engineers be armed to enable them to take their place with the troops in any future emergency which brought them again face to face with the foe. The French Government was so impressed with their performance that it sent the following communication to Washington:

"We must remark upon the conduct of certain American soldiers, pioneers and workmen on the military railroad in the sector of the German attack west of Cambrai on November 30, 1917. They exchanged their picks and shovels for rifles and cartridges and fought with the English. Many died thus bravely, arms in hand, before the invader. All helped to repulse the enemy. There is not a single person who saw them at work who does not render warm praise to the coolness, discipline, and courage of these improvised combatants."

Their exploit stirred the American camp to enthusiasm mingled with envy. The British front at Cambrai was a long step from the American trenches in the Lorraine sector, and tidings

War St. 7—G

of the happenings at Gouzeaucourt impressed the troops with the fact that not on them only was the glory of the Stars and Stripes being upheld on the soil of France. An infantry sergeant voiced the general feeling of his comrades thus:

"We stay in the trenches for a spell and let Fritz shoot his artillery at us and have never really had a chance to use our rifles except to snipe and pot Fritz out in no-man's-land on dark nights. These railroaders managed to run their trains right into a good, thick scrap, and if this isn't luck, I don't know what it is."

Casualties continued to grow with the constant shelling. Sporadic raids over no-man's-land and visitations of German airships added to them. Bombs were dropped on a party of engineers, killing one of them, and two privates were victims of a German aviator's explosive over a wood in which they were camped.

Winter set in with a snowfall that impeded the training of the troops and communications. Roads became impassable by drifts, and many motor trucks, after crawling at a snail's pace over the hilly roads, became stranded in the snow. A thaw in January turned icy roads into river beds. Torrential streams flowed from melting snows in the hills, and together with a downpour of fine rain combined to make weather conditions on the American front the worst the troops had encountered since their arrival in France. The roads were cluttered in places with ditched motor trucks. Here and there mule-drawn vehicles were mired. Transport trains drawn by mules suffered most before the thaw, the animals slipping and falling on the icy roadbeds, and were unable to rise except by the aid of thick layers of branches and twigs placed under their hoofs. The beginning of 1918, in short, found the American army in France, like their allied comrades on the rest of the front, stalled by the weather, and little tidings came of their accustomed activities.

CHAPTER IX

POPE AND PRESIDENT

PEACE efforts, assiduously pursued in Berlin, and culminating in the Reichstag resolution recorded in the previous volume, had meantime taken a new turn; but they encountered a new element in the United States as a resolute belligerent.

The Vatican interposed with an olive branch. The Pope tread cautiously, sensible of the delicacy of his task in seeking to effect world peace; but his proposals were hopelessly futile and died in the borning. Their only welcome came from the Central Powers, and even there dissentient voices were heard. The Allies' reception of his note was cold, unresponsive, suspicious, and resentful. "As you were," the Pope virtually proposed to the two groups of belligerents, running directly counter to the chief aim of the Allies, which was to overturn the *status quo ante*, and establish a European concert of nations on a new, safer, and enduring foundation.

The Papal note, communicated to the various belligerent powers on August 1, 1917, invited their governments to agree on the following points, which seemed to his Holiness, "to offer the basis of a just and lasting peace":

"First, the fundamental point must be that the material force of arms shall give way to the moral force of right, whence shall proceed a just agreement of all upon the simultaneous and reciprocal decrease of armaments, according to rules and guarantees to be established, in the necessary and sufficient measure for the maintenance of public order in every State; then, taking the place of arms, the institution of arbitration, with its high pacifying function, according to rules to be drawn in concert and under sanctions to be determined against any State which would decline either to refer international questions to arbitration or to accept its awards.

"When supremacy of right is thus established, let every obstacle to ways of communication of the peoples be removed by insuring, through rules to be also determined, the true freedom and community of the seas, which, on the one hand, would eliminate any causes of conflict, and on the other hand, would open to all new sources of prosperity and progress.

"As for the damages to be repaid and the cost of the war, we see no other way of solving the question than by setting up the general principle of entire and reciprocal conditions, which would be justified by the immense benefit to be derived from disarmament, all the more as one could not understand that such carnage could go on for mere economic reasons If certain particular reasons stand against this in certain cases, let them be weighed in justice and equity.

"But these specific agreements, with the immense advantages that flow from them, are not possible unless territory now occupied is reciprocally restituted. Therefore, on the part of Germany, there should be total evacuation of Belgium, with guaranties of its entire political, military, and economic independence toward any power whatever; evacuation also of the French territory; on the part of the other belligerents, a similar restitution of the German colonies.

"As regards territorial questions, as, for instance, those that are disputed by Italy and Austria, by Germany and France, there is reason to hope that, in consideration of the immense advantages of durable peace with disarmament, the contending parties will examine them in a conciliatory spirit, taking into account, as far as is just and possible, as we have said formerly, the aspirations of the population, and, if occasion arises, adjusting private interests to the general good of the great human society.

"The same spirit of equity and justice must guide the examination of the other territorial and political questions, notably those relative to Armenia, the Balkan States, and the territories forming part of the old Kingdom of Poland, for which, in particular, its noble historical traditions and suffering, particularly undergone in the present war, must win with justice, the sympathies of the nations."

The deep esteem in which the Allies and the rest of the nations held the Pontiff assured an attentive and respectful hearing of his appeal. But his intervention was nevertheless denounced as an espousal of a German peace, in that it would enable Germany to take her place at the peace council table with all her lost colonies restored, exempt from every demand for reparation for the ruin she had wrought, secure in the possession of all her territory, and with the future of Alsace-Lorraine, Trent, Trieste, Poland, Rumania, and Serbia left for settlement by negotiation by the parties in conflict. The Papal proposals were also objected to in making no distinction between the combatants, but placed them all on the same footing as apparently "stricken by a universal madness."

It soon became apparent that the Allied Powers, including the United States, were a unit in agreeing that the Papal note, because it overlooked the issues for which the Entente was fighting, must be respectfully rejected. President Wilson became their spokesman in a note he addressed to the Pontiff on August 27, 1917. While recognizing the Pope's "moving appeal" and the "dignity and force of the humane motives which prompted it," the President considered it would be folly to take the path of peace the Pope pointed out if that path did not in fact lead to the goal proposed. As to the Pope's proposals generally, he said:

"It is manifest that no part of this program can be successfully carried out unless the restitution of the *status quo ante* furnishes a firm and satisfactory basis for it. The object of this war is to deliver the free peoples of the world from the menace and the actual power of a vast military establishment, controlled by an irresponsible Government, which, having secretly planned to dominate the world, proceeded to carry the plan out without regard either to the sacred obligations of treaty or the long-established practices and long-cherished principles of international action and honor; which chose its own time for the war; delivered its blow fiercely and suddenly; stopped at no barrier, either of law or of mercy; swept a whole continent within the tide of blood—not the blood of soldiers only, but the blood of innocent women and children also and of the helpless poor; and now stands balked, but not defeated, the enemy of four-fifths of the world.

"This power is not the German people. It is the ruthless master of the German people. It is no business of ours how that great people came under its control or submitted with temporary zest to the domination of its purpose; but it is our business to see to it that the history of the rest of the world is no longer left to its handling.

"To deal with such a power by way of peace upon the plan proposed by his Holiness, the Pope, would, so far as we can see, involve a recuperation of its strength and a renewal of its policy; would make it necessary to create a permanent hostile combination of nations against the German people, who are its instruments; and would result in abandoning the newborn Russia to the intrigue, the manifold subtle interference, and the certain counter-revolution which would be attempted by all the malign influences to which the German Government has of late accustomed the world.

"We cannot take the word of the present rulers of Germany as a guaranty of anything that is to endure unless explicitly supported by such conclusive evidence of the will and purpose of the German people themselves as the other peoples of the world would be justified in accepting. Without such guaranties treaties of settlement, agreements for disarmament, covenants to set up arbitration in the place of force, territorial adjustments, reconstitutions of small nations, if made with the German Government, no man, no nation, could now depend on.

"We must await some new evidence of the purposes of the great peoples of the Central Powers."

In other words, the Pope's proposals were regarded as untenable because the Allies could not trust the kaiser and his government to respect any covenants that might flow from them. There was no responsible person to negotiate with. The Vatican was disappointed, the German press greeted the President's answer with abuse, and the Allies found the American note so comprehensive and satisfying in expressing their views that they paid no further attention to the proposal.

Germany and Austria were more responsive; but the Allies' rejection through President Wilson of the papal suggestions imparted something of an anticlimax to the Teutonic replies when they were forthcoming a month later. Both reflected an earnest desire for peace; both gave whole-hearted support to the Vatican's efforts. Austria was especially eager to enter into negotiations on the basis the Pope proposed. But neither was specific. The Austrian emperor favored disarmament and arbitration in a cloud of platitudes. The kaiser accepted the Pope's general aims, but was mute on particularizing the German aims. Both suppressed whatever terms of peace they longed to offer. Sifted down to essentials, and extricating their meaning from a welter of unctuous verbiage, the Teutonic answers merely conveyed an eager desire to reach a peace conference, withholding terms for submission until such parleys could begin. As each evaded any suggestion of definite concessions on vital points, the absence of which constituted the principal obstacles to peace, and as the Allies had already refused to negotiate with the German Government in any event, the Teutonic answers lost all significance except as diplomatic courtesies in response to the Pope's well-meant mediation. That was probably their main purpose.

Germany proposed nothing except that the war be ended by a promise on her part to reduce her army reciprocally with other nations—a promise she would not fulfill; by a promise that Great Britain reduce her navy—a promise she would expect Great Britain faithfully to fulfill; and a promise of the nations to arbitrate in future—a promise Germany would ignore if conditions favored a new war. She saw "the freedom of the seas" as the issue of the war; but the seas were as free to Germany in time of peace as they were to Great Britain, their reputed mistress. The rest of the world saw the German Government as the real issue of the war.

The next peace manifestation, which caused a momentary disturbance in Allied circles, came from the Marquis of Lansdowne, a former British Foreign Secretary, who had also been Viceroy of India and Governor General of Canada. Fearing that the prolongation of the war might lead to "the ruin of the civilized world," he besought the Allies to make a restatement of their war aims in order to bring about peace before that catastrophe came.

The Lansdowne communication to the press looked like a plea for Germany, and coming as it did from a British noble of ingrained toryism, who had done his share as a Cabinet Minister to develop British imperialism, was startling enough. To forestall any suspicion that he was voicing unofficial sentiments of the British Government, Bonar Law and Lord Robert Cecil declared that Lord Lansdowne only spoke his own views. The Government repudiated them, as did the Unionist party. Lord Lansdowne himself was obliged to acknowledge that his proposals were solely his own and that he consulted no one in formulating them. It was realized that his note only encouraged the German war party, which construed it as evidence of divided counsels in Great Britain, and that the British were weakening in their determination to conquer. The air was quickly cleared and showed that no peace movement was possible in England while Germany remained impenitent and unbeaten.

CHAPTER X

AMERICA'S WAR AIMS

NEVERTHELESS, the Papal and Lansdowne letters were not entirely fruitless. It brought the Allies a step nearer to restating their war aims through Lloyd-George and President Wilson. But their utterances pointed to a steadfast continuance of the war until those aims were achieved, not a slackening of hostilities to effect an inconclusive peace lenient to Germany.

Addressing a body of trades-union delegates at Westminster on January 5, 1918, the British Premier faced a situation—an apparent outgrowth of the Lansdowne letter—where national unity in the prosecution of the war was perceived to be in jeopardy. A suspicion was rife that the war was being pursued for objects which could not be openly avowed. Lloyd-George therefore saw the need of a restatement of war aims:

"We may begin by clearing away some misunderstandings and stating what we are not fighting for.

"We are not fighting a war of aggression against the German people. Their leaders have persuaded them that they are fighting a war of self-defense against a league of rival nations, bent on the destruction of Germany. That is not so. The destruction or disruption of Germany or the German people has never been a war aim with us from the first day of this war to this day.

"Nor did we enter this war merely to alter or destroy the imperial constitution of Germany, much as we consider that military and autocratic constitution a dangerous anachronism in the twentieth century. Our point of view is that the adoption of a really democratic constitution by Germany would be the most convincing evidence that her old spirit of military domination has, indeed, died in this war and would make it much easier for us to conclude a broad, democratic peace with her. But, after all, that is a question for the German people to decide.

"We are not fighting to destroy Austria-Hungary or to deprive Turkey of its capital or the rich lands of Asia Minor and Thrace, which are predominantly Turkish.

"The settlement of the new Europe must be based on such grounds of reason and justice as will give some promise of stability. Therefore, it is that we feel that government with the consent of the governed must be the basis of any territorial settlement in this war. For that reason also, unless treaties be upheld, unless every nation is prepared, at whatever sacrifices, to honor the national signature, it is obvious that no treaty of peace can be worth the paper on which it is written."

The British Premier then restated the Allies' specific war aims, which did not materially differ from the first declaration recorded in a previous volume of this history, except with regard to Russia, conditions in that country having called for a suspension of judgment on territorial questions affecting her.

Three days later (January 8, 1918), President Wilson gave to the world the peace terms of the United States in an address to

Congress. His declaration was the most advanced doctrine of internationalism pronounced by any of the Allied statesmen. It definitely committed the United States not only to promoting and safeguarding the peace of Europe but the peace of the world. The frequent question: What was America fighting for? was answered. It was not merely to uphold American rights. The aims of the United States had developed far beyond nationalism. It was to uphold the rights of all the peoples menaced or outraged in the world war.

The purpose of the President's address appeared to be threefold:

To drive a wedge into the political structure of Germany by encouraging the Socialists and liberal elements, and exhibiting the military party as the single obstacle to democracy and world peace.

To expose the insincerity of Germany's pretensions of liberality in her peace offers to Russia and thus bring Russia back into partnership with the democracy of the Allies, which she showed symptoms of abandoning.

To show the agreement of the United States with the speech of Lloyd-George and to develop further the principles of world peace for which America stood.

The Entente Allies welcomed the President's pronouncement as putting the seal of American approval on their war aims, as reiterated by Lloyd-George, and as committing the United States to the Allied cause till it was won. The necessity for any restatement of war aims by the United States was regarded as a question for the President to determine, and he had done so at a time when the need was clearly urgent in Great Britain. Hence his address, echoing and, indeed, amplifying that of Lloyd-George, buttressed British solidarity on the war by definitely establishing an abiding Anglo-American Entente while the war lasted.

Far from opening a way to peace, the Papal and Lansdowne pleas produced a sequence of utterances which were in effect renewed war declarations from the spokesmen of the Allies. Lord Lansdowne sought a reiteration of war aims as a basis for

peace negotiations. President Wilson's answer to that suggestion was not confined to a reassertion of America's war objects.
While the dove of peace was fluttering a pair of weak wings he
went to Congress (December 4, 1917) and called for war against
Austria-Hungary to remove an "embarrassing obstacle" in the
conduct of hostilities against Germany.

"Austria-Hungary," he told Congress, "is for the time being
not her own mistress, but simply the vassal of the German Government. We must face the facts as they are and act upon them
without sentiment in this stern business.

"The Government of Austria-Hungary is not acting upon its
own initiative or in response to the wishes and feelings of its
own peoples, but as the instrument of another nation. We must
meet its force with our own and regard the Central Powers as
but one. The war can be successfully conducted in no other way.
The same logic would lead also to a declaration of war against
Turkey and Bulgaria. They also are the tools of Germany. But
they are mere tools and do not yet stand in the direct path of
our necessary action."

Both branches of Congress responded by passing a joint war
resolution with only one dissentient House vote, and on December 7, 1917, war with Austria-Hungary was declared.

Germany meditated. There was an answer to be made to
Lloyd-George and President Wilson, but what? The military
situation, as seen through German eyes, and the political situation in Germany, as dominated by the Junkers and annexation-
ists, duly supplied it. Germany seemed to have become convinced that a German peace was certain. Her confidence was
stated to be based on the war map, added to a belief that a
lack of cohesion and community of spirit prevailed among the
Allies, in contrast with her own unified will to victory, and
that the United States was merely gesturing in entering the
war. There was obvious camouflage in affecting to question
the solidarity of the Allies and to asperse the sincerity of
American intervention; but no posturing was perceived in Germany's reliance on the war map as a tangible basis for a
German peace.

The kaiser's new chancellor, Count von Hertling, addressing the Reichstag main committee on January 22, 1918, emphasized this reliance in a speech which constituted a tardy response to the war aims reaffirmed by Lloyd-George and President Wilson. Demanding that the Entente Powers abandon their attitude that Germany was the guilty party who must do penance and promise improvement, he said:

"They may take it from me that our military position was never so favorable as it now is. Our highly gifted army leaders face the future with undiminished confidence in victory. Throughout the army, in the officers and the men, lives unbroken the joy of battle.

"Our repeatedly expressed willingness for peace and the spirit of reconciliation revealed by our proposals must not be regarded by the Entente as a license permitting the indefinite lengthening of the war.

"If the leaders of the enemy powers really are inclined toward peace let them revise their program once again. If they do that and come forward with fresh proposals, then we will examine them carefully."

This was by way of preface to answering President Wilson's fourteen requirements if the United States was to lay down its arms. The first four, in the chancellor's view, were susceptible to agreement. Germany accepted in principle the abolition of secret diplomacy and favored open covenants of peace. The chancellor saw no difference of opinion on the subject of freedom of navigation upon the seas; but it was "highly important for the freedom of shipping in future if strongly fortified naval bases on important international routes, such as England has at Gibraltar, Malta, Aden, Hongkong, the Falkland Islands, and many other places, were removed." Further, Germany was in accord with the President regarding the removal of economic barriers that interfered with international trade. She also affirmed that the limitation of armaments desired by President Wilson was "discussable."

The fifth clause of the Wilson peace aims, which called for self-determination by colonial peoples as to whose sovereignty they should recognize, was less easily disposed of. The chancellor evaded the issue by throwing the onus of putting the proposal in practice upon Great Britain:

"I believe that for the present it may be left for England, which has the greatest colonial empire, to make what she will of this proposal of her ally. This point of the program also will have to be discussed in due time, on the reconstitution of the world's colonial possessions."

Thus Germany submitted, as one of the foundations of peace, that England should not only abandon her naval bases but assent to the dismemberment of her colonial empire.

The President's demand for the evacuation of Russian territory was met by a refusal. The Entente Powers having declined to participate in the negotiations between the so-called Russian Government and the Teutonic Powers, the matter was one to be decided between the negotiators alone.

Belgium was not to be evacuated and restored as a condition insisted upon by the United States. The settlement of the Belgian question, the chancellor said, belonged to the peace conference:

"So long as our opponents have unreservedly taken the standpoint that the integrity of the Allies' territory can offer the only possible basis of peace discussion, I must adhere to the standpoint hitherto always adopted and refuse the removal in advance of the Belgian affair from the entire discussion."

The chancellor took the same attitude toward the question of freeing and restoring the invaded French territory and of the return of Alsace-Lorraine to France to right an old wrong. "The occupied parts of France are a valued pawn in our hands," said the chancellor. "The conditions and methods of procedure of the evacuation, which must take account of Germany's vital interest, are to be agreed upon between Germany and France. I can only again expressly accentuate the fact that there can never be a question of dismemberment of imperial territory."

The next four Wilson requirements (VIII to XI), relating to readjustment of the frontiers of Italy, autonomy for the subjugated races of Austria-Hungary, the restoration and integrity of Rumania, Serbia and Montenegro were not Germany's immediate concern, and the chancellor airily relegated them to Austria-Hungary for consideration. As to Turkey, for whose subject races the President demanded self-government, as well as a free Dardanelles, the chancellor intimated that her integrity vitally concerned the German Empire, while the future of Poland was to rest entirely in the hands of Germany and Austria-Hungary. Finally, President Wilson's proposed league of nations admitted of basic consideration only when all other pending questions had been settled.

The chancellor's answer was a mere repetition of the defiant and arrogant presentations of the German position with which the Allies had become familiar. The war aims of the President to which Count von Hertling could assent were of trivial importance compared to the Allies' chief aim—the overthrow of Prussian militarism. Peace gropings had produced another declaration of war. Germany openly announced that she was engaged on a war of conquest. Chancellor von Hertling's address admitted of no other interpretation. The fate of Poland was to be decided by the kaisers, that is, annexed in substance, if not in form. The Baltic provinces of Russia were earmarked for Germany, and Russia, thus cut off from the western seas, was to have icebound Archangel and distant Vladivostok as her only ports. The disposition or division of Rumania, Serbia, and Montenegro was to be left to Austria-Hungary, with Germany pledged to support her decisions. Armenia, Palestine, and Arabia, were to be returned to the Turks, while as to Constantinople and the Dardanelles no settlement could be permitted that was not agreeable to German imperialism. As to Belgium, the conclusion was that it would receive the same status as Luxemburg had before the war, with railroads, ports, commerce, and army in German hands. Not even the return of northern France was promised this being a question to be discussed, not with the Allies, but only between Germany and France, and Alsace-Lorraine was to be kept on the fraudulent claim that it was and always had been German territory. The question of Italia Irredenta was remitted to Austria-Hungary, and the German colonies were to be restored regardless of the wishes of their inhabitants or the safety of their neighbors.

When this grandiose scheme of conquest was ratified and realized, then, and then only, would Germany consider entering into a league of peace, or discuss mutual disarmament, or other of the Allies' proposals for safeguarding peace when it came. Germany sought to be placed in possession of doubled power before she would even talk about creating conditions making for a durable peace. She must be able to reject flatly any scheme proposed, and then, snapping her fingers, defy the Allies to do what they would, for she in no wise bound herself to disarm a single soldier or spike a single gun.

The Austrian Reichsrat heard a speech of a different tenor by Count Czernin, Foreign Minister, on the subject of President Wilson's peace aims. The contrast in tone from that of Chancellor von Hertling was so marked and significant as to revive the preexisting belief that the road to peace negotiations would eventually be opened through Austria. Though Count Czernin's speech resolutely upheld the integrity of Austria-Hungary and the preservation and development of her neighboring interests without dictation from the Entente Powers, he held out an olive branch that seemed less of an imitation than those offered by Berlin.

"I think," he said, "there is no harm in stating that I regard the recent proposals of President Wilson as an appreciable approach to the Austro-Hungarian point of view, and that to some of them Austria-Hungary joyfully could give her approval.

"Our views are identical not only on the broad principles regarding a new organization of the world after the war, but also on several concrete questions, and differences which still exist do not appear to me to be so great that a conversation regarding them would not lead to enlightenment and a rapprochement.

"This situation, which doubtless arises from the fact that Austria-Hungary on the one side and the United States on the other are composed of States whose interests are least at variance with one another, tempts one to ask if an exchange of ideas between the two powers could not be the point of departure for a personal conversation among all States which have not yet joined in peace negotiations."

This conciliatory overture— significantly addressed, the Allies quickly noticed, only to the United States—was clearly governed by expediency. Count Czernin revealed a recognition of the critical condition of internal affairs in Austria-Hungary, and sought to make advances that would placate the restless and war-worn people of the dual monarchy without offending the autocratic rulers in Berlin. If peace could come by compromise, then let there be compromise, and approaches to the United States seemed to afford a line of least resistance.

Austria's sincerity, however, was questioned alike in Washington, Paris, and London. Count Czernin was suspected of dangling a familiar bait to split the Allies. The Administration view was that his endeavor to single out the United States as a party with whom to begin preliminary peace conversations was so naive as to be amusing if the situation were not so serious. His invitation was not acceptable. The American Government had thrown in its lot with Great Britain, France, and Italy, and was determined to stand or fall with them. His attempt to promote a separate peace between Austria and the United States was viewed as inspired by a hope that its consideration would either lessen the effectiveness of America's part in the war or provide an opportunity for the pacifists in the Allied countries to extend such a peace movement to the other powers before the war's purposes had been achieved.

The French view was that while the deliverances of Count von Hertling and Count Czernin disclosed that a real cleavage on peace sentiment existed in the two Central Empires, and that the Austrian minister was the first of their spokesmen to show breadth and detachment, the contrast between the two speeches indicated Germanesque stage play. Germany's move was not to show a conciliatory spirit; she left Austria to perform that rôle. The Allies could take their choice in measuring the negotiable value of the two outgivings.

The Allies decided that the war must proceed. Germany regarded herself as a conqueror, was determined upon aggression, and would listen to no peace terms except her own. Count Czernin's conciliatory tone was discounted by his declared fidelity to Austria's alliance to Germany. The two speeches were believed to have been concocted in collusion with the object of springing a combined diplomatic offensive against the Entente Allies.

"The attack," said the London "Times," "obviously was intended to shake the solidarity of our defense at several points, but President Wilson manifestly was the chief objective of the converging forces. Neither speech discloses the least readiness to make any concessions which the Allies declare to be indispensable."

The effect of the Austro-German pronouncements on Great Britain was to stiffen her resolution to continue hostilities. Little weight was attached to what Austria, the tool of Germany, had to say; the former's peace yearnings, set against the latter's aspirations, were impotent unless energized by a revolution in the dual monarchy. The British only took cognizance of Count von Hertling's words, which confirmed the prevalent belief that Prussian militarism considered itself more firmly seated in the saddle than ever, and that although the chancellor seemed to hold the reins, the team which drew the German car of state was at the mercy of Ludendorff's whip and Hindenburg's spur.

CHAPTER XI

MOVING THE MILITARY MACHINE

WHEN Congress closed an epochal session on October 6, 1917, it had appropriated over twenty-one billion dollars. Except for $7,000,000,000 loaned to the Allies, and another billion for the normal expenses of the Government, the amount voted was placed at the service of the Administration as America's sinews of war for defeating the Central Powers. No nation had applied such a huge sum to war purposes in a like period.

War St. 7—H

The loans to the Allies were not considered as part of the American war outlays. The Allies gave their own bonds to the Government as collateral for the loans, bearing the same rate of interest, and a condition attached to the loans was that the money be spent in the United States for war equipment. Hence the loans were allocated for the purchase of material in this country and substantially aided American industries.

Included in the work of Congress was final agreement on a war revenue measure after six months of debate (with wide divergence of taxation plans between the House and Senate) estimated to produce $2,534,870, of which $851,000,000 was to be levied on incomes, and $1,000,000,000 on excess profits.

On October 1, 1917, the Government appealed for popular subscriptions to the second Liberty Loan for $3,000,000,000. As in the case of the first Liberty Loan the response at the outset flagged. Two weeks later only 14 per cent of the maximum total had been subscribed and a daily subscription of $358,000,000 was needed to make the loan a success within the time allotted for receiving subscriptions. A period of apprehension and misgiving followed; but that had happened during the floatation of the first loan, and no European war loan had been asked without a similar experience. It was not an easy task to draw three billion dollars from the public purse, and the purse was leisurely, even lax, in loosening its strings. It needed a nation-wide advertising propaganda to open it. The President entered the fray by naming a Liberty Day, fixed for October 24, on which he asked the American people to assemble in their respective communities and pledge to one another and to the Government the fullest measure of financial support.

"The might of the United States," he declared in his proclamation, "is being mobilized and organized to strike a mortal blow at autocracy in defense of outraged American rights and of the cause of liberty. Billions of dollars are required to arm, feed and clothe the brave men who are going forth to fight our country's battles and to assist the nations with whom we are making common cause against a common foe. To subscribe to the Liberty Loan is to perform a service of patriotism.

"Let the result be so impressive and emphatic that it will echo throughout the empire of our enemy as an index of what America intends to do to bring this war to a victorious conclusion."

The Government's efforts to brace popular interest in the loan, aided by hundreds of thousands of voluntary workers throughout the country who formed Liberty Loan organizations, bankers, boy scouts, girl scouts, the newspapers and magazines, and patriotic, commercial, and fraternal bodies, produced a flood of subscriptions at the last moment which dissipated all fear of failure. The people needed driving, knew that their procrastination called for a dinning advertising campaign to translate intentions into deeds, and finally yielded good-humoredly to the impetus. They responded in such good measure that on October 27, 1917, when the loan closed, $4,617,532,300 had been subscribed, or $1,617,-532,300 over the amount asked. The oversubscription exceeded that which the first loan yielded. Approximately 9,400,000 shared in applying for the loan. Of this number, it was estimated, 9,306,000, or 99 per cent, subscribed in amounts ranging from $50 to $50,000, the aggregate of such subscriptions being $2,488,469,350.

The loan proved to be popular in a degree of which the world afforded no equal. Never had there been a loan taken by 9,400-000 subscribers. It surpassed all previous experience of Government loans. The single offering was larger than the total takings in all subscriptions made in the four years of the Civil War. It far exceeded the response to any government loan of the other belligerents.

With an ample treasury to draw from, provided by Congress and the public, the Government proceeded with the war preparations, but in face of inevitable obstacles and friction. The American military establishment was not designed for making war on a huge scale, and, like the British War Office at the beginning of hostilities, was swamped and confused by an avalanche of new responsibilities. There were admitted shortages in clothing, artillery, and machine guns in the cantonments, and delays in the construction of new shipping also produced impatient criticism. Congress interposed by investigations into the general conduct of the war, with the result that the air was cleared and defects of organization located. The investigations appeared to have developed primarily not so much from ineffective and wrong decisions in meeting war needs as from delays due to indecision and procrastination. The result was a change of administrative methods aiming at a centralization of authority, which England and France had early found imperative in conducting the war, instead of depending on a bureaucratic system with its complicated channels of distributed authority. The friction which had arisen seemed to be substantially due to a clash between the methods of business men, whom the administration had requisitioned into war service, and the red tape of an established governmental system. The Administration recognized at length that an infusion into the Government ranks of capable business organizers, bent on conducting their share of the war with expedition, could not blend with departmental systems clogged by traditions, customs, rules, and regulations, written and unwritten. The whole Government became engaged in a process of introspection. The investigations compelled it to see itself as others saw it, and were salutary in that respect alone. In other directions the inquiries revealed, in spite of departmental shortcomings, that an enormous amount of work had been accomplished in a short time. When war was declared the country was wholly unprepared; it was working at full capacity in many war fields to maintain the largest foreign commerce reached in its history. Its industries being thus occupied on the outbreak of war, they could not readily digest a flood of orders, aggregating more than ten billion dollars in value, which the Government suddenly superimposed upon their capacities, with their equipments already driving at top speed under forced draft. On one point at least there was agreement—that the task so far accomplished could not have been done in the same period by any other nation.

In Secretary Baker's view, much of the criticism leveled at the War Department was due to a natural and praiseworthy impatience of the people at large to build a war machine worthy of their country's power. "Every one of us," he said, "wants to se our country hit like a man at the adversary." Answering the charge that the War Department had fallen down the Secretary set out to remove the impression prevalent in the country that the failures and delays were disproportionate to what had been achieved. He thereupon disclosed the results accomplished.

On April 1, 1917, a few days before the United States declared war on Germany, the army stood at 9,524 officers and 202,510 men. On December 31 of that year this force had grown to 110,-856 officers and 1,428,650 men, composed of the regular army, the National Guard, and the National Army. In other respects the work accomplished by the War Department at the close of 1917 was summed up by Secretary Baker as under:

"1. A large army is in the field and in training; so large that further increments to it can be adequately equipped and trained as rapidly as those already in training can be transported.

"2. The army has been enlisted and selected without serious dislocation of the industries of the country.

"3. The training of the army is proceeding rapidly, and its spirit is high. The subsistence of the army has been above criticism; its initial clothing supply, temporarily inadequate, is now substantially complete, and reserves will rapidly accumulate. Arms of the most modern and effective kind—including artillery, machine guns, automatic rifles, and small arms—have been provided by manufacture or purchase for every soldier in France, and are available for every soldier who can be gotten to France in the year 1918.

"4. A substantial army is ready in France, where both men and officers have been additionally and specially trained and are ready for active service.

"5. Independent lines of communication and supply and vast storage and other facilities are in process of construction in France.

"6. Great programs for the manufacture of additional equipment and for the production of new instruments of war have been formulated."

An outcome of the investigation was the creation of a War Council within the War Department, composed of the Secretary of War, the Assistant Secretary of War, and five general officers. Its purpose was to supervise and coordinate the supplies of the field armies and the military relations of those armies with the War Department.

The National Army, composed of civilians enrolled under the selective draft law, was the most ambitious experiment in constructive military organization any country had ever attempted. It presented innumerable problems for which no solutions could be found in available textbooks, and the celerity with which it was converted into a real army rested wholly upon the skill with which the problems were grappled by the cantonment commanders and drill officers. Before the magnitude of a training organization could be considered and the drilling set in motion, much groundwork had to be covered in preparing the cantonments. There were sixteen of them, situated in various sections of the country, each roughly housing 40,000 men, and cost the Government at least $100,000,000. Their sites generally were in rugged, partially cleared country, marked by scrubby timber, dirt roads, wooden buildings, occasional patches of canvas, clouds of dust or acres of mud. They sprang up, in brief, out of wilderness tracts, usually some miles away from large centers of population. Their construction meant the creation out of the void of sixteen fully equipped cities, furnished with water supply, sewage systems, electric installations, governing organizations, police, and transportation. Standardization of construction was the only method by which the camps could be brought into being with dispatch. Each type of building, and every stick and board, ventilator and window sash used therein for all the cantonments were shaped to identical measurements, and produced by the enormous driving power of modern engineering, working under contract. Out of industrial plants, devising standardized material, came the camps. The number of buildings in the camps varied from 1,200 to 1,600, and included, besides the barracks proper, kitchens, shower baths and sanitary units, hospitals and administration offices, churches, schools, clubs and lodges, laundries, commissary stores, and even moving-picture theaters.

The first stage of training the men was confined largely to elementary military drill, which was a test of their physical capacity to withstand the driving routine of marching fifteen to twenty miles a day, burdened with a sixty-pound pack, ammunition, and rifle. The second stage embraced advanced military drill, involving several weeks of Swedish exercises, manipulating the army Springfield and marching and countermarching in close or extended order. The third phase was specialized warfare as taught abroad, with British and French trench instructors.

Military tactics having been revolutionized by modern trench warfare, no time was wasted in the open-country maneuvers formerly employed to accustom the troops to actual field service. The National Army was trained for the single purpose of effective trench fighting. On adjacent hillsides and plains extensive field fortifications were prepared, equipped with barbed-wire entanglements, artillery, and machine-gun emplacements, bombproof dugouts, communication trenches, support trenches, listening posts, and every other device which had been evolved from the war operations in Europe. The men were taught how to enter and leave a trench, to repel attacks, make raids in pursuit of information, surprise forays by day or night behind the protection of barrage fire, and how to take care of themselves, repair artillery damage, and reenforce the barbed-wire barriers.

The training was intensive and embraced a sixteen weeks' course crowded with manifold detail, which was vigorously observed. More attention was paid in the curriculum to drilling individual men, platoons, and companies than to conducting brigade, divisional, and regimental exercises, these latter being deferred until the smaller units were fit for advanced warfare. The platoon, commanded by a lieutenant, was the fighting unit in trench operations, and upon the lieutenants was therefore imposed the responsibility of training less than company units in order to effect an intimate and sympathetic cooperation between officers and men when they encountered the stern realities of warfare in Europe.

Camp conditions formed a chief subject of the Congressional investigation. The War Department had been confronted with the task of providing for a new army which had to be rushed into training, and had to depend upon congested railroad facilities to equip the camps. But everything had been done, Secretary Baker told the committee, to care for the men, and where defects had occurred they were quickly removed.

"And where, I want to know, in all history can you find an achievement comparable to that of America's in raising this great army from her citizenry in this period of time?" asked the Secretary of War. "It has never been done before, and it is to America's credit that she has accomplished it in the nine months we have been at war."

The outlook, as viewed by Secretary Baker, was that if adequate transport facilities were available, 1,500,000 men could be shipped to France during 1918. He indicated that a third of that number would be on the western front early in the year as a forerunner of the main body.

The country appeared satisfied by this prospect. The War Secretary had revealed much information regarding the military preparations to the Senate investigators; but he had to suppress much more to keep Germany—who was anxious to learn General Pershing's plans—in the dark, especially as to the number and disposition of American troops already there. The conclusions drawn from the progress of war preparations at the beginning of 1918 were that greater advances had been made than was expected. American troops would be in the thick of the fighting in the early spring and would be greatly reenforced just as soon as the Entente Allies pooled their tonnage resources.

The Administration's critics in Congress, nevertheless, were not pacified. A bill was proposed in the Senate creating a War Cabinet, the purpose of which was to divest the executives of Government departments of all authority in the conduct of the war. The new body was to be composed of "three distinguished citizens of demonstrated ability," to be named by the President and indorsed by the Senate. They were to control the administrative Cabinet officers and other department heads in the war's conduct, and adjust all differences, subject to the President's review.

The President saw in the proposed new war administration nothing but "long additional delays" and the turning of the Government's experience into "mere lost motion." He said as much to Senator Chamberlain, the author of the measure, in a letter which stoutly defended the Government's military preparations.

"The War Department," he wrote, "has performed a task of unparalleled magnitude and difficulty with extraordinary promptness and efficiency. There have been delays and disappointments and partial miscarriages of plan, all of which have been drawn into the foreground and exaggerated by the investigations which have been in progress since the Congress assembled. . . . But by comparison with what has been accomplished, these things, much as they were to be regretted, were insignificant, and no mistake has been made which has been repeated."

CHAPTER XII

FLEETS IN THE MAKING

THE navy was not exempt from the searchlight Congress cast upon the manifold war preparations of the Government. But nothing was adduced before the investigating subcommittee to indicate that the Navy Department had not met the abnormal situation produced by American belligerency. The outstanding development disclosed was that the navy had more than 1,000 ships commissioned in the winter of 1917, as against 300 two years ago; that 425 vessels were under construction, exclusive of 350 submarine chasers; and that contracts had been let for building hundreds of other small craft.

The expansion of the navy occasioned by the war was notable in other directions. Since January 1, 1917, the naval force increased from 4,500 officers and 68,000 men to 15,000 officers and 254,000 men; the number of stations operated by the navy from 130 to 363; the number of civil employees from 35,000 to 60,000;

the strength of the Naval Reserve from a few hundreds to 49,-246 men; the average monthly expenditures from $8,000,000 to $60,000,000; the Hospital Corps from 1,600 to 7,000; the National Naval Volunteers from zero to 16,000 men; the Marine Corps from 344 officers and 9,921 men to 1,197 officers and 30,000 men.

The navy placed great reliance on destroyers to fulfill the part allotted to it in the sea warfare against German submarines. A formidable fleet of these vessels was planned at a cost of $350,-000,000, and contracts for the construction were placed with five shipbuilding concerns in October, 1917. Their actual number was guarded as a military secret. It was the largest project the navy department had undertaken, and would probably give the United States a destroyer fleet exceeding those of all other countries. The expenditure embraced the expansion of existing shipbuilding plants and the building of additional engine and boiler factories, as the destroyer program taxed the full capacity of the shipbuilding industry.

The destroyer had proved to be the deadliest weapon utilized against the submarine, and was superior to the submarine chaser, even for harbor and in-shore patrol work, besides having better seagoing qualities. Submarine chasers were regarded as a necessity, but the navy evinced little enthusiasm for them as a weapon of permanent effectiveness, and rather pinned its faith to an overwhelming destroyer armada to combat the U-boats.

In aviation the Government made no less impressive strides. The building of 20,000 aeroplanes, for which Congress had voted $640,000,000, was undertaken for the creation of a great American aerial force to operate against Germany. Their types covered the whole range of training machines, light, high-speed fighting airships, and powerful battle and bombing planes of heavy design. The training of aviators, the building of motors, and the assembling and framing of the wings proceeded uniformly so that men and equipment would be ready for service simultaneously.

Numbers of American aviators were already abroad undergoing intensive training behind the battle fronts. The thousands in training at home were coached by a corps of Allied air experts of various nationalities, forming virtually an international aviation general staff for organizing the American aerial force.

The United States had set out resolutely to do its part in wresting the air spaces over the western front from Germany. The arrival in France in the autumn of 1917 of a group of American aviators with American-built airships brought an administration announcement which viewed the event as of signal importance. The opportunity rested with the United States to give its Allies such a great preponderance of airships that the enemy would be driven from the skies altogether, impotent either to give battle or defend himself. With this aim in view, Congress was asked for further funds for developing aviation during 1918 and 1919 to the amount of $1,138,000,000, of which it was proposed that $1,032,294,260 be expended on aviation: $553,219,120 on extra engines and spare parts, $235,-866,000 for airplanes and hydroaeroplanes, $77,475,000 for machine guns, $8,050,000 for schools for military aeronautics, and the balance for stations, depots, equipment, upkeep, and pay for instructors, inspectors, mechanics, engineers, accountants, &c.

There was an army of aviators to meet all this development in equipment, numbering, at the beginning of 1918, 3,900 officers and 82,120 men.

Perhaps the shipping situation called most for legislative investigation. The paramount need of the Allies was for 6,000,000 tons annually, and the British Shipping Controller warned that if the United States could not produce this tonnage to replace the losses by submarines the Allies' military and naval efforts would be crippled. The construction of new tonnage in American shipyards had been beset by personal conflicts in the shipping administration, resulting in reversals of policy and retarded operations. Edward J. Hurley, chairman of the Shipping Board, told the Senate investigating committee that one obstacle to the expeditious pursuit of the vast program of ship construction was that it had been superimposed on an equally extensive naval program. When war was declared 70 per cent of the eighteen prominent shipyards then in existence were overtaxed by the naval program, while only the remaining 30 per cent of the yards could be utilized to proceed with the mercantile ship program. The task was to bring an adequate merchant marine into being to assist the Allies and he assured the committee (December, 1917) that it was being accomplished with the utmost dispatch despite past dissensions and many obstacles. The number of ships under construction or contract was 1,427, representing 8,573,108 dead-weight tons. Of this number 431 were ships embracing 3,056,000 tons which were in course of building in the yards for private and foreign owners and had been commandeered for war service under Government order. The rest were composed of 559 steel ships of 3,965,200 dead-weight tons, 379 wooden ships of 1,344,900 dead-weight tons, and 58 composite ships of 207,000 tons. The main need in proceeding with this huge program was shipyard space. New yards constructed and tonnage contracts awarded to each called for a constant expansion in the shipping organization, so that by the end of 1917 the Shipping Board controlled 132 yards, of which only 58 were old establishments, the remainder, 74, being new.

The burden imposed on American shipyards can be realized by contrasting their output in the prewar period with the total tonnage under construction for both the navy and the Shipping Board. The navy program was the equivalent in value, and therefore in shipbuilding effort, of 2,500,000 tons of merchant shipping. The mercantile marine program represented a tonnage of over 8,500,000. Here was 11,000,000 tons being produced by American shipyards whose greatest previous output in one year had only amounted to 615,000 tons according to Mr. Hurley. For 1918 he promised an output of 6,000,000 tons. Of the vessels under contract a good proportion were of 7,500 tons or more, classified as cargo steamers, and of these a number were designed specially for transports.

Tonnage being the immediate need, the Shipping Board did not wait for the completion of the new construction to supply it. As a war emergency measure it requisitioned all American ocean cargo and passenger-carrying vessels over 2,500 tons.

This step was taken as a means to control freight rates as well as to enable the Government to command the tonnage it needed for war purposes. American merchant vessels for oversea traffic exceeded 2,000,000 tonnage. Some had already been requisitioned by the army and navy. With the exception of craft taken over for Government service, the vessels were left in their owners' hands for operation on Government account as the Shipping Board directed.

Between 600,000 and 700,000 tons of German shipping seized in American ports had already been utilized as troop transports and freighters for reenforcing the American army in France. These vessels included the *Leviathan*, formerly the *Vaterland*, which was capable of carrying 10,000 troops on a single voyage, but the number was limited to 8,000 to insure comfort. In January, 1918, it was disclosed that the *Leviathan*, with fifteen other former German ships, had safely reached Entente ports laden with men and supplies. The announcement was made from the American army headquarters in France to disprove false reports circulated in Germany belittling the assistance rendered the Entente cause by the use of these vessels. They had, on their first voyage, escaped the submarines, a feat which was not palatable to Germany, who sought to bolster up a waning popular confidence in the U-boat campaign. The German vessels which had run the gantlet, besides the *Vaterland*, were the *Covington* (ex-*Cincinnati*), *America* (ex-*Amerika*), *President Grant*, *President Lincoln*, *Powhatan* (ex-*Hamburg*), *Madawaska* (ex-*König Wilhelm II*), *George Washington*, *Mount Vernon* (ex-*Kronprinzessin Cecilie*), *Agamemnon* (ex-*Kaiser Wilhelm II*), *Aeolus* (ex-*Grosser Kurfürst*), *Mercury* (ex-*Barbarossa*), *Pocahontas* (ex-*Princess Irene*), *Huron* (ex-*Friedrich der Grosse*), *Von Steuben* (ex-*Kronprinz Wilhelm*), *De Kalb* (ex-*Prinz Eitel Friedrich*).

A further step to expedite the shipment of men and supplies to Europe was the formation of a Committee of Shipping Control, composed of American and Allied membership. Its chief object was to endeavor to fulfill Secretary Baker's expectation that 1,500,000 American troops and their requisite equipment could be landed in France in 1918 if sufficient shipping was available. It was endowed with power of absolute control in the allocation of all tonnage on both sides of the Atlantic, and aimed to end the complications and delays that had hitherto prevented the fullest use of American shipping for war purposes.

The Shipping Board had succeeded in turning over to the War Department over 1,000,000 tons of ships on the bare board basis for the transportation of soldiers, live stock, and munitions. Much of this tonnage was commandeered by the Government for that purpose, the shipyards not being sufficiently advanced in their work to provide much new construction. To facilitate the production of the enormous amount of new tonnage under way the Board sought a further appropriation of $800,000,000, increasing the amount Congress had authorized for the shipping program to $2,100,000,000.

CHAPTER XIII

FOOD AS A WAR FACTOR

ECONOMIC conditions generally had been shaped and dictated by the nation's entry into the war. The financial advantages which the country enjoyed in the two previous years through being neutral and not belligerent, disappeared with the war declaration; but the accumulated resources of the country's previous neutrality remained a continuing bulwark, and its distance from the theaters of war gave the country certain economic advantages of a neutral.

The situation greatly changed upon the United States throwing its entire resources into the common stock of the Entente Allies. The Government's enormous advances of credits to them took place when its own war requirements were even larger. Shipments to the Allies of maximum consignments of food and equipment proceeded in face of heavy home demands for the same products. The abnormal efforts with which the Shipping

Board set about building new ships to repair the ravages of the submarines coincided with unexampled calls upon the mills for domestic needs. Such developments could not occur without profoundly affecting American finance and production; especially in view of the intensified economic strain on belligerent Europe by the continuance of the war through another year and the reliance of the Allies on American aid.

There came an immediate and violent rise in commodity prices, due largely to the Government's new demands, coming in the wake of the increased needs of the Allies. As a consequence maximum prices on many products were imposed either by imperative Government orders or by agreement between the Government and the producers. The wheat crop failed in volume, being barely eleven million bushels above the deficient yield of 1916, and except for that season was the smallest in half a dozen years. On the other hand, corn and oats yielded record-breaking crops, and there was such an excellent harvest of other cereals that the total out-turn of the five leading grains, including wheat, exceeded by 970,000,000 bushels that of 1916. Except for 1915 the general crops surpassed in yield that of any other year. The war, however, robbed the country of the fruit of its own fertility. The effect of full granaries was offset by a European wheat harvest worse even than that of 1916 and by the difficulty of sparing ships to bring Australia's wheat to Europe. The demand on American wheat for export became so urgent that the Government was compelled to place the wheat trade virtually in the hands of a paramount commission.

Governmental food control became a reality on November 1, 1917, when the manufacture, storage, importation, and distribution of practically all essential foodstuffs came under the jurisdiction of the Food Administration headed by Herbert C. Hoover, and could only be conducted under license from that body. Probably the Government had never before undertaken such a step in commercial regulation which came so close to the lives of the people. About twenty important and inclusive classes of food were brought under Federal control. Virtually the whole machinery of their manufacture and distribution be-

came subject to Federal pressure. All food brokers, commissio
men, wholesalers, jobbers, warehousemen, importers, and grai
elevator men not previously licensed were required to take ou
permits, in most cases without reference to the size of thei
business. Only meat packers, canners, millers, egg packers
ginners, etc., whose business was small, were exempted. Al
retailers whose gross sales of food exceeded $100,000 yearl
were licensed. The control affected small retailers also, for i
was expressly provided by Mr. Hoover that no licensee sha
"knowingly sell any food commodity to any person who shal
after this regulation goes into effect, violate the provisions" o
the Food Administration Act; and wholesalers and jobbers wer
to be furnished information concerning small retailers wh
hoarded or extorted. It also affected manufacturers and dealer
whose merchandise was not included in the specified classes o
food controlled.

The object, of course, was to keep food prices down to th
minimum. The Food Administration Act forbade manipulatio
or speculation, excessive profits, discriminatory practices, an
waste. The licensing system was simply a means of enforcin
these prohibitions. Mr. Hoover looked for their successful opera
tion not so much by formulating strict regulations as by awaken
ing a spirit of public service among food traders.

The grocers undertook to concentrate their efforts upon sellin
substitutes for white flour and meat, in view of the Allies' call
on American produce and the consequent shortage for hom
purposes. Retailers promised to encourage the sale of "article
of food cheap but good in quality in place of high-priced staples.
Wholesale grocers were urged to arrange with manufacturer
for larger supplies of corn meal, rye, and oat products. Foo
distributing and selling organizations throughout the countr
began a campaign to induce retailers to stop soliciting order
to reduce deliveries to one daily for a family or route, and t
stimulate the sale of prunes, oats, corn meal, and rice in bul
and for cash. Mr. Hoover had laid down the principle that i
was the delivered cost of food to jobber, wholesaler, and mer
chant that determined the price on resale, and not market con

ditions at the time of resale. No one was to profit by fluctuations upward while he held goods in stock.

The Food Administration's task was to awaken millions of families to recognize the necessity of food conservation, to educate millions of producers to maximum effort, and to banish greed from the business of thousands of distributors. The last presented the greatest difficulty. Yet the readiness of dealers to be content with living-profit margins and to increase efficiency, the eagerness of commission men to discourage all speculation and to help constructively in effecting adequate deliveries on full cars, and the assurances of most distributors that they would aid in bringing recalcitrants into subjection, promised that the problem was not impossible of solution. Profiteering had been one of the banes of the war in Europe, and the Government sought to check this rapacious method of using war conditions to acquire ill-gotten gains by traders who preyed upon public necessities.

Mr. Hoover thus presented the situation in the autumn of 1917:

"There is plenty of food in this country, and our problem is one of surplus and not a deficit. This does not mean that we can send to the Allies all they need, for there is not enough when considered from the war point of view. The wheat we export will be the direct amount that the people save out of their bread, or we have shipped our surplus and must keep the bread supply or the country. We will ship wheat or flour from month to month, but such shipments will not be allowed except our supply warrants them. Through conservation we are gaining a 20 per cent surplus of wheat. This means literally that every one who saves a slice of bread is giving a slice of bread to our Allies. We are consuming 20 per cent less wheat than last year.

According to Mr. Hoover, the Allies' wheat requirements from the United States amounted to 210,000,000 bushels. The country's production of wheat in 1916 was 670,000,000 bushels, of which 590,000,000 bushels was consumed at home, leaving only 0,000,000 bushels available for export. There were thus 130,-00,000 bushels to be found to fulfill the Allies' needs, that is, by saving that much from the normal consumption of flour by the people. The Food Administration found a spokesman in President Wilson, who, in a proclamation, called on the people at large to observe more wheatless days, and on wheat traders to curtail their stocks and sales.

The application of the slogan, "Food will win the war," was extended to neutral countries contiguous to Germany. If food was to win the war, then victory would come by the weakening of Germany through being unable to obtain American food, since the United States had virtually become Europe's chief food source, and Germany could always obtain American supplies through the neutrals. The President stopped further trading in American food between the neutrals and Germany by a proclamation ordaining that after August 30, 1917, no exports from American ports could be shipped, except under a strict license of the Exports Council, to any country in the Eastern Hemisphere. The restraint, though made of universal application, was specifically aimed at the European neutrals which flourished upon trading with Germany.

A large number of Dutch and other neutral vessels lying in New York harbor were chartered by the American Government and added to the available merchant shipping.

CHAPTER XIV

TRANSPORTATION AND FUEL

THE war was gradually being brought home to the nation not by tidings of American troops taking their places side by side with their Allies in Europe, but by internal changes. The Government stretched forth an expropriating arm in all directions where public and private service could be utilized for war purposes, and it duly took charge of the railroads.

As a war measure, the President's intervention in assuming control of the country's transportation systems was the mo sweeping step he had taken under the extraordinary powers vested in him by Congress. The railroad authorities themselves realized its need. The war had received many designations, but analyzing its conduct down to fundamentals, it was a railroad war. So Marshal Joffre had termed it in recalling how the railroad had enabled him to win the Battle of the Marne by rushing troops and munitions where they were critically needed.

The American railroads were already overtaxed when war was declared, and lacked facilities for proper repairs and new equipment. Early in 1915 and thenceforth they became swamped by a flood of traffic in munitions, food, and other supplies from the interior to the seaboard for transshipment overseas to the Allies. They needed more locomotives and cars for this huge traffic; but the day of reasonable prices had passed, labor was costly and uncertain, and engine and car builders were absorbed in producing for the Allies. When the war drew in the United States the railroad's burdens were swollen manifold by the transportation problem incident to the mobilizing of an army of 1,500,000 men. Troop trains had to be operated by the tens and hundreds and even thousands; for every troop train there were ten, fifteen, and twenty trains of camp equipment; ore and fuel had to be carried; more and more material called for transit to the seaboard for the Allies. The traffic grew 50 per cent above that of 1914, the year the European war started, and it was operated with little more than 3 per cent of additional equipment. The working forces of the railroads, in addition, were depleted, not only by numerous volunteer enlistments to the regular army, but by the selective draft, and by the creation of nine full regiments of railroad engineers for service in France.

Reviewing the situation in December, 1917, the Interstate Commerce Commission recommended immediate unification of the railroads into one system, operated under government control, as the only solution of the problem of conducting the war traffic.

The President by proclamation took over the railroads on December 28, 1917. He exercised this power both under the resolutions declaring war against Germany and Austria-Hungary, wherein he was authorized to employ the resources of the

Government and of the country to bring the conflict to a successful termination, and under an army appropriation bill passed on August 29, 1916 (eight months before the United States entered the war), which provided:

"The President, in time of war, is empowered, through the Secretary of War, to take possession and assume control of any system or systems of transportation, or any part thereof, and to utilize the same, to the exclusion as far as may be necessary of all other traffic thereon, for the transfer or transportation of troops, war material and equipment, or for such other purposes connected with the emergency as may be needful or desirable."

The President, explaining his action in a supplementary statement, told the country:

"This is a war of resources no less than of men, perhaps even more than of men, and it is necessary for the complete mobilization of our resources that the transportation systems of the country should be organized and employed under a single authority and a simplified method of coordination which have not proved possible under private management and control.

"The Government of the United States is the only great government now engaged in the war which has not already assumed control of this sort. It was thought to be in the spirit of American institutions to attempt to do everything that was necessary through private management, and if zeal and ability and patriotic motive could have accomplished the necessary unification of administration, it would certainly have been accomplished; but no zeal or ability could overcome insuperable obstacles, and I have deemed it my duty to recognize that fact in all candor now that it is demonstrated and to use without reserve the great authority reposed in me. A great national necessity dictated the action, and I was therefore not at liberty to abstain from it."

The Government undertook to guarantee to each company such net earnings as would amount to the ascertained average of the three-year period ending with June, 1917. The right of stockholders and bondholders and other creditors of the railroads were not to be impaired by the change in control, and th roads were to be kept in as good repair and equipment as when taken over. For their upkeep and betterment the President sought an appropriation of $500,000,000 from Congress.

The Secretary of the Treasury, William G. McAdoo, was appointed director general. His first act was to order that all terminals, ports, locomotives, rolling stock and other transportation facilities be utilized in the common cause of serving the country. By this course he ended all railroad compacts apportioning the distribution of traffic, and pooled the terminals for the common use of all carriers whose lines or cars could reach them.

Meantime a coal famine, due to freight congestion of unexampled proportions, had been gradually developing. At the beginning of December the country, except in the northwest, faced a serious shortage of fuel, not through lack of coal, but through lack of means to transport it. Dr. H. A. Garfield, the Federal Fuel Administrator, took steps to have coal and coke given the right of way over general freight, which in turn was subordinate to the transit of actual war supplies. Traffic priority of coal shipments was the remedy sought to loosen the congestion of coal cars at mines and terminals. But sufficient coal did not reach the various points of distribution for normal winter use, nor, what was as serious, for war purposes. It was solely a transportation problem, involving a general freight problem, and its solution would also solve the fuel problem. The navy and factories alone required 100,000,000 tons more than they needed before, and could get little above half that quantity. There came an imperative call for fuel economy from Dr. Garfield, who warned the country that unless it could save 50,000,000 tons by retrenchment, the Government would have to stop the operation of nonessential industries where coal was a big factor in order to apply the use of fuel so saved for essential war industries.

In the end Dr. Garfield resorted to heroic measures. Without prior notice he issued a closing order to the industries east of the Mississippi, which were thus made to feel the full force of the coal famine. The operation of all factories, except those engaged in the manufacture of foodstuffs, was suspended for five days (from January 18 to January 22, 1918), and they were also to close every Monday from January 28 to March 25 inclusive. Coal merchants were required in selling fuel to give preference to railroads, domestic, and public service consumers, ships for bunker purposes, Government departments, national and local, and manufacturers of perishable food. On the five days named and on the succeeding Mondays, no fuel was to be delivered to any other person or corporation for any purpose except for plants which must be operated seven days a week to avoid injury to their equipment, and printing establishments. The curtailment of the use of fuel was further prescribed on the Mondays named to an extent that virtually made them holidays. All private, business, and professional offices, except those of banks and trust companies, physicians and dentists, were forbidden to be heated or lighted at all except to avert the danger of damage from frozen apparatus. Wholesale and retail stores (except those selling food), business buildings, saloons, theaters, dance halls and all other places of amusement came under this ban.

The country was startled by the sweeping order. Protests poured into the White House; Congress was in a ferment; the Senate passed a resolution urging a postponement of such a drastic step. But Dr. Garfield remained firm. He insisted that the inadequacy of the coal supply and transportation facilities to meet the enormous war demands, coupled with unprecedented adverse weather, had made immediate restrictive measures imperative. The order, with a few modifications, was enforced in the face of a rising storm of indignation from a multitude of objectors who saw nothing but industrial chaos in its operation.

The protests subsided as quickly as they arose. Industry had received a violent shock; confusion and uncertainty followed; but the order was obeyed. It fell with stunning effect upon an unprepared public opinion which in some directions exploded with symptoms of a panic-stricken hysteria. But presently it began to dawn on the public mind that if a cessation of business for a few days helped the railroads to move coal and war freight, whereby ships could get fuel and cargoes to depart to Europe, and also removed the tantalizing spectacle (one of many like situations elsewhere) of a coalless New York while 350,000 tons were traffic-bound a few miles away, the fuel-curtailment order would be remembered as marking a decision of great courage and statesmanship. The congestion of the railroads and their terminals had produced a condition bordering on transportation immobility. The arteries of commerce, as it were, had become frozen. Factories and plants piled their daily output in railroad yards and near the docks in rising quantities. The accumulations of undelivered freight grew and grew and the panting railroads, working beyond the limits of what their traffic would bear, could only reduce the incubus piecemeal. The tardy recognition came that, even had there been no coal shortage, which was the primary cause of the shutdown, a temporary cessation of manufacture was necessary to clear the loaded tracks and empty the groaning storehouses before they were burdened with further accretions from the hives of industry.

The antagonism provoked by the closing order soon gave way to a cordial spirit of cooperation, and many industries affected undertook to assume in large part the financial burdens incident to enforced idleness. Manufacturing was halted and further merchandise was kept from cluttering the crowded railroads. Improved transportation conditions followed, due largely to milder weather. The way was rapidly cleared for a steady movement of coal to tidewater for bunkering ships loaded with supplies for the American oversea forces and for the Allies, as well as for supplying domestic fuel needs.

1391

PART III—REVOLUTIONARY RUSSIA

CHAPTER XV

THE LAST DAYS OF KERENSKY

VIEWED in the light of later events, there can now remain no doubt of that the overthrow of the Russian czar was as much a reaction against war as it was a revolution against autocracy. In July, 1917, Premier Kerensky, representing the radical intellectuals, rather than the people as a mass, had attempted to stimulate the enthusiasm of the armies for another general offensive against the Austro-German forces. The effort had failed disastrously, not through any tactical mistakes or through any great lack of equipment or material support, but because the stiffness had gone out of the backbone of the Russian soldier. The propaganda of the Bolsheviki had created this situation, it was said, but propaganda can only crystallize a sentiment: it can never create it. The rank and file of the Russian armies accepted the Bolshevist agitators and their doctrines only because their state of mind was in sympathy. Ivan was willing to face any alternative to further fighting.

This fact Kerensky evidently realized better than anyone after the collapse of the midsummer offensive. Either one of two things an army must possess to fight effectively: iron discipline or enthusiasm. The latter Kerensky had tried to awaken. He had failed. Hastily he tried to establish the other: a rule of "blood and iron," as he termed it. But Kerensky was not of the stuff of which dictators are made. Like Madero of Mexico, he possessed too abundantly the quality of mercy to play the rôle of the Prussian.

Kerensky, undoubtedly, knew of the growing antiwar sentiment in the rank and file of the army. This sentiment prevailed
to a much less extent behind the lines, especially among the
intellectuals of all shades of opinion, and among the commercial
classes. Or, perhaps, it would be more correct to say that these
elements saw the necessity of continuing the war more clearly
than did the soldiers at the front and therefore feared the
results of a premature, or separate, peace.

To give the prowar elements an opportunity to express themselves, to transmit their enthusiasm to the army, perhaps,
Kerensky and his associates of the Provisional Government had
called a national conference, to be held in Moscow in the latter
part of August, 1917. All kinds of organizations and social
bodies were invited to send delegates; the zemstvos, the cooperative societies, the Red Cross, the labor unions, the professional
leagues and the army itself, through the councils and several of
the commanding officers. It was, in fact, a sort of a provisional
general assembly whose authority, Kerensky hoped, would be
strong enough to impress the army.

The scene in the ancient capital on the gathering of this notable conference, on August 26, 1917, was a picturesque one,
especially in the neighborhood of the Grand Opera House, where
the sessions were being held. As demonstrations on the part
of the Bolsheviki had been threatened, the building itself was
surrounded by a chain of soldiers and picked officers were stationed at every few yards, the majority of the guards being
cadets from the military academies, notable for their loyalty
to the Provisional Government, as distinguished from the
Soviets, or soldiers' councils.

The interior of the Opera House was elaborately decorated,
the footbridge connecting the auditorium with the stage being
hung with festoons of revolutionary red. Among the delegates
present, numbering several hundreds, could be distinguished
the various national types and costumes of Russia; Tartars in
peaked caps, white-robed mullahs from the Volga, Georgians
with their gorgeous cassocks and bearded priests with long
hair and beards.

The most notable event of the three days' sessions of the conference, which, on the whole, accomplished nothing but an excited debate, was the appearance and speech of General Kornilov, the Cossack chief. As he mounted the platform, the great majority of the delegates in the auditorium rose *en masse* and cheered loudly. The delegates from the soldiers' councils remained stolidly seated, however, in the boxes where they were grouped together. Officers shouted at them indignantly.

"Rise to your feet and show respect!" they cried.

But the soldiers' delegates paid no heed, or some few shouted back:

"We are done with that! We are a free people now!"

General Kornilov made an impassioned plea for the reestablishment of the death penalty, as the basis for that discipline without which the army could no longer stem the Teutonic invasion.

"The old régime bequeathed to Russia," he said, "an army which, despite the defects in its organization, nevertheless was animated by a fighting spirit and was ready for sacrifices. The measures taken by those who are completely foreign to the spirit and the needs of the army have transformed it into a collection of individual groups which have lost all sense of duty and only tremble for their personal safety. If Russia wishes to be saved, the army must be regenerated at any cost."

Here again the general was cheered by all but the representatives of the army itself, who remained stolidly silent.

None of the elements hid its disappointment over the results of the conference. And the general disappointment was more or less centered on Kerensky. His position was, indeed, a difficult one. He realized the need of a united nation, if the war was to be continued. A radical himself, affiliated with the Socialist Revolutionary Party, at one time the most radical of all factions, he now felt drawn toward the comparatively conservative elements, represented by the Cadets, or Liberals, on account of their prowar attitude. Yet his human sympathies were all with the recalcitrant mujiks who, soldiers now at the front, no longer felt any desire for fighting. Endeavoring to draw these two greater elements together, he stood between and lost the support of each.

The last day of the Moscow Conference marked the beginning of Kerensky's downfall.

Throughout the rest of the month and during the beginning of September, 1917, there was ample evidence that Kerensky was keenly alive to the dangers about him; counter-revolutions from two directions. On the one hand were the conservatives, now thoroughly disgusted with the new régime and the disorganization which it seemed to them to represent. During the first week of September, 1917, it was reported that a plot to reestablish, if not the autocracy, at least a modified form of it, had been uncovered, and a number of titled personages were arrested, among them Grand Duke Michael Alexandrovitch, brother of the former czar, and Grand Duke Paul. General Gurko, too, was accused of writing compromising letters and was exiled from the country.

But more portentous, considering later events, was the reported results of a municipal election held in Petrograd, wherein the Bolsheviki polled an unusually large vote; 174,000, as compared to 182,000 by the more moderate Socalists and 101,000 by the Constitutional Democrats. It was from this quarter that the second counter-revolution threatened.

The conservative elements were to be heard from first. Whether they really attempted a genuine counter-revolution remains to this day somewhat of a mystery. The facts, as reported, bear very much the aspect of an intrigue against the conservatives themselves.

On September 10, 1917, it was announced that General Kornilov, commander in chief, had asked the Provisional Government to eliminate itself and hand over its power to him; that he proclaimed himself dictator. Kerensky himself supplied the first details in a personal proclamation.

Already the next day it was reported that Kornilov was moving troops on the capital and that he had even begun bombarding government positions with heavy guns. All the councils were issuing appeals to their constituents, the soldiers, to refuse support to Kornilov and to rally to the support of the Government, while this danger lasted, at least. And then, on the second day, Kerensky proclaimed himself commander in chief of the Russian military forces, with General Alexiev, chief of the General Staff, as his second in command.

Kornilov now issued a proclamation, or statement, from his headquarters at Mogilev, in which he declared that Kerensky's account of his interview with the emissary, Lvov, was a fabrication in that he, Kornilov, had not sent Lvov to Kerensky, but that Kerensky had sent Lvov to him, Kornilov, with the deliberate purpose of creating a misunderstanding.

"I, General Kornilov, the son of a peasant," added he, in a later proclamation, "declare to all that I require nothing personally; nothing, save the salvation of mighty Russia. I swear to lead the nation by the road of victory over the foe to a constituent assembly, through which the nation will decide its own fate and choose the organization of its own political life."

From later accounts it appears that no fighting of any sort ever took place, or even threatened. A body of Caucasians and other soldiers of other non-Slavic races, all Moslems and speaking no Russian, did indeed appear near Petrograd, and created considerable alarm among councils. Being met by a body of Government troops, a misunderstanding arose and threats of arrest were exchanged. Then came some Caucasians from Petrograd, loyal to the Provisional Government, and interpreted, whereupon it appeared that the supposed rebels had heard of no rebellion and had no intention of attacking. Nevertheless, much capital was made of the incident at the time.

On the 14th General Kornilov was arrested or, rather, he gave himself up to a commission of inquiry which arrived at Mogilev, and henceforward little is heard from him. On the following day Kerensky issued a proclamation definitely declaring Russia a republic, in the following terms:

"General Kornilov's rebellion has been quelled, but great is the confusion caused thereby and again great is the danger threatening the Fatherland and its freedom. Holding it necessary to put an end to the external indefiniteness of the state's organization, remembering the unanimous and rapturous approval of the republican idea expressed at the Moscow Conference, the Provisional Government declares that the constitutional organization, according to which the Russian state is ruled, is a republican organization, and it hereby proclaims the Russian Republic."

To this document Kerensky signed his name as "Minister and President," though the latter title may have referred to his presidency of the Ministry.

Meanwhile almost daily changes were taking place in the personnel of the Cabinet, members of which were resigning, withdrawing their resignations and again resigning. Finally this body was reduced to five members, with Kerensky still at the head, with practically plenary powers. Every official utterance, whether by the premier or any one of his associates, sounded one note: the need of stricter discipline. Evidently there was now a genuine effort being made to counteract the laxness which had been continually increasing since the July defeat.

It was at this time that the name of Kaledine, the hetman of the Don Cossacks, first began to appear prominently in the reports of events. Kaledine had evidently shown himself in sympathy with Kornilov, for an order was now sent to the Don Cossacks to arrest their chief and send him on to Petrograd. To this demand the Cossacks returned an evasive reply, saying that they were holding a congress at which the presence of Kaledine as presiding officer was necessary. One of the accusations against Kaledine was that he was attempting to organize a separate government among his people in southern Russia.

During these exciting days the soldiers' and workmen's councils had indeed given their full support to the Provisional Government against the Kornilov movement. But if Kerensky had hoped thereby to silence the voices of the extremists, the Bolsheviki, and to create solidarity among the radical groups, he was to be strongly disappointed. The effect was directly contrary; within the councils, and especially in the Petrograd Council, there was a strong reaction in favor of the extremists. For at a meeting of that latter body, held in the evening of the 13th, in which the policy of the Council was being discussed, the Bolsheviki for the first time gained a substantial majority, numbering 279 against 150. The resolution bringing out this vote demanded the absolute exclusion from participation in the government of all representatives of the propertied classes, with the usual invitation to all the warring states to come together at a general peace conference. Already the second counter-revolution was lifting. Nor was the developing situation any more reassuring when, on the 19th, Chiesde, Skobeliev, Tsertelli, Chernov and the rest of the Executive Committee of the Petrograd Council resigned on account of the majority vote polled by the Bolsheviki on the 13th.

Meanwhile, from Finland and from the Ukraine, or Little Russia, came rumors of secret conferences wherein was discussed the establishment of separate governments. In Kiev was held a congress of non-Slavic peoples inhabiting Russia, which declared for a "democratic federal republic," in which the separate nationalities should each enjoy a large measure of autonomy.

On September 28, 1917, there assembled in Petrograd what was known as the "Democratic Congress," a conference called by the councils to offset the Moscow Conference. About 1,200 delegates attended, representing, first of all, the various provincial councils, then the zemstvos, labor unions, cooperative societies, peasant organizations, etc.

Kerensky spoke from the platform during the opening session, though he made it plain that he did so in his private capacity, and not as the representative of the Government, which, he declared, would recognize no other authority than that of the Constituent Assembly, when that should have been created.

His tone was aggressive, as though he were facing an opposition, and, indeed, from the volume of the applause accorded him it was obvious that he had only a minority heartily with him. He expressed himself strongly in favor of a cabinet in which should be represented the Constitutional Democrats, and he denounced the local council of Helsingfors, which had refused to prevent the opening of the Finnish Diet, which had been forbidden by the Provisional Government, for it was known that the Finns contemplated the declaration of a separate state. At this point the speaker was hissed from the left.

"You may hiss, my friends," declared Kerensky, "but bear in mind that a German fleet is moving up the Baltic."

At a later session a resolution was passed demanding that there should be no change made in the Cabinet without consulting the Congress. In open defiance of this order Kerensky, on October 4, 1917, completely reorganized his Cabinet, appointing a number of Constitutional Democrats. Three days later there was another reorganization of the Cabinet, after a conference between representatives of the Democratic Congress, the Constitutional Democrats and Premier Kerensky, in which it seemed they had arrived at some sort of a compromise by which they could work together.

One definite result of the Democratic Congress was the organization of a sort of a makeshift constitutional assembly, called the "Temporary Council of the Russian Republic," in which "nondemocratic elements were to have 120 representatives."

At first the Congress insisted that the Cabinet should make itself responsible to this body. This suggestion Kerensky and his associates promptly refused to consider. Finally a compromise was effected by which it was agreed that the temporary council should work together with the Cabinet in an advisory capacity and should have certain initiative powers.

This body was then organized and finally held its first meeting on October 20, 1917.

Meanwhile the Soldiers' and Workmen's Council had held an election to fill the vacancies created by the resignation of most of its officers and executive committee. What political complexion the Council had now assumed may be judged from the fact that Leon Trotzky was elected to the chairmanship. He and several of his political associates had also been elected members of the Temporary Council, or Preliminary Assembly, as it was also called, but this election they utilized only as a means to making an effective demonstration, for at the first session of the body Trotzky made a fiery speech denouncing the Cabinet and the Temporary Council itself as being in the hands of the "bourgeoisie."

"We will have nothing to do with you!" he shouted. "We will go among the soldiers and the workers and the peasants and tell them that you are endangering the revolution." Having concluded, Trotzky and the other Bolshevist members walked out in a body.

Whatever else may be said against the Bolsheviki, they do most assuredly give their opponents sufficient warning of their intended acts. In fact, so continuously did they declare their intention of seizing the powers of government, even to fixing the date, that they gave the superficial impression of being mere boasters.

After being elected chairman of the Petrograd Soviet, Trotzky caused to be formed a military revolutionary committee. In the evening of Sunday, November 4, 1917, a delegation from this committee appeared at the Government staff offices and demanded the right of entry, control, and veto. This demand was flatly refused.

"What you will not concede voluntarily we will take by force," replied the delegates, and went. Thus the events beginning three days later could have been no surprise to the Kerensky Government.

CHAPTER XVI

THE BOLSHEVIST REVOLUTION

ON November 7, 1917, the Bolsheviki took their first violent action. An armed naval detachment, under orders from the military revolutionary committee of the Soviet, which had established itself in the Smolny Institute building, occupied the offices of the official Petrograd Telegraph Agency and the Central Telegraph Office, the State Bank and the Marie Palace, where the Preliminary Assembly was holding its sessions. In a communication to the Municipal Duma, Trotzky stated that it was not the intention of the Soviet to seize full power, but only to assume control of the city.

Kerensky immediately took measures to oppose these overt acts, but within the next twenty-four hours it became obvious that he had little support among the soldiers in the capital. By next morning he had disappeared, fleeing, as was presently to develop, to the military forces at the front, which he believed might be loyal to the Government.

Meanwhile Trotzky declared the Preliminary Assembly dissolved and issued a proclamation that it was the intention of the new government, when established and in control, to open negotiations with the Germans for a "general democratic peace."

As yet the Bolsheviki had not met with any serious opposition. Orders issued by the Kerensky Government for the opening of the spans of the bridge across the Neva were not carried out. Bolshevist patrols paraded the streets and maintained order. A number of outbursts on the part of the criminal elements, having as their object robbery and looting, were severely suppressed and the ringleaders shot.

Late in the afternoon of the 8th the following proclamation was issued:

"To the Army Committees of the Active Army and to all Councils of Workmen's and Soldiers' Delegates and to the Garrison and Proletariat of Petrograd:

"We have deposed the Government of Kerensky, which rose against the revolution and the people. The change which resulted in the deposition of the Provisional Government was accomplished without bloodshed. The Petrograd Council of Workmen's and Soldiers' Delegates solemnly welcomes the accomplished change and proclaims the authority of the Military Revolutionary Committee until the creation of a government of the Workmen's and Soldiers' Delegates. Announcing this to the army at the front, the Revolutionary Committee calls upon the revolutionary soldiers to watch closely the conduct of the men in command. Officers who do not join the accomplished revolution immediately and openly must be arrested at once as enemies. The Petrograd Council of Workmen's and Soldiers' Delegates considers this to be the program of the new authority:

"First—The offer of an immediate democratic peace.

"Second—The immediate handing over of large proprietarial lands to the peasants.

"Third—The transmission of all authority to the Council of Workmen's and Soldiers' Delegates.

"Fourth—The convocation of an honest Constituent Assembly.

"The national revolutionary army must not permit uncertain military detachments to leave the front for Petrograd. They should use persuasion, but where this fails they must oppose any such action on the part of such detachments by force without mercy.

"The actual order must be read immediately to all military detachments in all arms. The suppression of this order from the rank and file by the army organizations is equivalent to a great crime against the revolution and will be punished by all the strength behind the revolutionary law.

"Soldiers! For peace, for bread, for land, and for the power of the people!

"THE MILITARY REVOLUTIONARY COMMITTEE."

Meanwhile, simultaneously with the uprising, a General Congress of the Soviets of all Russia convened. When Trotzky had stated that there was no intention to take over the powers of the government, he had spoken only for the Petrograd Soviet. This Congress was responsible for the more ambitious program.

Of the 560 members of the Congress, 250 were Bolsheviki, 150 Social Revolutionists, 60 were Minimalists, or Socialist of the Kerensky type, while the rest belonged to the various other minor radical groups.

The order of business for the Congress was:

First—Organization of Power.

Second—Peace and War.

Third—A Constituent Assembly.

Among the officers elected were Lenine and Trotzky.

The Minimalists immediately presented a motion proposing a working compromise with the Kerensky Government, but this was voted down.

The general result of the first session of the Congress was approval of the action of the Petrograd Soviet and the declaration of a new revolutionary government through the Congress. The Bolshevist element were triumphant, completely so.

CHAPTER XVII

THE SIEGE OF THE WINTER PALACE

THE new government was not to gain control without some fighting, however. When the forces of the Soviet attempted to take possession of the Winter Palace, the headquarters of the Kerensky Government, they found the building in possession of a military force determined to give some resistance. Among the troops stationed here was the Women's Regiment, the Death Battalion, whose fame had been spread all over the world. The women immediately surrendered without firing a shot. It seems highly probable that this body was never intended for fighting, and that its surrender was with the full consent of the defenders within the building. The women were marched off and later disarmed; then the fighting began.

Within the square before the palace were stacked great quantities of firewood. Behind these woodpiles the Bolshevist forces immediately took shelter and opened up a steady fire at the windows of the palace.

Eventually, later in the night, the defenders of the Winter Palace surrendered.

Next day the bullet-spattered palace, the only visible sign of the revolution, drew vast throngs of the populace to the vicinity of the structure. On the Nevsky Prospect, where machine guns and armored cars and infantry had been massed were to be seen only the usual moving throng of pedestrians, among whom might be seen an occasional bandaged soldier or sailor, who had been wounded during the fight. Of the defenders of the Winter Palace about thirty had been killed or wounded, while the forces of the Soviet had lost only one sailor killed and several were wounded.

In spite of the fact that dispatches were announcing that the Bolsheviki were in a majority only in Petrograd, similar uprisings were taking place all over Russia, notably in Moscow. There the fighting seems to have been of a more determined nature, however, the casualties amounting to seven hundred on both sides. Eventually the Bolsheviki were triumphant.

After Kerensky left Petrograd, he managed, a few days later, to obtain the support of a small force of Cossacks, numbering three or four thousand, under General Krasnov, and with these he began an advance on Petrograd, reaching Gatchina, a few miles distant. Here he was joined by an additional force of military cadets, some light and heavy artillery, and an armored train.

Here he was attacked on Saturday, the 10th, and the fighting which then began lasted until Monday night. The Bolshevist forces included four of the famous Petrograd guard regiments, several battalions of sailors from the fleet, and a large number of armed workmen, known as the Red Guard.

"Our forces," reported a Bolshevist colonel, "were under a continuous shell fire, and many of our men were wounded, though few were killed. At one time a squadron of Kerensky's Cossacks attempted a charge near Tsarskoe Selo. They evidently were not familiar with the fact that officers of veteran regiments were with the Bolshevist forces, and, to their surprise, they were met by organized resistance. A heavy volley, which toppled over many of their horses, caused them severe losses. This was the last active attempt of the Kerensky forces to attack, and afterward they retreated."

Later reports seemed to indicate that the fighting had not been very severe and that the commander of the Kerensky forces, General Krasnov, was only half-hearted in his support of the former Premier. Or it may have been the attitude of his own soldiers which compelled him to begin parleying with the Bo shevist commander, the result of which was that the Cossacks joined the forces of the latter. General Krasnov joined them and made the following report regarding Kerensky:

"At 3 o'clock in the afternoon of November 1 (November 14, new style) I called at Kerensky's headquarters. He appeared nervous and excited.

"'General,' he said to me, 'you have betrayed me. Your Cossacks say they will arrest me and hand me over to the sailors.'

"'Yes,' I answered, 'such a discussion is now going on.'

"'Do the officers feel the same way?' he asked.

"'Yes.'

"'What shall I do? Will I have to commit suicide?'

"'If you are an honest man you will go to Petrograd under a white flag and appear before the Revolutionary Committee, where you will negotiate as head of the Government.'

"Kerensky agreed to this and he was promised a guard. He objected to a guard of sailors on the ground that he had enemies among them. He wanted to wait until night, but finally agreed to go in daytime. I ordered Colonel Kishkov, of the Tenth Don Cossacks, to appoint a guard of eight men. A half hour later the Cossacks told me that Kerensky could not be found. I raised the alarm, thinking he could not have left Gatchina."

It is evident that Kerensky could not trust himself to the Bolshevist leaders. There were rumors, but no authentic news came as to his whereabouts. Some reports placed him in Siberia; others with the Cossacks in southern Russia.

CHAPTER XVIII

THE BOLSHEVIKI AND THEIR LEADERS

BUT before the final defeat of the Kerensky forces the Bolsheviki had consolidated their hold on the political situation and had organized a government. Most of the ministers of the former Kerensky Cabinet had been arrested and were imprisoned in the St. Peter and St. Paul Fortress; they were with the forces which had defended the Winter Palace. On the occasion of their arrest Trotzky made the statement that they would be tried for complicity in the Kornilov revolution, or attempt at revolution, indicating that the Bolsheviki took the attitude that the affair had been the result of an intrigue of Kerensky's.

Nikolai Lenine, whose return to Russia at the beginning of the Revolution had been effected with the aid of Germany, headed the new cabinet as Premier. Leon Trotzky, who posed as an internationalist, was assigned the Department of Foreign Affairs. It may be well to discuss briefly the origin and aims of the political party which had suddenly achieved control.

The Bolsheviki are simply a faction of the Socialist party which may be found in every country where the Socialists are organized. In the United States they are known as the "Impossibilists," signifying that they will accept no compromise in their struggle against capitalism, as compared to their more moderate opponents, the "Opportunists," who are not averse to playing politics with the more conservative parties. In Russia the Bolsheviki are the "Impossibilists," the word Bolshevik being derived from "Bolsho," meaning large, or great. Literally the name indicates "all or nothing." The word was first coined in the summer of 1903, when the split in the Russian Social Democratic party occurred at a general convention, Lenine heading the secessionist movement. It is claimed that the Maximalists of the Social Revolutionists who, during the turbulent period that began in 1904, advocated violent expropriation and committed robberies against the Government to obtain funds, were a different faction.

Fundamentally the Bolsheviki are Marxian Socialists, believing that all history is simply a record of the varying phases of the eternal class struggle between the ruling classes and the oppressed proletariat. Compared to this struggle, between the rulers and the ruled, all other struggles, even the present war, are to them of no significance; they consider them simply quarrels between the capitalist groups of the various countries, while the soldiers forming the armies of the various belligerents are simply—so the Bolsheviki believe—dupes. From the same point of view, if those dupes, the working classes of all nations, were really "class-conscious," realizing their true interests, they would understand that nationalism and patriotism are only tricks of the ruling classes to keep them separated, so that they may be all the more easily controlled.

Theoretically all Socialists of the Marxian school believe this. But when the present war broke out, such Socialists as Kerensky and Tchernov and a great many more in this country, England and France were convinced that the situation was exceptional and that, though the Allied countries were not, from their point of view, thoroughly democratic, in that the industries are controlled by private persons for private profit, they did, nevertheless, relatively speaking, represent democracy as against such rank autocracy as the German and Austrian Governments.

The Bolsheviki, true to their name, would grant no such concessions. All governments, in their eyes, were against the people, the difference between them being only a question of degree so slight as not to matter materially. The real fight, according to their opinion, is between the great masses of the workers on the one hand and the exploiting traders and other capitalists on the other. Therefore they called on the masses of all countries to unite in a great world-wide brotherhood and overthrow all the governments.

The intellect, the chief exponent, of the Russian Bolsheviki was and is Vladimir Illitch Ulyanov or, as he is more generally known, Nikolai Lenine. He was born in Simbirsk, central Russia, forty-eight years ago, being a scion of the minor landed nobility. His father was an official in the Department of Public Instruction and Lenine received his early education in his native city. After graduating from the local gymnasium he went to Petrograd where he continued his studies in the university, specializing in economics. The early and the picturesque phase of the Nihilist movement was past then, but its seed was sprouting and very many students were radicals and revolutionists, Lenine among them.

But what made Lenine more determined in his revolutionary activities was a tragedy which happened in the family when he was only seventeen years of age. It was then, in 1887, that his elder brother, also a student in the Petrograd University, was arrested for suspected complicity in a revolutionary plot and, after a secret trial, was condemned to death and hung.

Like all men of his type, Lenine was intensely emotional and this tragedy in his life made a deep impression on him and was probably one of the chief factors in determining him to devote his whole career to the revolutionary movement. By this time he had become a convert to the Socialist theories of Karl Marx, and thenceforth he spent all his spare time spreading the propaganda among the working people. At the same time he also continued his studies of economics and various kindred subjects. At the age of twenty-five he published his first essay, "The Economic Significance of the People's Movement." Four years later appeared a historical treatise, "The Development of Capitalism in Russia," just at the moment when two important factions in the general revolutionary movement were carrying on a controversy as to whether the economic development of Russia would be the same as in western Europe. Even as the result of mere research the work was a scholarly masterpiece and was regarded as one of the landmarks in the literature of Russian industrial development.

It was not long before Lenine's activities caused him to become involved with the police, and not only was he compelled to change his name often, as did all revolutionists, but he was finally forced to leave Russia and could only return on short visits on false passports. Most of his time abroad was spent in Switzerland, France, and Austria.

Naturally, he took an active part in the disturbances of 1905, but did not specially distinguish himself, as it was the Social Revolutionists with their program of terrorism who were the most energetic during that period. Then followed the reaction and little was heard of Lenine or his Bolsheviki for a while. But in 1911, when Russian revolutionary activities showed signs of reawakening, Lenine and his associates founded the prominent Socialist daily paper, "Pravda," and took up their propaganda work with renewed activity. In 1913 the Leninites had developed such strength that they were able to elect six representatives to the Duma.

When the war broke out Lenine was in Cracow. He was immediately arrested by the Austrians as a Russian subject, but it was a moment when his past career stood him in good turn, and he was easily able to prove himself an enemy of the Russian Government. Being released, he went to Switzerland, where he remained until March, 1917. On the outbreak of the revolution which resulted in the overthrow of the Czar he at once set out for Russia. The Germans were only too glad to offer him facilities for crossing over to Russian territory, for they were well acquainted with his antiwar theories and had every reason to hope that he would play their game in the Russian capital.

But if Lenine was the scholar, the theorist, of the Bolsheviki, the dynamic power was undoubtedly Leon Trotzky. His real name is Leber Braunstein, and as the name indicates, he is of Jewish origin. He was born in Kherson, a province bordering on the Black Sea, about forty-five years ago. Of well-to-do parents, he obtained an excellent university education and, like Lenine, became active among the university revolutionary societies.

During the disturbances in 1905 he was at the head of the Workmen's Council which directed the general strike, but after the attempted revolution had been suppressed he was arrested and exiled to Siberia. After a few years he escaped by way of Japan, thence to Europe, where he became a familiar figure in the Russian exile colonies in Switzerland and other European countries.

When the war broke out he was in Berlin. Not liking his brand of Socialism for home consumption, the German Government sent him across the frontier into Switzerland. But Switzerland proved too quiet for a man of his turbulent temperament, so he managed to find his way to Paris, where he began publishing a Socialist paper. Here he was allowed to remain until the Russian troops were sent to France. His paper fell into the hands of the Russian soldiers. Trotzky's doctrines were quite as uncompromising as were those of Lenine, so, at the suggestion of the Russian Government, he was requested to move on. He thereupon went to Spain. But the Spanish Government would not tolerate a man of his radical opinions, so he was put aboard a steamer bound for Cuba. From Havana he at once took passage to New York, where he received a cordial welcome from the radical Jewish elements, landing in January, 1917.

During the three months that Trotzky remained in New York he lived in the Bronx section of the city, his friends supplying him with the furniture for a small flat. As a means of livelihood he wrote editorials for the Socialist Jewish papers and was one of the editors of "Novy Mir," a Russian paper published in New York. He also wrote articles for the German Socialist paper, the "Volkszeitung."

Shortly after the news of the March revolution in Petrograd Trotzky, together with a number of other exiles, took passage for home. At Halifax he was taken off the ship by the British authorities, who knew his record. Here he was detained until, at the request of the Kerensky Government, he was released and allowed to proceed to his destination. In Petrograd he joined Lenine and was the executive head of the Bolsheviki.

Of the domestic, the internal, program of the Bolsheviki little need be said, for it could not be brought into effective application until the international problems should be solved. Like other Socialists, they stand for the collective ownership of all public industries and natural resources, including the land. It is part of their doctrine that the big estates of the church and the bigger landlords who live off their rents should be expropriated at once. They hold that all army officers should be elected; that once elected, they should be respected and obeyed so far as military organization is concerned, but they should be made subject to sudden recall, or ejection. Unlike many Socialists, the Bolsheviki do not believe in centralization, even in a democratic government. In other words, they are keen partisans of "states' rights," and believe in local autonomy, superimposed by loose federation. For this reason, they recognize the right of secession on the part of any distinct section of the people who may have special sectional interests, such as radical, religious or national interests.

These are the general principles underlying the Bolshevik movement, apart from the sinister leadership of Trotzky and Lenine, whose treacherous connection with Germany and German gold finally betrayed their party as well as their country and her Allies.

CHAPTER XIX

FIRST BOLSHEVIKI PEACE MOVE

THE first informal notice of the peace negotiations which the Bolsheviki proposed to initiate was issued on November 20, 1917, when the following announcement was issued:

"By order of the All-Russian Workmen's and Soldiers' Congress, the 'Council of the People's Commissaries' had assumed power, with obligation to offer all the peoples and their respective governments an immediate armistice on all fronts, with the purpose of opening pourparlers immediately for the conclusion of a 'democratic peace.'

"When the power of the Council is firmly established throughout the country, the Council will, without delay, make a formal offer of an armistice to all the belligerents, enemy and ally. A draft message to this effect has been sent to all the people's commissaries for foreign affairs and to all the plenipotentiaries and representatives of Allied nations in Petrograd.

"The Council also has sent orders to the citizen commander in chief that, after receiving the present message, he shall approach the commanding authorities of the enemy armies with an offer of a cessation of hostilities for the purpose of opening peace pourparlers, and that he shall, first, keep the Council constantly informed by direct wire of pourparlers with the enemy armies and, second, that he shall sign the preliminary act only after approval by the Commissaries Council."

These instructions were, in fact, sent that same day to General Dukhonin, who had assumed command of the armies at the front since Kerensky's disappearance and seemed to be well inclined toward the new régime, since he had given out an order forbidding the movements of any troops toward Petrograd. But Dukhonin made no response to the above instructions. Finally, three days later, on the 23d, Lenine and Krylenko, the "Commissary of War," got into direct telephone communication with Dukhonin, and asked the meaning of his silence and whether he intended to obey the instructions.

"Before replying," returned Dukhonin, "I would like information on the following points: Has the Council of the People's Commissaries had an answer from the Powers to its appeal to belligerent nations regarding a peace decree? Is it intended to open negotiations regarding an armistice, and with whom—only with Germans or with Turks—or are negotiations to be opened for a general truce?"

"These are questions not to be decided by you," replied Lenine; "all that remains for you is to obey instructions."

"I can only understand," replied Dukhonin, "that immediate negotiations with the Powers are impossible for us; still less are they possible for me in your name. Only the central Government, supported by the army and the country, can have sufficient weight with our enemy to make such negotiations authoritative and to secure results. I, also, consider that it is to the interest of Russia that a general peace should be concluded as soon as possible. But I repeat that the peace necessary for Russia can only be concluded by the central Government."

The reply to this expression of opinion was:

"In the name of the Government of the Russian Republic and of the Council of the People's Commissaries, we dismiss you from your post for disobeying the Government's orders and for conduct that brings unheard-of calamities to the working classes of all countries, and especially to the armies. Krylenko is appointed commander in chief."

A proclamation was immediately issued, addressed to the army and the navy, authorizing regiments at the front to elect delegates to open negotiations with the enemy, though the power to sign an agreement for an armistice could only be exercised by the Council in Petrograd. The soldiers were urged not to allow their generals to stand between them and the attainment of their ends. Care should be taken, however, that they should be in no danger from unlawful violence. They were urged to maintain the strictest military discipline.

On the following day Trotzky sent a notification of the effort being made to open negotiations with the Germans to the ambassadors of the Allied nations, the text of which was as follows:

"I herewith have the honor to inform you, Monsieur Ambassador, that the All-Russian Congress of Soldiers' and Workmen's Delegates has organized a new Government in the form of a Council of National Commissioners. The head of this Government is Vladimir Illitch Lenine. The direction of the foreign policy has been intrusted to me in the capacity of National Commissioner of Foreign Affairs.

"Drawing your attention to the text of an offer of an armistice and a democratic peace on the basis of no annexations or indemnities and the self-determination of nations, approved by the All-Russian Congress of Soldiers' and Workmen's Delegates, I have the honor to beg you to regard the above document as a formal offer of an immediate armistice on all fronts and the immediate opening of peace negotiations—an offer with which the authoritative Government of the Russian Republic has addressed itself simultaneously to all the belligerent peoples and their governments.

"Accept my assurances, Monsieur Ambassador, of the profound respect of the Soldiers' and Workmen's Government for the people of France, which cannot help aiming at peace, as well as all the rest of the nations, exhausted and made bloodless by this unexampled slaughter."

CHAPTER XX

THE PEACE PARLEYS BEGIN

AT four o'clock in the afternoon of November 28, 1917, a Russian delegation crossed over into the German lines under a flag of truce and asked the German commander of that sector to communicate their request for immediate negotiations for an armistice to German headquarters.

The official Russian report of this first parley was as follows:

"We crossed the line, preceded by a trumpeter carrying a white flag. Three hundred yards short of the German entanglements we were met by German officers. Our eyes were blindfolded and we were conducted to a battalion staff of the German army, where we handed over our credentials to two officers of the German General Staff, who had been sent to meet us.

"The conversation was in French. Our proposals to carry on negotiations for an armistice on all the fronts as a preliminary to a general peace were immediately handed over to the staff of the division, whence it was sent by direct wire to the staff commander of the eastern front and to the chief in command of the German armies.

"At 6.20 we were taken in a motor car to the Minister's house on the Dvinsk-Ponevyezh road, where we were received by the Divisional General von Hoffmeister, who informed us that our proposal had been handed to the highest commander, and that a reply would probably be received within twenty-four hours. But at 7.30 the first answer from the chief of the general command already had been received, announcing agreement to our proposals, and leaving the details of the next meeting to General von Hoffmeister and the parliamentarians. After an exchange of opinion and further communication by wire from the chief of the general command, at midnight a written answer to our proposal was given to us by Von Hoffmeister. In view of the fact that ours was written in Russian, the answer was given in German. The reply was:

" 'The chief of the German eastern front is prepared to enter into negotiations with the Russian chief command. The chief of the German eastern front is authorized by the German commander in chief to carry on negotiations for an armistice. The chief of the Russian armies is requested to appoint a commission with written authority to be sent to the headquarters of the commander of the German eastern front. On his side the German commander likewise will name a commission with special authorization.

" 'The day and the hour of the meeting are to be fixed by the Russian commander in chief. It is demanded that the German commander be warned in due time to prepare a special train for the purpose. Notice must be given at which part it is intended to cross the line. The commander of the German eastern front will place at the disposition of the Russian commission the necessary apparatus, so that it may keep in communication with its chief command.'

"The Russian parliamentarians decided to appoint as the place the junction of the Dvinsk-Vilna line, whence the Russian representatives will be conducted to the Brest-Litovsk headquarters of the German commander. The time appointed is midnight of December 2, 1917. At the same time we were informed that no firing would occur unless prompted, and that enemy fraternization would be stopped. We were blindfolded again and conducted to our lines."

Meanwhile the elections for the Constituent Assembly had been called, and on November 26, 1917, the returns for Petrograd were made public. It was announced that the Bolsheviki polled 272,000 votes, the Constitutional Democrats 211,000 and the Social Revolutionists 116,000. There was considerable discrepancy between this report and others which were issued through various press agencies, though in all the Bolsheviki were the leading party, but they still fell far short of a working majority. They obtained six seats, the Constitutional Democrats four and the Social Revolutionists two. Later reports covering the elections as a whole indicated that the Bolsheviki polled about 40 or 45 per cent of the total vote.

CHAPTER XXI

PUBLICATION OF SECRET TREATIES

IT was during this period, before the end of the month, that Trotsky carried out his threat to publish all the secret state documents, consisting largely of the treaties agreed to between the old Russian autocracy and the other Entente governments.

The first of these was an official communication from Russia to the Allies expressing the desire of the Russian Government to acquire the Dardanelles, Constantinople and the west shore of the Bosporus, also certain limited territories over in Asia Minor. In reply France and England demanded that Russia agree to the freedom of Constantinople for cargoes not to or from Russian ports, the independence of certain Mussulman territories in Arabia, and the right of England to include certain parts of Persia under her sphere of influence. The Russian sphere of influence was also defined, and an agreement regarding the northern boundary of Afghanistan was discussed.

In the second installment of published documents was a telegram from the Russian ambassador in France, Izvolsky, dated March 11, 1917, indicating France's recognition of Russia's right to define her own western frontiers. This was followed by a telegram from Sergius Sazonov, former Minister of Foreign Affairs, assuring Izvolsky of Russia's approval of the agreement with England and France regarding Constantinople and the Dardanelles, and also stated the willingness of Russia to give France and England the right to define the western frontiers of Germany, but insisted on the exclusion of the Polish question for international discussion. There was also reference to the future exclusion of Germany from the Chinese markets, which was held subject to further discussion with Japan.

Another series of documents, published December 1, 1917, related to the concessions which had been offered Greece to bring her into accord with the Allies. One of these offered Greece all of Albania south of Avlona; another defined concessions in Asia Minor at the expense of Turkey. Another document discussed the handing over of Kavala to the Bulgarians on condition that they join the Allies.

One document referred to a conference of financiers held in Switzerland, in which the German delegates insisted that the Baltic Russian provinces should be ceded to Germany, and Finland should become an independent state. Another telegram, sent by the Russian ambassador at Rome on October 31, 1917, expressed a desire on the part of the Italians to have the Russians relieve the pressure on the Italian front by creating a diversion on the Galician front.

There was also published the text of a treaty between France, Great Britain, Italy, and Russia, whereby Italy was promised certain territories for joining the Alliance; also, Italy was to disregard all attempts on the part of the Pope to bring about peace discussions. Italy, according to another agreement, was to have the active assistance of the British and French fleets in destroying the Austrians on the Adriatic. After peace Italy was to receive the Trentino or southern Tyrol to the Brenner Pass, Trieste, Istria, and Dalmatia. In case Albania should be granted independence, it should be under the protection of Italy, but Italy should not oppose should it be decided to apportion parts of Albania to Montenegro, Serbia, and Greece. The agreement also recognized the principle of Italian control of the balance of naval power in the Mediterranean. Italy was also to have rights in Libia enjoyed by the Sultan on the basis of the Treaty of Lausanne, but Italy agreed to recognize the right of independence of those Mussulman territories including sacred places. Should France and Great Britain increase their African colonial possessions, Italy should have the right to increase hers at the cost of Turkey. On the whole, it will be obvious that Trotzky's promise of sensational revelations fell rather flat. The main features of all these treaties and agreements had been common knowledge before.

During the last days of November, 1917, the press dispatches seemed to indicate the possibility of a counter-revolution against the Bolsheviki within a very brief time. It was reported that the more conservative elements were organizing and were preparing to assert themselves. Much significance especially was attached to the action of the Cossack General Kaledine, who had declared the territory of his people, in the south of Russia, an independent state with headquarters at Rostov. It was said that he controlled the coal fields of Russia and would be able to force the Bolsheviki to terms economically. But subsequent events seem to indicate that these dispatches pictured the hopes of their senders, rather than actual facts, for gradual recognition of the authority of the Lenine-Trotzky Government was spreading and deepening. By the first days of December, 1917, the Bolsheviki were in full control of army headquarters, at Mogilev. General Dukhonin did, indeed, protest their authority, but obviously he had no support from the rank and file of his men, for the Bolsheviki, under Abram Krylenko, their new military chief, took possession without bloodshed. General Dukhonin himself was killed, under circumstances described by Krylenko himself in his official report, as follows:

"I cannot be silent on the sad act of lynch law practiced upon the former highest commander in chief, General Dukhonin. Popular hatred surpassed the limits of reason, and in spite of all attempts to save him, he was thrown out of a railroad train at the Mogilev station and killed. The flight of General Kornilov, the day before the fall of headquarters, was the cause of this excess. I cannot allow the banner of the revolution to be stained, and it is necessary strongly to condemn such acts. A revolutionary people are fearful in a struggle, but they should be soft after victory."

The tendency of the old Russian Empire to break up into separate and independent territories, or nationalities, which had been manifesting itself even during the days of the Kerensky régime, now showed itself in its full course. As already stated, the Bolshevist program was favorable to this tendency as a matter of fundamental principle, therefore no effort was made to check it, other than to give support to the Bolshevist elements in the seceded territories.

On the outbreak of the revolution a committee had been elected by the Soviets in Kiev, the metropolis of Little Russia, or the Ukraine, to "safeguard the revolution." The military staff in Kiev attempted to suppress this organization, but troops arriving from the Galician front upheld the committee and the military staff was forced to flee. Thereupon all power, civil and military, was vested in this committee.

On November 26, 1917, the temporary popular assembly, which had meanwhile been called together, known as the Rada, proclaimed itself the supreme authority throughout Ukrainia, and elections were called for a legitimate constituent assembly. This new republic covered a vast territory, including some of the best agricultural sections of Russia; the governments of Kherson, Ekaterinoslav, Kharkov, Taurida, and parts of the governments of Voronesh and Kursk; it extended to the Black Sea, Odessa, and the Crimea, and eastward to the territory of the Don Cossacks, where Kaledine had organized his people. At least part of the Black Sea fleet attached itself to the Ukraine Government, recognizing its authority.

But the Ukraine Government, though revolutionary, was not Bolshevist. Here the Bolsheviki did not gain control, though they continued the same agitation which had been carried on up in Petrograd for so many months. Occasionally there were open attacks and violent fighting between the two factions, in which the Bolsheviki from the Great Russian sections assisted them, giving the general impression that the two republics were at war and raising the hope in the Allied countries that, through the triumph of the Ukrainians, assisted by the Cossacks, the Bolsheviki and their peace policy would yet be ousted. But, as subsequent events have since shown, there was no less danger of a separate peace on the part of the conservative Ukrainians than from the Bolsheviki.

CHAPTER XXII.

THE PEACE NEGOTIATIONS

MEANWHILE the Central Powers were responding to the Russian proposals for peace negotiations with poorly concealed avidity. On November 30, 1917, Czernin, the Austro-Hungarian Foreign Minister, replied to the Russian proposals as follows:

"The guiding principles announced by the Russian Government for negotiations for an armistice and a peace treaty, counterproposals to which are awaited by the Russian Government, are, in the opinion of the Austro-Hungarian Government, a suitable basis for entering upon these negotiations. The Austro-Hungarian Government therefore declares that it is ready to enter upon negotiations as proposed by the Russian Government regarding an immediate armistice and a general peace."

Thus Austria-Hungary was the first government to extend to the Lenine-Trotzky Cabinet official recognition.

The Allied representatives, in protesting against the peace negotiations which had already been initiated, had addressed themselves to the commander in chief at Mogilev. So much did Trotzky resent this attitude that he issued the following warning on November 30, 1917:

"The Government cannot permit Allied diplomatic and military agents to interfere in the internal affairs of our country and attempt to excite war. Further steps in this direction will result in the gravest complications, responsibility for which the Government now disclaims."

Nevertheless, Trotzky did not confine his attacks to Russia's allies. On the same day, while addressing the Soviet meeting, he made some extended remarks regarding the impending negotiations.

"We shall be on our guard in the negotiations," he said, "and will not permit distortion of those principles of universal peace for which the Russian revolution is fighting. We shall allow no evasions and will make most categorical demands, both to our allies and to our enemies. . . . In no case shall we allow a wrong interpretation of our principles for a general peace. We shall confront our enemies with questions which will admit of no ambiguous answers. Every word spoken by us or by them will be written down and sent by wireless to all nations, who will be the judges of our negotiations. Under the influence of the working classes the German and Austrian Governments have agreed to place themselves in the dock. Be assured, comrades, that the prosecuting attorney, in the persons of the Russian revolutionary delegation, will speak with thunderous accusation against the diplomacy of all imperialists. It is all the same to us how the Allied and enemy imperialists treat us. We will carry on our independent class policy whatever they do. . . . Our Allies and our enemies must learn once for all that the Czars, the Kerenskys and the Miliukovs have passed. . . ."

On December 2, 1917, as agreed, the Russian peace delegates again crossed the lines and were escorted to Brest-Litovsk by the Germans, where the first session of the conference was opened. Three days later the Russian official version of the conference was issued from Petrograd:

"The conference opened in the presence of the representatives of Germany, Austria-Hungary, Turkey, and Bulgaria. Field Marshal von Hindenburg and Field Marshal Hoetzendorf charged Prince Leopold of Bavaria with the negotiations, and he in his turn nominated his chief of staff, General Hoffmann. Other delegates received similar authority from their highest commander in chief. The enemy declaration was exclusively military.

"Our delegates opened the conference with a declaration of our peace aims, in view of which an armistice was proposed. The enemy delegates replied that that was a question to be solved by the politicians. They said they were soldiers, having powers only to negotiate conditions of an armistice, and could add nothing to the declaration of Foreign Ministers Czernin and Von Kühlmann.

"Our delegates, taking note of this evasive declaration, proposed that they should immediately address all the countries involved in the war, including Germany and her allies, and all States not represented at the conference, with a proposal to take part in drawing up the terms of an armistice on all fronts.

"The enemy delegates again replied evasively that they did not possess such powers. Our delegation then proposed that they ask their governments for such authority. This proposal was accepted, but no reply had been communicated to the Russian delegation up to 2 o'clock, December 5, 1917.

"Our representatives submitted a project for an armistice on all fronts elaborated by our military experts. The principal points of this project were: first, an interdiction against sending forces on our fronts to the fronts of our allies, and, second, the retirement of German detachments from the islands around Moon Sound.

"The enemy delegation submitted a project for an armistice on the front from the Baltic to the Black Sea. This project is now being examined by our military experts. Negotiations will be continued to-morrow morning.

"The enemy delegation declared that our conditions for an armistice were unacceptable, and expressed the opinion that such demands should be addressed only to a conquered country."

On December 6, 1917, a slightly different version of the conference was issued by the German Government, as follows:

"Yesterday the authorized representatives of the chief army administrations of Germany, Austria-Hungary, Turkey, and Bulgaria concluded in writing with the authorized representatives of the Russian chief army administration a suspension of hostilities for ten days for the whole of the mutual fronts. The beginning is fixed for Friday noon. The ten days' period will be utilized for bringing to a conclusion negotiations for an armistice. For the purpose of reporting verbally regarding the present results, a portion of the members of the Russian deputation has returned home. The sittings of the commission continue."

On this same day, December 6, 1917, Trotzky sent to all the Allied embassies in Petrograd a note intimating that the armistice negotiations with the Central Powers and the initiative of the Russian delegation had been suspended for seven days for the purpose of providing opportunity for informing the peoples and the governments of the Entente nations of the existence and the details of such negotiations and their tendency. The note added that the armistice would be signed only on condition that the Central Powers agreed not to transfer troops from the front affected by the armistice to the other fronts where fighting was still in progress, and that the German troops evacuated the islands around Moon Sound. The note concluded with:

"The period of delay thus given, even in the existing disturbed condition of international communication, is amply sufficient to afford the Allied Governments opportunity to define their attitude toward the peace negotiations—that is, their willingness or refusal to participate in negotiations for an armistice and peace. In case of refusal they must declare clearly and definitely before all mankind the aims for which the peoples of Europe may be called to shed their blood during the fourth year of the war."

To this communication the Allied Governments made no official reply.

CHAPTER XXIII

AN ATTEMPTED COUNTER-REVOLUTION

IT will be noted that one of the outstanding characteristics of the Bolshevist Government was the publicity with which it carried on all its business. A history of the Bolshevist régime might almost be compiled from the proclamations of Trotzky alone. Even facts and events which one might suppose would be advantageously suppressed are announced. It was this policy which gave significance to the rumors of an attempt on the part of the conservative elements, backed by the Cossacks, to overthrow the Bolsheviki, for on December 7, 1917, Trotzky issued a proclamation, or announcement, stating that "Generals Kaledine and Kornilov, assisted by the imperialists and Constitutional Democrats and bourgeoisie," were precipitating a counter-revolution and were "raising a revolt in the Don region against the people and the revolution."

"The Workmen's and Soldiers' Delegates," added the announcement, "have ordered the necessary movements of troops against the counter-revolution and issued decrees authorizing the local revolutionary garrisons to attack the enemies of the people without awaiting orders from the supreme authorities and forbidding any attempts at mediation."

Kornilov, according to previous reports, had escaped from his confinement at military headquarters at Mogilev the day before the surrender to Krylenko, together with an escort of four or five hundred Cossacks, and apparently he had succeeded in reaching the territory of the Don Cossacks, where Kaledine had established his authority.

Further details indicated that Kaledine and his forces were advancing against Ekatrinoslav, Kharkov, and Moscow. In the province of Orenburg the Bolsheviki were attacked by General Dutov, at the head of an army of Ural Cossacks, and he was now besieging Tcheliabinsk, an important railroad junction. In the Caucasus General Karaulov was reported to be attacking at two important points.

"While representatives of the Congress of Workmen's and Soldiers' Delegates," continued Trotzky's announcement, "and the Congress of Peasants' Deputies were negotiating to secure an honorable peace for the exhausted country, the enemies of the people, the imperialists, the bankers, the landowners, and their allies, the Cossack generals, have undertaken a final attempt to destroy the cause of peace, wrest the power from the hands of the soldiers and workmen and the land from the peasants, and to compel soldiers, sailors, and Cossacks to shed their blood for the benefit of the Russian and Allied imperialists.

"General Kaledine on the Don and General Dutov in the Ural province have raised the flag of revolt. The Constitutional Democratic party is supplying the necessary means to enable them to carry on the fight against the people. The Rodziankos, the Miliukovs, the Gutchkovs and the Konovalovs seek to regai power, and, with the aid of the Kaledines, the Kornilovs, and the Dutovs are endeavoring to turn the Cossack laborers into an instrument for achieving their criminal aims.

"General Kaledine has declared a state of war in the Don region, is hindering the supply of bread to the front, and collecting his forces. General Kornilov, who fled from prison, has arrived at his side—Kornilov who in July introduced the death penalty and conducted a campaign against the revolutionary power in Petrograd. In Orenburg General Dutov has arrested the executive and the military revolutionary committee, has disarmed the soldiers and is endeavoring to capture Tcheliabinsk, in order to cut off the supply of bread from Siberia to the front and the towns. . . . The bourgeois Central Committee of the Ukrainian Republic, which is waging a struggle against the Ukrainian Workmen's and Soldiers' Councils, is assisting General Kaledine in drawing troops to the Don region and is hindering the Workmen's and Soldiers' Councils from distributing the necessary military forces throughout the Ukraine for the suppression of the Kaledine rebellion.

"The Constitutional Democrats, the worst enemies of the people, who, together with the capitalists of all countries, prepared the present world war, are hoping that as members of the Constituent Assembly they may be able to come to the assistance of their generals, the Kaledines, the Kornilovs, and the Dutovs, in order to strangle the people with their aid."

The document then concluded with a decree declaring a state of siege in the Ural and Don regions, outlawing leaders of the rebellion, etc.

In typical Russian revolutionary fashion, the fighting, which now took place between the forces of the Cossack generals and the soldiers of the Soviets, seems to have been largely limited to mutual threats of arrest and general argument. The Cossack leaders retired and the Bolsheviki did not pursue them. One report stated that Kaledine had been wounded.

For some time the Rumanians had been very busy issuing official proclamations from their temporary capital, Jassy, denouncing the peace negotiations and declaring their intention

of fighting the Central Powers, "to the last man." But in spite
of the admiration these proclamations aroused, there was little
hope that the small Balkan country could actually continue the
struggle if Russia made peace. On December 7, 1917, the Rumanians consented to associate themselves with Russia in the
proposed armistice. The Ukrainian Rada, also, agreed to a suspension of hostilities, by a vote of 29 to 8. On the Caucasus
front, where the Russians were opposed by the Turks, it was
the latter who took the initiative.

On December 11, 1917, the Constituent Assembly, on which
the conservative elements had based so much hope, attempted
to meet in Petrograd. But of the more than 600 delegates who
had been elected only about fifty were present.

Meanwhile the negotiations for an armistice continued. The
original deputation from Petrograd was now joined, on the side
of the Russians, by delegations from the other fronts farther
south, representing the Ukrainians and the Rumanians. The
two points that created discussion and disagreement were the
demands of the Russians that all movements of troops by the
Germans from their eastern fronts should be suspended during
negotiations and the right of the Russians to carry on unlimited
fraternization with the German and Austrian soldiers. The
Teutons were especially disinclined to allow the former; it was
obvious that they wanted to reenforce the Italian and the western fronts with the soldiers they had to spare on the Russian
fronts. But finally an agreement was reached, on December 16,
1917, and an armistice was signed by the two sides involved,
the armistice to begin on noon, December 17, 1917, and last for
four weeks, until January 14, 1918.

CHAPTER XXIV

LEGISLATION BY DECREES

SO far, as already recorded, the Constituent Assembly had proved a fiasco; it could not gather together a quorum. Therefore the Lenine-Trotzky Cabinet really represented all the authority there was. Nor did they hesitate to exercise this power to promulgate certain laws which were in accordance with their program, or principles.

One of the first of these which they proclaimed, on November 26, 1917, was the abolition of all class titles, distinctions, or privileges; like the French revolution, every individual was resolved into the simple "citizen," whatever his position. The corporate properties of the nobles, large merchants and other "capitalists" were confiscated by the state.

On December 17, 1917, a similar decree was proclaimed against the church. This institution in Russia, it must be admitted, had played a sinister part in Russian politics in the earlier days of the czars and had been, if that were possible, more reactionary and despotic than the military or civil authorities. Now, according to the decree, the properties of the church, in land, money, and other treasure, was completely confiscated and its jurisdiction over the schools was ended.

Perhaps the most radical decree was that which was promul gated on December 16, 1917, in regard to army organization.

Henceforward all officers were to be elected by their men, and those which were not reelected automatically were degraded to the rank of privates, with corresponding pay. Nor did such officers have the relief of resignation, for, having become privates, they were now subject to the penalties for desertion during war time. In a sense this was only a natural reaction, for nowhere, perhaps not even in Germany, were the caste lines drawn so sharply between officers and private. In the days of the autocracy no soldier could hope to become an officer, for it was the law that officers must be of noble birth; they must be

members of the aristocratic families.   The natural result was
that the common soldier was regarded as a degraded creature
and his officers treated him as such.   Now came the opportunity
for revenge, and the reports of correspondents seem to indicate
that this was taken full advantage of.   Colonels exchanged places
with their orderlies; captains and majors were forced to clean
out the stables.   And in not a few cases violence and lynch
law were applied to officers who had been, in former days,
hard taskmakers.

Meanwhile, throughout the passing days, there were continuous reports of passive resistance against the authority of the
new government.   It was especially among the employees of the
administrative departments of the Government machinery that
this resistance arose in the form of strikes.   The officials of the
state banks especially proved recalcitrant and refused to surrender Government moneys.   Parties of drunken soldiers also
created disorders, it was reported, breaking into wine shops
and helping themselves to the merchandise.   But when all these
minor events are viewed in the retrospect of a month or two,
summed up, it is remarkable how little disorder there really has
been in Petrograd, comparatively speaking.   Conditions certainly
in no way approached those existing in France, or Paris, during
the French Revolution.

It was in the Ukraine, not yet in the hands of the Bolsheviki,
that disorder reigned, though they were, apparently, responsible
for it in that they made efforts to gain control.   In Odessa,
during a few days around December 16, 1917, something very
closely approaching a violent revolution broke out.   Here the
Rada had apparently established the capital of the republic.
The Bolshevist element among the troops made a determined
attack on the arsenal, where the Rada was in session.   The
officials of the Rada summoned loyal troops by telephone and a
pitched battle ensued in the streets.   Then the sailors from the
Black Sea were summoned, but on arriving on the scene part
of them went over to the Bolsheviki.   The fighting spread from
the arsenal, where the loyal troops had taken up a strong
position, the Bolsheviki getting possession of the Municipal

Theater, close at hand. Here some fierce hand-to-hand encounters took place, the theater building changing hands several times. Finally the Bolsheviki gained full possession of the water front, the shipping district, whereupon this section of the city was bombarded by the loyal artillery. The final outcome of the fighting was not reported, but apparently the Bolsheviki were suppressed, for the time being.

But this did not immediately concern the Petrograd Government. Under the direct supervision of Lenine and Trotzky vast quantities of Socialist literature were being published in German for the purpose of distribution along the front. Of one pamphlet it was said that a hundred thousand copies were carried to the German lines and distributed in one day. Special newspapers, printed in German, were issued for the sole purpose of propaganda among the German soldiers. According to the account of a prominent Belgian Socialist, who visited Russia, hoping as many Socialists had in other countries of the world that their principles were to receive a fair trial in the new Russia, the Bolshevik propaganda in German was hardly calculated to make converts among intelligent people, for it was written in schoolboy language, with trivial arguments. Meantime, German propaganda in Russia was couched in irreproachable Russian and calculated to appeal to the educated and the unlettered alike.

At 4 o'clock in the afternoon, on December 23, 1917, the peace negotiations were resumed at Brest-Litovsk. The meeting was attended by the following delegates:

Germany—Dr. Richard von Kühlmann, Foreign Minister; Herr von Rosenberg, Baron von Hock, General Hoffmann, and Major Brinckmann. Austria-Hungary—Count Czernin, Foreign Minister; Herr von Merey, Freiherr vonWisser, Count Colleredo, Count Osaky, Field Marshal von Chisceries, Lieutenant Polarny, and Major von Gluise. Bulgaria—Minister Popov, Former Secretary Kossev, Postmaster General Stoyanovitch, Colonel Gantchev, and Dr. Anastasov. Turkey—Former Minister of Foreign Affairs, Nessimy Bey, Ambassador Hakki, Under Foreign Secretary Hekmit Bey, and General Zekki Pasha. Russia—Citizens Jaffe, Kaminev, Bisenko, Pokrosky, Karaghan, Lubinski, Weltman Pawlowitch, Admiral Altvater, General Tumorri, Colonel Rokki, Colonel Zelpett, and Captain Lipsky.

Prince Leopold of Bavaria, as commander in chief of the German forces in the east, welcomed the delegates and invited Hakki Pasha, as the senior delegate, to open the conference. Hakki Pasha, after a speech, declared the conference formally open and proposed Dr. von Kühlmann as president. The German Foreign Minister was thereupon elected to the chair unanimously. In his opening speech he said:

"The purpose of this memorable meeting is to end the war between the Central Powers and Russia and reestablish a state of peace and friendship. In view of the situation it will be impossible in the course of these deliberations to prepare an instrument of peace elaborated in its smallest details. What I have in mind is to fix the most important principles and conditions on which peaceful and neighborly intercourse, especially in the cultural and economic sense, can be speedily resumed, and also to decide upon the best means to healing the wounds caused by the war.

"Our negotiations will be guided by the spirit of peaceable humanity and mutual esteem. They must take into account, on the one hand, what has become historical, in order that we may not lose our footing on the firm ground of facts, but, on the other hand, they must be inspired by the new and great leading motive which has brought us here together.

"It is an auspicious circumstance that the negotiations open within the sight of that festival which, for centuries past, has promised peace on earth and good will to men. I enter upon the negotiations with the desire that our work may make speedy and prosperous progress."

Having concluded his address, Dr. von Kühlmann proposed the following rules, which were adopted:

Questions of precedence will be decided according to the alphabetical list of the represented powers.

Plenary sittings will be presided over by the chief representative of each of the five powers in rotation.

The following languages may be used in debate: German, Bulgarian, Turkish, and Russian.

Questions interesting only part of the represented powers may be discussed separately.

Official reports of the proceedings will be drafted jointly.

At the President's invitation the Russian delegates now presented, in a long speech, the basic proposals for peace terms, already familiar in the forms of the various resolutions passed by the Workmen's and Soldiers' Delegates.

The Russian demands comprised fifteen paragraphs, or points, as follows:

1. Evacuation of all Russian territory now occupied by Germany, with autonomy for Poland and the Lithuanian and Lettish provinces.

2. Autonomy for Turkish Armenia.

3. Settlement of the Alsace-Lorraine problem by a free plebiscite.

4. The restoration of Belgium and indemnity through an international fund for damages.

5. Restoration of Serbia and Montenegro with a similar indemnity, Serbia gaining access to the Adriatic. Complete autonomy for Bosnia and Herzegovina.

6. Other contested Balkan territory to be temporarily autonomous pending plebiscites.

7. Restoration of Rumanian territory with autonomy for the Dobrudja; the Berlin convention concerning equality for Jews to be put into full force.

8. Autonomy for the Italian population of Trent and Trieste, pending a plebiscite.

9. Restoration of the German colonies.

10. Restoration of Persia and Greece.

11. Neutralization of all maritime straits leading to inland seas, including the Suez and Panama Canals.

12. All belligerents to renounce indemnities; contributions exacted during the war to be refunded.

13. All belligerents to renounce commercial boycotts after the war or the institution of special customs agreements.

14. Peace conditions to be settled at a congress composed of delegates chosen by a national representative body, the condition

being stipulated by the respective parliaments that the diplomats shall sign no secret treaty; all such secret treaties to be declared null and void.

15. Gradual disarmament on land and sea and the establishment of militia to replace the standing armies.

At almost precisely the same moment that this conference was in session Trotzky was publicly delivering an address to the members of the Executive Committee of the Soviet, in Petrograd, in the following terms:

"We have called you here to ask your support. You must help us in our efforts to make peace with nations, and not with German militarism. If our delegation meets, eye to eye, representatives of the German emperor, without the people, then peace will be impossible. If dead silence should continue in Europe, if the German emperor should be enabled to offer offensive terms of peace, we should fight against it. I do not know to what extent we could fight, because of economic conditions, utter exhaustion, and the disorganized state of the army. But I think we would fight. We would release all elderly soldiers and call the youth of the country to fight to the last drop of their blood. The Allies must understand that we did not overthrow czarism to bend our knees before the kaiser. They know our game is not yet ended.

"If they should offer unacceptable terms directed against our basic principles, then we shall submit the question to the Constituent Assembly. But our party takes its position for a holy war against militarism in all countries. But if, exhausted as we are by this unprecedented slaughter, we must accept the terms of the German emperor, we would accept them only in order to rise together with the German people against German militarism, as we did against czarism."

Meanwhile during Christmas the peace conference was proceeding, the representatives of the Central Powers deliberating over the Russian proposals.

The German Socialist leaders, Haase, Ledebour, and Kautsky had attempted to procure passports that they might go to Stockholm, there to meet representatives of the Russian Bolsheviki to learn at first hand what conditions the latter demanded. But passports were refused them. Trotzky, hearing of this, telegraphed to the Russian delegates at Brest-Litovsk, stating that if this refusal were persisted in, the popular indignation in Petrograd would rise to such a pitch as to seriously hamper the prospects of success of the negotiations. Nevertheless, the passports were not granted.

On Christmas Day the Central Powers made their reply to the Russian peace proposals, and that reply was one which immediately attracted world-wide attention, for it took in all the Entente Powers.

Through Count Czernin the Central Powers offered a general peace based on the Russian demands; no annexations, no indemnities, etc. According to their interpretation, however, the question of the subjection of nationalities who have not independence, to another country, must not come under the scope of "self-determination"; such questions must be decided by each government and its people according to the constitution of each government.

In the event of mutual renunciation of claims for indemnities for war costs and war damages, Count Czernin continued, each belligerent would have to bear only the expense incurred by its subjects made prisoners, and to pay for damage caused in its territory to property of civilian subjects of an enemy country by violations of international law. The creation of a special fund for this purpose, as suggested by the Russians, could be discussed only in the event that the other belligerents joined in the peace negotiations within a certain time.

The chairman of the Russian delegation, Jaffe, while expressing his pleasure at the acceptance of the Russian basic proposals, demurred over the vagueness of the definition of self-determination of small nationalities; it was incomplete. He said that the war could not end without the reestablishment of the violated rights of small and oppressed nationalities, and Russia would insist on guaranties that their lawful rights would be protected in a general peace treaty.

War St. 7—L

"By renouncing the application of the right of the stronger nations with regard to territories occupied during the war," he continued, "the Central Powers at the same time give all their opponents an immediate peace ground. They affirm that the right of the stronger, after unprecedented bloodshed, shall be preserved with all its integrity within each of the countries with no regard for little and oppressed nationalities. The war cannot end without the violated rights of those nationalities being reestablished. The Russian delegation insists that those nationalities must in the very next peace treaty establishing a general peace among all nationalities receive, on the basis of international agreement, guaranties that their lawful rights shall be protected. The lapse of time in no case legalizes the violation of one people by another."

Germany also demanded the return of her overseas colonies, contending that the valor with which the natives of those colonies had fought for the German flag testified to their loyalty. While apparently not strongly impressed with this manifestation of loyalty, the Russians agreed that Germany had the right to make this demand. The Russian chairman then proposed that the next session of the conference be postponed until January 8, 1918, to allow ample time for the circulation of the German proposals among the Entente nations. At the end of that time the negotiations should be resumed, whether the Entente nations responded or not.

The terms of Germany, as submitted in detail to Petrograd several days later, were substantially as follows:

Article 1.—Russia and Germany are to declare the state of war at an end. Both nations are resolved to live together in the future in peace and friendship on conditions of complete reciprocity. Germany will be ready, as soon as peace is concluded with Russia, and the demobilization of the Russian armies has been completed, to evacuate her present positions in occupied Russian territory, in so far as no different inferences result from Article 2.

Article 2.—The Russian Government having, in accordance with its principles, proclaimed for all peoples, without exception, living within the Russian Empire the right of self-determination, including complete separation, takes cognizance of the decisions expressing the will of people demanding a full state of independence and separation from the Russian Empire for Poland, Lithuania, Courland, and portions of Esthonia and Livonia, the Russian Government recognizes that in the present circumstances these manifestations must be regarded as an expression of the will of the people, and is ready to draw conclusions therefrom. As in those districts to which the foregoing stipulations apply, the question of evacuation is not such as provided for in Article 1, a special commission shall discuss and fix the time and other details in conformity and in accordance with the Russian idea of the necessary ratification by a plebiscite on broad lines and without any military pressure whatever of the already existing proclamation of separation.

Article 3.—Treaties and agreements in force before the war are to become effective if not directly in conflict with changes resulting from the war. Each party obligates itself, within three months after the signing of the peace treaty, to inform the other which of the treaties and agreements will not again become effective.

Article 4.—Each of the contracting parties will not discriminate against the subjects, merchant ships, or goods of the other parties.

Article 5.—The parties agree that with the conclusion of peace economic war shall cease. During the time necessary for the restoration of relations there may be limitations upon trade, but the regulations as to imports are not to be of a too burdensome extent and high taxes or duties on imports shall not be levied. For the interchange of goods an organization shall be effected of mixed commissions, to be formed as soon as possible.

Article 6.—Instead of the commercial treaty of navigation of 1894-1904, which is abrogated, a new treaty will accord new conditions.

Article 7.—The parties will grant one another during at least twenty years the rights of the most favored nations in questions of commerce and navigation.

Article 8.—Russia agrees that the administration of the mouth of the Danube be intrusted to a European Danube commission, with a membership from the countries bordering upon the Danube and the Black Sea. Above Braila the administration is to be in the hands of the countries bordering on the Danube.

Article 9.—Military laws limiting the rights of Germans in Russia, or Russians in Germany, are to be abrogated.

Article 10.—The contracting parties are not to demand payment of war expenditures, nor for damages suffered during the war, this provision including requisitions.

Article 11.—Each party is to pay for damage done within its own limits during the war by acts against international law with regard to the subjects of other parties, in particular, their diplomatic and consular representatives, as affecting their life, health, or property. The amount is to be fixed by mixed commissions with neutral chairmen.

Article 12.—Prisoners of war who are invalids are to be immediately repatriated. The exchange of other prisoners is to be made as soon as possible, the time to be fixed by a Russian-German commission.

Article 13.—Civilian subjects, interned or exiled, are to be immediately released and sent home without cost to them.

Article 14.—Russian subjects, of German descent, particularly German colonists, may within ten years emigrate to Germany, with the right to liquidate or transfer their property.

Article 15.—Merchantmen of any of the contracting parties, which were in the ports of any of the other parties at the beginning of the war, and also vessels taken as prizes which have not yet been adjudged, are to be returned, or, if that be impossible, paid for.

Article 16.—Diplomatic and consular relations are to be resumed as soon as possible.

When these terms were read in Petrograd, the strongest indignation prevailed; it was Article 2 especially which the Russians were unwilling to accept.

The Russians had indeed emphasized the right of small nationalities to determine their own fates, even to separate from Russia, if so they desired. They also recognized their right to join any other national organization, if they chose.

Of this stand the Germans took full advantage, in rather a clumsy way. Germany insisted that those certain nationalities specified, Poland, Esthonia, Livonia, Lithuania, and the others, having declared their separation from Russia, could, and undoubtedly would, now declare themselves a part of the German Empire. At any rate, this was to be assumed.

The Germans had also explained, through General Hoffmann, that Germany would not evacuate Riga, Libau, and other occupied points until certain that all Russia sanctioned peace.

Germany's imperialistic schemes in the direction of Russia were very plainly revealed. Trotsky vaunted it as a signal success for his so-called diplomacy that he had forced Germany to make manifest her real purposes. But it was only in Russia that people hoped for any other attitude on the part of the Central Powers, with Russia's military power destroyed. Naturally, the peace offer made by Germany to the Allies was rejected with derision; or, at least, no official reply was made to it. But it did inspire a speech by President Wilson, on January 8, 1918, in which the war aims of the United States were definitely stated and the Russian peace deputation was given credit for at least the unmasking of German hypocrisy.

It was not until January 2, 1918, that the Russian Government made known its rejection of the German counterproposals for peace. This was done through a resolution passed by the Executive Committee of the Soviet, which was worded as follows:

"This assembly confirms the fact that the program proclaimed by the representatives of the Central Powers at Brest-Litovsk recognizes in principle the conclusion of a peace without annexations or indemnities. This recognition establishes the basis for further pourparlers, with the view of a general democratic peace.

"However, already in this declaration the representatives of the German Government have refused to admit the free right of oppressed nations and colonies seized before the beginning of the war in 1914 to dispose of their own destinies. This restriction, which was immediately reported by the Russian delegation, signifies that the dominant parties in Germany, compelled by a popular movement to grant concessions to the principle of a democratic peace, nevertheless are trying to distort this idea in the sense of their own annexationist policy.

"The Austro-German delegation, in setting forth the practical conditions of peace in the East, alters still further its idea of a just democratic peace. This declaration is made in view of the fact that the Austrian and German Governments refused to guarantee immediately and irrevocably the removal of their troops from the occupied countries of Poland, Lithuania, and Courland and parts of Livonia and Esthonia.

"In fact, the free affirmation of their will by the people of Poland, Lithuania, Courland, and all other countries occupied by the troops of other states is impossible until the moment of the return of the native population to the places they have evacuated. The allegation of the German delegation that the will of the people of the said countries has already been manifested is devoid of all foundation.

"Under martial law and under the yoke of the censorship the peoples of the occupied countries could not express their will. The documents on which the German Government could base its allegation at best only prove the manifestation of the will of a few privileged groups, and in no way the will of the masses in those territories.

"We now declare that the Russian revolution remains faithful to the policy of internationalism. We defend the right of Poland, Lithuania, and Courland to dispose of their own destinies actually and freely. Never will we recognize the justice of imposing the will of a foreign nation on any other nation whatsoever.

"This joint session insists that the peace pourparlers communicated later to the neutral states and instructs the Soldiers' and Workmen's Councils and the Commissioners to take measures to bring this about.

"We say to the people of Germany, Austria-Hungary, Bulgaria, and Turkey:

"Under your pressure your Governments have been obliged to accept the motto of no annexations and no indemnities, but recently they have been trying to carry on their old policy of evasion. Remember, that the conclusion of an immediate democratic peace will depend actually and above all on you. All the people of Europe look to you, exhausted and bled by such a war as there never was before, that you will not permit the Austro-German imperialists to make war against revolutionary Russia for the subjection of Poland, Lithuania, Courland, and Armenia."

Simultaneously with the issue of this declaration a pamphlet in German was prepared and published by the hundred thousand copies, wherein the trickery of the German peace parleys was set forth and their pretensions denounced as "unconscionable lies." After a description of the wholesale recruiting of labor forces from Poland and Lithuania carried on by the Germans, amounting to over 300,000 noncombatants, the pamphlet continued:

"The German Government only found support in Courland from the hated slave owners, the German barons, who have their prototypes in the Polish landowners."

The document further declared that the Germans only desired to free the peoples of those border countries that they might be exploited as laborers by German capital, impose an Austrian monarchy in Poland and make Lithuania and Courland German provinces. "On such a basis," added the pamphlet, "we shall never continue negotiations."

The Russian people themselves did not understand the manner in which they had been tricked and betrayed by Trotzky and Lenine and hoped much from the distribution of quantities of these pamphlets among German and Austrian soldiers. Indeed, the German and Austrian commanders are said to have endeavored to have this literature confiscated and destroyed, though it seemed to have little effect on the soldiers of their armies.

On the same date that the official rejection of the German proposals was issued, January 2, 1918, the chairman of the

Russian peace delegation sent an official telegram to the German, Austrian, Turkish, and Bulgarian delegations stating that the Russian Government desired to continue the negotiations on foreign soil, in a neutral country, and therefore suggested that the next conference be held in Stockholm. A revision of Articles 1 and 2 of the German-Austrian terms must be discussed, these messages added.

The next session of the peace conference was held at Brest-Litovsk, on January 10, 1918. Trotzky himself now attended, as head of the Russian delegation, to assume direct charge of the deliberations. The Ukrainians were now, for the first time, represented by an independent deputation, their independence being recognized by both the Russians and the representatives of the Central Powers. Bolubovitch, the head of the Ukrainian delegation, said that he had been instructed to hand the following note to the members of the conference:

"The Ukrainian Republic brings the following to the knowledge of all belligerents and neutral states: The Central Rada, on November 20, 1917, proclaimed a People's Republic, and by this act acquired an international status. It has as its ideal the creation of a confederation of all the republics which have arisen in the territory of the former Russian Empire. The Ukrainian People's Republic, through its General Secretariat, proceeds to enter into independent relations pending the formation of a Federal Government in Russia."

The head of the Ukrainian deputation further added that Ukrainia also desired that the peace to be established be on a general democratic basis, in which the rights of the smallest nationalities be recognized.

At the session held on January 11, 1918, it was agreed to prolong the period of the armistice another month, until February 12. A German report dated January 14, 1918, stated that a subcommittee of Austrians, Germans, and Russians had held three sittings in order to arrange territorial adjustments. The one point of difference on which no agreement could be reached was the border provinces. These the Germans were obviously determined to hold, and here was the deadlock. On January 21, 1918, the conference adjourned, the Russian delegates refusing to accept the Teutonic proposals, yet willing to meet again within a week's time.

At Petrograd Trotzky delivered his report and made his recommendations before a Congress of the Workmen's and Soldiers' Delegates, on January 28, 1918, the day before returning to Brest-Litovsk to resume negotiations. He pretended opposition to accepting the German proposals, and the sentiment of the delegates supported him. Already Krylenko had been calling for volunteers to form a Russian army of "Red Guards" to carry on a "holy war" against the imperialism of the Central Powers.

Meanwhile, during the last two weeks of January, 1918, other important events had taken place, the most notable of which was the final dissolution of the Constituent Assembly.

This famous body was scheduled to hold its first meeting on January 18, 1918, about 500 delegates being now assembled in Petrograd, to judge from the voting. The Bolsheviki had almost a majority; they were, at any rate, the leading element, but they now contended that the delegates had been elected on issues now dead, or at least that the candidates had not yet been able to declare themselves before the election.

Tchernov, the former Minister of Agriculture in the Kerensky Cabinet, was elected chairman at the first session, by a vote of 244 against 151. Several others of Kerensky's old supporters, now in prison, were allowed to attend under guard. The first day's session was marked by considerable disorder, in the midst of which the Bolshevist members withdrew in a body.

On the following day the Executive Committee of the Soldiers' and Workmen's Council issued a decree dissolving the Constituent Assembly, which order was accordingly enforced by the necessary display of armed force. The explanation of the reason for this action was, as usual, couched in the phraseology of ultra-Socialism, but in this instance was absolutely unconvincing, even from the Socialist point of view.

During the latter part of January, 1918, the relations between Petrograd and Finland became extremely unpleasant. As far back as December 5, 1917, Finland had declared itself independent, and according to their principles, this declaration the Bolsheviki had acknowledged. But, as it was also the case in Ukrainia, there was a very strong Bolshevist element in Finland, which immediately precipitated a state of civil warfare against the conservative elements. The Baltic fleet, being in the hands of the Bolsheviki, naturally gave its support to the Finnish Bolsheviki, who were enabled to establish themselves in the capital, Helsingfors. The Conservatives immediately protested to other nations, including even Germany, that though Russia had recognized Finnish independence, she was still interfering in domestic affairs, and that with armed force. A call for active armed assistance was also made on Sweden, and at the end of the month Sweden seemed inclined to respond.

Similar trouble was experienced with Rumania, except that the Petrograd Government stood in a reversed position; the Rumanians were taking aggressive action against the Bolsheviki along the southern front. Rumania, whose military effort had been checkmated, not so much by the Teutons as by the treachery of pro-German Russian officials, distrusted the Bolsheviki and entered Bessarabia. The Bolshevist Russians in Bessarabia resisted this action, whereupon the Rumanians shot them. The Petrograd Government took immediate action; it arrested the Rumanian ambassador in Petrograd, Constantine Diamandi, and together with his staff threw them in prison, on January 14, 1918. Against this rather irregular procedure the whole diplomatic body in Petrograd protested to Lenine, and two days later Diamandi was released. On that same day, however, an ultimatum was sent to Rumania, demanding the release of certain Russians whom the Rumanians were holding. On January 20, 1918, the Russian forces, established at the southern extremity of the front, at Galatz, were cut off from communication with Russia, then attacked by the Rumanians. A pitched battle ensued, with the result that the Russians, much inferior in number, were hemmed in. On the 26th Rumanian troops attacked and captured Kishinev, the chief city in Bessarabia. In these maneuvers Rumania had the active assistance of General Dimitri Tcherbatchev, commanding a section of the adjacent front. On January 28, 1918, the Petrograd Government broke off relations with Rumania and declared General Tcherbatchev "an outlaw and an enemy of the revolution and of the Russian people." The Rumanian gold reserves, deposited in Moscow and amounting to 1,200,000,000 rubles, were seized, "to be returned to the Rumanian people when they shall assert their authority."

But in Ukrainia, during this same period, the Bolshevist elements were making rapid headway. On the same day that Rumania occupied Kishinev, the Black Sea fleet definitely swung over to the Bolsheviki and seized the Rumanian transport ships and other shipping belonging to the Rumanian Government, consisting of about forty steamers and several old warships. Then cooperating with the Bolshevist land forces, the city of Odessa was attacked, and on the last day of the month not only this city, but Kiev as well, were reported to be in the hands of the Bolshevist Soviets, thus placing them in control of affairs in Ukrainia.

Among the Cossacks of the Don region the partisans of the Soviets were also said to be gaining in general support. Here, too, a republic had declared itself, with Kaledine as president. One report had it that he had resigned on account of his unpopularity with his own men. At any rate, he had shown no further aggressive activity against the Petrograd Government; as the hoped-for regenerator of Russia he proved a decided failure.

On the first day of February, 1918, the peace parleys were again in session at Brest-Litovsk, with Trotzky at the head of the Russian deputation, strengthened now by the Bolshevist deputation from Ukrainia.

PART IV—ITALIAN FRONT

CHAPTER XXV

THE CAPTURE OF MONTE SANTO

DURING the first three weeks of August, 1917, little of importance happened on the Italian front. The comparative inactivity which had prevailed during most of July, 1917, continued, interrupted only occasionally by local engagements of no particular moment at various points in the different sectors of the entire front. There were plenty of rumors, though, concerning preparations that were being made on the Italian side for a resumption of activities, and on August 19, 1917, the first definite reports were received to the effect that the Italians had begun a new and powerful offensive movement in the Julian Alps along a front of some thirty-five miles.

It will be recalled that their successes in 1916, which gained for them Goritz, had left them still without possession of the heights, rising from 1,800 to 2,200 feet to the northeast and east of that town and had brought them to the edge of the mountains to the west of the Carso Plateau. In a twenty-five days' campaign, begun May 14, 1917, they had then improved this position by crossing the Isonzo to the north of Goritz, by capturing Monte Cucco on its east bank and by extending their positions along this bank so as to include the Vodice Ridge, bringing them right up against the slopes of Monte Santo. On the Carso, too, they had succeeded in advancing so that their artillery could reach the heights west of it, including the Hermada Hills.

Their line then, as constituted in August, 1917, began some miles southwest of Tolmino, ran for a little more than five

186

miles along the west bank of the Isonzo, crossed it west of the village of Decla, ran along the east bank for about five more miles, then opposite a bend in the river turned south for about another five miles to the San Marco, running at a distance of about one and one-half miles east of Goritz, and then twisted in a general southern direction for some fifteen miles, crossing in its course the valley of the Vippacco River, down to the Gulf of Trieste where it ended about two miles southeast of Monfalcone.

It appears that in the new drive, now started, there were engaged: The Third Army, under General Cappello, in the north, on the Bainsizza Plateau, Monte Santo, Monte San Gabriele, and the approaches to San Daniele; the Second Army, under the Duke of Aosta, operating south to the sea, in the valleys of Vippacco and Brestovizza, on the Carso, and before Hermada; British and Italian monitors, which bombarded Hermada and the Austrian ships and arsenals at Trieste and Pola; the great Caproni aerial machines, which both on the battle line and over Trieste and Pola aided the work of the soldiers and warships.

Not until August 19, 1917, did it become known that for many weeks prior to the beginning of the offensive the Italians at sundown every night had by a great engineering feat diverted the water of the Isonzo above Anhovo, and had built in the shallow stream thus left 10-foot bridges, which were concealed from view when the water resumed its natural course each morning. On the eve of the crossing they supplemented these with four pontoon bridges laid while their searchlights blinded the eyes of the Austrians on the opposite cliffs. These bridges extended from Anhovo up to Loga, a distance of four miles. That night, August 18, 1917, the stream remained diverted and the army of Cappello crossed, while the Duke of Aosta performed a diversion on the Carso.

In the morning of August 19, 1917, after a twenty-four hours' bombardment, during which Italian artillery shelled the Austrian positions with ever-increasing intensity, the masses of Italian infantry commenced the advance toward their objectives.

From Plava, between Anhovo and Goritz, as far as the sea, after having crossed the Austrian first line, which was completely destroyed, Italian troops brought pressure to bear upon the Austrians, who, resisting strongly and being supported by considerable artillery and a large number of machine guns, offered a desperate resistance.

Altogether 208 Italian aeroplanes participated in the battle, attacking repeatedly with bombs and machine guns the troops assembled to the rear of Austrian positions.

The enemy's losses were very serious. The booty, even during the first day, was very considerable. Some guns and a large number of machine guns were taken by the Italians and more than 7,500 men and about 100 officers had passed into Italian collecting stations by the end of the first evening.

During the next few days severe fighting continued. By the evening of August 20, 1917, the number of Austrians taken by the Italians had increased to over 10,000 men and about 250 officers.

On the night of August 19-20, 1917, the Austrians attempted a diversion by concentrating fire and carrying out local attacks at various points on the Trentino and Carnia fronts. They were everywhere repulsed. One of their storming parties was destroyed in the Lagarina Valley, and another which had succeeded in gaining a foothold in one of the Italian advance posts southeast of Monte Maio was driven back by a prompt counterattack.

During August 19, 1917, cooperating with the advance of the army, floating batteries of the Italian navy and British and Italian monitors effectively bombarded the Austrian positions and communications on the lower Isonzo. Simultaneously Italian monitors were bombarding the Austrian dockyards south of Trieste. Austrian batteries replied vigorously, but the Allies' units were entirely unharmed. At nightfall they were attacked unsuccessfully by Austrian aeroplanes. One of these was brought down by antiaircraft guns and captured in the Grado Lagoon, mouth of the Isonzo.

During the continuation of the fighting in the northern part of the line, the Austrian lines on the Carso Plateau and on the coastal zone began to bend and give way at various points. Italian forces succeeded in carrying the well-organized Austrian defenses between Korite and Selo, near the strongly fortified position of Stari Lokva.

During the night of August 24, 1917, the Austrians evacuated Monte Santo, which, soon afterward, was occupied by Italian forces.

By August 25, 1917, the number of prisoners taken amounted to more than 600 officers and 23,000 men. The number of guns captured had risen to seventy-five, including two 305-millimeter, (twelve inches) mortars and many guns of medium caliber.

On August 26, 1917, on the Bainsizza Plateau, northeast of Goritz, the intensity of the struggle increased. With extreme desperation and a greater employment of forces, the Austrians sought to prevent the Italians from progressing toward the eastern edge of the plateau.

Not only did the Austrian resistance stiffen considerably, but the Italians also had to overcome great natural difficulties.

It must be remembered that the first part of their advance after the crossing of the Isonzo was a climb of 2,000 feet, and that the upland of Bainsizza is not flat but traversed by ridges which rise to a considerable height above the general level. One peak, for instance, northeast of Na Kobil, is over 3,100 feet above the sea, and the range that runs farther to the north along the eastern rim of the plateau above the upper Chiapovano Valley reaches a height of over 3,500 feet.

In spite of these conditions, however, fighting continued on the Bainsizza Plateau. After having overcome the Austrian rear guards, Italian troops on August 28, 1917, encountered a powerful line of resistance which had been previously organized and which the Austrians were defending with desperation. On the heights beyond Goritz the Italians made some gains. During the day they captured more than 1,000 prisoners and several machine guns. Altogether 247 airplanes participated in the battle.

A squadron of forty Caproni machines, which took part in the action east of Goritz, dropped many tons of projectiles on Austrian batteries in the Panovizza Wood.

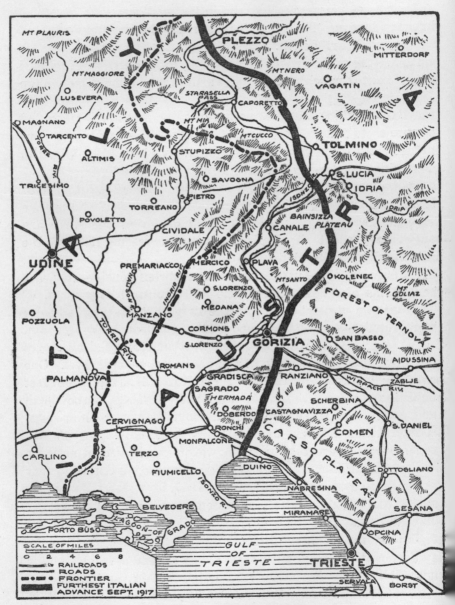

THE ITALIAN ADVANCE IN ISTRIA

On the Carso only an artillery duel and patrol action occurred.

In the Stelvio region, on the Trentino front, the Austrians attacked one of the Italian advanced posts on the glaciers in the upper Zebru Valley and succeeded in penetrating it. The Italian forces, however, were able to occupy a higher summit, from which they kept their old position under fire.

The next day, August 29, 1917, the Austrians attempted on the Bainsizza Plateau and east of Goritz, by counterattacking in force, to retake positions recently captured. They were driven back everywhere. The Italian lines held firmly, and advanced at some points.

Italian aircraft successfully renewed bombardment of Austrian batteries in Panovizza Wood, on the Carso. An Austrian attack between Vippacco and Dosso Faiti broke down.

On the Trentino front, from Stelvio to Carnia, concentrated fire and numerous reconnoitering actions kept the Austrians busy. In the Tofane region the Austrians, after intense artillery preparation, attacked the Italian positions at the mouth of the Travenanzes Valley three times and with great violence, but were repulsed.

All this time the most determined struggle was going on for the possession of Monte San Gabriele, which changed hands a number of times. Both on August 30 and 31, 1917, very brisk fighting occurred on the northern slopes of Monte San Gabriele and east of Goritz, where the Austrians with repeated violent counterattacks attempted to drive back the Italians. They were repulsed with heavy losses. On the Carso, in the Brestovizza Valley, the Italians carried other elements of trenches.

The total number of prisoners taken from the beginning of the Italian offensive to the end of August, 1917, had risen to 720 officers and 26,582 men.

Trieste, too, was continuously a point of attraction to the Italians. Hardly a day passed without an attack being made on it by Italian airmen.

Throughout the next few days the fighting continued without abatement. Again Monte San Gabriele was the center of it. Following the Italian success of August 30, 1917, the Austrians had attempted a number of times to regain their positions there.   But the Italians held on and continued their preparations for further attacks.   The final storming of this important and desperately contested position was described by the London "Times" correspondent, attached to Italian headquarters, in part as follows:

"The attack came on the morning of September 3, 1917, when the Italians went forward in three columns.   One column attacked straight along the crest, one worked along the northeastern slope, while the third advanced on the right, where the first precipitous fall of the ridge meets the steep slope that comes up from Salcano past the jutting spurs of Hill 343 and Santa Caterina.   The left-hand column was held up southeast of Hill 552 by a rocky bastion that juts out eastward from the main massif, but it kept the Austrians in this sector very busy and diverted their attention from the flank and center columns. The right-hand column got well forward and performed the same service for the other flank of the main attack, which was brilliantly successful.

"Nothing could stop the center column, which was made up of volunteer storming troops.   These broke down all resistance. They stormed the machine-gun positions, careless of loss, and reached the caverns, where the Austrian reserves were caught like rats.   In less than an hour the Italians were in possession of the main peak.

"They had thrust a wedge into the enemy position on the mountain, but their own position was precarious.   The enemy still lay round them east, south, southwest, on the lower grounds, indeed, but for that very reason they were half protected from the terrific hail of shells that had pounded the crest to fragments.

"Altogether the center column took nearly 1,500 prisoners— more than the whole number of the 'forlorn hope' that had stormed the peak.   Think of what they had done.   They had rushed a steep glacis that rises about 300 feet in 600 yards, a glacis not more than 200 or 300 yards wide.   At the end of the last abrupt rise they had stormed trenches cut in the rock and full of machine guns."

The day following the capture of Monte San Gabriele, September 4, 1917, the battle on the Julian front was violently renewed. On the Bainsizza Plateau the Italians obtained new advantages, capturing an important position southwest of Corogio.

On the Carso Plateau the Austrians, after most violent bombardment, launched infantry forces against the Italian positions from Castagnevizza to the sea. On the northern section of the line, between Castagnevizza and Korite, the attack, after varying fortunes, was repulsed. In the center, between Korite and Celle, the Italian troops resisted seven furious assaults and maintained their positions.

To the south, between the Brestovizza Valley and the sea, the Austrians were able to gain an initial success between Hill 146, to the northeast of Flondar and the railway tunnel northeast of Lokavac, where the Italians were compelled to withdraw temporarily from a few advanced positions. In the afternoon, by energetic counterattacks, the Italian line was reestablished, with the capture of 402 prisoners, including fourteen officers.

Two hundred and sixty-one Italian airplanes participated in the battle, bombing the Austrian troops and their communication lines.

CHAPTER XXVI

THE STRUGGLE ON THE ISONZO FRONT

IMMENSE quantities of booty had been captured by this time by the Italians as a result of their successful offensive movement. On the Bainsizza Plateau, near Santo Spirito and Laska, whole convoys of arms and munitions were abandoned by the Austrians in such haste that there was no time to destroy them. At one point thousands of boxes of projectiles, hand grenades, rockets, shoes, rifles, and helmets were strewn everywhere.

Mule paths and the adjacent side hills were littered with unexploded projectiles which the Austrians had thrown away, together with daggers, swords, and iron-studded maces used for dispatching the wounded. On Hill 652 the Italians captured three 105-millimeter cannon. Two of them were perfectly serviceable, and the Italians turned them on their former owners.

In an armored dugout near Ravena the Italians discovered the entire equipment of an Austrian staff of brigade. The extraordinary variety of objects found testified to the haste of the retreat. It included electric lights, official documents, toilet articles, kitchen utensils, ventilators, and even love letters. Ravena was the Austrian center of supplies for engineer troops, and near by were found stores of picks, shovels, hoes and wire cutters, entire outfits of electric equipments, miles of steel rails, and innumerable rolls of barbed wire.

During the next few days the fighting was chiefly done by the artillery on both the Bainsizza and the Carso Plateaus. The Austrians attempted a number of counterattacks, all of which, however, fell short of the desired results. During the period, devoted by the Italians to the consolidation of the newly conquered territory, they found time to count their prisoners and to list their booty. The result was the announcement that during the actual offensive there had been captured 30,671 Austrians, including 858 officers, and that the Austrians also had lost: 145 guns, including about eighty of medium caliber, ninety-four trench mortars and bomb throwers, 322 machine guns, 11,196 rifles.

Besides their attempts at counterattacking the Austrians also tried to relieve the Italian pressure on the Isonzo front, by launching a number of local attacks on some of the other fronts. In no case, however, were they successful. Thus on September 7, 1917, in the Concei Valley, west of Lake Garda, local attacks against two Italian advanced posts were repulsed.

Again on September 9, 1917, on the Trentino front Austrian reconnoitering parties were put to flight by Italian advanced posts in Cima di Cady, Tonale, in the Zurez region, east of Lake Garda and on Col di Lana. In the Carnia an attack against Italian positions of Monte Granuda and Cuel Tarond completely failed, though carried out in force after careful artillery preparation.

West of Lake Garda the Austrians, after intense artillery preparation, attacked Italian advanced posts on September 10, 1917, between the Concei Valley and the Lake of Ledro, succeeding in gaining a foothold in one of them, but were immediately driven out.

At the mouth of the Timavo, upper end of Gulf of Trieste, Austrian storming parties, which, with the support of infantry waves, moved against the Italian positions on the extreme right wing, were stopped and put to flight with severe losses caused especially by barrage fire.

The Austrians now began a series of most desperate counter-attacks in the attempt to drive the Italians from Monte San Gabriele which they had gained after terrific fighting some days ago. Various attacks were launched on September 11, 1917, against the Italian lines on the Bainsizza Plateau, afterward concentrating their greatest efforts in the region northeast of Goritz.

After having kept under most violent fire for several hours the Italian positions occupied along the crest of Monte San Gabriele, and on the western slopes of the mountain descending toward Salcano, they attacked from the east and south. The bitter struggle, which began at dawn, became more pronounced around the western edge of the table-land of Santa Caterina. Finally toward midday the Austrians, beaten and repulsed, gave up their fruitless attempts.

The crest of Monte San Gabriele is distant about one and a half miles east by north from Salcano, and the western edge of the Santa Caterina table-land is about half a mile from Salcano, Santa Caterina being somewhat to the south of a line drawn between Monte San Gabriele and Salcano. It appears, therefore, that the Italian front must make a sharp salient at San Gabriele.

On the following day, September 12, 1917, northeast of Goritz, the Austrians employing units recently sent to the front, renewed with greater intensity and with a larger number of forces their attempts to dislodge the Italians from Monte San Gabriele.

Their furious attacks were successful in a few advanced posts, but were stopped by the Italian main line of occupation, which could not be shaken or penetrated.

On September 13 and 14, 1917, the Italians succeeded in extending their previous gains on the Bainsizza Plateau. On the former date this was accomplished near Log, in the northern zone of the plateau, and on the latter date in the southeastern corner. During the night of September 15 to 16, 1917, the Austrians attempted, without success, by four successive counter-attacks to regain this ground. Other counterattacks, made September 16, 1917, were equally unavailing. During this period there was also considerable artillery and aerial activity on the other sectors of the Isonzo front.

Local actions of limited extent also occurred on the Trentino front.

On September 15, 1917, greater activity of Austrian artillery provoked a brisk reaction on the part of the Italian artillery in the Upper But and Fella Valley in Carnia. On the Carso Plateau, too, there was considerable artillery action during all these days.

A comparative lull set in during the next week, September 16 to 23, 1917. Though the Austrians had gained some ground on the summit of Monte San Gabriele, this was of little import, because the position was so located that neither side could possibly hold it for any length of time. On the other hand the Italians had captured two more heights on the Bainsizza Plateau near Volnik, which they succeeded in holding against repeated Austrian attacks and heavy artillery fire.

In the Marmolada region, on the night of September 21-22, 1917, by exploding a mine which had been prepared with long tunneling work, Italian parties were enabled to penetrate two advanced Austrian positions and to establish themselves there.

In the neighborhood of Raccogliano and Selo in the Carso, on the same day, the Italians succeeded in making a slight advance.

During September 23, 1917, the railway line in the Bazza Valley, east of Tolmino, was the objective of Italian air forces. In the morning one of the Italian bombarding squadrons arrived over the railway station of Grahovo, about five or six miles east-southeast of Tolmino, at a moment when intense railway movements were going on, and four tons of bombs were dropped there. In the night an Italian airship, by dropping numerous high-explosive bombs, greatly damaged the establishments in the neighborhood of Podmelec, midway between Tolmino and Grahovo. At the same time another Italian airship once again bombarded the numerous Austrian troops in the Chiapovano Valley.

In the Monte Nero region, upper Isonzo, the Austrians exploded on September 24, 1917, a powerful mine under Italian positions, upon which they then concentrated violent artillery fire. Prompt and effective barrage fire, hindering the advance of the infantry, prevented the Austrians from gaining any advantage. The damage done was slight.

Another let-up set in for the next few days. However, on September 28, 1917, Italian storming troops made a surprise attack toward the southeastern edge of the Bainsizza Plateau, capturing some of the high ground south of Podlaka and southeast of Madoni, and forty-nine officers and 1,360 men. Subsequent violent enemy counterattacks accompanied by heavy bombardment were repulsed and the positions maintained.

On the night of September 28-29, 1917, and on the following day, fresh attempts on the part of the Austrians to dislodge the Italians from the positions occupied between Sella di Dol and the northern slopes of Monte San Gabriele failed. On the remainder of the front considerable artillery activity and numerous good patrol actions were reported.

Air fighting was very brisk along the whole Julian front. Italian air squadrons bombarded the enemy depots at Berje, northeast of Nabresina, Gulf of Trieste, and during the night the known military works of the fortress of Pola with excellent results. The response of the enemy was vigorous everywhere.

The following day, September 29, 1917, Italian troops, by means of another successful surprise attack, rectified their line between the Sella di Dol and the northern slopes of Monte San Gabriele. Eight officers, 216 men, and a few machine guns were captured. The position was maintained and strengthened, not withstanding that the Austrians repeatedly counterattacked.

Italian air attacks were concentrated on the military zone of Voiscizza, Carso, which was effectively bombarded, and on the fortified maritime center of Pola, where the submarine base and the arsenal were again bombed with numerous projectiles by a strong Italian bombardment squadron. During the night Austrian aircraft dropped incendiary bombs on the town of Palmanova, causing slight damage, but no casualties. Austrian aircraft also dropped bombs on Aquileja, Monfalcone, and other localities of the lower Isonzo, without doing much damage. During September 30, 1917, the Austrians renewed their attacks against the Italian positions, recently occupied by them on the Bainsizza Plateau, but were repulsed. On the other hand the Italians reported that they had taken prisoners, in their offensive actions during September 28-30, 1917, a total of 2,019 Austrians, including sixty-three officers.

In Val di Fumo, Adamello, Austrian parties attempting to reach Italian positions between the Passo della Porta and the Forcel Rosso Pass were repulsed and pursued by Italian patrols, who captured a quantity of ammunition and explosives.

The first three weeks in October, 1917, passed without any happenings of much significance. Weather conditions began to become unfavorable and it looked at this time as if affairs were about to settle down to the accustomed trench warfare of past winters. Only a few engagements are worthy of special mentioning.

At dawn of October 2, 1917, the Austrians once more attacked the Italian positions on the western slopes of Monte San Gabriele. The attack failed. An assault company was destroyed and the battalion following it, caught in its turn under the fire of Italian batteries and attacked by Italian troops, was dispersed. On the remainder of the Bainsizza Plateau front there were only patrol actions.

Air activity was very lively. During the day one of the Italian squadrons carried out a bombardment on the railway station of Grahovo, Bazza Valley, northeast of Goritz. During the previous night in two successive raids the military objectives of Pola were bombarded and damaged.

During the night of October 3-4, 1917, one of the Italian bombarding squadrons, composed of a large number of machines, flew over the naval base of Cattaro. The Austrians replied by a violent fire. The Italian airmen on several occasions, and with visibly good results, hit torpedo boats and submarines lying in the harbor.

On October 4, 1917, from the Giudicaria, as far as the Brenta, Italian patrols were operating, and captured some prisoners. Artillery bombardments were more frequent and more lively on the Asiago Plateau.

In the region of San Gabriele repeated attacks launched by the Austrians were repulsed. To the east of Goritz the Italians improved a point in our line by a coup de main, and held it, in spite of violent Austrian counterattacks. On the Carso intermittent artillery actions took place as well as attempts to attack on the part of Austrian patrols, which were repulsed.

Snowstorms and gales now began to prevail in the Trentino, while the Isonzo and Carso lines were inundated by rain, and the valleys transformed into lakes of mud. The torrents were so swollen and impetuous as often to be impassable.

During the night of October 11-12, 1917, in the Costabella region, San Pellegrino Valley, an attempted Austrian attack was crushed. On the Julian front Italian patrols effectively harassed Austrian working parties and brought in some prisoners. Artillery activity was considerable from the Rombon, upper Isonzo, to the sea.

During the next day, October 13, 1917, there was considerable artillery activity from the Stelvio to the Rombon, as well as on the Bainsizza Plateau and on the southern front of the Carso. At Vrhovec, west of Chiapovano, Austrian parties attempting to approach the Italian positions were repulsed.

Along the whole Julian front there were lively local actions of the infantry on October 14, 1916. On the southern slope of Monte Rombon, north of Piesso, by a successful coup de main the Italians captured some prisoners. Between Castagnavizza and Selo, Carso, an Italian raid brought other prisoners. In the Brestovizza Valley large Austrian parties, protected by violent artillery and machine-gun fire, approached the Italian lines, but were driven back. Near Lokavac, southeast of Monfalcone, after a lavish artillery preparation extending from the west of Flondar to the sea, an Austrian attack was broken up.

Throughout October 15, 1917, on the Trentino front there was moderate activity. North of Lenzumo, Lake Ledro, in an encounter of advanced posts, Austrian patrols were driven back. On the Carso and Julian fronts, from the Paralba, Carnia, to the Rombon, upper Isonzo, there was desultory artillery fighting, on the Bainsizza Plateau intense artillery duels, on the front lines and on the lines of communication of the Carso the usual destructive and harassing fire.

CHAPTER XXVII

THE AUSTRO-GERMAN OFFENSIVE IN ITALY

IN the preceding chapters we have been told of the Italian successes gained in the summer of 1917 and the spasmodic fighting following them. The latter was frequently interrupted by periods of comparative quiet, and sometimes during the early fall of 1917 very vague rumors would be heard to the effect that they ought to be interpreted as the proverbial calm before the storm. However, as time passed and nothing of any import occurred, it began to look as if the Central Powers had decided to maintain the positions they occupied during the winter.

It will be recalled that the last fighting of any extent took place about October 15, 1917. This was followed by about a week of comparative quiet. Suddenly on October 21, 1917, reports came from Rome that Italian observers had noticed the removal of troops from the Trentino and Carso fronts to the

Bainsizza Plateau, as well as the arrival of fresh contingents from the Russian front, where evidently the Germans apparently expected no further serious developments. Usually activity was also reported in the Austrian trenches.

On the preceding day, October 20, 1917, notwithstanding adverse atmospheric conditions on the Trentino front, brisk engagements with rifle fire took place here and there. Northeast of Laghi Pesinar Austrian parties were driven back and counterattacked by Italian patrols. In the Booche region in the Pellegrino Valley Austrian parties came in contact with the garrisons of the Italian advanced posts, but after a fierce struggle they were forced to withdraw to their positions. On the Julian front the Austrian artillery showed spasmodic activity. Italian batteries replied with well-directed bursts of fire and effective concentration.

The air continued to be full of rumors. On October 23, 1917, it was semiofficially reported that "General Cadorna is making preparations on an extensive scale for an important military movement, but that there could not be any disclosure, for military reasons, of the objective, extent, or character of the movement or when the Italian offensive will be resumed."

Another report had it "that British and French soldiers, guns, munitions were being sent by train to the Italian front."

Still another bit of gossip was that reports of an impending Austrian offensive had proved to be unfounded and that "General Cadorna desired to start a new offensive against Austria and as a consequence there had been an extreme enlivenment of trench, mortar, and artillery firing from the Tolmino to the southern Carso and over the entire area of the Bainsizza Plateau, which was still in progress. Although the firing was uninterrupted on the part of the Italians, it was declared not to be the prelude of a fresh attack."

The reports covering events at the front during the preceding day, October 22, 1917, showed that the Italian positions on Monte Piana, in the Cadore, were strongly attacked by Austro-German forces. After heavy fighting the enemy was driven back with severe loss. On the following morning, October 23,

1917, Italian storming parties recaptured a portion of their intrenchments which the Austrians had temporarily occupied.

On the remainder of the front there were lively local engagements. In the Cordevole Valley and at the head of the Padola Valley the Italians repulsed enemy detachments.

On the Julian front the artillery action continued intense the whole day. The weather conditions were favorable also to aerial activity.

From then on events as reported from the front made it clearer and clearer day by day that the Austrians, supported by strong German reenforcements, were about to launch an important offensive movement, the extent of which, of course, at that time could not be predicted. By October 23, 1917, the fighting activity had been perceptibly revived in the Tyrolean, Carnia, and Isonzo regions. German artillery took part in the artillery battle, and German and Austro-Hungarian infantrymen captured the foremost Italian positions near Flitsch and Tolmino and in the northern portion of the Bainsizza Plateau, taking some thousands of prisoners.

On October 24, 1917, after an interval of a few hours, the Austrians resumed the violent bombardment all along the front, with a specially destructive fire on that portion between the southern slopes of Monte Rombon and the northern edge of the Bainsizza Plateau, where afterward a strong infantry attack was launched. The Narrows of Saga resisted the hostile blow; but farther south, favored by a thick mist which rendered useless the Italian barrage fire, the Austrians succeeded in breaking through the Italian lines on the left bank of the Isonzo.

Taking advantage of the bridgehead of Santa Maria and Santa Lucia, they then brought the battle on to the slopes of the right bank of the river.

At the same time, powerful attacks were made to the west of Volnik, on the Bainsizza Plateau, and on the western slopes of Monte San Gabriele, but they were kept in check by the Italian troops, which in the course of successful counterattacks captured a few hundred prisoners.

On the Carso, a violent Austrian bombardment was effectively countered by Italian batteries. The Germans claimed that up to the end of the day more than 10,000 prisoners, including divisional and brigade staffs, and rich booty in guns and war material had been taken.

The offensive against the Italian left wing on the Julian front continued during the night and on October 25, 1917, conducted by powerful forces. From Montemaggiore to the west of Auzza the Italians were forced to withdraw to their boundary line, in consequence of which they had to provide for the evacuation of the Bainsizza Plateau. East of Gorltz and on the Carso the situation remained unchanged.

This meant that the Germans, profiting by their success in breaking through the line near Flitsch and Tolmino, were advancing beyond Caporetto and Ronzina. They were already fighting at many places on Italian territory. The number of prisoners had increased to more than 30,000, of whom 700 were officers. The booty amounted to more than 300 guns, including many heavy ones.

The Austro-German offensive now began to gain more and more momentum almost every hour. It became known that Von Mackensen was in supreme command of the forces of the Central Powers. Favored by good weather, the German and Austro-Hungarian divisions pressed forward irresistibly over heights and through the valleys. The steep mountain ridge of Stol was captured and soon afterward the strongly fortified summit of Monte Matajur, 1,641 meters high, fell.

The Germans claimed that by now the number of prisoners had increased to 60,000 and the captured guns to 450 and that inestimable quantities of war materials were yet to be salved from the captured Italian positions.

After having crossed the boundary line between Monte Canin and the head of the Judrio Valley, the Austrians, by October 26, 1917, were attempting to reach an opening on the plains. On the Carso their effort was increasing. Strong offensive thrusts, however, were repulsed by the Italian troops.

The worst fears now began to be realized and with stunning swiftness the Austro-German forces forced back the Italians from territory which the latter had gained only by fighting most valiantly for months. In spite of determined resistance, which only in some instances was not all that might have reasonably been expected, the Italian forces were thrown back by powerful thrusts. In the evening of October 27, 1917, German troops forced their way into the burning town of Cividale, the first town in point of position in the plain. The Italian front as far as the Adriatic Sea was now wavering. The Austro-German troops were pressing forward on the whole line. Goritz, the much-disputed town in the Isonzo battles, was taken early on October 28, 1917, by Austro-Hungarian Divisions.

Cividale is a town of about 5,000 inhabitants, nine miles northeast of the important railroad center of Udine. It is near the entrance to the valley of the Natisone River, along which the Austro-German forces which broke the Italian line in the Tolmino region battered their way. Cividale is in the foothills of the Julian Alps, beyond which lie the plains of northern Italy.

Goritz was captured by the Italians on August 9, 1916. It is a town of 31,000 inhabitants on the Isonzo, halfway down the river from Tolmino to the sea. It is strongly situated among hills of great defensive value, in which there was heavy fighting before the Italians reached the city itself. Goritz is twenty-two miles northwest of Trieste, Austria's big seaport at the head of the Adriatic, the capture of which is one of the principal Italian aspirations in the war.

By October 28, 1917, the defeated second Italian army was retreating toward the Tagliamento. The third Italian army, it was claimed, offered only brief resistance to the attack against their positions from Wippach to the sea and hastily retreated along the Adriatic coast. North of the broad sector which had been pierced, the Italian front also was now yielding as far as the Ploecken Pass.

Italian rear guards vainly endeavored to stem the advance of the armies of the Central Powers. Austro-Hungarian troops were then standing before Udine, hitherto the grand

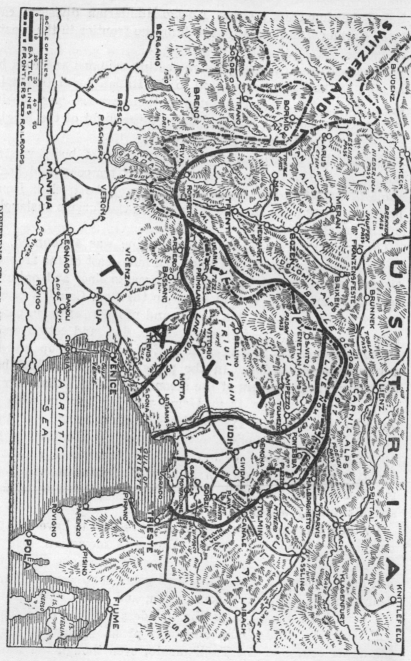

DIFFERENT STAGES OF THE ITALIAN RETREAT

Italian headquarters. Other Austro-Hungarian divisions captured Cormons, and were approaching the frontier in the coastal region.

All roads were covered with retreating columns and cars belonging to the Italian army and to the Italian population, who, overcome by the sudden disaster to their armies, were fleeing in a pathetic disorder, matched only by the flight of the Belgian civilians in the early part of the war.

The number of prisoners and the quantity of booty was reported as continually increasing. Violent tempests and heavy rains prevailed on the vast fighting area of the twelfth Isonzo battle, but seemed to have no influence on the furious onslaughts of the invading hordes.

On October 29, 1917, the fall of Udine was announced. It is sixty miles northeast of Venice, ten miles east of the frontier, sixteen miles west of the new Tagliamento line, and only 300 feet above sea level. It is situated on the Roia Canal, a branch of the Torre River. It is a quaint and prosperous town, chiefly interested in the manufacture of hemp, flax, and cotton goods, is the capital of the province, the seat of an archbishop, and has a population of 25,000. In the present war Udine had been the general headquarters of the second and third Italian armies. Five railways radiate from Udine west to link up with the Venetian-Quadrilateral system, by which the second and third armies have been supplied; north, across the frontier, to link up with the Vienna-Trentino line; northeast only as far as Cividale, whence the town was invested; southeast, via Goritz to Trieste; and due south, over the lower plains to a small steam tramway which skirts the marshes.

By then, too, the Italian Carnia front seemed to have collapsed on the most important sectors. During a snowstorm Austrian troops wrested from the Italians frontier positions which they had built up during two and a half years southwest of Tarvis, near Pontafel, in the Ploecken region, and on St. Pal. Advancing out of the Carnic Alps the invaders set foot on Venetian soil along the entire front, and were pressing forward against the upper course of the Tagliamento, even though the Italians

The officer responding to salutes is the Italian commander in chief, General Diaz, who succeeded General Cadorna in November, 1917. Next beside him is the French General Fayolle

destroyed, wherever possible, bridges and other means of communication in order to delay the hostile advance.

In spite of valiant efforts on the part of the Italians to stem the tide of invaders, the latter gained new successes on the last day of October, 1917. Portions of the Italian army made a stand at the Tagliamento. Austro-Hungarian forces, however, stormed the last Tagliamento bridgehead, near Latisana, on the lower reaches of the river, south of Codroipo. The bridgehead positions at the latter place and at Dignano were taken by storm by German troops. The Germans claimed that as a result of these operations more than 60,000 Italians, cut off and outflanked on both sides, laid down their arms, and that the number of prisoners taken by them had increased to more than 180,000 and that the number of guns captured had increased to more than 1,500. Late that day such Italian forces as were still maintaining themselves on the eastern bank of the Tagliamento near Pinzano and Latisana were either driven back or taken prisoners. In less than a week's fighting the troops of the Central Powers had pushed forward a thirty-mile front an average distance of thirty miles, making the total of the territory wrested from the Italians some 1,000 square miles.

On November 1, 1917, it was reported that Anglo-French reenforcements had reached the Italian front. Of course, these were comparatively small in number and were sent more for the moral effect their arrival would have than for any actual military value. The battle continued without let-up. Along the middle and lower Tagliamento the opposing armies were in continuous fighting contact. By evening the left bank of the river had been cleared of Italians from the Fella Valley to the Adriatic Sea. That the Italian armies were not totally annihilated was due solely to the efficient rear-guard actions which parts of them had fought against terrific odds.

During November 2 and 3, 1917, the fighting along the Tagliamento was chiefly done by the artillery of both armies. The Germans again claimed large increases in the number of prisoners and guns captured. On the other hand the Italians claimed that a great many of the 200,000 so-called prisoners were mainly workmen or other units of a noncombatant nature and that of the "more than 1,800 guns" the majority were machine guns.

CHAPTER XXVIII

THE ITALIANS AT BAY ON THE PIAVE

EVER since Udine had fallen into the hands of the Central Powers, there had, of course, been much speculation as to what the real German objective was and how and where the Italians were finally going to make a stand against the Austro-German onslaught. For some time it seemed as if the Central Powers were going to try to capture Venice and as if the Italians were going to attempt to prevent it by making a stand at the Tagliamento River. When, however, the fighting along that river, as described in the latter part of the last chapter, gradually but definitely went against the Italians, it soon became clear that the Tagliamento line could not be held for any length of time.

This assumption was proved to be correct very soon. On November 4, 1917, German and Austro-Hungarian divisions succeeded in crossing the middle course of the river and immediately began to press the advantage gained. General Cadorna's line now was broken again and a continued resistance in its present position had become too dangerous to be feasible. It was, therefore, not much of a surprise when news came that the Italians had begun a new retreat on November 5, 1917, especially in view of the fact that Austro-German pressure in the northern, mountainous section of the line had also become so strong that it resulted in evacuation of territory on the part of the Italians.

However, the few days' resistance offered on the Tagliamento had served its purpose. It enabled the Italians to rearrange their shattered armies to a certain extent, so that their withdrawal had been changed from a rout to an orderly retreat. It was made in the direction of the Livenza River, some fifteen miles west of the Tagliamento. The Livenza, however, did not offer the necessary natural defenses to make a determined and extended defense possible, and its only purpose was to delay the enemy sufficiently long to make it possible for the Italians to withdraw in good order behind the next line of defense, the Piave. The Livenza line was reached on November 6, 1917. But so close were the Austro-Germans that the Italians immediately proceeded to cross the Livenza. Indeed, by November 7, 1917, some Austro-German forces, too, had forced their way across the river at some points.

In spite of this, however, the Italians succeeded in extricating themselves from their dangerous position and in withdrawing the great bulk of their forces behind the next line of defense, the Piave River. There it had been determined to face the foe. The Italians, it is true, continued to lose a considerable number of men as prisoners. But compared with their losses of the two preceding weeks, the present losses were slight and showed a decided revival of the Italian resistance and a slowing up of the Austro-German advance.

It also became known now that General Cadorna, who had been in command of the Italian armies since the beginning of the war, had been relieved of this command and had been appointed as the chief military representative of Italy on the permanent interallied military committee. His successor in chief command of the Italian armies was General Diaz, and under him were to be Generals Badoglio and Giardino. The new commander in chief was fifty-six years old, eleven years the junior of General Cadorna. At the outbreak of the war, in 1914, he was a colonel. The second in command was only forty-six years old and had risen since the beginning of the war to his present rank from that of a major of artillery.

By November 9, 1917, the Italians had reached their more or less prepared positions on the lower Piave and frantically began digging themselves in. In the north, however, matters did not go well with the Italians. Austro-Hungarian troops succeeded in pressing forward in the Sugana Valley and in the upper Piave valley. After desperate fighting in the streets

Asiago was captured by them. This town is some twenty miles west of the Piave and only a few miles across the Austro-Italian border. On the lower Piave the Italians crossed to the west bank, blowing up behind them all bridges and established themselves fairly firm behind the river from Susegana, in the foothills of the Alps, to the Adriatic, a line of some forty miles.

The Austrians extended their gains in the north on November 10, 1917. Belluno, on the upper Piave, was taken by them, and so was Vidor and its bridgehead, some twenty-five miles downstream, not, however, until the bridge itself had been blown up by the Italians. Fighting on the lower Piave was restricted to artillery and machine-gun firing.

As a result of their gains in the Belluno sector, the Austro-Germans claimed on November 12, 1917, to have captured about 14,000 prisoners and numerous guns and to have reached Feltre, a small town at a bend of the middle Piave.

Heavy fighting occurred on November 12, 1917, on the Asiago plateau. But the Italian line, established there from Monte Gallio-Longara-Meletta di Gallio, held. Between the Brenta and the Piave the Austro-Germans occupied territory previously evacuated by the Italians and reached contact with the Italian lines. On the lower Piave the Italian line held, except at one point, about twelve miles northwest of the mouth of the Piave. There, near Monte San Dona di Piave, about twenty-three miles northeast of Venice, enemy groups succeeded, with the aid of large boats, in crossing to the west bank of the Piave. Italian counterattacks, however, promptly drove them back and the Italian lines were reestablished without a break.

On November 13, 1917, the Central Powers again registered successes. They took Primolano on the upper Brenta and Feltre on the middle Piave. Near the Adriatic they crossed the lower Piave and gained a slight foothold on its western bank, which, however, they were unable to extend in width in spite of determined efforts. A surprise attack against the Italian rear from the north in the region of Lake Garda failed.

New attempts on the part of the Austro-German forces to cross the lower Piave, made repeatedly during November 14

1917, were promptly repulsed by the Italians, whose power of resistance gradually seemed to stiffen. The same fate met renewed Teuton attacks along the entire front from Asiago to the Piave River, attempted on November 15, 1917. In this the Italians were assisted by opening the floodgates of the Piave River.

The following day, November 16, 1917, the forces of the Central Powers succeeded at two points in crossing the Piave, but were unable to maintain their gains against the fierce counterattacks of the Italians, though they captured Prassolan.

Again on November 17, 1917, the enemy attempted to get across the Piave. Everywhere however, the Italian line held like a wall of steel. Between the Brenta and the Piave the Austro-Germans were even forced to withdraw slightly.

The heaviest kind of fighting raged for the next four weeks in the Alps between Asiago and the Piave. From day to day the fortune of battle wavered. With admirable tenacity the Italians held every position to the very limit of their power and gave up only against overpowering strength, giving way occasionally almost foot by foot, only to come back with strong counterattacks as soon as they regained their breath. The difficulties under which this fighting was done beggars description. For not only were there the natural difficulties of the mountainous terrain, comparatively bare of means of communication, except the wonderful Italian mountain roads, but it must also be remembered that winter had set in long ago and that snow and gales added their share of hardships.

To recite in detail this tremendous struggle would cover page after page and, in a way, would involve much repetition. The complete story would read more like an ancient epic poem than the description of a modern battle. We must be satisfied with an outline of events as they happened day by day.

On November 18, 1917, the Austro-Germans captured Quero, a little town on the Piave, south of Feltre, Monte Cornelle and Monte Tomba. Four times they tried to storm Mt. Monfenera on the 19th, and four times the Italians drove them back. The following day, November 20, 1917, they were no more successful in their attacks against Monte Pertica, and again on November

21, 1917, they failed in their attempts, both against Monte
Pertica and Monte Monfenera. However, on that day they
succeeded in wresting from the Italians Monte Fontana Secca
and Monte Spinoucia, farther to the north and east.

An encircling movement against Monte Meletta, northeast of
Asiago, attempted by the Austrians on November 22, 1917, was
thwarted by the Italians and numerous attacks against various
points between the Brenta and Piave Rivers also failed.

The Italians did not restrict themselves to defending their
positions. Whenever the chance offered they undertook offensive
movements and as a result of one of these they recaptured, on
November 23, 1917, both Monte Tomba and Monte Pertica.
They also made some slight gains in the region of Monte Meletta
during November 24, 1917. Between that date and December
3, 1917, the Austro-Germans made many attacks along the entire
Asiago-Quero front. None of them succeeded in gaining their
objectives.

On December 4 and 5, 1917, the Italians were driven from
strong positions which they held between Monte Tondarecar
and Monte Badenecche, some miles east of Monte Meletta. But
when the enemy attempted to extend his operations still farther
west he was checked. However, as a result of his success, he
he was able, on December 6, 1917, to take Monte Sisemol, farther
south. Still farther south the Italian line held in spite of repeated attempts to break it.

For the next few days the fighting in the hills slowed down
considerably. But on December 11, 1917, the Austro-Germans
again began to pound away against the Italian positions. Attacks
were launched that day against Col di Beretta and Col dell'Orso,
and once more Monte Spinoucia was stormed. Three days later,
December 14, 1917, Col Caprille, just southwest of Col di Beretta,
was reached by the Austrians.

In the latter part of December, 1917, we hear from time to
time of separate actions of the English and French forces which
had been rushed to the assistance of the Italian armies. Thus
an English attack was launched on December 16, 1917, against
Monte Fontana Secca, but failed to accomplish the desired result.

The French, supported by British and Italian artillery and airplanes, were more successful on December 30, 1917, when they took by storm some important positions on Monte Tomba.

In the meantime the Italians had continued their struggle to keep the Austro-Hungarians from breaking into the plains from the north, with varying success. On December 18, 1917, they lost their positions on Monte Asolone, south of Col Caprille. Strong counterattacks during December 20 and 21, 1917, promptly regained them. On December 23, 1917, the Teutons made some gains near Monte Valbella, and on the following day they took the hills as well as Col de Rosso. On December 25, 1917, the Italians recaptured both, but eventually had to give them up again and permit the enemy to pass even slightly farther toward the south.

During the first two weeks of January, 1918, the Italians at all times held their lines in the Asiago sector. On January 14 and 15, 1918, they registered some gains in the region of Monte Asolone. On January 23, 1918, the Austro-Germans were forced to evacuate positions in the Monte Tomba region and to move back to Monte Spinoucia. During the last week of January, 1918, the Italians succeeded in pushing back the enemy at many points between the Piave and Asiago and thus establish beyond all doubt that, for the time being at least, the way into the Italian plains was closed to the invaders from the north.

Things had been going even better for the Italians on the lower Piave, between November 15, 1917, and January 31, 1918. Some isolated attempts of the Austro-Germans to gain the west bank, it is true, were successful. But at no time did these successes last. Almost as soon as a position had been taken by them, the Italians threw themselves against it and drove the invaders back to the east bank. From all sides thus Venice and the Italian plains were held safely against all Austro-German attacks at the end of January, 1918, and confidence regained by the Italians through their success in stopping the Teutonic onslaught promised that the future, too, would keep the balance of Italy free from the enemy, if not, indeed, he should be thrown back once more beyond his own frontier.

PART V—CAMPAIGNS IN PALESTINE, ARABIA, MESOPOTAMIA, AND AFRICA

CHAPTER XXIX

THE PALESTINE CAMPAIGN

IN midsummer, 1917, it will be remembered, a change had been made in the command of the British forces in Palestine, officially known as the Egyptian Expeditionary Force, and General Allenby was made commander in chief.

At that time the Turkish army in southern Palestine held a strong position extending from the sea at Gaza, roughly along the main Gaza-Beersheba road to Beersheba. Gaza had been made into a strong modern fortress, heavily intrenched and wired, offering every facility for protracted defense. The remainder of the enemy's line consisted of a series of strong localities, viz.: the Sihan group of works, the Atawinek group, the Baha group, the Abu Hareira-Arab el Teeaha trench system, and, finally, the works covering Beersheba. These groups of works were generally from 1,500 to 2,000 yards apart, except that the distance from the Hareira group to Beersheba was about four and one-half miles.

The enemy's force was on a wide front, the distance from Gaza to Beersheba being about thirty miles; but his lateral communications were good, and any threatened point of the line could be very quickly reenforced.

The British forces were extended on a front of twenty-two miles, from the sea, opposite Gaza, to Gamli.

Owing to lack of water the British were unable, without preparations which would require some considerable time, to approach within striking distance of the enemy, except in the small sector near the seacoast opposite Gaza.

According to official reports the British general had decided to strike the main blow against the left flank of the main Turkish position, Hareira and Sheria. The capture of Beersheba was a necessary preliminary to this operation, in order to secure the water supplies at that place and to give room for the deployment of the attacking force on the high ground to the north and northwest of Beersheba, from which direction the British intended to attack the Hareira-Sheria line.

The difficulties to be overcome in the operations against Beersheba and the Sheria-Hareira line were considerable, and careful preparations and training were necessary. The chief difficulties were those of water and transport, and arrangements had to be made to insure that the troops could be kept supplied with water while operating at considerable distances from their original water base for a period which might amount to a week or more; for, though it was known that an ample supply of water existed at Beersheba, it was uncertain how quickly it could be developed or to what extent the enemy would have damaged the wells before the British succeeded in occupying the town. Except at Beersheba, no large supply of water could be found till Sheria and Hareira had been captured.

The transport problem was no less difficult; there were no good roads south of the line Gaza-Beersheba, and no reliance could therefore be placed on the use of motor transport. Owing to the steep banks of many of the wadis which intersected the area of operations, the routes passable by wheeled transport were limited, and the going was heavy and difficult in many places. Practically the whole of the transport available in the British force, including 30,000 pack camels, had to be allotted to one portion of the eastern force to enable it to be kept supplied with food, water, and ammunition at a distance of fifteen to twenty miles in advance of the railhead. Arrangements were also made for the railhead to be pushed forward as rapidly as possible toward Karm, and for a line to be laid from Gamli toward Beersheba for the transport of ammunition.

A railway line was also laid from Deir el Belha to the Wadi Ghuzze, close behind the sector held by another portion of the eastern force.

Considerable strain was thrown on the military railway from Kantara to the front during the period of preparation. In addition to the normal requirements of the force, a number of siege and heavy batteries, besides other artillery and units, had to be moved to the front, and large depots of supplies, ammunition, and other stores accumulated at the various railheads.

During the period from July to October the Turkish force on the Palestine front had been increased. It was evident, from the arrival of these reenforcements and the construction of railway extensions from El Tine, on the Ramleh-Beersheba railway, to Deir Sincid and Belt Hanun, north of Gaza, and from Deir Sincid to Huj, and from reports of the transport of large supplies of ammunition and other stores to the Palestine front, that the Turks were determined to make every effort to maintain their position on the Gaza-Beersheba line.

The date of the attack on Beersheba, which was to commence the operations, was fixed as October 31, 1917.

On the morning of October 27, 1917, the Turks made a strong reconnoissance toward Karm from the direction of Kauwukah, two regiments of calvary and two or three thousand infantry, with guns, being employed. They attacked a line of British outposts near El Girheir, covering railway construction. One small post was rushed and cut up, but not before inflicting heavy loss on the enemy; another post, though surrounded, held out all day, and also caused the enemy heavy loss. British reenforcements succeeded in coming up in time, and on their advance the Turks withdrew.

The bombardment of the Gaza defenses commenced on October 27, 1917, and on October 30, 1917, warships of the Royal Navy, assisted by a French battleship, began cooperating in this bombardment.

On the evening of October 30, 1917, the portion of the British eastern force, which was to make the attack on Beersheba, was concentrated in positions of readiness for the night march to its position of deployment. The night march to the positions of deployment was successfully carried out, all units reaching their appointed positions up to time.

The plan was to attack the Turkish works between the Khalasa road and the Wadi Saba with two divisions, masking the works north of the Wadi Saba with the Imperial Camel Corps and some infantry, while a portion of the 53d (Welsh) Division farther north covered the left of the corps. The right of the attack was covered by a cavalry regiment. Farther east, mounted troops took up a line opposite the southern defenses of Beersheba.

As a preliminary to the main attack, in order to enable field guns to be brought within effective range for wire cutting, the enemy's advanced works at 1,070 were to be taken. This was successfully accomplished in the early morning of October 31, 1917, after a short preliminary bombardment. By about 1 p. m. the whole of the works between the Khalasa road and the Wadi Saba were in British hands.

Meanwhile the British mounted troops, after a night march, had arrived early in the morning of October 31, 1917, about Khasim Zanna, in the hills some five miles east of Beersheba. From the hills the advance into Beersheba from the east and northeast had to be be made over an open and almost flat plain, commanded by the rising ground north of the town and flanked by an underfeature in the Wadi Saba called Tel el Saba.

A British force was sent north to secure Bir es Sakaty, on the Hebron road, and protect the right flank; this force met with some opposition, and was engaged with hostile cavalry at Bir es Sakaty and to the north during the day. Tel el Saba was found strongly held by the enemy, and was not captured till late in the afternoon.

Meanwhile attempts to advance in small parties across the plain toward the town had made slow progress. In the evening, however, a mounted attack by Australian Light Horse, who rode straight at the town from the east, proved completely successful. They galloped over two deep trenches held by the enemy just outside the town, and entered the town at about 7 p. m,, October 31, 1917.

About 2,000 prisoners and 13 guns were taken, and some 500 Turkish corpses were buried on the battle field. This success laid open the left flank of the main Turkish position for a decisive blow.

After the complete success of the Beersheba operations, the attack on Gaza was ordered to take place on the morning of November 2, 1917.

The objectives of this attack were the works from Umbrella Hill (2,000 yards southwest of the town) to Sheikh Hasan, on the sea (about 2,500 yards northwest of the town). The front of the attack was about 6,000 yards, and Sheikh Hasan, the farthest objective, was over 3,000 yards from the British front line. The ground over which the attack took place consisted of sand dunes, rising in places up to 150 feet in height. This sand is very deep and heavy-going. The Turkish defenses consisted of several lines of strongly built trenches and redoubts.

Umbrella Hill was attacked and captured during the night of November 1, 1917.

The main attack was successful in reaching all objectives, except for a section of trench on the left and some of the final objectives in the center. Four hundred and fifty prisoners were taken and many Turks killed. The enemy also suffered heavily from the preliminary bombardment.

Meanwhile on the British right flank the water and transport difficulties were found to be greater than anticipated, and the preparations for the second phase of the attack were somewhat delayed in consequence.

However, in the early morning of November 1, 1917, the 53d Division, with the Imperial Camel Corps on its right, had moved out into the hills north of Beersheba, with the object of securing the flank of the attack on Sheria. Mounted troops were also sent north along the Hebron road to secure Dhaheriyeh.

The 53d Division took up a position from Towall Abu Jerwal (six miles north of Beersheba) to Muweileh (four miles northeast of Abu Irgeig). Irish troops occupied Abu Irgeig the same day.

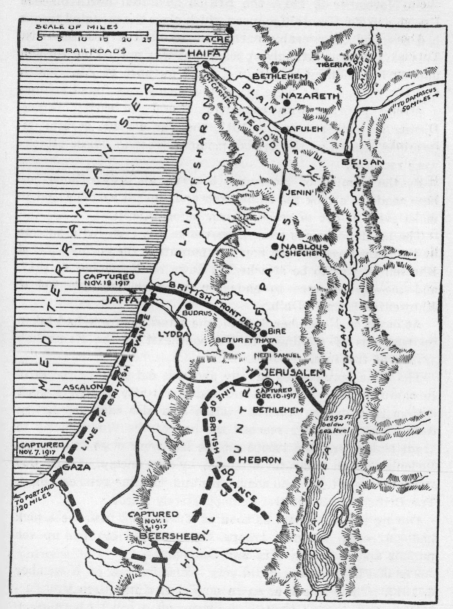

THE CAMPAIGN IN PALESTINE

On November 3, 1917, the British advanced north on Ain Kohleh and Tel Khuweilfeh, near which place the mounted troops had engaged considerable enemy forces on the previous day. This advance was strongly opposed, but was pushed on through difficult hill country to within a short distance of Ain Kohleh and Khuweilfeh. At these places the enemy was found holding a strong position with considerable and increasing forces. During November 4 and 5, 1917, the Turks made several determined attacks on the British mounted troops. These attacks were repulsed.

By the evening of November 5, 1917, all preparations had been made to attack the Kauwukah and Rushdi systems and to make every effort to reach Sheria before nightfall.

The mounted troops were prepared in the event of a success by the main force to push north in pursuit of the enemy. Tel el Khuweilfeh was to be attacked at dawn on November 6, 1917, and the troops were to endeavor to reach the line Tel el Khuweilfeh-Rijm el Dhib.

At dawn on November 6, 1917, the attacking force had taken up positions of readiness to the southeast of the Kauwukah system of trenches.

The attack progressed rapidly and was completely successful in capturing all its objectives, and the whole of the Rushdi system in addition. Sheria Station was also captured before dark. The Yeomanry reached the line of the Wadi Sheria to Wadi Union; and the troops on the left were close to Hareira Redoubt, which was still occupied by the enemy. Some 600 prisoners were taken and some guns and machine guns captured. The British casualties were comparatively slight.

During the afternoon, as soon as it was seen that the attack had succeeded, mounted troops were ordered to take up the pursuit and to occupy Huj and Jemmamah.

The 53d Division again did very severe fighting on November 6, 1917. Their attack at dawn on Tel el Khuweilfeh was successful, and, though they were driven off a hill by a counterattack, they retook it and captured another hill, which much improved their position.

The bombardment of Gaza had meanwhile continued, and another attack was ordered to take place on the night of November 6-7, 1917.

The objectives were, on the right, Outpost Hill and Middlesex Hill, and on the left the line Bellah Trench-Turtle Hill.

During November 6, 1917, a certain amount of movement on the roads north of Gaza had been observed by British airmen and fired on by British heavy artillery.

The attack on Outpost Hill and Middlesex Hill met with little opposition, and as soon, after they had been taken, as patrols could be pushed forward, the enemy was found to be gone. Other British troops on the left also found at dawn that the enemy had retired during the night, and early in the morning the main British force occupied the northern and eastern defenses of Gaza. Turkish rear guards were still occupying Beit Hanun and the Atawineh and Tank systems, from whence Turkish artillery continued to fire on Gaza and Ali Muntar till dusk.

As soon as it was seen that the Turks had evacuated Gaza a part of the British force pushed along the coast to the mouth of the Wadi Hesi, so as to turn the Wadi Hesi line and prevent the enemy making any stand there. British cavalry had already pushed on round the north of Gaza, and became engaged with an enemy rear guard at Beit Hanun, which maintained its position till nightfall. The force advancing along the coast reached the Wadi Hesi by evening, and succeeded in establishing itself on the north bank in the face of considerable opposition, a Turkish rear guard making several determined counterattacks.

On the extreme right the situation remained practically unchanged during November 7, 1917; the Turks made no further attempt to counterattack, but maintained their positions.

In the center the Hareira Tepe Redoubt was captured at dawn. The London troops, after a severe engagement at Tel el Sheria, which they captured by a bayonet charge at 4 a. m. on November 7, 1917, subsequently repulsing several counterattacks, pushed forward their line about a mile to the north of

Tel el Sheria; the mounted troops on the right moved toward Jemmamah and Huj, but met with considerable opposition from hostile rear guards.

During November 8, 1917, the advance was continued. The Turkish rear guards fought stubbornly and offered considerable opposition. Near Huj a British charge captured twelve guns, and broke the resistance of a hostile rear guard. It soon became obvious that the Turks were retiring in considerable disorganization.

By November 9, 1917, operations had reached the stage of a direct pursuit by as many troops as could be supplied.

On the evening of November 9, 1917, there were indications that the Turks were organizing a counterattack toward Arak el Menshiye by all available units of the force which had retired toward Hebron, with the object of taking pressure off the main force, which was retiring along the coastal plain.

The British, however, decided to press the pursuit and to reach the Junction Station as early as possible, thus cutting off the Jerusalem Army, while the Imperial Camel Corps was ordered to move to the neighborhood of Tel el Nejile, where it would be on the flank of any counterstroke from the hills.

Operations on November 10 and 11, 1917, showed a stiffening of the enemy's resistance on the general line of the Wadi Sukereir, with center about El Kustineh; the Hebron group, after an ineffective demonstration in the direction of Arak el Menshiye on the 10th, retired northeast and prolonged the enemy's line toward Beit Jibrin. Royal Flying Corps reports indicated the total Turkish forces on this line at about 15,000.

British progress on November 10 and 11, 1917, was slow; the troops suffered considerably from thirst, as a hot, exhausting wind blew during these two days.

November 12, 1917, was spent in preparations for the attack on the enemy's position covering Junction Station. British forces were now operating at a distance of some thirty-five miles in advance of their railhead, and the bringing up and distribution of supplies and ammunition formed a difficult

On December 9, 1917, a White Flag party came out of Jerusalem to meet the nearest British outposts and surrender the city. The Mayor of Jerusalem is the man with the walking cane and cigarette

problem. The routes north of Wadi Hesi were found to be hard and good going, though there were some difficult Wadi crossings, but the main road through Gaza and as far as Beit Hanun was sandy and difficult.

CHAPTER XXX

THE FALL OF JERUSALEM

ON the morning of November 13, 1917, the Turks had strung out their forces, amounting probably to more than 20,000 rifles, on a front of twenty miles, from El Kubeibeh on the north to about Beit Jibrin to the south. The right half of their line ran roughly parallel to and only about five miles in front of the Ramleh-Junction Station railway, their main line of supply from the north, and their right flank was already almost turned.

The advance guard of the 52d Division had forced its way almost to Burkah on November 11, 1917, on which day also some mounted troops pushed across the Nahr Sukereir at Jisr Esdud, where they held a bridgehead. During November 12, 1917, other British forces pushed north up the left bank of the Nahr Sukereir, and eventually seized Tel-el-Murreh on the right bank near the mouth.

The Australian mounted troops, extended over a wide front, secured the British flank and pressed forward on November 12, 1917, toward Balin, Berkusie, and Tel-es-Safi. Their advance troops were counterattacked and driven back a short distance, but the Turks made no effort to press farther forward. The British then decided to attack on November 13, 1917.

The country over which the attack took place is open and rolling, dotted with small villages surrounded by mud walls with plantations of trees outside the walls. The most prominent feature is the line of heights on which are the villages of Katrah and El Mughar, standing out above the low flat ground which separates them from the rising ground to the west, on

War St. 7—O

which stands the village of Beshit, about 2,000 yards distant. This Katrah-El Mughar line forms a very strong position, and it was here that the Turks made their most determined resistance against the turning movement directed against their right flank. The 52d Division, assisted by a charge of mounted troops, who galloped across the plain under heavy fire and turned the Turkish position from the north, captured the position. Some 1,100 prisoners, three guns, and many machine guns were taken here. After this the Turkish resistance weakened, and by the evening the Turks were retiring east and north.

The British infantry, who were sent forward about dusk to occupy Junction Station, met with some resistance and halted, for the night, not much more than a mile west of the station. Early next morning (November 14, 1917) they occupied the station.

The Turkish army had now been broken into two separate parts, which retired north and east respectively.

In fifteen days the British force had advanced sixty miles on its right and about forty on its left. It had driven a Turkish army of nine infantry divisions and one cavalry division out of a position in which it had been intrenched for six months, and had pursued it, giving battle whenever it attempted to stand, and inflicting on it losses amounting probably to nearly two-thirds of its original effectives. Over 9,000 prisoners, about eighty guns, more than 100 machine guns, and very large quantities of ammunition and other stores had been captured.

After the capture of Junction Station on the morning of November 14, 1917, the British secured a position covering the station, while the mounted troops reached Kezaze that same evening.

The mounted troops pressed on toward Ramleh and Ludd, On the right Naaneh was attacked and captured in the morning, while on the left the New Zealand Mounted Rifles had an engagement at Ayun Kara (six miles south of Jaffa). Here the Turks made a determined counterattack and got to within fifteen yards of the British line. A bayonet attack drove them back with heavy loss.

Flanking the advance along the railway to Ramleh and covering the main road from Ramleh to Jerusalem, a ridge stands up prominently out of the low foothills surrounding it. This is the site of the ancient Gezer, near which the village of Abu Shusheh now stands. A Turkish rear guard had established itself on this feature. It was captured on the morning of November 15, 1917, by mounted troops, who galloped up the ridge from the south. A gun and 360 prisoners were taken in this affair.

By the evening of November 15, 1917, the mounted troops had occupied Ramleh and Ludd, and had pushed patrols to within a short distance of Jaffa. At Ludd 300 prisoners were taken, and five destroyed aeroplanes and a quantity of abandoned war material were found at Ramleh and Ludd.

Jaffa was occupied without opposition on the evening of November 16, 1917.

The following situation had now developed: The Turkish army, cut in two by the capture of Junction Station, had retired partly east into the mountains toward Jerusalem and partly north along the plain. The nearest line on which these two portions could reunite was the line Tul Keram-Nablus. Reports indicated that it was the probable intention of the Turks to evacuate Jerusalem and withdraw to reorganize on this line.

The British mounted troops had been marching and fighting continuously since October 31, 1917, and had advanced a distance of seventy-five miles, measured in a straight line from Asluj to Jaffa. Other troops, after heavy fighting at Gaza, had advanced in nine days a distance of about forty miles, with two severe engagements and continual advance-guard fighting. The 52d Division had covered sixty-nine miles in this period.

The railway was being pushed forward as rapidly as possible, and every opportunity was taken of landing stores at points along the coast. The landing of stores was dependent on a continuance of favorable weather, and might at any moment be stopped for several days together.

A pause was therefore necessary to await the progress of railway construction, but before the British position in the plain could be considered secure it was essential to obtain a hold of the one good road which traverses the Judean range from north to south, from Nablus to Jerusalem.

The west side of the Judean range consists of a series of spurs running east and west, and separated from one another by narrow valleys. These spurs are steep, bare, and stony for the most part, and in places precipitous. Between the foot of the spur of the main range and the costal plain is the low range known as the Shephelah.

On the line intended for the British advance only one good road, the main Jaffa-Jerusalem road, traversed the hills from east to west. For nearly four miles, between Bab el Wad (two- and one-half miles east of Latron) and Saris, this road passes through a narrow defile, and it had been damaged by the Turks in several places. The other roads were mere tracks on the side of the hill or up the stony beds of wadis, and were impracticable for wheeled transport without improvement. Throughout these hills the water supply was scanty without development.

On November 17, 1917, the Yeomanry had commenced to move from Ramleh through the hills direct on Bireh by Annabeh, Berfilya, and Beit ur el Tahta (Lower Beth Horon). By the evening of November 18, 1917, one portion of the Yeomanry had reached the last-named place, while another portion had occupied Shilta. The route had been found impossible for wheels beyond Annabeh.

On November 19, 1917, the British infantry commenced its advance. One portion was to advance up the main road as far as Kuryet el Enab, with its right flank protected by Australian mounted troops. From that place, in order to avoid any fighting in the close vicinity of the Holy City, it was to strike north toward Bireh by a track leading through Biddu. The remainder of the infantry was to advance through Berfilya to Beir Likia and Beit Dukka, and thence support the movement of the other portion.

After capturing Latron and Amnas on the morning of November 19, 1917, the remainder of the day was spent in clearing the defile up to Saris, which was defended by hostile rear guards.

On November 20, 1917, Kuryet el Enab was captured with the bayonet in the face of organized opposition, while Beit Dukka was also captured. On the same day the Yeomanry got to within four miles of the Nablus-Jerusalem road, but were stopped by strong opposition about Beitunia.

On November 21, 1917, a body of infantry moved northeast by a track from Kuryet el Enab through Biddu and Kulundia toward Birch. The track was found impassable for wheels, and was under hostile shell fire. Progress was slow, but by evening the ridge on which stands Neby Samwil was secured. A further body of troops was left at Kuryet el Enab to cover the flank and demonstrate along the main Jerusalem road. It drove hostile parties from Kustul two and one-half miles east of Kuryet el Enab, and secured this ridge.

By the afternoon of November 21, 1917, advanced parties of Yeomanry were within two miles of the road and an attack was being delivered on Beitunia by other mounted troops.

The positions reached on the evening of November 21, 1917, practically marked the limit of progress in this first attempt to gain the Nablus-Jerusalem road. The Yeomanry were heavily counterattacked and fell back, after bitter fighting, on Beit ur el Foka (Upper Beth Horon). During the following day the Turks made two counterattacks on the Neby Samwil ridge, which were repulsed. Determined attacks were made on November 23 and 24, 1917, on the strong positions to the west of the road held by the Turks, who had brought up reenforcements and numerous machine guns, and could support their infantry by artillery fire from guns placed in positions along the main road. British artillery, from lack of roads, could not be brought up to give adequate support to their infantry. Both attacks failed, and it was evident that a period of preparation and organization would be necessary before an attack could be delivered in sufficient strength to drive the Turk from his positions west of the road.

By December 4, 1917, all preparations had been completed and the British held a line from Kustul by the Neby Samwil ridge, Beit Izza, and Beit Dukka, to Beit ur el Tahta.

During this period of preparation attacks by the Turks along the whole line led to severe local fighting. On November 25, 1917, British advanced posts north of the river Auja were driven back across the river. From November 27 to 28, 1917, the Turks delivered a series of attacks directed especially against the high ground position in the hills from Beit ur el Foka to El Burj, and the Neby Samwil ridge. An attack on the night of November 29, 1917, succeeded in penetrating the British outpost line northeast of Jaffa, but next morning the whole Turkish detachment, numbering 150, was surrounded and captured by Australian Light Horse. On November 30, 1917, a similar fate befell a battalion which attacked near El Burj; a counterattack by Australian Light Horse took 200 prisoners and practically destroyed the attacking battalion. There was particularly heavy fighting between El Burj and Beit ur el Folka, but the British troops successfully resisted all attacks and inflicted severe losses on the enemy. At Beit ur el Foka one company took 300 prisoners. All efforts by the Turks to drive the British off the Neby Samwil ridge were completely repulsed. These attacks cost the Turks very dearly. The British took 750 prisoners between November 27 and 30, 1917, and the Turkish losses in killed and wounded were undoubtedly heavy.

Favored by a continuance of fine weather, preparations for a fresh advance against the Turkish positions west and south of Jerusalem proceeded rapidly. Existing roads and tracks were improved and new ones constructed to enable heavy and field artillery to be placed in position and ammunition and supplies brought up. The water supply was also developed.

The date for the attack was fixed as December 8, 1917. Welsh troops, with a cavalry regiment attached, had advanced from their positions north of Beersheba up the Hebron-Jerusalem road on December 4, 1917. No opposition was met, and by the evening of December 6, 1917, the head of this column was ten miles north of Hebron.

On December 7, 1917, the weather broke, and for three days rain was almost continuous. The hills were covered with mist at frequent intervals, rendering observation from the air and visual signaling impossible. A more serious effect of the rain was to jeopardize the supply arrangements by rendering the roads almost impassable.

In spite of these difficulties, the British troops moved into positions by night, and, assaulting at dawn on December 8, 1917, soon carried their first objectives. They then pressed steadily forward. The mere physical difficulty of climbing the steep and rocky hillsides and crossing the deep valleys would have sufficed to render progress slow, and the opposition encountered was considerable. Artillery support was soon difficult, owing to the length of the advance and the difficulty of moving guns forward. But by about noon some British troops had already advanced over two miles, and were swinging northeast to gain the Nablus-Jerusalem road, while others had captured the Beit Iksa spur, and were preparing for a further advance.

As the British right column had been delayed and was still some distance south of Jerusalem, it was necessary for the advanced British forces to throw back their right and form a defensive flank facing east toward Jerusalem, from the western outskirts of which considerable rifle and artillery fire was being experienced. This delayed the advance, and early in the afternoon it was decided to consolidate the line gained and resume the advance next day, when the right column would be in a position to exert its pressure. By nightfall the British line ran from Neby Samwil to the east of Beit Iksa, through Lifta to a point about one and one-half miles west of Jerusalem, whence it was thrown back facing east. All the Turkish prepared defenses west and northwest of Jerusalem had been captured, and the British troops were within a short distance of the Nablus-Jerusalem road.

During the day about 300 prisoners were taken and many Turks killed. British casualties were light.

Next morning the advance was resumed. The Turks had withdrawn during the night, and the British forces driving back rear guards, occupied a line across the Nablus-Jerusalem road four miles north of Jerusalem, while other troops occupied a position east of Jerusalem across the Jericho road. These operations isolated Jerusalem, and at about noon the enemy sent out a parlementaire and surrendered the city.

At noon on December 11, 1917, General Allenby made his official entry into Jerusalem.

In the operations from October 31 to December 9, 1917, over 12,000 prisoners were taken. The captures of material included about 100 guns of various calibers, many machine guns, more than 20,000,000 rounds of rifle ammunition, and 250,000 rounds of gun ammunition. More than twenty aeroplanes were destroyed by British airmen or burned by the Turks to avoid capture.

This ended four centuries of Turkish rule over the Holy City of Jews and Christians. General Allenby, after his entry, issued the following noteworthy proclamation:

"To the inhabitants of Jerusalem the Blessed and the people dwelling in the vicinity. The defeat inflicted upon the Turks by the troops under my command has resulted in the occupation of your city by my forces. I therefore here and now proclaim it to be under martial law, under which form of administration it will remain so long as military considerations make it necessary. However, lest any of you should be alarmed by reason of your experience at the hands of the enemy who has retired, I hereby inform you that it is my desire that every person should pursue his lawful business without fear of interruption.

"Furthermore, since your city is regarded with affection by the adherents of three of the great religions of mankind, and its soil has been consecrated by the prayers and pilgrimages of multitudes of devout people of these three religions for many centuries, therefore do I make known to you that every sacred building, monument, holy spot, shrine, traditional site, endowment, pious bequest, or customary place of prayer, of whatsoever form of the three religions, will be maintained and protected according to the existing customs and beliefs of those to whose faiths they are sacred."

An eyewitness of the memorable event, the special correspondent of the London "Times" with the British forces describes it in part as follows:

"It was a picturesque throng. From the outskirts of Jerusalem the Jaffa road was crowded with people who flocked westward to greet the conquering general. Somber-clad youths of all nationalities, including Armenians and Greeks, stood side by side with Moslems dressed in the brighter raiment of the East. The predominence of the tarboosh in the streets added to the brightness of the scene. Many of the Moslems joined aloud in the expression of welcome, and their faces lighted up with pleasure at the general's approach.

"Flat-topped roofs and balconies held many, crying out a genuine welcome; but it was in the streets, where the cosmopolitan crowd assembled, that one looked for and obtained the real feeling of all the peoples. What astonished me were the cries of 'Bravo' and 'Hurrah' uttered by men who could have hardly spoken the words before. . . .

"General Allenby entered the city on foot. Outside of Jaffa gate he was received by the military governor and a guard of honor formed by men who have done their full share in the campaign. On the right of the gate were men from English, Scottish, Irish, and Welsh counties. Opposite them were fifty men afoot, representing the Australian and New Zealand horsemen who have been engaged in the Empire's work in the Sinai Desert and Palestine almost since the war broke out. Inside the walls were twenty French and twenty Italian troops from the detachments sent by their countries to take part in the Palestine operations.

"General Allenby entered by the ancient gate which is known to the Arabs as 'The Friend.' Inside the walls was a crowd more densely packed in the narrow streets than was the crowd outside.

"The commander in chief, preceded by his aids-de-camp, had on his right the commander of the French detachment, and on his left the commander of the Italian detachment. The Italian, French, and American military attachés followed, together with a few members of the General Staff. The guards of honor marched in the rear. The procession turned to the right into Mount Zion and halted at Al Kala (the Citadel).

"On the steps, at the base of the Tower of David, which was standing when Christ was in Jerusalem, the Proclamation of Military Law was read, in the presence of the commander in chief and of many notables of the city.

"Re-forming, the procession moved up Zion street to the barrack square, where General Allenby received the notables and the heads of the religious communities. The mayor and the mufti—the latter also a member of the Husseiny family—were presented, likewise the sheiks in charge of the mosques of Omar and Aksa, and Moslems belonging to the Khaldieh and Alamieeh families, which trace their descents through many centuries. The patriarchs of the Latin, Greek, Orthodox, and Armenian Churches, and the Coptic bishop, had been directed by the Turks to leave Jerusalem, but their representatives were introduced to General Allenby, as were also the heads of the Jewish committees, the Syrian Church, the Greek Catholic Church, the Abyssinian bishop, and a representative of the Anglican Church. The last presentation was that of the Spanish consul, who is in charge of the interests of almost all the countries at war, and is a busy man."

CHAPTER XXXI

PALESTINE—ARABIA—MESOPOTAMIA

ALTHOUGH the British had accomplished their main objective in Palestine with the capture of Jerusalem, they did not rest on their laurels. Within a few days after their occupation of the Holy City, by December 12, 1917, they had advanced their lines to the north and some detachments of Indian troops had carried positions as far north as the mouth of the Midieh

During the night of December 20-21, 1917, British troops crossing the Nahr-el-Auja on rafts and light bridges, seize

Khurbet Hadrah, Sheikh Muannis, Tel-er-Rekkeit, and later El Makhras.

These localities are near the mouth of the river, and include commanding ground two miles to the north of it. Three hundred and five prisoners, of whom eleven were officers, and ten machine guns were captured.

Other forces captured Ras-ez-Zamby, two miles northeast of Bethany, which itself is two miles east of Jerusalem, taking thirty prisoners and two machine guns and beating off three Turkish counterattacks.

By this time the booty captured by the British since the beginning of the operations had been counted and had been found to total ninety-nine guns and howitzers with carriages, about 400 limbers, wagons and other vehicles; 110 machine guns, more than 7,000 rifles, 18,500,000 rounds of small-arm ammunition, and over 58,000 rounds of gun and howitzer ammunition, besides various other stores.

On December 22, 1917, troops on the extreme left of the British forces, with naval cooperation, continued their advance north of the Nahr-el-Auja, reaching the line Sheik-el-Ballutah-El Jelil, some four miles north of the river. Pushing eastward south of the river Fejja and Mulebbis, center of a Jewish colony, were occupied. This was followed by the capture of Rantieh on the Turkish railway to the north, and Kh.-el-Beida, and Kh.-el-Bireh, four miles southeast of Rantieh.

The Turks, with German assistance, on December 27, 1917, made a determined attempt to retake Jerusalem. Repeated attacks were pressed with vigor and continued from two a. m. on the 27th for twenty-six hours. General Allenby at once launched a counterattack against the west flank of the Turkish attack.

On the 27th this attack progressed two and one-half miles over very difficult country. Seeing that the Turkish attack was spent, on December 28, 1917, the British made a general advance. British troops on the Nablus road advancing north and the troops on their left advancing east drove the Turks back before them. By the morning of December 29, 1917,

General Allenby had secured the line Burkah, Ras-et-Tahunieh, Ram Allah, El Tireh, Wadi-el-Kelh.

On December 30, 1917, British troops occupied Beitin, or Bethel, two miles northeast of Bireh, El Balua, one mile north of Bireh, on the Nablus road, and Kh.-el-Burj, about one mile west of El Balua, Janiah and Ras Kerker, six and seven miles respectively northwest of Bireh.

In the coastal sector of the line a patrol reached Kuleh, twelve miles east of Jaffa, and there found a Turkish gun ammunition depot, which it destroyed. Kuleh is two miles east of Rantieh, on the Damascus Railway, which had recently been occupied by the British.

The Turks suffered heavily in killed and wounded, the killed alone being estimated at about 1,000. About 600 prisoners were taken and twenty machine guns.

The British line was now, at its nearest point, twelve miles north of Jerusalem. The right wing reached some four miles east of the Sheehem road; the center extended across that road north of Beeroth, Bireh, and along the Ram Allah Ridge and the Wadi-el-Kalb, which lies north of and parallel to the Jerusalem-Beth Horon-Joppa road. On the coast the left wing of the British was north of the Auja, in the plain of Sharon.

In describing the Turco-German attempt to regain Jerusalem the special correspondent of the London "Times" attached to the British forces in Palestine said in part:

"The first objective was Tell-el-Ful, a high conical-shaped hill just east of the Sheehem road dominating our lines east and west for a considerable distance. During daylight on Boxing Day the Turks made no movement, but just before midnight our post north of El Ful was driven in. At twenty minutes past one a. m. the first attack on El Ful was made, and at the same time an advance began against Beit Hannina, about a mile west of the road. This line was defended by London Territorials, who added to their grand record by meeting attack after attack with magnificent steadiness, standing like rocks against most furious onslaughts, and never once yielding an inch of ground. Two companies defending Hanbna were attacked

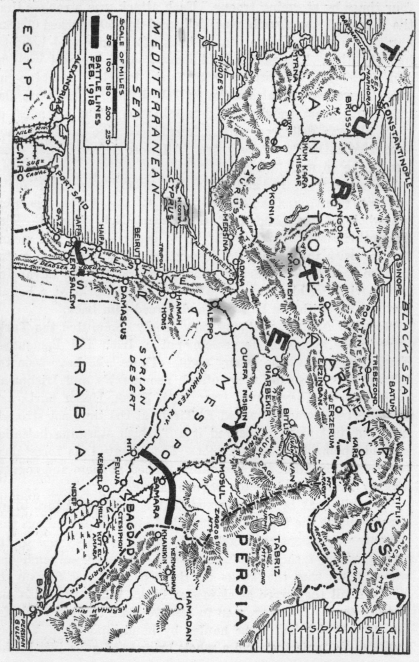

THE BRITISH ADVANCE IN MESOPOTAMIA AND PALESTINE

four times by storming troops. Each attack was stronger than the last, and the fourth was delivered by 500 picked Turks, but all the attacks were beaten back after prolonged hand-to-hand fighting. The enemy dead showed many bayonet wounds, and the hillside was strewn with Turks killed by machine-gun fire. There were eight attacks on Tell-el-Ful. These were also made with great weight and determination. The strongest of them all was delivered with a reenforced line at dawn, and supported by heavy artillery fire. All were defeated with great loss to the enemy.

"Between 7 a. m. and noon the enemy organized for a last big effort, and about half-past 12 the Turks assaulted the whole of the Londoners' line except Nebi Samwil. This final attack was pressed right up to our positions, the enemy fighting with the bravery of desperation. He proved no match for the London Territorials, who, after raking the advancing waves with machine guns, cleared his breastworks at a bound, met the foe with the bayonet, and forced him back.

"General Allenby, realizing how deeply committed the Turks were to the attack on Jerusalem, put in Irish and dismounted Yeomanry against the enemy right. Those who have seen the terrain marvel at the dismounted Yeomanry's and Irishmen's achievement. They moved from Beth Horon Upper northeastward. The Yeomen attacked El Tireh, at the time not strongly held, but just as they secured it a Turkish storming battalion was advancing to the same spot. The enemy, thus forestalled, counterattacked, but the Yeomanry rushed at them and counted seventy Turks killed by the bayonet alone.

"The hill near by was so steep that it took two hours to get supplies up to the top. Another hillside was so precipitous that the only way troops could get up the terraced slopes was by the men standing on each other's shoulders. So nearly perpendicular was the hill that the Turks on the top could not fire on the climbers till they were at close quarters. While the Irish and Yeomen were advancing, men in reserve were making roads for the guns, which had to be hauled by hand, and when Yeomen captured Beitunia they had a whole brigade of guns just behind their front line, though it was sometimes necessary for a whole company of infantry to haul one gun, which at moments was dangling in the air.

"Welsh and Home Counties troops also took part in beating off the attack on Jerusalem. They had taken Zanby and White Hill, north of the Jericho road, and held White Hill against three counterattacks. On the 27th the Turks attacked all day, and White Hill became no-man's-land, but Zanby was held. Fighting was at bombing distance. At dusk the enemy tried to take White Hill, but the Welshmen charged with the bayonet and killed over a hundred Turks. Farther south a post at the village of Obeid was attacked by 700 of the enemy, who surrounded it and fired 400 shells into the monastery, but the Middlesex men, who were the garrison of the post, held out, their casualties being trifling."

Immediately following the defeat which the British inflicted on the Turks, the former succeeded in advancing their lines north of Jerusalem still another mile.

During January, 1918, there was little activity on the Palestine front. In the last week of the month there was, however, considerable aerial activity. On January 22, 1918, the Turkish camps and depots on the railway west of Sebustieh, Samaria, were raided.

On January 24, 1918, two Turkish aeroplanes were wrecked in aerial combats.

On January 25, 1918, British bombing squadrons surprised a body of some 2,000 Turkish troops in close formation near Hawara, on the Jerusalem-Nablus road four and one-half miles south of Nablus. Half a ton of bombs were dropped on the column before it could disperse. At the same time a camp of mounted troops was bombed and the animals were stampeded.

Twelve Turkish aeroplanes were destroyed during the month of January, 1918.

During the night of January 30, 1918, the British line was again advanced slightly in the vicinity of Arnutieh, a ruined site, on the Sheehem road, twelve miles north of Jerusalem.

On the morning of January 31, 1918, a British reconnoiter-ing detachment penetrated the village of Mukhmas, eight miles north-northeast of Jerusalem, repulsed Turkish counterattacks, and withdrew during the following night, having accomplished its object. During the night of February 2, 1918, Turkish patrols were active between Arnutieh and Sheikh Abdulla, one mile east of Arnutieh. Attempts to penetrate the British lines at these points, however, were repulsed.

In the meantime the Arab revolt in the Hedjaz, that part of Arabia adjoining the Red Sea, was spreading. It will be re-called that it had been announced in July, 1917, that the Turks had been defeated at Maan and that the Arabs had occupied the enemy positions between Maan and Akaba, the latter place being at the head of the Red Sea gulf of the same name, and just east of the Egyptian frontier. The town of Maan, which is on the Hedjaz Railway, is about 120 miles southeast of Gaza.

Late in August, 1917, it became known that forces operating under the orders of the King of the Hedjaz, the Grand Sherif of Mecca, had carried out a series of extensive operations against Turkish detachments and posts in Arabia. According to the information available, the Arab forces had been working on a carefully thought out plan, resulting in the destruction of part of the railway line north of Medina, which is 230 miles north of Mecca, and in the capture of isolated Turkish posts.

In the Maan district alone, over 700 Turks were killed in action and a similar number taken prisoner, in addition to four guns.

The Arab movement, originating with the Sherif of Mecca, apparently was gaining the support of almost all the Arab tribes in the Hedjaz, and was spreading eastward.

During September, 1917, no news came from the Hedjaz. Early in October, 1917, it was reported that Arab forces had successfully raided the railway communications north of Medina on the Hedjaz Railway.

Not until late in December, 1917, did it become known that the Arabs had been quite active during the latter part of Novem-ber, 1917, though definite news was lacking concerning their activities during October, 1917, and the early part of November, 1917.

Between November 8 and November 12, 1917, a section of Arabs attacked the railway from Deraa to Amman, that part of the Hedjaz line running parallel to the Jordan. Two locomotives, a number of coaches and trucks, and a bridge were destroyed, and traffic was interrupted for six days.

On November 11, 1917, a train in which Djemal Pasha was traveling to Jerusalem was blown up with a mine and destroyed. Djemal escaped, but his aid-de-camp and the staff officers accompanying him were killed. The Turkish casualties amounted to 120, while the Arabs lost seven killed and four wounded.

On November 22, 1917, a Turkish lancer patrol from Maan attacked some Arab tents in the neighborhood of Batra, fifteen miles southwest of Maan, but were driven off with losses. Arab forces later took the posts of Fuweila and Basta, southwest and west of Maan respectively. These points had been fortified by the Turks in August last in the hope of confining the Arabs in the Akaba area.

A few days later it was announced that an Arab force under Sherif Feisal, son of the King of Hedjaz, had destroyed a troop train south of Tebuk, on the Hedjaz Railway, some 350 miles north of Medina.

The whole of the Turkish detachment in the train were killed or captured, amongst the former being Suleiman Pasha Rifada, paramount chief of the Billi tribe. Three hundred rifles were captured as well as a large quantity of ammunition, also £24,000 Turkish in gold.

On January 11, 1918, it was announced that the Arab forces in Hedjaz had made a successful raid on the railway some twenty miles south of Maan, and that still farther to the south the entire Turkish garrison of an important post on the railway had fallen into the hands of the Arabs.

A few days later the Arabs occupied the Turkish post of Tafile, forty-five miles north-northeast of Maan and eighteen miles southeast of the Dead Sea, capturing the entire garrison. On January 26, 1918, a body of Turkish troops moving on Tafile from El Kerak, twenty miles northeast of the southern end oɪ the Dead Sea, was routed on the Seil-el-Hesa, eleven miles north of Tafile, by the Arabs, and driven back in disorder with the loss of many prisoners, a mountain gun, and seven machine guns.

On the same day another Turkish force advancing westward from Maan was repulsed by Arab troops near Ain Uheid, seven miles west of Maan.

Still farther south, in the Aden sector of Arabia, little of importance transpired between August, 1917, and February, 1918, though the British troops near Aden continued to be in constant contact with the Turks, engaging in numerous outpost and patrol skirmishes.

On November 22, 1917, an action was fought on a larger scale than usual, in which British troops attacked and captured the Turkish post at Jabir, fifteen miles north of Aden, and its neighboring pickets. Losses were inflicted on the Turks and their defenses were destroyed.

On January 5, 1918, a strong reconnoissance was made toward Hatum and Jabir, the defenses of the former being destroyed by British troops. Aeroplanes cooperated with the British artillery, who inflicted considerable damage on the Turkish infantry.

In Mesopotamia there had been very little activity since the fall of Bagdad on March 11, 1917. Soon after that event a British column had been sent westward to Feluja on the Euphrates, a town almost on a line with Bagdad, but about thirty-five miles farther west. The Turks had offered no resistance and the town had been occupied by the British. The Turkish forces in the meantime had been withdrawn to Ramadie, about twenty-five miles northwest from Feluja and also on the Euphrates. In July 1917, a British column had successfully pushed forward about twelve miles in the direction of Ramadie, but after inflicting considerable losses on the Turks had to stop farther advance on account of the extreme heat.

Early in October, 1917, came the news that Ramadie had fallen on September 29, 1917. During the night of September 27, 1917, the British had moved in two columns from an advanced camp on the Euphrates, west of Feluja, one column on the right, the other on the left, and at dawn they attacked Mushaid Ridge, a low line of dunes running north and south from the Euphrates to Habbanie Canal.

At dawn they bombarded the main crest of the ridge, but the Turks had evacuated it, and they replied with a counterbombardment a few minutes afterward, expecting apparently that the British would follow up the barrage with an assault. The British, however, as soon as it became clear that the Turks were evacuating Mushaid Ridge, changed their line of attack. The right column was withdrawn and, swinging round west behind the left column, became the left wing of the force.

As soon as the infantry had carried Mushaid Ridge British cavalry made a wide sweeping movement across the desert round the right flank of the Turks. They left the battle area at 8 a. m. and by 4 p. m. they were established astride the Aleppo road on a regular line of hills running at right angles with the river five miles west of Ramadie.

By this move the Turks were cornered. The net which the British had flung round them was complete. They had no bridge behind them and were cut off from all hope of reenforcement or supplies. Their only chance was to drive in determined counterattacks, and to break through before the British drew the ring in closer and drove them out from their trenches with their artillery.

Meanwhile the British infantry were closing in. At 1 o'clock, after bombardment, one column attacked Ramadie Ridge, on the right, while the other was working round to Azizie Ridge, on the left. The capture and holding of Ramadie Ridge by British and Indian infantry was a difficult achievement. This low pebbly rise is perfectly smooth, a long and gentle gradient barely seventeen feet above the plain level. It offered no cover of any kind, and the British infantry became visible to the Turks a full 200 yards before they reached the top of the rise. As soon as they came into view the Turks opened concentrated rifle and machine-gun fire on the British front and right flank, while their guns opened intense enfilade fire from the batteries on the left. The British and Indian soldiers hung on to their positions and at night dug themselves in. Their action so occupied the Turks that the left column was able to work round and seize the Azizie Ridge before dusk with very little opposition.

At night British cavalry, who occupied strong points on a front of three miles along the ridge, prepared for a desperate struggle. The expected attack began the battle after 3 o'clock, when the Turks tried to break through between the cavalry and the river. The action continued for two hours till dawn, when it degenerated into casual sniping. The nearest Turkish dead were found within fifty yards of the cavalry trenches.

In the meantime the infantry soon after daybreak had taken up the attack again and in face of well-directed fire and against repeated counterattacks, had carried the last outlying defenses of the Turks on the British left, until 8 o'clock, September 29, 1917, they had seized and were holding the bridgehead of the Azizie Canal. After this new repulse an intense bombardment was opened on the Turkish trenches. The British line of cavalry, far away west, soon saw the dark masses of the enemy approaching and apparently prepared for bloody battle. They watched this advance, as they thought, for over an hour, but there came a moment when, to their astonishment, they saw the Turks turn and walk in mass formation toward the British. The Turkish guns were silent and white flags went up all along the line.

It was a general surrender. Ahmed Bey, the Turkish commander, who had been on the Euphrates all through the campaign from the battle of Shaiba, March, 1915, came out and surrendered with his whole force.

The British captured 3,455 prisoners, thirteen guns, ten machine guns, 1,061 rifles, a quantity of ammunition, some railway material, two steam launches and a large quantity of miscellaneous engineering material, equipment, and military stores. When the British entered Ramadie they found that such Turkish forces as had not surrendered had hurriedly fled.

To the north and east of Bagdad the British forces, too, succeeded in advancing in the direction of the Persian border. In this undertaking they had for some time the cooperation of Russian troops still fighting in this region.

On August 19, 1917, British columns attacked the Turks near Shahroban on the left bank of the Dialah, about fifty miles northeast from Bagdad. The Turks made little resistance and retreated hastily to the Hamrin Hills, and British troops remained in possession of Shahroban.

In an action fought on October 20, 1917, the British occupied Deli Abbas, about ten miles northwest from Shahroban, and established themselves on the Jebel Hamrin range on the left bank of the river Dialah. The Turks retreated across the Dialah River in the vicinity of Kizil Robat, burning the bridge behind them, and continued to hold a position in the hills on the right bank of that river, north of Deli Abbas, which is on the Bagdad-Kifri road.

This position was attacked on the morning of December 3, 1917, by converging columns, one of which successfully bridged the Dialah near Kizil Robat, sixty miles northeast of Bagdad, on the road to Khanikin.

The Turks attempted to delay the British advance by flooding the area between the Nahrin and Dialah Rivers close to their junction, six miles east of Deli Abbas, but by the morning of December 4, 1917, British troops had driven back the Turks and were in possession of the Sakaltutan Pass, eleven miles north of Deli Abbas, and between the Dialah and the Nahrin, a northern tributary of the Dialah, flowing through the Jebel Hamrin, and crossed on the main road between Deli Abbas and Kifri at an elevation of 600 feet above sea level. Through the Sakaltutan Pass the road from Deli Abbas leads to the north to Kifri and Mosul.

A force of Russians, under the command of Colonel Bicharakoff, operated on the British right flank and rendered valuable assistance.

Immediately after the capture of the pass, the Turks were pursued as far as the village of Kara Tepe, thirteen miles north of the pass and about twenty-five miles north of Deli Abbas, through which the Turks were driven on December 5, 1917, after a sharp engagement. The pursuit was carried out over difficult country containing bogs and intersected by numerous watercourses.

On the morning of December 7, 1917, British aeroplanes bombed Tuz Kurmatli, on the Mosul road, thirty-five miles north of Kara Tepe, with good results. It was reported that the Turks set fire to the Kifri coal mines on December 5, 1917, and the British observed that fires were burning there on the following day.

No further news came from the Mesopotamian theater of war during the balance of December, 1917, or during January and February, 1918.

On December 1, 1917, it was officially announced by the British authorities, that reconnoissances had definitely established the fact that German East Africa had been completely cleared of all German troops and that the German commander, General von Lettow-Vorbeck, with the force under his command, estimated at 2,000 rifles, had crossed the Rovuma River into Portuguese East Africa.

During December, 1917, after driving the Germans across the border into Portuguese territory, the British forces were busy in preparing for the new task of hunting out General Lettow-Vorbeck in Portuguese East Africa. British patrols by December 25, 1917, were forty miles south of the Rovuma River, which marks the frontier.

Von Lettow's force had been broken up into small foraging parties; and it was expected that they would be rounded up before the big rains set in.

However, during the last few days of December, 1917, the German forces in Mozambique, consisting of 2,000 men with two fieldpieces and ten machine guns, attacked the Portuguese positions on Mt. M'Kula, occupied by Captain Curado, with 250 men and five machine guns, and after three days' fighting succeeded in carrying the positions by assault.

This did not change the fact that the last vestige of the German Colonial Empire had fallen into the hands of the Allies.

PART VI—THE BALKANS

CHAPTER XXXII

THE BALKANS: GREECE AND MACEDONIA

ON the Macedonian front the military situation has had all the appearance of a deadlock, not only since last summer, but for the past year. On November 24, 1917, the Austrians were reported to be making a general offensive attack on the Italian lines in southern Albania, between the Voyusa and Osum Rivers, which was followed by a strong Italian counterattack, but neither side was able to announce any gains of territory or any notable capture of prisoners or material. Again, barely two weeks later, on December 5, 1917, violent fighting was said to have begun for several miles along the front near the Struma, with the net result that "several Bulgarian patrols were captured." Compared to what we have come to regard as fighting in this war, therefore, these few sporadic efforts in Macedonia and Albania have been very little more than outpost affairs, mere raids.

On November 15, 1917, there was published in London a report on the military activities of the British by General G. F. Milne, commanding the British forces covering the past year, which seems in part to have a significant bearing on a later event.

In the latter part of February, 1917, a year ago, General Milne was instructed by General Sarrail to prepare for a forward push against the Bulgarians in the first week of April. A corps was, accordingly, sent forward shortly afterward to take a position on the high ridge between Lake Doiran and the River

Vardar. By April 8, 1917, General Milne was ready, whereupon General Sarrail found it necessary to postpone action until the 24th. On that day the British were sent forward and succeeded in occupying the front-line trenches of the enemy almost along the entire front of the attack. The British were now in a commanding position, of which great advantage could have been taken, but at this juncture General Milne was instructed to retire, "on account of the unhealthful conditions of the terrain."

General Milne was next informed that the advance would begin over again on May 8, 1917. So another assault on the enemy lines was begun between Lake Doiran and the "Petite Couronne" Hill. In spite of the powerful opposition of the Bulgarians some progress was made, and twelve days later the new advance line was consolidated. A farther advance was in progress, with every prospect of success, when on May 24, 1917, General Milne received instructions from Sarrail to cease all offensive operations.

By itself this report might at least indicate unpleasant relations between the British and the French commanders, but further significance is added by the announcement made December 19, 1917, that General Sarrail had been recalled from his supreme command on the Macedonian front, to be succeeded by General Guillemet.

A serious charge, it will be remembered, had been made against Sarrail in France before his appointment to Saloniki, in July, 1915. This charge had been made by General Dubail and had been indorsed by General Joffre and Millerand, then Minister of War in the French Cabinet. It had to do with certain maneuvers against the German Crown Prince, directed by Sarrail under the command of Dubail. Subsequently these charges were dropped, and until his sudden appointment to the Saloniki command Sarrail dropped from view.

The specific reason for Sarrail's removal has not been officially stated, but there are rumors throwing doubt on his loyalty and suggesting his connection with the Caillaux scandal, which would imply that Sarrail had deliberately made no efforts to proceed seriously against the Bulgarians and the Austrians, even that he had secretly connived in the destruction of the Rumanians when he should have created a diversion by a general attack in Macedonia.

The double part played by Constantine, King of Greece, in the dealings with the Entente Powers, had always been a matter of grave suspicion, in spite of his repeated denials and protestations of friendship, published through his frequent newspaper interviews. Even after his removal from the throne by the Allies there still remained a doubt in the minds of many people that he had been justly treated. But then his duplicity has been conclusively proved beyond all question.

Early in November, 1917, there were discovered in Athens the records of a number of telegrams which had been exchanged between Constantine and Queen Sophia on the one hand and her brother, the kaiser, on the other. These telegrams were in a cipher code unknown to the Greek foreign office. The key was discovered later and the contents of the telegrams revealed clearly, exposing a series of plots which had been initiated by the Greek sovereigns against their supposed friends, the Allies.

Those sent early in 1916, by both the king and the queen, urgently requested the kaiser to institute an energetic military movement in the Balkans toward Greece, that Greece might be relieved from the presence of the Allied troops in the neighborhood. Then came the affair in which the Greek military authorities surrendered Fort Rupel to the Bulgarians, showing conclusively that the king had connived in the surrender.

At the time of the crisis, in the first days of December, 1916, when the Greek army attacked Entente representatives in Athens and caused an ultimatum to be delivered against the Greek Government, Queen Sophia, in a long telegram to her brother, described the "splendid victory" which the Greeks had achieved over "four great powers." In this telegram she demanded a strong German and Austrian offensive with the object of relieving Greece. In reply the kaiser urged Constantine to declare war against Sarrail's forces and begin active military operations against them. In reply the queen explained the impossibility of doing this on account of the lack of equipment and ammunition and again urged a German relief expedition. To this the German Emperor answered that this was impossible, but urged that Constantine take measures to organize guerrilla bands in the neighborhood of Lake Ochrida, to cooperate with the Austrian forces. This suggestion was complied with, no less a person than the Master of the King's Horse being intrusted with the supervision of this task. The following telegram, sent on January 10, 1917, is a notable example of this correspondence in general:

"For the Kaiser from Queen Sophia (through the Greek Minister in Berlin):

"I thank you for your telegram, but we are without sufficient food for the duration of such an undertaking, and the shortage of ammunition and many other things compel us unfortunately to abstain from such offensive action. You can realize my position. How I suffer. Thank you warmly for your welcome words. *May the infamous swine receive the punishment they deserve.* I .embrace you heartily. Your exiled and unhappy sister, who hopes for better times. (*Signed*) SOPHIA."

Another telegram from Sophia, sent on this same day, stated to the kaiser "I am grateful and happy for having at any rate spoken to Von Falkenhausen at Larissa on the telephone, as well as having received direct news of you. I was afaid the ultimatum would have to be accepted. We were obliged to accept it, although we desired to enter the war on the side of Germany on account of the political advantages, in order to rid ourselves of our bitter enemies, and to respond to the sympathy already shown by the Greek people to the cause of Germany, but we lack food and ammunition for such a campaign. . . . Finally, the immediate menace to the capital and to our only means of communication by the British forces reported to be at Malta for the expedition against Greece obliged us to our great regret to abandon this project. . . ."

On January 6, 1917, King Constantine sent a telegram to Von Hindenburg, in which the following passages occur:

"The present situation must be seriously considered, as it is probable that a declaration of war might come before mobilization could be effected. Probably the Entente desire to involve Greece in immediate war so as to destroy her before the German occupation could begin. Already Greece is faced with a fresh Entente note demanding her complete disarmament. The transport of the whole of the artillery and war material to the Peloponnesus is being maintained by the pressure of the blockade. The Government and the people are resisting with constancy, enduring all sorts of privations, but the situation is growing worse from day to day. It is urgent that we should be informed if a German attack on the Macedonian front is contemplated, and when it is likely to begin."

That these intrigues were not confined to Constantine and Sophia alone is obvious, from the following telegram, sent by Theotokis, the Greek Minister in Berlin, on December 10, 1916:

"Let Von Falkenhausen await at Berlin the decision which will be taken at Athens. In case it is neutrality he will proceed to Podgradetz; in case of rupture with the Entente he will go by aeroplane to Larissa. In any case, it is of the greatest importance to develop as quickly as possible the question of Caravitis's bands and matters relative thereto. Pray inform me with all speed what assistance in the way of munitions, money, and provisions you would want. The object of Caravitis should be to cut the railroad from Monastir to Saloniki, and harass Sarrail's rear. One should not lose sight of the fact that even this unofficial action by the bands will powerfully help Greece when the time for negotiations comes to put forward large territorial claims which, naturally, can be larger in case action is taken than in case of mere neutrality. Falkenhausen is awaiting instructions, upon which he will act immediately."

On December 2, 1916, Sophia telegraphed to General von Falkenhausen:

"Owing to the continuance of the blockade there is only bread left for a few days longer, and other foodstuffs are also growing scarcer. The idea of war against the Entente is now out of the question. Negotiations are now proceeding on the note. I consider the game lost. If the attack is not made immediately, it will be too late."

CHAPTER XXXIII

RUMANIA

FOR six months the Rumanian troops engaged in no important military operations. They held their lines against the Austrian forces, and these latter, apparently, made no strong efforts to advance. Indeed, the entire collapse of the military power of Russia made it practically certain that the Rumanians could not continue the war effectively. When the Bolsheviki came into power, their course toward Rumania was openly hostile, so that the Rumanians were compelled to guard themselves against their one-time allies as well as against the enemy.

Finally Rumania joined in the armistice initiated by the Petrograd Bolsheviki. There seemed to be no question of the desire of the Rumanians to remain loyal to their western allies; but the Balkan country was now surrounded by enemies, and there was apparently little hope that she could maintain her warfare against the Central Powers. Reports from Austrian sources stated that negotiations for a separate peace between Austria and Rumania were going on at Fokshani. Peace with Germany, Turkey, and Bulgaria would naturally follow to save the country from utter destruction.

On January 20, 1917, a Berlin dispatch announced that the Rumanian Premier, Bratiano, had resigned, and was to be succeeded by General Averescu, former Minister of War and commander in chief of the Rumanian forces which had operated in Dobrudja. This report has not since been verified.

That Bulgaria is not completely under German control and is a member of the Quadruple Alliance on terms peculiarly her own has been manifested in more than one way during recent months. As previously stated, in earlier editions of this work, there is a very strong popular opinion in Bulgaria against the alliance with Germany which at times has seemed on the point of manifesting itself in a material way. Occasionally rumors have come through of wholesale military executions, following attempts at mutiny on the part of the troops. Thus Bulgaria's position as an uncertain quantity in the Teutonic alliance is not due to any disloyalty on the part of the king, Ferdinand, but to the disposition of the people, who are interested only in a Macedonia free from Serbia or Greece, and not in the German plans for empire. Though successfully suppressed so far, these subterranean movements do limit the policy of the Bulgarian ruling clique, however loyal to German rule it may be in itself.

During the past November there were frequent rumors of proposal from Bulgaria to the Entente for separate peace, but nothing definite was known at the time. That definite negotiations were at least begun only became known in December, 1917, when the Petrograd Bolsheviki began the publication of secret treaties and correspondence found in the Government archives on their stepping into power. Among these many revelations appeared a telegram from the Russian embassy in Berne, Switzerland, which described a meeting in the embassy office in the latter part of September, 1917, between a Bulgarian representative, said to be the exarch of the Bulgarian church, and a British representative, whose name was not given. The latter asked for a statement of the Bulgarian terms.

The Bulgarian demanded, in return for severing the alliance with Germany and Austria, that Bulgaria be granted all of Dobrudja, an expanded Bulgaria down to the old Media-Rodosto line, with a western frontier along the Morava River, in Serbia, from the junction of that river with the Danube, down through Nish, Pristina, and Uskub; and Macedonia, including Monastir and Saloniki.

This demand the British representative refused to consider, but made the tentative counterproposal of an independent Macedonia, with Saloniki as the capital.

That Bulgaria should have refused this offer is only another illustration of the duplicity of Ferdinand and his governing clique. His one hold on the Bulgarian people has been his pretended espousal of the cause of the Macedonian Bulgars. For long years past the Macedonians strove for an independent Macedonia, but this was made impossible by the policies of the great powers interested. They were, however, on the verge of achieving this ideal after the First Balkan War, when the interference of Austria in Albania caused Serbia and Greece to demand a revision of the treaty which had provided for Macedonian freedom. Against this demand the Macedonians protested, and their leaders were largely instrumental in precipitating the Second Balkan War. The result was their defeat and the Treaty of Bucharest, which forced the Macedonian patriots under the wing of the Bulgarian Government, the only refuge left them.

That Bulgaria should now have refused terms including an independent Macedonia was, indeed, a matter to be kept secret. Ferdinand, naturally, desires Macedonia as an extension of his own territory, although the Macedonians are very little in sympathy with his Greater Bulgaria imperialism and would only accept it as an alternative between freedom on the one hand and subjection to Greece and Serbia on the other.

On October 12, 1917, Emperor William of Germany, accompanied by Prince August Wilhelm and Foreign Secretary Dr. von Kühlmann, paid an official visit to Ferdinand in Sofia. The streets and houses were profusely decorated and much festivity prevailed.

PART VII—NAVAL AND AIR WARFARE

CHAPTER XXXIV

ON THE SEA

AS in the past, naval warfare during the six months' period, August, 1917, to February, 1918, consisted primarily of attacks by German submarines on units of the allied merchant marine. There was again a wide discrepancy between the figures published by the allied and German governments. An example of this are the respective totals of monthly tonnage losses for the year 1917.

	German Claim	Allied Claim
January	439,500	. . . . .
February	781,000	812,000
March	885,000	600,000
April	1,091,000	788,000
May	869,000	549,000
June	1,016,000	758,000
July	811,000	463,000
August	808,000	591,000
September	673,000	455,000
October	674,000	470,000
November	607,000	435,000
December	816,000	514,000
	9,470,500	6,435,000

Continuous detailed figures of losses are available only regarding the British and American merchant marines. Between

August, 1917, and February, 1918, the British weekly losses
were as follows:

Week ending	1,600 tons and over	Under 1,600 tons	Fishing vessels
August 5	21	2	0
August 12	14	2	3
August 19	15	3	2
August 26	18	5	0
September 2	20	3	0
September 9	12	6	4
September 16	8	20	1
September 23	13	2	2
September 30	11	2	0
October 7	14	2	3
October 14	12	6	1
October 21	17	8	0
October 28	14	4	0
November 4	8	4	0
November 11	1	5	1
November 18	10	7	0
November 25	14	7	0
December 1	16	1	4
December 8	14	7	0
December 15	14	3	1
December 22	11	1	1
December 29	18	3	0
January 6	18	3	4
January 13	6	2	2
January 20	6	2	0
January 27	9	6	1
	334	116	30

On August 14, 1917, it was also officially stated in the House
of Commons that since the beginning of the war and up to June
30, 1917, a total of 9,748 lives were lost on British merchantman
as the result of U-boat attacks, mine and other explosions. Of

these 3,828 were passengers of all nationalties and 5,920 officers and seamen.

During the same period the following twenty-six American vessels were sunk by submarines:

			Gross tons	Lives lost
August	6.	Campana	3,695	4
August	7.	Christine	964	0
August	23.	Carl F. Cressy.......	898	0
August	29.	Laura C. Anderson...	960	0
September	8.	William H. Clifford...	1,593	0
September	12.	Wilmore	5,398	0
September	15.	Platuria	3,445	10
September	16.	Ann J. Trainer......	426	0
September	23.	Henry Lippitt........	895	0
September	25.	Paulina.............	1,337	0
October	3.	Annie F. Conlon......	591	0
October	11.	Lewis Luckenbach....	3,905	10
October	16.	Jennie E. Richter....	647	0
October	16.	St. Helens...........	1,497	24
October	17.	Antilles	6,878	64
October	25.	Fannie Prescott.......	404	0
October	27.	D. N. Luckenbach....	2,933	5
November	2.	Rochester	2,551	7
November	7.	Villemer	....	2
November	9.	Rizal	2,744	3
November	16.	Margeret L. Roberts..	535	0
November	21.	Schuylkill	2,720	0
November	25.	Actaeon	4,999	37
December	10.	Owasco	4,630	2
December	20.	Suruga	4,374	1
January	6.	Harry Luckenbach....	2,798	8

This meant a loss of about 61,000 tons and of 177 lives.

Unrestricted submarine warfare was initiated by the Germans, it will be remembered, on February 1, 1917. During the first twelve months of it, February, 1917, to February, 1918, a total of sixty-nine American ships, representing about 170,000

War St. 7—Q

tons, were sunk by submarines, mines, and raiders. Over 300 lives were lost with these boats.

Figures in regard to the French and Italian losses are incomplete. From available sources, however, it appears that during the six months' period, August, 1917, to February, 1918, the French merchant marine lost by U-boat attacks seventy-three steamers of over 1,600 tons, fifty-two steamers of under 1,600 tons and thirty fishing boats. In the same period U-boats sank sixty-one Italian steamers and forty-six Italian sailing vessels.

Regarding neutral losses figures are even less definite. Only Norway, which again is by far the heaviest loser amongst neutral nations, has published official statements covering her losses. For six months, July to December, 1917, her losses were 127 boats of 216,000 tons. For the entire year 1917, they amounted to 434 boats of 686,800 tons and involved the death of 401 sailors, while 258 more were missing or unaccounted for.

Holland, amongst other losses, reported the sinking by a mine off the Dutch coast on August 3, 1917, of the steamer *Moordam* of 12,531 tons. Mines in one case, and an explosion in the other, were responsible for the sinking of two British steamers: *City of Athens*, of Cape Town, of 5,600 tons, on August 10, 1917, with the loss of nineteen lives, of which five were Americans; and *Port Kembla*, of 4,700 tons, on September 18, 1917, off Cape Farewell.

Regarding the German losses in U-boats, practically no definite information is available. Only occasionally has any news managed to get by the censors of the Allies, and the Germans, of course, are entirely silent on the subject. On November 24, 1917, one U-boat was sunk by the United States destroyers, *Fanning* and *Nicholson*, while on patrol service in European waters. Her crew were captured with the exception of a few members who were drowned. Two other U-boats were reported to have been sunk during December in the Ionian Sea by a French destroyer. This, of course, does not represent the total losses inflicted by the Allies on the German U-boat forces.

Indeed, it has been stated officially that the average loss amounts to thirty-eight U-boats per month.

Naval engagements between units of the various belligerents were comparatively few and unimportant. As a result the losses incurred by the different navies, at least as far as they became known, were likewise comparatively slight.

During August, 1917, British monitors cooperated with the Italian navy in bombarding successfully Austrian positions in the Gulf of Trieste. On August 16, 1917, there was also a slight engagement between British and German destroyers in the North Sea without result.

On September 1, 1917, British destroyers destroyed four German armed mine-sweeping vessels off the coast of Jutland. Three days later, September 4, 1917, a German submarine bombarded Scarborough, killing three persons, wounding five, and doing some material damage.

During the successful German attack against Riga in the early part of September, 1917, German submarines appeared in the Gulf of Riga and bombarded the city.

In October it also became known that the German raider *Seeadler* had run ashore on Lord Howe Island (Society Islands) in the Pacific Ocean, leaving forty-seven prisoners on the island in a state of destitution. The crew of the raider afterward seized a motor sloop and a French schooner on which they carried out some further raids. It was later reported that the motor boat had been captured by an unarmed merchantman in one of the outlying islands of the Fiji group.

The armored British cruiser *Drake* was torpedoed on the morning of October 2, 1917, off the north coast of Ireland. Though she was able to make harbor, she sank later in shallow water. One officer and eighteen men were killed by the explosion of the torpedo. The *Drake* was a ship of 14,100 tons with a speed of 24.11 knots and had been launched in 1902. She was a sister ship of the *Good Hope* sunk off Coronel in November, 1914, during the battle with the German Pacific fleet.

Strong German naval forces participated in the fighting in the Gulf of Riga which took place in the middle of October,

1917. They were prominent in enabling German troops to land on Oesel and Dagö Islands and later on Moon Island. It was reported that during an engagement between German and Russian naval forces the Germans lost two destroyers, not, however, before they had sunk a Russian destroyer. A few days later the Russian battleship *Slava* was also reported as having been sunk, while the balance of the Russian Baltic fleet was trapped in the Gulf of Riga.

Amongst the French losses during September, 1917, was the steamer *Media* of 4,770 tons, which was torpedoed late that month in the western Mediterranean in spite of the fact that she was being convoyed while in use as a transport. Of her crew of sixty-seven and of 559 soldiers on board 250 were reported missing.

Two fast German cruisers on October 17, 1917, attacked a convoy of merchantmen, escorted by two British destroyers, at a point about midway between the Shetland Islands and Norway. The two destroyers as well as nine of the merchantmen were sunk with a total loss of about 250 lives.

On November 1, 1917, a German warship was reported to have been sunk by a mine off the coast of Sweden. British naval forces, operating in the Cattegat, on November 3, 1917, sank a German auxiliary cruiser and ten German patrol vessels. On November 17, 1917, during an engagement off Helgoland one German light cruiser was sunk and another damaged.

A German submarine, during November, 1917, attacked British naval forces, cooperating with the British expeditionary force in Palestine and sank one destroyer and one monitor.

On November 22, 1917, it was announced that the German Government had included in its "barred zone" waters around the Azores and the channel hitherto left open in the Mediterranean to reach Greece, and had extended the limits of the zone around England.

On November 29, 1917, a German torpedo boat struck a mine off the coast of Belgium and sank, all of her crew with the exception of two being lost.

During the night of December 9-10, 1917, Italian naval forces entered the harbor of Trieste and successfully torpedoed the Austrian battleship *Wien,* which sank almost immediately.

A German submarine bombarded on December 12, 1917, for about twenty minutes Funchal on the island of Madeira, destroying many houses and killing and wounding many people.

On the same day German destroyers attacked a convoy of merchantmen in the North Sea and sank six of them as well as a British destroyer and four armed trawlers.

Two days later, December 14, 1917, the French cruiser *Château Renault* was sunk in the Mediterranean by a submarine which itself was destroyed later on.

During the night of December 22-23, 1917, three British destroyers were lost off the Dutch coast with a total loss of lives of 193 officers and men. On December 30, 1917, the British transport *Aragon* and a British destroyer, coming to her assistance, were torpedoed and sunk. The following day, December 31, 1917, the auxiliary *Osmanieh* struck a mine and sank. The total loss involved in these three sinkings was 809 lives, of which forty-three were members of the crew and officers, and 766 military officers and soldiers.

During the night of January 12, 1918, two British destroyers ran ashore off the coast of Scotland. All hands were lost. Yarmouth was bombarded on January 14, 1918, for five minutes by German naval forces and four persons were killed and eight injured.

British naval forces fought an action at the entrance to the Dardanelles on January 20, 1918. As a result the Turkish cruiser *Midullu,* formerly the German cruiser *Breslau,* was sunk and the battle cruiser *Sultan Selim,* formerly the *Goeben,* damaged and beached. The British lost two monitors and, a week later, a submarine which attempted to enter the Dardanelles in order to complete the destruction of the *Goeben.*

On January 28, 1918, the British torpedo gunboat *Hazard* was lost as the result of a collision. The day before the big Cunard liner *Andania* of 13,405 tons was attacked off the Ulster coast. Her passengers and crew were saved, the boat, however, sank a few days later. Another severe loss was the sinking of the British armed boarding steamer *Louvain* in the Mediterranean with a loss of 224 lives on January 21, 1918.

Two German destroyers sank off the coast of Jutland during the same week.

The United States Navy, during the six months' period covered in this chapter, fared comparatively well, in spite of the fact that large forces were engaged in patrol duty in European waters and many transports crossed from the States to Europe and vice versa. Of the latter only one was lost. On October 17, 1917, the *Antilles* while returning to the United States was torpedoed and sunk. Of those on board sixty-seven were drowned, including sixteen soldiers.

The United States destroyer *Cassin* had an encounter with a German submarine on October 16, 1917. Though struck by a torpedo, she was not seriously damaged and made port safely, after having first attempted, until night broke, to discover her attacker, without succeeding, however.

The patrol boat *Alcedo*, formerly a steam yacht, belonging to G. W. C. Drexel of Philadelphia, was torpedoed and sunk on November 5, 1917. She was the first fighting unit of the United States Navy to be lost since the war begun. Two weeks later, on November 19, 1917, the United States destroyer *Chancey* was sunk as a result of a collision, twenty-one lives being lost.

On December 6, 1917, the United States destroyer *Jacob Jones* was sunk by a U-boat and 60 lives were lost.

CHAPTER XXXV

THE WAR IN THE AIR

AEROPLANES, dirigible and other balloons are no longer considered freaks and curiosities, as they were at the beginning of the war. Their use has become an integral part of all military and most naval operations. On all fronts they are employed regularly and extensively, just as any other branch of the military and naval services. In considering, therefore, aerial operations at the various fronts during the six months' period—August 1, 1917, to February 1, 1918—in this chapter we shall treat only of such undertakings in the air which were carried out independent of the general military operations. Those events in the air which formed part of offensive or defensive actions have been mentioned in their proper place as part of the general narrative. In this direction it must suffice to state here that all forms of aerial activities were continuously carried on by all belligerents at all fronts to even a greater extent than before. Statistics as to losses of aeroplanes and of members of the various flying services are very incomplete and more or less unreliable, primarily because each side has been trying to keep the other in the dark as to actual increases or decreases in the effectives of their air service. Such figures as are available, however, will be given a little farther on. They must not be taken as final, even though it has been attempted to compile them with the utmost care.

As in the past, air warfare, independent of military operations, consisted, of course, of German and Austrian attacks on French, English, and Italian territory behind the actual front, and of similar operations on the part of the French, English, Italian, and American air services against German and Austrian territory.

As compared with previous performances, the Zeppelin attacks against English and French territory decreased considerably in number, though apparently not in effectiveness, except that the losses suffered by the attackers were much heavier as a result of improved conditions in aerial defense. There were only two raids over England and none over France. The first Zeppelin raid over England occurred on August 21, 1917. It was directed against the Yorkshire coast, caused little damage and killed one man. On the same day British aeroplanes brought down one of the monster airships off the Danish coast.

During the night of October 19-20, 1917, thirteen Zeppelins raided the eastern and northeastern counties of England.

Thirty-four persons were killed and fifty-six injured. On their return journey they were attacked by French airmen and it was announced later that four were destroyed and three captured. Amongst the latter, one, the L-49, was brought down intact, the first one to be captured in this manner since the war had begun.

Figures regarding Germany's Zeppelin strength and losses are, of course, hard to obtain. From German sources there are none. But at the end of 1917, French and English authorities semiofficially published the following data:

Destroyed before the war......................	2
Destroyed in Germany........................	5
Destroyed in neutral countries.................	5
Destroyed in England or on the way home.......	15
Destroyed at sea.............................	2
Out of use..................................	5
In use at training schools.....................	4
In use in the North Sea......................	9

Though Zeppelins apparently had practically reached the end of their usefulness, a considerable increase took place in the number and extent of aeroplane raids, especially over England.

A number of watering places on the southeast coast of England were raided on August 12, 1917. Twenty-five persons were killed, fifty-two injured, and two German machines were brought down. Dover, Margate, and Ramsgate were visited on August 22, 1917, killing eleven persons and injuring thirteen. Eight of the attacking machines failed to return home.

The east coast was again raided on September 2, 1917. The following day, September 3, 1917, an English naval station at Chatham, near London, was bombed. One hundred and eight persons were killed and ninety-two wounded, most of them members of the English naval service. The first moonlight raid of London was carried out during the night of September 4-5, 1917. It resulted in the death of eleven persons and in the wounding of sixty-two.

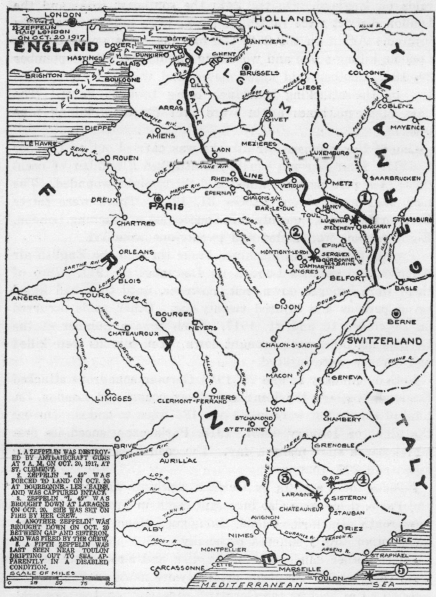

FIVE ZEPPELINS DESTROYED AFTER THE AIR RAID ON LONDON,
OCTOBER 19-20, 1917

The end of September, 1917, brought a large number of raids on England. On the 24th the southeast coast and the London district were raided. Fifteen were killed and seventy injured. Again on the 25th German machines appeared over London, killing seven and wounding twenty-six. On September 29, 1917, another raid killed eleven and wounded eighty-two; two of the attacking machines being brought down. The next night machines again were over England, killing nine persons.

One of the strongest air attacks was carried out on October 1, 1917. Four German squadrons attacked a number of coast towns, ten persons were killed and thirty-eight wounded. The next raid occurred on October 31, 1917. There were thirty German machines, but only three succeeded in reaching London. Eight persons were killed and twenty-one wounded.

Twenty-five German machines broke through the English air defenses and reached London on December 6, 1917. Two of them were brought down, not, however, until they had killed seven persons and injured twenty-one. Other raids occurred on December 18 and 21, 1917. Each time a number of the German machines were brought down. Ten persons were killed and seventy were injured.

Both on January 28 and 29, 1918, German squadrons attacked England, bombing the Kent and Essex coasts and London. A total of sixty-eight were killed and 183 were wounded. During the night of January 30-31, 1918, Paris experienced its first aerial attack since many a day. The casualties were forty-five killed and 207 wounded.

Besides these attacks by German machines against England and Paris, there were also incessant raids on French cities near the front. Dunkirk, Calais, Boulogue, Nancy, Belfort, and many other towns suffered especially.

On the other hand both the English and French air service were very active. Frequent attacks were made on French and Belgian cities held by the Germans, especially on Lille, Bruges, Ostende, and Zeebrugge. Some of the near-by German cities, such as Metz, too, were frequently attacked. German airdromes also were subjected to continuous attacks, hampering German operations to a considerable extent.

In retaliation for the German attacks on English cities, both French and British air squadrons made many successful raids on German inland cities. Few details are available regarding these raids, however, the German Government having adopted a policy of more or less silence concerning the results achieved. Amongst the German cities attacked were especially: Colmar, Frankfort-on-Main, Freiburg, Stuttgart, Tübingen, Saarbrücken, Lahr, Mannheim, Rastatt, Ludwigshafen, Thionville, Treves, Pirmasens, Kaiserslautern, Karlsruhe.

On the Italian front, too, there was greater aerial activity than ever. Pola, the Austrian naval base in the Adriatic, south of Trieste, was the chief aim of the Italian attacks, in which British airmen, having come to the support of the Italians, frequently participated. It was visited many times and much damage was done, both to ships and naval establishments. Trieste, too, was bombarded a number of times with good results.

The Austro-German air services made a number of attacks against Italian cities back of the front. Venice was one of the chief sufferers. The first attack occurred on August 14, 1917. Unfortunately many of these raids on Italian cities resulted in serious damages to churches, palaces, and other monuments of historic fame and value. Another attack against Venice was made on September 7, 1917. Again on November 25, 1917, Austrian or German airplanes bombed the ancient city of the Doges.

In December, 1917, Padua, not very far from the New Austro-Italian front, was the principal recipient of Austrian attentions. It was bombed on December 28, 30, and 31, 1917. About twenty persons were killed and some seventy wounded. Considerable damage was done to the cathedral, many other churches and numerous houses.

During the first few days of January, 1918, Vicenza, Bassano, Treviso, and Padua were bombed, almost continuously. About fifteen persons were killed, and fifty wounded and great damage was done to some of the wonderful old churches and palaces in these towns. During the night of January 26, 1918, Treviso and Mestre were bombed. In the latter city two Americans, William Platt and R. C. Fairfield, attached to the American Red Cross, were killed.

Figures regarding losses of the various air services were growing continuously more scarce and unreliable, a considerable amount of secrecy being imposed on all sides for military reasons.

In August the Germans claimed that during July, 1917, they had brought down 213 Allied aeroplanes and twenty-four balloons, but had lost only sixty machines themselves. From this source it was claimed that during August, 1917, the Germans lost sixty-four against 295 Allied machines, and that during December, 1917, the corresponding figures were eighty-two and 119.

The only official announcement regarding losses suffered by the German air services was made by the French authorities, who claimed that French airmen had accomplished the following results against the Germans:

1917	Brought down in French lines	Brought down in German lines	Seriously damaged
August	3	53	59
September	7	60	80
October	15	27	61
November	2	15	17
December (1-15)	16	21	28
	43	176	245

For the period January to December 15, 1917, French airmen claimed the following figures, brought down in German and French lines: 586 machines; seriously damaged, 583. In practically the same period in 1916 (January–December 31) the corresponding figures had been only 417 and 185.

Some interesting figures also were published from combined English and French calculations regarding the strength of the

German air service at the end of 1917. It was claimed that it consisted of more than 200 squadrons with a total of about 2,500 machines, divided as follows:

Bombing squadrons		23
Chaser "		40
Protecting "		30
Patrol "		80
Artillery "		100

There were also said to be numerous separate squadrons of aeroplanes and hydroplanes belonging to the German Navy, and about twelve squadrons each for garrison and training purposes.

Amongst other events in the various aerial services a number deserve especial mention. On September 7, 1917, German machines bombed a number of Allied hospitals on the French coast. As a result four Americans, belonging to a Harvard unit, were killed and ten wounded, and another American, a member of a St. Louis, Mo., unit, was killed.

On September 11, 1917, the famous French "ace," Captain Georges Guynemer, was killed in an air battle, after having brought down shortly before his 53d enemy plane.

On November 22, 1917, the British Admiralty announced that a successful air attack in the vicinity of Constantinople had been carried out by a large British bombing airplane, which flew from England to a British base in the Mediterranean in a series of eight flights. The stopping places included Lyons and Rome, and the total distance covered was nearly 2,000 miles. The machine was actually in the air thirty-one hours. This is believed to be a world's record for a cross-country journey and for the weight carried. During some parts of the flight strong winds and heavy rainstorms were experienced, and there was one stretch of 200 miles over a mountainous country where it would be impossible for any machine to land.

Another record long-distance flight was that made by Captain Laureati of the Italian air service in a S. T. A. machine with a 200 H. P. Fiat engine, from Turin to London, a distance of 650 miles. The distance was covered in seven hours, twenty-two minutes, and thirty seconds. No stops were made and one passenger, a mechanician, was carried.

In the latter part of January, 1918, the former German cruiser *Goeben*, then the Turkish *Sultan Selim*, having been beached after a fight with British naval forces at the entrance to the Dardanelles was bombed repeatedly by British naval aviators who also bombed Constantinople with success.

As a result of a raid, carried out during the latter part of August, 1917, a member of the famous Lafayette Squadron, Corporal H. B. Willis, Harvard '17, was captured by the Germans after his plane had been shot down behind the German lines.

Another member, Sergeant Douglas MacMonagle of San Francisco, who had joined the Lafayette Squadron in June, 1917, and had received the French war cross on August 9, 1917, was killed in a fight on September 24, 1917.

PART VIII — THE WESTERN FRONT

CHAPTER XXXVI

PREPARING FOR THE GREAT OFFENSIVE — THE ATTACK MARCH 21 — FIRST PHASE OF THE BATTLE

WITH the coming of bright, springlike weather on the western front in the first weeks of February, 1918, the contending forces displayed a new activity. The sodden fields were drying out; the snow and mud which made roads impassable had disappeared. If the fine weather continued to hold, the much advertised German offensive could not be long delayed.

The Allies were constantly engaged in trench raids for the main purpose of gaining information from prisoners as to the movements of the enemy. It was learned that the Germans were making intense preparations for a big operation. Fresh troops and many guns were constantly arriving on the front. Certain back areas were being cleared for action. Every day large bodies of troops were practicing attacks under the tutelage of experts.

The Allies meanwhile awaited the promised blow hopefully if not calmly. As far as could be ascertained they had a preponderance of men and guns, and the most elaborate preparations had been made during the winter months for the anticipated offensive.

But the much heralded "great push" did not start in February. The Germans were cautiously "feeling out" the ground, by means of trench raids and bombardments, and gathering information through their aerial observers regarding the disposition of the

Allied forces, while the intense activity which prevailed within their own lines foreshadowed the nearness of a mighty attack, and what might prove to be the most sanguinary period of the war.

During the first days of March the Germans were engaged daily in raids all along the French and British fronts, but in every attempt they were repulsed with considerable losses. Determined efforts were made by the enemy to obtain possession of Fort La Pompelle to the southeast of Rheims, which would give them a dominating position from which to complete the destruction of that martyred city. Along a front of nearly ten miles extending from Loivre to Sillery the German infantry advanced from five different points. Some troops succeeded in reaching Alger Farm, a fortified position fronting on Fort La Pompelle, but none was able to enter the fort itself.

The French regiment holding the position in a spirited counterattack drove the Germans back, and regained every inch of ground, though bombarded by thousands of gas shells which filled the air with poisonous fumes. It was during this bombardment that a number of French prisoners escaped their captors and sought refuge in a shell crater where they discovered a large supply of hand grenades. With these they were able to hold off the enemy who tried to capture them and after killing a number succeeded in regaining their own lines.

On March 6, 1918, the Germans made a strong attack on Belgian positions in the flooded zone northwest of Dixmude. At daybreak Beverdyk and Reigersvliet were bombarded by explosives and gas shells and an infantry attack in force followed.

The Belgian artillery replied with a heavy barrage and the fine work of their gunners and riflemen checked the German advance at Beverdyk and eventually drove them back to their own lines. At Reigersvliet the Germans won a footing at several points owing to the fact that the floods in some places had largely subsided, and made an advance comparatively easy.

It was here that a Belgian commander with only nine men and a machine gun, and occupying a bridgehead, held back hundreds of Germans and twelve machine guns until a patrol

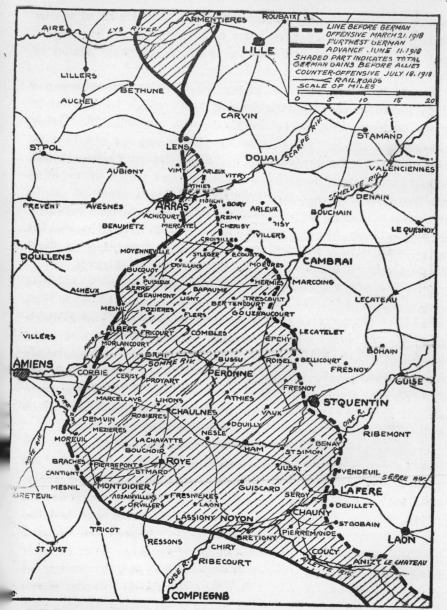

THE GERMAN OFFENSIVE FROM ARRAS TO THE OISE, MARCH-JUNE, 1918

arrived. With this slight reenforcement the Belgian officer took the offensive and by a dashing attack recaptured the position which the Germans had won in front of the bridgehead. Belgian chasseurs had meanwhile been organizing for a counterattack. To reach the German positions it was necessary to cross the flooded area by a single plank walk which was completely dominated by German artillery and machine-gun fire. But the Belgians went forward as coolly as if on parade amid a tempest of shells, and attacked the invaders with reckless bravery. Close and sanguinary fighting ensued, but by 1 o'clock in the afternoon the Belgians had succeeded in capturing the first of seven posts which lay in a semicircle in front of the bridgehead. For hours the fighting raged back and forth, but the stubborn German resistance broke down before the flaming fury of the Belgian spirit and late in the afternoon the last post was regained from the enemy. The German losses were heavy. Large numbers were found dead on the barbed wire. Belgian gunnery had been remarkably effective. The Germans lost as prisoners five officers, 111 men, and a dozen machine guns.

On March 8, 1918, after a bombardment that lasted all day, the Germans launched an attack on the British lines on a front of nearly a mile from south of the Menin road to north of the Polderhoek Château. The assault was vigorously pressed, aided by intense artillery fire, but the Germans were driven back at all points except in the neighborhood of Polderhoek, where they penetrated British advanced posts on a front of about 200 yards. Here the fighting continued for the greater part of the night, with the result that the British recaptured all the positions they had lost.

In the first ten days of March the Germans made twenty hard-driven raids along the French front, most of which were repulsed without difficulty. In the region of the Butte-du-Mesnil they regained some trenches which the French had won from them in February.

The British on their front continued to hold the initiative, carrying out successfully minor operations along the Ypres salient as well as at many points south.

The Germans continued to make swift dashes into the British lines at a number of points. As subsequently developed, the purpose of these continued raids was to search out the weak spots in the British defense. During two successive nights the Germans undertook no less than ten minor operations along the British front, some of which were of more importance than mere raids.

In the midst of this continued activity the great offensive was not forgotten. It was a period of great tension for the Allied forces, and more than once there were rumors that the great push had started, and no-man's-land was deluged with shells and the night was bright with star shells and illuminants, to be followed by comparative calm only broken by raids and minor operations.

As described in another place, the American troops took an active part in many of these minor engagements which tried their courage and served as excellent schooling in the art of active warfare.

At 8 a. m. on March 21, 1918, the Germans launched the great offensive on a front of over fifty miles extending from the river Oise in the neighborhood of La Fère to the Sensée River about Croisilles. When the attack was made the position of the Allied armies was as follows: The British Fifth Army under General Sir Hubert Gough held the front from the Oise at La Fère to a point north of the Omignon River, where the defense line was taken up by the Third Army under General Sir Julian Byng, whose left rested on the Scarpe River, joining here the First Army under General Sir Henry Horne. Sixteen divisions held this line of about 100,000 yards, which gave to each division (9,000 rifles) about 6,000 yards.

Facing the British were three German armies. The Seventh, under General Otto von Below, on the right held the front from north of the Scarpe to the Scheldt at Cambrai where General von der Marwitz with the Second Army prolonged the line down to north of St. Quentin. General von Hutier, commanding the Eighth Army, held the line on Marwitz's left between Omignon River and the Oise, where an army under

General Böhm faced the Third French Army under General Humbert.

The German offensive had been prepared with the greatest care; every division had rehearsed the part it was to play when the hour of attack should come. Before the push the British lines were deluged with shells, and this was followed by showers of projectiles that liberated poisonous gases. The infantry now went forward in waves following each other closely. The first wave of troops would be swept almost away by the British gun and rifle fire, but those that remained alive hung on until joined by more waves of men, when using flame projectors they proceeded to drive the British out of the trenches.

The Germans were prodigal in the waste of man power, counting on weight of numbers to crush their opponents. After they had captured the first British line, the rear lines were deluged with fire from the machine guns, rifles, and every form of small artillery. This overpowering avalanche of death-dealing projectiles prevented the British in the rear from coming to the rescue of their fellow soldiers in the first line. Under the protection of this storm of bullets the Germans advancing in waves penetrated the British second line. After they had gone some distance the first ranks of infantry lay down, and permitted other waves of men to pass through their ranks. Great numbers of three-inch guns and small cannon on low carriages that could be swiftly moved were now brought up behind the infantry and the attack went on.

The German attack was directed against the center of the Allies' position. Their aim was to drive a great salient on a front of fifty or sixty miles through the occupied lines which would divide the French and British, after which they were to be dealt with separately.

The German objective was Amiens, which, situated astride the Somme, is on the main trunk-line railroad from Paris to the Channel ports of Boulogne and Calais, the most important strategical point in northern France.

If the Germans succeeded in gaining their objective, Sir Douglas Haig's troops separated from their French allies would be penned up in a northwestern corner of France with their backs to the sea, or they would be forced to retreat behind the lower Somme in order to cover their communications with Havre.

The Germans began their great offensive by an intense bombardment of both high explosives and gas shells, while a powerful infantry attack was launched on a front extending from Croisilles to La Fère. The misty weather that prevailed in the morning of March 21, 1918, was favorable for an assault, and the Germans were close to the British lines before they were discovered. In the course of the first onrush they broke through all the British outpost trenches and south of Cambrai penetrated some battle positions.

Forty German divisions were identified by the British as taking part in the first day's attack, but it was believed that at least fifty in all entered the battle before the day closed. At several points the British were heavily outnumbered. Nine German divisions were hurled against three British at one part of the line and eight against two at another.

The German storming troops, including the Guards, made a brave appearance in new uniforms. They advanced in solid ranks until their formation was broken by the intense British machine-gun fire.

Over the dead and wounded the supporting troops swept in countless waves and there was no faltering as the hurricanes of shells swept through their ranks. As hundreds fell others closed in and filled the gaps and the human tide rolled relentlessly on.

The Germans were exceedingly strong in guns. At some points in the line they had one to every twelve or fifteen yards. No less than a thousand confronted three British divisions. With heavy long-range guns they were also well provided and back areas to a distance of twenty-five miles and more were under shell fire.

Among the places against which the Germans first directed their efforts were Bullecourt, Lagnecourt, and Noreuil west of Cambrai, the St. Quentin Ridge on the right of the Cambrai salient, and Ronssoy and Hargicourt south of the Cambrai salient.

The Germans reported that they had captured the British first line between Arras and La Fère and 16,000 prisoners and 200 guns.

On the following day (March 22, 1918,) the fighting reached the greatest intensity in two sectors—one north of Cambrai and the other southwest. The fighting on the northern front was about Bullecourt, while Hargicourt was the southern center. Before attacking the sector between the Canal du Nord and Croisilles the Germans for four hours deluged the British with every kind of projectile and high explosive that a gun could throw.

The British were compelled to fight for hours with their gas masks on, but despite this drawback they were in high spirits because they were able to create such havoc when the Germans advanced in massed formation.

Around Mory on the northern end of the battle field the Germans attacked with superior numbers and the fighting was especially fierce. The British held on during the day, but toward evening the Germans gained a foothold in the village after close fighting that lasted some hours. The Germans advanced for this attack from Croisilles and for a long time were held back by a company of British gunners who were stationed on high ground, from which point of vantage they mowed down the enemy with a grilling fire.

The most critical period for the Allies since the offensive was launched was in the afternoon and the night of March 22-23, 1918, when the British lost important positions one after another as German divisions in successive masses carried everything before them, regardless of losses. General Gough's Fifth Army especially suffered, being hit by Von der Marwitz on the north, and Von Hutier on the east. Under these sustained hammer blows the entire front gave way and the British were forced to retire across the Somme, pursued by Generals Lüttwitz and Öttingen. Lower down Generals Webern and Von Conta, with troops of the Seventh Army under Von Gayl, captured Ham, and forced the French who had crossed the Oise back to Chauny.

This was the blackest hour for the Allies. Von Hutier had rolled up the British right wing. The road to Paris down the Oise was no longer a doubtful adventure. Unless the broken link between the French and British could be restored the Germans had accomplished what they set out to do.

In this crucial hour for the Allies, when the demoralization of the Fifth British Army was complete, General Carey with a scratch division kept it in touch with General Byng's Third Army on the north over an eight-mile gap, and the French General Fayolle saved it in the south over a thirty-mile gap between it and the Sixth French Army.

As the result of the first two days' fighting the Germans claimed to have captured 25,000 prisoners, 400 guns, and 300 machine guns. It was also claimed that between Fontaine-les-Croisilles and Mœuvers German forces had penetrated into the second British positions and captured Vaulx-Vraucourt and Morches, the former being about three and a half miles, and the latter two and a half miles, behind the former British front. It was further claimed by the Germans that the British after evacuating their positions in the bend southwest of Cambrai were pursued through Demicourt, Flesquières and Ribecourt. Between Gonnelieu and the Omignon stream the first two British positions were penetrated and the heights west of Gouzeaucourt, Heudicourt, and Villers-Faucon were captured.

The German official report stated that the battle of attack against the British front was under command of the kaiser.

The Germans sprung a new form of frightfulness on the Allies when at 8 o'clock in the morning of March 23, 1918, they bombarded Paris with long-range guns. At intervals of about twenty minutes shells of 240 millimeters (about 9.5 inches) reached the capital, killing ten persons and wounding others. The shortest distance from Paris to the front was over sixty-two miles. The first daylight aeroplane raid followed this bombardment, but did little damage. Public interest was centered on the mysterious gun that could drop shells on the city from such a great distance. Pieces of shells examined were found to bear rifling marks showing that they had not been dropped, but were fired from some kind of gun. Later the French located several of these "mystery guns," and some were destroyed. The only purpose they could serve was to terrify the people of Paris, otherwise they were of no military importance.

While the British front was being overrun by the German hordes the French front was subjected to violent artillery fire, especially south of the Oise in the Rheims region, in Lorraine, between Harracourt and the Vosges mountains and the heights of Alsace. The Germans made only one attack on the French lines in the region of Blemeray, where they were dispersed with considerable losses in dead and prisoners.

South and north of Péronne the Germans renewed their attacks on the British front throughout the day of March 24, 1918. South of the city they succeeded after heavy fighting in crossing the Somme at some points.

North of Péronne violent attacks were directed against the line of the Tortille River (a tributary of the Somme), where the British were finally forced to withdraw to new positions. Although fighting continued at different points during the night, the situation had not changed. British troops held the line of the Somme River to Péronne. German troops that attempted to cross the river at Pargny were driven back. The British right was now in touch with the French, and continued to hold their positions to the north of the Somme at Péronne after beating off a number of attacks made by the Germans on this front during the early hours of the night.

The Allies, despite considerable losses and the yielding of some miles of territory, were undismayed. The Germans had not attained their objectives at any point. Hard fighting was still in progress, but the British were holding strongly the whole front line to which they had withdrawn. The British had used only a few troops besides those that held the front lines. The brave defense maintained by these shock troops enabled the British main body to fall back on the positions they had established a long time before the German offensive was started.

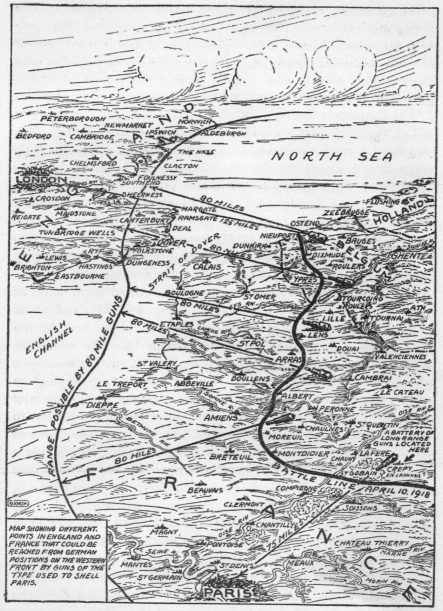

THE RANGE OF THE GERMAN 80-MILE GUN

Owing to the German methods of advancing in dense masses their losses had been terrific. The British identified fifty German divisions that had been hurled into the sea of fire made by the Allied artillery, machine guns, and rifles. The British losses were considerable, but principally in prisoners. They also lost a number of guns, but very few pieces of artillery were captured by the Germans after the first day of the offensive.

The hardest fighting on March 25, 1918, was around Bapaume. The British artillery on the heights west of the town broke up every attack which the Germans launched. Later in the day the British were forced to withdraw to the west, leaving the town in enemy hands. On the following day the Germans renewed their attacks, but by afternoon these had ceased, and the British took advantage of the comparative calm to retire in good order to their old positions behind the Ancre which they held in July, 1916, when the battle of the Somme began.

The Germans began their attacks on the Allied front south of the Somme early in the morning of March 26, 1918, and about 10.30 had captured Roye. West of this place and Noyon the British, French, and American troops held the enemy in check. Fresh German divisions brought forward pressed the attack all along the Somme. The assaults around Chaulnes and on the front northward from there to Bray were especially violent. The German troops displayed a reckless bravery in these attacks and were heavily punished. Their losses were so considerable that reenforcements were brought up from all parts of the western front. It was established by the British that more than seventy divisions (about 840,000) men were engaged.

The net results to the Germans during the seven days' fighting may be briefly summed up as follows: They had won back most of the line they lost when retreating from the Somme line of 1916 on the fifty-mile front between the Oise and the Scarpe and this stretch of territory is from twenty to twenty-five miles wide along about forty miles of front. Though the Germans had failed to gain all their objectives and the offensive had not proved as successful as they hoped for, the Allies were not disposed to minimize the seriousness of the situation. They found comfort in the fact that in the seven days' fighting the British who had borne the brunt of the blows had lost in killed, wounded, and missing not more than 100,000 men while the German losses were nearly 600,000. It was also believed that at least one half of the remaining German troops had reached such a point of exhaustion that they could no longer do effective fighting. At the close of the seven days' struggle the battle line took in Fenchy, Boyelles, Hebuterne, Albert, Chapilly, Bray-sur-Somme, Avre, and Noyon.

After an all-day battle north and south of the Somme, with Arras as the chief center, the British forces beat off the Germans, inflicting heavy losses. The attack on this new sector, delivered on a wide front north and south of the river Scarpe, was opened with an intense bombardment, and under cover of smoke clouds. The Germans were unable to break or even bend the British front and they lost a large number in killed and prisoners. South of the Somme, the British, subjected to fierce assaults, maintained their positions throughout the day, but the Germans brought forward fresh troops, and by sheer weight of numbers forced the British about nightfall to fall back on Chapilly. North of the Somme the British maintained their line intact.

On the same day the French made substantial gains on the front from Lassigny to Noyon, advancing their line about ten kilometers (6.21 miles) to a depth of about a mile and a quarter. During the entire morning the Germans pressed vigorous assaults in the region of Montdidier in attempts to enlarge their gains west and south of the town. The French troops in spirited counterattacks drove the Germans out of the village of Courtemanche, Mesnil-St. Georges, and Assainvillers, and proceeded to occupy these places solidly.

On the following day fresh German troops were thrown against the French Army maintaining the junction between the French and British lines. The French made a determined stand, but the German pressure forced them to retire toward the west. The Germans broke through at Montdidier and occupied that place. In order to keep in touch with the British the French were pushing northward to relieve part of the line of their ally which had been thrown back. At the same time the Germans made a demonstration at the point where the British and French lines joined. Employing large forces, they were able to make a breach in the British line, but the French sent forward cavalry and infantry into the gap and closed it.

The salient which the Germans had now been pushing westward since the beginning of the offensive was now forty miles long at its farthest point, from Vimy Ridge, three miles south of Arras, to two miles south of Lassigny. Its greatest width was thirty miles, from the old line west of La Fère westward to Montdidier, the junction of the new western and southern fronts. On the north the territory was flanked by a semicircular ridge lying north and northeast of Arras, beginning with Notre-Dame-de-Lorette, six miles southwest of Lens, and ending at the much-fought-over Vimy Ridge.

The base of the German salient ran from Montdidier east and a little south, by way of Noyon, and linked up with the old line between St. Gobain and Anizy-le-Château, nine miles west of Laon, a distance of thirty-two miles in all. Just as the northern extremity of the German salient was flanked by the Arras ridges, so the southern extremity of thirty-two miles was flanked in the east by the watershed of the Oise and the Aisne, and eastward from the valley of the Oise, where it is joined by the ridge lying parallel to the Chiry-Lassigny highway.

The Allies holding the ridges north and south of the German salient were in a favorable position, and it seemed unlikely that the Germans would attempt to push farther westward without trying to capture the high approaches on their flanks.

It was known to the Allies through their aerial observers that the German armies, reenforced by new divisions that had been brought from Russia, were massing for another powerful attack.

On March 28, 1918, strong German forces drove back the British line south of the Somme to a line running west of Hamel, Marcelcave, and Demuin in the direction of Amiens. On the same date the Germans launched a terrific drive in the Scarpe sector with the purpose of capturing Arras and Vimy Ridge.

Six German divisions were flung against the British positions, while four were held in reserve, but they failed to break through. To the south between Boiry and Serre eleven divisions attacked the British positions, but were forced back.

On the same date, in the Montdidier region, the French under Pétain not only held their ground but made gains. In the course of the evening and part of the night the Germans made violent attacks in the endeavor to eject the French from the villages of Courtemanche, Mesnil-St. Georges, and Assainvillers, which were won the day before, but in every instance were driven back with heavy losses. The French followed up their success by driving the enemy out of Monchel, which they occupied.

To the north of Montdidier Franco-British troops continued to hold the Germans on the Avre River and in front of Neuville, Mezières, Marcelcave, and Hamel.

It was evident that the great German offensive was losing force. The fighting was still intense at some points, but no operations were attempted on such a colossal scale as marked the fighting in the first week of the battle. At many places along the front of attack the Germans were being driven back and at others French and British were holding their positions firmly. Artillery battles had now taken the place of infantry fighting to a great extent, a sure sign that the German armies were in an exhausted condition and needed time to re-form and recuperate. As the Germans had been unable to drag much artillery with them during their advance the French had the advantage.

On March 28, 1918, the news that General Ferdinand Foch, chief of the French General Staff had been made generalissimo of all the Allied forces in the western theater of war was received with general satisfaction by the Allied nations. The Allies had long suffered from lack of coordination, while the Germans had not only profited by their own united direction, but were also advantaged by the frequently unrelated efforts of their enemies. General Foch, who was born in 1851, began mastering the strategy of war in 1870. He had studied German mentality. He counted on their repeating in future conflicts the maneuvers that had succeeded, and also expected them to make some of the old mistakes. Foch led the Ninth French Army at the Battle of the Marne, where, according to some military critics, he won first honors. In the spring of 1915 he led his army in the offensive between Armentières and Arras. After these operations he was surpassed in public opinion of the French army chiefs by Generals Pétain and Nivelle, whose wonderful leadership before Verdun made them famous throughout the world. When General Pétain succeeded Nivelle in May, 1917, as commander in chief in the field, General Foch took his place as chief of staff in Paris. President Wilson, who had been urging unity of command ever since the inter-Ally war conference at Paris in the winter of 1917, was among the first to congratulate General Foch on his appointment as generalissimo of all the Allied forces on the western front.

CHAPTER XXXVII

THE SECOND PHASE OF THE GREAT GERMAN OFFENSIVE

THE full force of the great German offensive having spent itself, though fighting still continued, it may be of great interest to consider how far the Germans succeeded in carrying out their carefully laid plans.

It was evident that their main purpose was not to capture Paris or reach the Channel ports, though these objectives were considered, but to destroy either the French or the British army. The British being the most powerful of the Allies' armies, owing to conditions that developed after the offensive started, was made the object of the Germans' most determined destructive efforts. They planned to strike a mighty blow along the Oise between St. Quentin and La Fère, at the junction of the French and British troops. Their purpose was to break through at this point regardless of the cost. This accomplished, they would push on up the Oise valley, and by throwing large forces across the British right turn it and roll it up. To accomplish this it would be also necessary to destroy the British salient at Cambrai, for unless this was done an advance down the Somme would have left the whole German flank exposed to attack from the north.

The first German attack was launched against the Cambrai salient from the north and the east, and was successful as the British were driven back.

In this preliminary assault the Germans employed some ninety divisions or over 750,000 men on a front of about fifty miles. This was the heaviest concentration of men to the mile that had so far been used in campaigns on the western front. Against these forces the British had only about 5,000 men to the mile or less than a third of the number the Germans had in action. Having disposed of the Cambrai salient the Germans had opened the way for the real attack south which was made in the angle between the Oise Canal and the Somme. The assault was carried out with great masses of men in close formation, and the Allies' lines were overwhelmed in the first rush. But the British and French made an orderly if hurried retreat and their front remained unbroken. The Allies made the Germans pay heavily for every gain, fighting on steadily from point to point. The British during the retreat still clung to the southern bank of the Oise, but were finally forced across the river at Noyon which fell to the Germans.

Meanwhile in the north the British were slowly falling back on the old battle field of the Somme. It was wisely decided by the British High Command to retire rather than bring forward the strong armies they held in reserve back of the lines. The use of these armies would eliminate the possibility of a great counterattack. Having reached the old battle field and after the Ancre valley was passed, the British ceased to retreat and established themselves strongly on the west bank of the river.

South of the town of Albert the Germans made more important gains. They had reached and passed the Allies' old line as it existed before the fighting on the Somme. But in the last days of March they made little progress as their artillery had not kept pace with the forward rush and until the guns arrived no important advance could be made.

The French had halted behind the Avre River, an excellent position, for there were wide marsh belts lining either bank of the stream. Before the French ceased to retreat the Germans had pushed their advance westward and encircled Montdidier, producing by doing this a salient in their lines with the town as the apex. One German flank extended eastward through Lassigny to the Oise and the other along the Avre and behind it. This salient marked almost the extreme limit of the German push.

North of the Somme and south of Arras the German advance was checked, because the British held such strong positions on Vimy Ridge and the heights of Notre-Dame-de-Lorette. The Germans could not push on north of the river before they had reduced these strong and commanding positions. To clear the way they made a determined attack with 90,000 men on a small front of not more than five miles east of Arras. After an intense artillery fire that lasted all day the Germans repeatedly attacked, but met with repulse. They gained a few hundred yards at several points, but the British line remained practically intact.

The net results of the German offensive showed that they had overrun considerable territory and were some miles nearer Paris. But they had not succeeded in crushing either the French or the British armies, and the real question in the war was the destruction of forces. Territorial gains were only of value as far as they contributed to that end. There was not the least doubt that the Germans had lost a far greater number of men than the Allies and that they could not continue for long a campaign on such a costly scale. Unless they found some other way out they were heading straight for defeat even if they should succeed in overrunning the greater part of France.

In the last two days of March the Germans resumed heavy fighting in the region between the Somme and the Avre and southward to Montdidier. Six villages around Montdidier were

British Official Photo

A remarkable group of British and French leaders photographed on the British front in 1918. King George is the center. At the king's right (left of picture) are Marechal Foch, General Debeney, and General Rawlinson. At the king's left (right of picture) are Field Marshal Haig, General Petain, and General Fayolle

wrested from the French—Ayencourt and Le Monchel south of the town, Mesnil-St. Georges, Cantigny, Aubevillers and Grivesnes. On the following evening the French recaptured Ayencourt and Le Monchel, a hundred prisoners, and fourteen machine guns.

On the Oise front German detachments, consisting of a battalion of storming troops, having succeeded in crossing the river at Chauny, attempted to establish a bridgehead on the left bank. The French launched a swift and vigorously pressed counterattack, with the result that the German battalion was completely annihilated, or taken prisoners.

Between Montdidier and Moreuil there was stiff fighting during the last two days of March. The Germans repeatedly attacked almost without ceasing. Moreuil, captured by them, was retaken by the French, again taken by the Germans, and finally carried in a brilliant bayonet charge by British and French troops. Between Moreuil and Lassigny the German check was complete. The French also advanced as far as the vicinity of Canny-sur-Matz. A division of picked French troops after a hot fight in which they took over 700 prisoners captured Plemon and held it firmly against repeated attempts made by the enemy to oust them.

On the British front the Germans were especially active. Attacks followed one another at different points unceasingly during March 30-31, 1918. All these assaults were costly and failed. The Germans' determined efforts were unsuccessful elsewhere, for they lost considerable ground near Feuchy, four miles east of Arras; and near Serre, seven miles north of Albert, the British made a notable advance, capturing 230 prisoners and forty machine guns. South of the Somme, by successful counterattacks, the British regained possession of the village of Demuin. There was heavy fighting in the sector to the south of the main highway leading from Péronne to Amiens, which proved costly to the Germans and brought no adequate returns.

At the close of the month it was the opinion of the French and British High Command that the offensive for the present was checked. The Germans were making strenuous efforts to rush forward their heavy artillery, and a formidable attack might be expected with all the reserves available, but the Allies viewed the future with confidence. At the same time they looked for a long struggle which might develop into such a contest as was fought at Verdun and the first battle of the Somme.

April 1, 1918, showed a slackening in the German pressure. There was brisk, and at times, violent fighting between the Germans and Allies around Moreuil and Hangard. Attacks and counterattacks followed each other in rapid succession, which resulted in the British gaining some ground. If it was the purpose of the Germans to make a drive on Amiens, this sector was of special importance, for it lay east of the city between the Somme and the Avre. What encouraged the Allies' High Command to believe that Amiens was the objective was the massing of great numbers of German troops in this area and in the district around Albert. In expectation of a heavy blow in these regions the Allies brought into the battle front as rapidly as possible a great number of guns. The Germans too were making artillery preparations, but their guns were arriving slowly and not in considerable numbers. All day long on April 1, 1918, they launched local attacks near Albert, but were unable to make any impression on the iron wall of British resistance.

On the same day the First German Guard Division, which had been severely punished by the French at Grivesnes, returned to the assault, but received such a warm reception that they were forced to seek shelter in their positions, leaving the French masters of the situation.

The British were active on the first of the month, carrying out some successful actions. German positions in a wood along the Luce River were stormed and after sharp fighting the enemy was forced to withdraw, leaving the field strewn with dead. The Germans shelled the wood after it was occupied by the British, and then organized two counterattacks with the purpose of retaking it. Both attacks were caught in the British artillery barrage and shattered. South of Hangard the British improved their position and smashed two German counterattacks which essayed to restore the situation.

Early in the morning of April 4, 1918, the Germans launched a new offensive. Amiens was evidently the objective toward which their forces moved from three directions. One attack was made from the northeast from the general direction of Albert, a second from the east along the line of the Amiens-Resières railroad, and the third along the Avre River where the French held the line. The Germans employed fifteen divisions against the French and fourteen divisions against the British, or nearly 350,000 men, attacking the Allies on a sixteen-mile front. All day long and through the night the French were assaulted with extreme violence. The Germans seemed determined to break through at whatever cost, their immediate aim being the Amiens-Paris railway. Despite their efforts, ten times repeated, the Germans, at the cost of heavy sacrifices, only succeeded in gaining a few hundred yards of territory, and occupied the villages of Mailly-Raineval and Morisel, while the French still controlled the heights in the neighborhood. Grivesnes was subjected to the fiercest attacks, but the French troops held it securely, and broke down every assault that was made by the enemy. The Germans were so badly battered in the fighting that raged all day and night in this region that they did not resume the offensive on the following day, and General Pétain took advantage of the lull to launch successful counterattacks, gaining ground notably in the region of Mailly-Raineval (south of Moreuil) and Cantigny.

The northern and western outskirts of Cantigny, which was captured by the Germans a few days before, were now in French hands.

While the French were stubbornly holding their own against superior numbers, the British front south of the Somme was the scene of heavy fighting. The battle raged all day and far into the night and the British were forced back to new positions east of Villers-Bretonneux, nine miles east of Amiens. North and south of Albert their lines were heavily attacked along a front of about 9,000 yards between Aveluy and Dernancourt. All that the Germans gained in the fighting in this region was a foothold on a small triangular bit of territory just southwest of

Albert, which brought the attacking troops close to the Albert-Amiens railway.

The net results of the Germans during the two days' fighting were a decided check and a very costly one.

On April 5, 1918, German forces engaged in massed attacks against the British lines just east of Corbie on the Somme. South of Hangard Wood the British were pushed back a short distance, but elsewhere the Germans achieved only costly failures.

Despite trifling gains here and there by the enemy, the Allies had every reason for feeling confident that the offensive would fail. In the vital sector between Montdidier and the Luce River, where the Germans were nearest to Amiens, their position was far from satisfactory, and in the north, where they must advance their lines if they wished to escape extreme danger, the situation was very bad indeed. The British were holding fast to their positions above Albert with indomitable courage, while the Germans were making a slow advance here and there at the cost of heavy sacrifice.

In the course of the fighting during April 7-8, 1918, the Germans made gains south of the Oise. Advancing toward the Ailette River they captured Pierremande and Folembray, driving the French to the western bank of the stream. The heights to the east of Coucy-le-Château were captured, and another force advancing from Verneuil-Barisis occupied the town of Verneuil.

Attacks and counterattacks continued along the British battle front. The little village of Cucquoy, near Serre, continued to be the center of the most determined German assaults. The place itself was nothing, a mere mass of ruins torn by artillery fire, but the hills around were occupied by the British, and the German advance was held up until these positions could be captured or disposed of.

On April 9, 1918, after a heavy bombardment in which over 60,000 gas shells were used, the Germans attacked British and Portuguese lines from La Bassée Canal to the neighborhood of Armentières (a distance of eleven miles).

The Portuguese in the center and the British on the flanks of the river Lys between Estaires and Bac St. Maur were forced to retire under the German pressure. Heavy fighting continued throughout the day in this sector. In the vicinity of Givenchy and Fleurbaix the British maintained their position and repulsed strong assaults. Richebourg St. Vaast and Laventie were occupied by the enemy.

In the morning of April 10, 1918, the Germans launched a new attack, with strong forces, against the British positions between the Lys River and Armentières and the Ypres-Commines Canal. The British were driven back to the line running through Wytschaete along the Messines Ridge to Ploegsteert.

South of Armentières, after a prolonged struggle, the Germans crossed the river Lys and established themselves on the left bank at a number of points east of Estaires and near Bac St. Maur. Southward from Estaires—the southern limit of the German offensive—the British continued to hold their lines. Givenchy was recaptured from the Germans, and 750 prisoners. The possession of this place was important to the Allies, as it stands on high ground, and is a gateway on the road to Bethune.

In the course of the two days' fighting in this region the Germans advanced in the center to a depth of about 5,500 yards, the British and Portuguese losing a considerable number of prisoners and guns.

In the retirement of the French forces to the line of the Ailette River two French battalions were cut off and the Germans took 2,000 prisoners. The retirement of the French was made on account of an awkward corner in the line.

The fighting during these days showed that it was the Germans' purpose to exhaust the British army. Their first plan had been to cut off the British from the French, but that failed. Now they attacked the British wherever they saw a favorable chance, hoping to destroy such large numbers that they would be unable to take the offensive.

During the night of April 9, 1918, the Germans made a strong assault on the French lines near Hangard-en-Santerre. The French retaliated with a counterblow that drove the enemy back

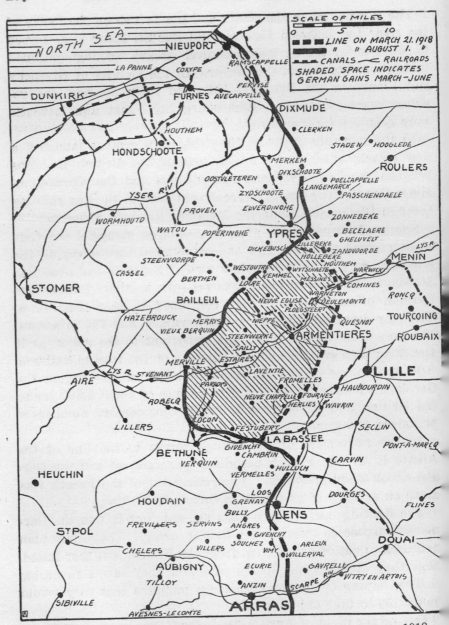

THE GERMAN ADVANCE BETWEEN YPRES AND ARRAS, MARCH–JUNE, 1918

in disorder. The village changed hands repeatedly, but early in the morning of April 10, 1918, the French gained possession of the place and of a cemetery near by, and established themselves strongly in the new positions.

All day long on April 11, 1918, the Germans were hurling great masses of troops against the British lines on the northern front, from La Bassée to the Ypres-Commines Canal southeast of Ypres. As the result of these heavy assaults Haig's troops were forced back north of Estaires and Steenwerck. The evacuation of Armentières followed. The German advance on the previous day between Warneton and the Lys on the north and their drive to the south of Armentières had subjected the place to attack from three sides. For the British to attempt holding the town under these conditions would have caused a useless sacrifice of troops. Armentières had no military importance, but the Messines-Wytschaete Ridge and the Passchendaele Ridge to the north of it were of great value. As long as these positions held out the British lines were safe. The Germans were confronted with the same situation that prevailed on the Somme front. The German push toward Amiens had been held up by the British possession of the Heights of Vimy and of the Notre-Dame-de-Lorette. These formed the hinge on which the whole British line swung as it moved westward. The same thing was happening in the north. The British center had given way under the fury of the German attacks, but the flanks held fast. On the north the Messines Ridge blocked the way of the German advance. For in case of a westward push both German flanks would be in great danger from this bastion which commanded the entire field of maneuver. Their front and rear as well as flanks would be subjected to destructive artillery fire from this ridge which therefore became the center of the fighting in the north.

The Germans recognizing the supreme importance of the ridge made determined and valiant efforts to capture the position. They launched one attack after another that were costly and brought no results. They entered the British lines in the village of Messines, but were promptly driven out in a brilliant

counterattack and the important positions remained in British
hands.

In the area west and northwest of Armentières the British
troops were forced back in the fighting that continued throughout the day on April 12, 1918. The British retired to the
neighborhood of the railway south of Bailleul, where the
heaviest fighting continued without respite. The Germans captured Merville and drove the British forces operating near
Ploegsteert to retire to new positions in the neighborhood of
Neuve Eglise.

In the Hangard-en-Santerre sector of the French front to the
southeast of Amiens the struggle was prolonged throughout the
day. The Germans attacked with large forces, but the French
held their own until late in the day, when the enemy, reenforced
by fresh troops in considerable numbers, gained a portion of
Hangard, while the French still held on to the western part of
the town. In the Noyon sector the Germans were active with
their artillery, but attempted no infantry attacks. Rheims,
the martyred city, was again bombarded, with the result that
a number of buildings were fired, especially in the vicinity of
the cathedral.

During the night of April 12-13, 1918, the Germans made a
determined drive for Neuve Eglise, three miles southwest of
Messines, and after a prolonged struggle occupied the village.
The British vigorously counterattacked in the morning and
drove the enemy out, capturing a battalion commander and a
number of prisoners. There was hard fighting at other points
on the British front, the Germans losing ground at Festubert.
On the French front all enemy attacks broke down. Northwest
of Orvilles-Sorel French forces broke into the German line on
a front of three quarters of a mile and won a strip of territory.

The Germans continued to bring up fresh divisions into the
Messines sector, until twenty-three divisions were engaged.
Neuve Eglise was wrested from the British during the night of
April 14, 1918. Seven attacks were made on the British lines
near Merville, only one of which pushed back the British line
and was successful in gaining ground. The British in a dash-

ing counterattack drove out the Germans and reoccupied the line. Bailleul and the neighborhood were the scene of violent fighting. The Germans seemed determined to carry the place at any cost. The town, which contained many handsome buildings, was reduced to a mass of ruins. The German pressure forced the British to evacuate the town in the night of April 15, 1918, after they had been driven from the heights to the south and southeast. The British troops fell back on the east and west line north of Wulverghem and Bailleul.

On this date (April 15, 1918) the Germans made other notable gains. Attacking the British on a nine-mile front, Haig's men were driven from Wytschaete and most of the Messines Ridge positions were taken. It will be recalled that this famous ridge was captured by the British from the Germans on June 7, 1917, after elaborate mining preparations had been made and 1,000,000 pounds of high explosives were used in blowing up the heights.

Intense fighting continued all day long on April 16-17, 1918, about the Messines Ridge and the Passchendaele Ridge to the north, forcing the British to retire to their lines east of Ypres.

In the Hangard sector on the French front, where since the beginning of the offensive the Germans had been hammering away in an effort to get astride the railway connecting Amiens with Clairmont, the British carried out a highly successful operation. At daybreak on April 17-18, 1918, along a front of about five miles between Thennes and Mailly-Renneval, the French launched a dashing assault that resulted in the capture of over 600 prisoners and the seizure of some important points which the enemy occupied. The ground over which the French had to charge had been transformed by recent rains into heavy mud into which the attackers sank at times up to their knees, but they pushed on undismayed. The commanding heights on the northern flank were carried amid victorious cheers. In the center bodies of infantry penetrated Senecat Wood and cleared up the gun emplacements which defended the approaches to Castel. Pressing forward, the French infantry established themselves on the outskirts of the town and prepared for an assault on the place.

Toward the south other French units captured dominating heights and advanced toward Anchin Farm on the road between Ailly-sur-Noye and Moreuil. The French advance met with the strongest opposition from the Germans, but their efforts were ineffective and their casualties heavy.

The main purpose of the Germans in their continued pounding of the French around Hangard was to prevent reenforcements being sent north. This they failed to accomplish. The French not only fought them off and gained ground, but were able to send a considerable force to the northern front.

The fighting around Hangard, which was prolonged for days, was of the most sanguinary description. Desperate hand-to-hand fighting took place in the streets of the town and inside the houses. Hangard changed hands again and again, but was finally occupied and strongly held by the French.

The fighting continued with undiminished fury on the northern front, but the Germans made no important gains. Attacks in the Mont Kemmel region were beaten off. At Givenchy, and at other points of the front, the Germans failed to gain ground, while great numbers were slaughtered by the British machine-gun and rifle fire. It was estimated that the Germans employed 137,000 men in their furious assaults on the Allied front extending from Givenchy, eleven miles northwest to the neighborhood of St. Venant. Important reenforcements of French troops strengthened the British resistance in the north, and German masses attempting to break through lost heavily.

During the week the Germans, employing picked troops, made violent attacks on the Belgian front between Kippe and Langemarck, but were unable to gain a foot of ground. The Belgians captured 714 prisoners, a 77-millimeter gun, and 42 machine guns. Documents found on captured German officers revealed the importance attached by the Germans to the operation. They had planned to capture Merckem, Luyghem, Aschoop, and neighboring towns, and after reaching the Ypres Canal purposed to push on in the direction of Poperinghe and envelop the left of the Allies.

At the close of the week (April 20, 1918) it was evident that the German offensive had broken down, and that no more important movement would be attempted for some time. In the Givenchy-Festubert region (west of La Bassée) the British forces expelled the Germans from some advanced points which they had occupied two days before.

A determined attack made by the Germans against the French lines north of Seicheprey, in which the American troops fought with valor and distinction, is described in another part of this work.

In summing up the operations of the week, it will be noted that the fighting in the Lys region absorbed most of the German energy, and that the British defense was strained at times nearly to the breaking point. The German advance from the south was diverted by indomitable British resistance encountered at Givenchy. Armentières was evacuated to avoid an encircling movement, after which the German armies on the north and south of the place joined hands. British divisions on the north and south flanks remained firm, but the attack in the center was pushed, and after the river Lawe was crossed Merville, Merris, and Neuve Eglise were captured, when the advance was checked. The struggle then narrowed down to Bailleul, Nieppe Forest, and Mont Kemmel, the main objective being the capture of Hazebrouck. In the course of the week's fighting these villages changed hands a number of times, but in the end Bailleul fell and the Germans occupied Meterne, Wulverghem, and Wytschaete, and an important section of Messines Ridge. This rendered the forward line eastward of Ypres untenable, and the British retired to new positions. The fighting at every point during the week was of the most desperate character. The Germans found it difficult to exploit their first successes in any direction but the most northern and northwestern sectors, where they discovered a weak point and concentrated a powerful attack. The Allied High Command had no reason to feel discouraged, for the situation, though serious, gave ground for confidence. The net result to the Germans was a small gain in territory, but their losses in men had been appalling. It was no longer a question of overrunning territory in France, but the destruction of man power that would count in the end.

CHAPTER XXXVIII

THE GERMAN OFFENSIVE RENEWED—YPRES THREATENED—THE ALLIES' HEAVY LOSSES

THE comparative quiet which had reigned for some days in the battle area was broken on April 23, 1918, when the Germans, using two divisions, attacked the whole British front south of the Somme, as well as the French forces on the British right. Villers-Bretonneux, the Germans' objective, stands on a ridge southeast of Amiens, an important position in reference to that place. A preliminary bombardment started at 3 o'clock in the morning and continued for nearly four hours, when their infantry advanced upon Villers-Bretonneux and the village of Cahy, from Hangard Wood, Marcelcave, and from below Warfusee. Among the German troops engaged were the Fortieth Guards Division, which had been fighting recently on this front, and the Seventy-seventh Division, fresh from Russia and in action here for the first time. At the hour the attack was launched a third German division, the Thirteenth, of Westphalian troops, fell upon the French near Castel to the south of the British forces. The Germans, after a fierce struggle, succeeded in gaining a little ground, when the French troops pivoted from the right and threw them back.

On the British front the Germans used tanks for the first time in an offensive, three of them advancing with the German infantry down the road to Cahy and Domart.

German attacks on the northern and southern sectors of this front were repulsed by the Allied troops, but the enemy made progress at Villers-Bretonneux. The fighting here continued throughout the day with unabated intensity and did not cease when the Germans captured the village in the early evening.

Their attacks broke down on the northern bank of the Somme and north of Albert. The British carried out a successful local operation northwest of Festubert, where they recaptured a post which the Germans had won on April 22.

British positions east of Robecq now came under strong enemy fire and were subjected to several strong attacks. The British line remained unbroken after every assault and the Germans were forced back, losing eighty-four men as prisoners and a number of machine guns.

In the night British and Australian troops launched several counterattacks against the positions the Germans had newly won in and around Villers-Bretonneux.

The Germans had been long enough in possession of the town and the neighborhood to set up strong defenses, and countless machine guns had been placed wherever they could do the most harm. When the British were driven out of the village after a hard fight it was late in the day and the Germans evidently thought that they would not attempt a counterattack until the following morning. But the British did not purpose to give the enemy any time to bring up fresh troops, and prepared for a night attack. They recognized the importance of Villers-Bretonneux, as it gave the enemy full observation of the British positions on both sides of the Somme Valley beyond Amiens.

The job of recapturing the village was given to the Australians who had made a brilliant record in carrying out night attacks and rarely failed of success. About midnight they set out, unpreceded by any artillery preparation, feeling their way along in the dark and relying solely on the weapons they carried with them.

The Australians broke into the village before the enemy woke up, and supported by several British battalions spent the night in clearing the Germans out of the place. The Germans were not disposed to surrender such an important observation point and put up a stiff fight, and the struggle raged for hours in the streets. Finally the British and Australians gained the upper hand and the village proper was freed of the enemy, who fell back on positions in the neighborhood. Fighting in the outskirts of the village continued in the morning. There was no gunfire even then, for the British, Germans, and Australians were so closely engaged in the struggle and so mixed up that the gunners on both sides were afraid of killing their own men.

On the western side of the village German machine gunners, cut off from their lines by the sudden counterattack, were stoutly defending themselves here and there among the remains of ruined buildings and dealt the British some shrewd blows before they could be driven out, or made prisoner. The British had escaped without severe casualties, while the German toll of dead was costly, especially in officers. In this operation the British captured between 700 and 800 prisoners.

In the Lys salient the Germans, employing large forces and aiming at Mont Kemmel, launched a succession of violent attacks from Wytschaete to Bailleul. The Allies made a brave resistance, but were compelled to fall back on prepared positions toward the Locre River.

Mont Kemmel is a hill of great tactical importance. It is almost covered with woods and stands out somewhat in front of the range of heights extending westward to the Mont des Cats, and to some extent dominating its western neighbors.

In the course of the fighting in this region (April 25-26, 1918) nine German divisions (about 120,000 men) were engaged, and the Allies, borne down by overwhelming numbers, were forced to give up the village of Kemmel, the near-by summit of Kemmel, and the village of Dranoutre to the south.

In the Somme-Avre battle area the French had been pitilessly hammered by overpowering numbers of German troops. The fighting in and around Hangard Wood was especially intense.

On April 25, 1918, the French repulsed seven assaults made on their lines north of the wood and in Hangard, which changed hands several times during the day. South of the Luce River the Germans were driven out of important positions which the French occupied and held firmly against repeated attempts made by the enemy to drive them out.

The Germans had by this time advanced to within three miles of Ypres, which was now threatened. The struggle for Voormezeele, the point at which the Germans had pushed closest to Ypres from the south, was prolonged and intense. They made a costly and futile effort to capture the wood southwest of the town on the 26th. The attack was desperately pushed, but met with disaster. Not only were their losses heavy in dead, but several hundred prisoners were taken by the Allied troops. Meanwhile the French were successful on their front from La Clytte to Locre (two miles west of Kemmel). Strong bodies of German troops under General von Arnim after four violent assaults captured Locre, but the French organized a strong counterattack and regained the village. They also won Hospice and Locrehof Farm, both strong points lying southeast of the place.

Ypres now came under heavy fire of the German guns; high explosives and gas shells rained down upon the ruins of the city for the first time in some months. Fields and villages around hitherto untouched by fire were showered with shells. The purpose was to catch the traffic on the roads and destroy soldiers' camps, but the only result was a few women and children killed.

Throughout the night of April 28, 1918, German batteries were active from the Belgian front down through Flanders to the districts about Béthune. About 6 o'clock in the morning, on the 29th, an attack was made according to the plan of General von Arnim after gaining Kemmel Hill; this was the capture of the chain of hills running westward below Ypres to Poperinghe, among them such familiar landmarks as Mont Rouge and Mont Noir. These hills, held at the time by the French, were of great tactical importance, forming the central keep, as it were, in the Allies' defense lines south of Ypres.

It was the purpose of the Germans, in case their frontal attacks against the French failed, to break the British lines on the French left between Locre and Voormezeele and on the French right near Merris and Meteren, but all their efforts failed.

On April 28, 1918, British flyers discovered the Germans massing troops on the road between Zillebeke and Ypres. A dense fog prevailed at the time, and a surprise attack was evidently planned. This never developed, for the assembly was promptly shelled by the British gunners and dispersed. After a tremendous bombardment that shook the whole country-side the German troops again assembled in the misty dawn and were again dispersed by British guns. The fighting in this area was almost continuous throughout the following day.

Around the Scherpenberg and Mont Rouge the Germans fiercely assailed the French lines and succeeding in making a wedge for a time, captured the crossroads, but were counter-attacked by General Pétain's men, who drove them out of most of the ground they had gained there.

A tremendous barrage was flung down by the German gunners from Ypres to Bailleul, and somewhat later they began the battle by launching an attack between Zillebeke Lake and Meteren. South of Ypres they crossed the Yser Canal near Voormezeele with the purpose of striking the British, while they tried to push past Locre against the French holding the three hills. As a result of the day's fighting the British lines remained intact, while General von Arnim's hosts were shattered and decimated. On the French front the Germans won a little ground, but it was unimportant in relation to the situation.

On April 29, 1918, French troops carried out a brilliant counterattack in the night, recovering ground on the slope of the Scherpenberg and advanced their line 1,500 yards astride the Dranoutre road. They alone drove the Germans out of positions around Locre and entered into full possession of the village itself.

The Germans still occupied Mont Kemmel, but their hold on the height was of little value, as the Allied artillery kept the summit smothered with shell fire, making it impossible for the enemy to maintain any considerable body of troops there.

The French and British were elated over the outcome, for the greatest effort made by the Germans in the Flanders offensive had failed. In addition to a large number of divisions in position at the beginning of the battle the Germans had employed about thirty fresh battalions of reserves. Von Armin's great thrust had been carefully planned and his troops fought with reckless bravery if not with distinction. The French and British had defeated him with relatively smaller forces and had shown that their men were more than equal to the best German soldiers. Owing to the close fighting and frequent hand-to-hand encounters, the Franco-British capture of prisoners (over 5,000) was less than might have been expected in a struggle of such magnitude.

While the Germans up to the first of May had failed to make any farther advance on the scale of the first days of the big offensive, they were still a menace to be reckoned with. It was estimated that they had already thrown 2,000,000 men into the line, but many fresh divisions were available for further efforts. They had enough men in their depots in the interior to fill all their gaps for some time; but reconstituted divisions, as is well known, never equal in fighting quality the original formation, as a large number of slightly wounded men after recuperation is included.

As the Germans did not publish their losses, no correct estimate could be formed. Conservative opinion placed the number as over 350,000 men. The Germans had 186 divisions on the western front when the offensive began, and reenforcements brought from Russia and other fronts raised the number to 210 divisions; a German division consisting of about 12,000 men.

For some time it was a mystery to the Allies as to how the Germans succeeded in bringing forward new divisions into the battle area and so often escaping the notice of the vigilant French and British observers. This the Germans accomplished by exercising the greatest precaution and cunning.

In the first place the territory occupied by each German army corps was divided into two zones, the first of which might be under observation of the Allies' lookouts, and the other only from captive balloons which had a wide radius of view. According to German army orders, infantry occupying the first zone were forbidden on clear days to move in any greater number than four men together, mounted men not more than two together, and vehicles not more than two at a time, with a minimum of 300 yards between groups. In heavy, misty weather, these restrictions were relaxed and the movement of groups of forty foot soldiers, twenty cavalrymen, and ten vehicles was permitted.

In the second zone it was permissible to form groups of the size allowed in the first zone, on days of poor visibility, but there must be intervals of 500 yards. It was in this manner that the Germans' military movements were often hidden from the Allies' observers. German divisions making forced marches in the night slept in the villages during the day, and were heavily punished if they showed themselves in the streets.

No infantry operations were attempted by the Germans on May 1-2, 1918, but German gunners continued at regular intervals to bombard the Franco-British lines. General Pétain took advantage of the lull in the fighting to advance his lines between Hailles and Castel (south of the Avre), meeting with little opposition, capturing Hill 82 and the wood near by bordering on the river.

The Germans became active again on May 3, 1918, when, after a heavy artillery barrage, they attacked British positions south of Locon (on the southern flank of the Lys salient). They were easily repulsed and made no further attempt that day to renew the attack. On May 4th, 1918, British and French troops carried out a successful operation between Locre and Dranoutre, gaining ground on a half-mile front to an average depth of 500 yards and capturing a number of prisoners. The Germans were driven from three ruined farms that were perfect strongholds, and high ground was won by the Allies near Koutkot (west of Dranoutre). All these local successes were of real value, for they strengthened the Allied defenses of the approach to Scherpenberg and Mont Rouge.

May 5, 1918, was a great day for those irrepressible fighters, the Australians, who gave the Germans a bad thrashing west and southwest of Morlancourt between the Ancre and the Somme Rivers.

The Australians' attack was made on a front of 2,500 yards unheralded by any preliminary bombardment, but the British guns became active after they were on their way, keeping roads and tracks under fire to prevent the enemy from bringing up supports.

The German garrison on this front did not occupy any definite trench system, but occupied scattered rifle pits and rifle trenches just large enough to afford shelter for small groups and machine-gun crews. These hornets' nests were dangerous things to tackle, but the Australians had dealt with such conditions before and went about their work in a cool and businesslike manner. With bombs and bayonets the Germans were killed or driven out of their holes, and as they were all picked men selected for their courage and long experience in warfare they made a gallant resistance. The Australian generally fights better when he has a desperate opponent, and the struggle became intense and at close quarters. In the end the men from overseas crushed all opposition, killing over 150 Germans and taking about 200 prisoners. The success of this minor operation was of some importance, as it enabled the Allies to advance their line 500 yards.

At this time, in the course of the offensive, the Germans introduced, as a new form of "frightfulness," a sneezing powder, that was fired by high explosive shells. The sneezing powder sifts down through the gas masks and causes sneezing when the wearer is forced to take off his mask and receives the full effect of the lethal gases which the Germans had spread abroad.

Preparations were now under way for a new offensive. It was known to the Allies that Ludendorff had already massed 70 divisions and that reenforcements of men and guns were daily brought into the fighting area. The Germans now sought for a basis for a new drive, feeling their way by making thrusts here and there on the Allies' front. On May 8, 1918, they made a drive at the British lines in the battle area north of Kemmel in the Lys salient, penetrating trenches between La Clytie and Voormezeele. About 25,000 German troops took part in this attack. In the night General Haig's men came back in force and drove them out, but the Germans contested the field again and again during the following day. They won a little ground here and there, but were eventually thrown back and the British remained in sole possession of the terrain.

North of Albert the Germans captured a small but important strip of trenches on high ground. Their temporary success was dearly won, for they suffered terrible slaughter from the rifle and machine-gun fire which poured into their ranks as they advanced up the slopes. By a brilliant counterassault the Germans were driven out of the position won before they could organize the defenses. East of Bouzincourt, where the British occupied positions on high ground, the enemy followed much the same tactics, but they were unable to gain even temporary foothold in the British defenses. The graycoats advanced, shouting in English "retire," in the hopes of confusing the British. The response of the defenders was such a fierce fire that the Germans acted on their cry and fell back in disorganized masses, leaving hosts of dead on the field.

Along the greater part of the front military operations were now confined to small enterprises. The Allies assumed a waiting attitude expecting that the enemy would show his hand. The Germans had brought a large number of divisions into the line facing Amiens, indicating an offensive in that direction. The attempts to "feel out" the Allies' strength had received so many setbacks that they hesitated to begin any new operation on a large scale.

Days passed and still the Germans failed to start a great offensive. It was a period officially called "quiet," though on many parts of the front the guns were active, and raids and minor operations were carried out every day and night. There was continued fighting between French and Germans for the possession of Mont Kemmel, which changed hands again and again. Its value lay in the fact that the hill dominates considerable territory, and for that reason was long a thorn in the flesh of the ambitious Germans.

The anticipated German offensive so long delayed was begun on May 27, 1918. At 1 a. m. a terrific bombardment in which gas shells predominated was opened along a forty-mile front between Noyon and Rheims.   The hurricane of fire continued undiminished for three hours when the Germans launched an assault with about 325,000 men against the Franco-British lines.

The German objective was the famous plateau, the Chemin-des-Dames, a long, bare ridge whose widest part is on the west and narrowest above Craonne.   It was against this narrowest point on the ridge that was held by a British division that the main blow was aimed.   The German forces, which far exceeded in numbers the defenders of the ridge, included some of the specially trained units that had fought in Von Hutier's army in March, two divisions of the Prussian Guards, and other crack formations. Having gained the ridge at a heavy cost, the Germans pressed on westward.   The Allies retreated toward the Aisne, inflicting, as they fell back, heavy losses on the Germans, who drove forward great masses of troops over their dead comrades' bodies.   The Germans pushed on over an eighteen-mile front in pursuit of the Allies and crossed the river.

North of the Aisne the Germans carried by storm a number of towns and drove a wedge southward from the Aisne to Fismes on the River Vesle, which the Germans crossed at several points. In the sector northwest of Rheims the British troops were forced back toward Berry-au-Bac and across the Aisne-Marne Canal. As a result of the first day's fighting the Germans advanced 10 miles and claimed the capture of 15,000 prisoners.

On the second day of the offensive the Germans continued their attacks on the French troops on the right wing of the Aisne offensive, and forced them to evacuate Soissons except for the western outskirts.   German forces of the center were now in possession of the territory between the Aisne and Vesle Rivers, and a considerable area to the south of the last-named stream, having extended their advance in this region four miles.

The fighting continued unabated all day on May 30, 1918, in the Aisne-Vesle area between Soissons and Rheims.   The German flanks near these two cities being firmly held by the French, the Germans were throwing their entire strength southward evidently with the intention of establishing themselves on the Marne.

This would enable them to direct their main efforts westward, counting on the river to protect their flank. On the whole southern front the fighting was of the most violent character, and it was here that the Allies had to give most ground. Fère-en-Tardenois, four or five miles south of the farthest point of the German advance on the 29th, was occupied by the Germans. They also captured Vezilly to the eastward. In the Rheims sector the crown prince's forces occupied the northern parts of La Neuvillete and Betheny, a mile nearer to Rheims on the northwest and northeast.

The most serious blow to the Allies in the German advance was not the loss of 35,000 men which the Germans claimed as prisoners, for that was a comparatively small number in an offensive of such magnitude, but the loss of artillery and stores which was enormous. The depth of the German advance had carried their lines beyond the positions of even the heaviest guns of the Allies. It is a slow process to move great cannon, as tractors are required, and so in the swift onrush, many were captured with ammunition dumps containing great stores of shells.

On May 31, 1918, the Germans extended their effort on the right as far as the Oise by heavy attacks in the region of the Ailette. The French were driven back, fighting, on positions to the north of the linc of Blerancourt-Epagny. In the region of Soissons, and farther south, the German assault was shattered by the brilliant fighting of the French, who maintained their position on the western outskirts of the town, and along the road to Château-Thierry. In the center the Germans were advancing north of the Marne and gained positions south of Fère-en-Tardenois. This forward movement of about eight miles, which the Germans had carried out in the space of twenty-four hours against strong opposition, was indeed a notable military achievement. They also forced the withdrawal of French lines northwest of Soissons toward Noyon, thus linking up the Aisne operations with those on the Picardy front.

In this advance the Germans had the advantage of superior numbers and moreover the French troops were tired out, having fought almost continuously day and night for nearly a week. As

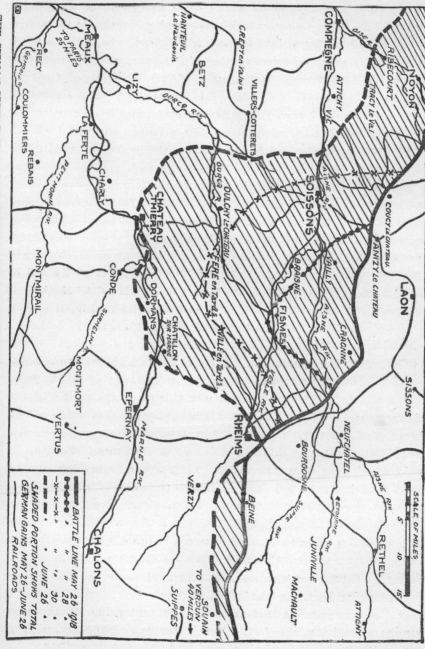

THE GERMAN DRIVE TOWARD PARIS WHICH BEGAN MAY 27, 1918.

an added advantage the Germans were well equipped with light and heavy machine guns, which were kept going all the time.

Eastward, in the neighborhood of Rheims, where the French and British were fighting together, the Germans were unable to make any progress of importance. South of Soissons they attempted to renew their advance. In this thrust they employed a number of tanks, but met with strong resistance from the French and were driven back without gaining a foot of ground.

The Germans claimed to have captured, in the course of the offensive, 45,000 prisoners, 400 guns, and several thousand machine guns.

CHAPTER XXXIX

DARK DAYS FOR THE ALLIES — THE GERMAN OFFENSIVE DECLINES — FRENCH GAIN IN THE RHEIMS REGION — BRITISH VICTORY AT HAMEL

THE situation that confronted the Allies had become serious. It was impossible to question the importance of the German advance. In the center of their new line of attack they had won their strategic objective, the Marne, there to establish a new front, and make preparations for pressing the fight on a new north and south line between Soissons and Château-Thierry.

If the Germans were successful, they would be able to advance westward toward Paris and complete the new front by joining up with their positions around Noyon at the head of the Oise Valley.

Continuing their successful advance to the Marne, they turned their energies toward the west and made an advance of five miles along the Ourcq River to the neighborhood of Neuilly and Cheny. In the region between Hartennes and Soissons farther north the Germans were unable to make any important gains, owing to the stubborn resistance of the French forces, increased by fresh troops brought into the battle area.

The Germans, though vastly superior in numbers over the Allies, continued to swell their fighting force. The formidable nature of their effort may be gauged from the identification of the Franco-British officers of nearly fifty of their divisions, or about 675,000 men. They had also many other divisions in immediate support. Opposing this mighty host the French and British had about a fifth of this number engaged, and although the Germans succeeded in throwing the Allies back, they had not been able to make a breach in their lines.

The German drive in the main area of activity between Château-Thierry and Soissons began to weaken during June 1-2, 1918, owing to the vigor of the French counterattacks, which continued day and night.

North of the Aisne the crown prince's forces succeeded in capturing Mont de Choissy (northwest of Soissons) after strong attacks, but only held it a short time when they were driven out by French bayonets.

During the night of June 1, 1918, operating between Soissons and Château-Thierry, the Germans with strong forces and operating in a five-mile front, made a gain of three miles over the previous day's advance, occupying the towns of Longpont, Corcy, Faverolles, and Troesnes. Later all these places but Faverolles were won back by the French.

On the Marne the situation remained unchanged. The Germans were in possession of the eastern half of Château-Thierry while the French occupied the western half of the town.

Northwest of this place, in the Neuilly St. Front region, the French made some headway, driving the Germans back on Passy-en-Valois and capturing an elevation known as Hill 163.

The German push had now slowed down. They continued local attacks that failed in every instance. The French held firm north of the Aisne, the most important sector of the battle front. The problem confronting the Germans was to link up the front in Picardy with that along the Aisne, which would extend their positions at Amiens, but this they had failed to accomplish. South of the Forest of Villers-Cotterets they had made repeated efforts to extend their positions along the Marne and throw the French back toward the Ourcq, but met only with defeat. It was along this stretch of the line that the American troops, as noted elsewhere, gave the French such valuable support.

In Flanders the situation of the German forces was much the same; they were held in a wedge, the sides of which they could not break through, one heel of the wedge being on high ground west of Kemmel and the other on the ridge in the rear of Béthune.

In the Aisne fighting area Germans were also held in a wedge much larger in extent, one heel of which was about Rheims, and the other west of Soissons. From this position the Germans must sooner or later endeavor to extricate themselves.

One of the most important factors in the battle, the mastery of the air, had passed to the Allies. German troops attacking or on the march were harried without respite by the Allies' pilots flying at tree-top level. Day and night centers behind the German lines were bombed on a scale hitherto undreamed of. In one day the French launched sixty-three tons of bombs at important points on the German bases.

June 6, 1918, on the Picardy front, the Americans made an advance of two and a half miles in the Château-Thierry sector. Details of the fighting here will be found in another place. Between the Ourcq and the Marne, French and American troops made an attack that resulted in the gain of two-thirds of a mile in the neighborhood of Veuilly-la-Peterie and the capture of nearly 300 prisoners.

The Franco-American forces continued to make gains with an advance in the Chezy sector northwest of the line. The Germans, it appeared, were in an exhausted condition and their resistance lacked spirit.

The Allies' reconquest of dominant points had greatly improved the tactical situation. German efforts in the Marne Valley were fading out now that they were confronted by the Allies' forces in numbers proportionate to their own.

An important attack was launched by the Germans early in the morning of June 9, 1918, on a front of more than twenty miles between Montdidier and Noyon. They gained ground in the center to a depth of two and a half miles and to a less degree on the wings of the attack. The southern limit of the German thrust was the villages of Ressons-sur-Matz and Mareuil. The French kept them from crossing the covering zone, and on the French right toward Noyon they were similarly held.

It was the opinion of experienced military observers that the war had witnessed no more severe fighting than in this sector, which resulted indeed in a German advance, but at what a cost! When the German infantry began coming over in dense masses they encountered a withering fire of machine guns and artillery that mowed them down in groups and cut great gaps in the moving wall. But as fast as the ranks melted away fresh waves of men swept forward and filled the empty spaces, and the massacre, for such it should be called, continued. Only the iron discipline of German military rule could have forced soldiers to face such tornadoes of fire.

It was evident that the prowess of the American soldier had stimulated the German command to take the most desperate chances, in the hope of forcing a decision before the Allies were further reenforced by the troops of the great republic. There could be no other explanation for the Germans' reckless waste of man power, the frenzied attempts to crush a foe by sheer weight of numbers.

Early in the morning of June 11, 1918, the French evacuated the Dreslincourt-Ribecourt angle, and fell back on the Matz. This region, with its numerous valleys and wooded hills, offered facilities for the tactics of "infiltration." Once it was turned by way of the Matz, the defenders, with the Oise behind them, could not continue to hold firm without risking great losses of men and material.

During the night of June 10, 1918, an enemy offensive, employing large numbers of fresh troops, attacked the French forces farther west, and flung them back along the Estrées Road as far as the Arende Valley. The French, however, had brought up reserves and in a dashing counterattack the enemy ranks were broken, an operation which brought them back to their former positions south of Belloy and Marqueglise.

By the prodigal waste of men (and it must be acknowledged that there was method in some of the madness) the Germans had obtained these results. By forcing their way down the Matz Valley at a prodigious cost the German columns had reached forward from Rassons to Marqueglise, Vandelicourt, and Elincourt, thus turning the wooded plateau of Thiescourt to the southwest.

These operations left the French cornered on the narrow range of hills before Ribecourt on the Oise, with another salient on the other side of the river, consisting of the woods of Ourscamp and Carlepont, which occupied low ground.

A strong effort was made on the German right to widen the front of the offensive movement. They had advanced from Mortemer and Cuvilly beyond Belloy and the hamlet of St. Maur. The columns of General von Hutier were now within a few miles of Estrées St. Denis and Compiègne, respectively, road and railway junctions of some importance.

During the night of June 10, 1918, Australian troops carried out a highly successful movement which advanced the British lines on the battle front north of the river Somme between Sailly-Laurette and Morlancourt.

The Australians drove forward along the high ground which runs east and west below Morlancourt. They attacked on a front of over a mile and a half, advancing the line south of the village about half a mile and capturing 233 prisoners, 21 machine guns and considerable war material.

Southeast of Montdidier, on June 11, 1918, the Germans were about to strike a hard blow with four divisions, when the French forestalled them by a sudden attack. The battle continued throughout the night and morning hours of the following day, the Allies advancing their line to the east of Mery, a point of considerable importance, as it commands the valley and surroundings. Toward the center the Germans struck a succession of hard blows at the line, but it held fast, although some enemy detachments succeeded in penetrating the Matz Valley through the woods. The French fought yard by yard as the Germans tried by overwhelming numbers to drive them back. The result of the fighting in this region, which lasted for two days and a night, was a small gain of ground for the Germans, but this was won at such a heavy price that the French considered they had won a victory.

Fighting continued on the Montdidier-Noyon battle ground on the following day, the French pushing forward around Belloy and St. Maur and gathering in prisoners, some cannon, and machine guns. In the center Foch's troops were holding fast, but on the right the Germans, after repeated efforts, gained a foothold on the southern bank of the Matz River, and occupied the village of Melicocq and the heights near by. East of the Oise along the line of Bailly, Tracy-le-Val and Nampœl the French troops withdrew under the protection of covering detachments without the enemy being aware of the movement. In the region east of Veuilly, where the French were fighting at the left of the United States marines and infantry, considerable ground was gained. Montcourt was occupied, and the southern portion of Bussières.

On June 13, 1918, the Germans gathered strong forces, between 30,000 and 40,000 men, and attacked the line from Courcelles to Mery. As a result, they were heavily punished and after eight hours of costly efforts were forced back, their ranks shattered and in an exhausted condition. The fifth day of the fighting marked a definite check of enemy operations. The Allies were well content since the Germans had paid such an enormous cost for the ground they had gained. The five-days' battle west of the Oise had ended for the Germans in a costly reverse after they had made an advance varying from two to six miles.

This last offensive showed that the Germans had not been able to maintain the driving power that characterized their first onrush. In their drive on Amiens, which lasted for ten days, the Allies lost a tract of territory forty miles deep, and their casualties were heavy. The German attack in the north was of about the same duration, but their gains were much less. After the conquest of the Chemin-des-Dames the crown prince's forces had pushed on to the Marne, twenty-five miles distant, but here they had been unable to carry out any successful operations. In studying the situation the Germans' gain in territory was not of first importance. They had failed to attain their object, which was to

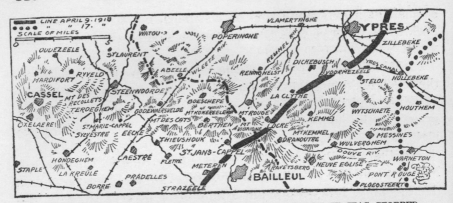

THE GERMAN THRUST SOUTH OF YPRES AND WHERE IT WAS STOPPED

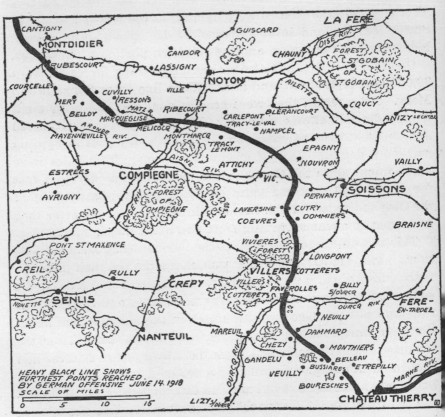

WHERE FOCH DEFINITELY STOPPED THE GERMAN OFFENSIVE, JUNE 14, 1918

divide the French and British army and then destroy one of them, and their attempt in a series of converging operations to crush both Allies was also a failure.

The German offensive for the time being was now definitely checked, and no important operations were undertaken. Trench raids and bombardments were of daily and nightly occurrence, but along the fighting front it was "a quiet period" in a military sense.

During the night of June 14-15, 1918, British and Scottish troops by a swift stroke attacked German outpost lines on a front of about two miles and won a long strip of ground, with 200 prisoners and about 25 machine guns. The scene of this interesting operation was before Hinges, and the Allies had a special grudge against the Germans occupying the posts in this neighborhood, for some of them belonged to the Eighteenth German Division of infamous memory; the first German division to enter Belgium at the beginning of the war, and active participants in the reign of terror at Louvain and Termonde. This division had been fighting ever since they were shooting civilians in Belgium, and there were probably few left of Von Kluck's original forces, for they had been marked out for special attention by the British and French.

This neat operation carried out by the British in the Lys sector was duplicated by the French on the following day when they attacked north and northwest of Hautebraye, between the Oise and the Aisne, and improved their positions there. The Germans counterattacked with fury, but were thrown back on their own lines. The French took 375 prisoners and 25 machine guns.

On June 18, 1918, the comparative quiet which had reigned for some days on the French front was broken. At 9 o'clock in the evening the First German Army under the command of General Fritz von Below made a frontal attack upon the salient of which the devastated city of Rheims formed the head. It was estimated that the Germans had 40,000 troops engaged in the assault along the front extending from Vrigny Plateau to Sillery.

The orders were to carry the city at all costs, a counterblow to compensate the Germans for their failure to capture Compiègne.

The counterbattery work of the French gunners dislocated all their plans and their losses were enormous. At every point the Germans were thrown back. So admirably was the French artillery served that the Germans gained nothing even in the first onrush, though hundreds of their cannon were busy and high explosives and gas shells were showered on the French lines.

The front of the new German attack was the semicircle they had drawn about Rheims in the recent offensive on the Aisne front. The Rheims region comprised the left flank of the German attack. The French had given ground on both sides of the city, but still held Rheims itself and the protecting forts near by. As the Germans hemmed in the city on three sides, it was only a question of time when they would attempt to drive out the defenders. The attack we have described was on a front from Viny, west of the city, to La Pompelle, and approximately fourteen miles.

In the Seicheprey region, and northwest of Montdidier, in front of Cantigny, and in the neighborhood of Belleau Wood, the American troops, as noted elsewhere, were fighting with valor and distinction.

For some days following trench and air raids constituted the principal activities on the French front. The Germans "lay low," but it was well known that they were preparing for a new offensive, as they were cunningly maneuvering into position their reserves for an attack. There were no sure indications where the blow would fall.

The Allies meanwhile were busy "nibbling" at the enemy lines whenever a chance offered, gaining ground and taking prisoners in minor operations that amounted to little when judged separately, but were of importance in the aggregate.

The Germans received a surprise and a shaking up, on June 28, 1918, when some British battalions attacked them opposite the Forest of Nieppe, to the west of Merville. The British advanced on a front of about three miles. Opposing them were two divisions of Saxons and Prussians, the 32d Saxon and the 44th German. They were making ready for breakfast when the

British bombardment opened upon them, preceding the advance of British infantry.

The surprise of the Germans was complete, for the British were upon them before they could do much. Some of the British troops found a trench that had been dug between two organized shell holes, where they captured forty of the enemy and a number of machine guns. These they procceded to turn on German positions ahead and in a short time it was all over, the British winning their objective with only light casualties. Everything had passed smoothly for the British; what their soldiers called "a romp." And the results were worth while. They had captured a strip of territory three miles wide and nearly a mile deep, and taken over 350 prisoners and 22 machine guns.

At the same hour the British launched this attack the Australians carried out a minor operation west of Merris which resulted in the capture of German outposts and a considerable number of prisoners and guns.

In the night of June 29, 1918, the French carried out a brilliant coup south of the Forest of Villers-Cotterets. Driving forward along a front of 1.8 miles, they advanced their line 800 yards, capturing a height of considerable strategic importance between Molloy and Passy-en-Valois. Nearly 1,200 Germans were taken and a number of machine guns.

On the same night the British made a drive at the German lines north of Albert, and forced them out of a strong position which they held on the tip of a crest overlooking the valley of the Ancre. The British assault was entirely successful. The important position was won and all the highest ground in the vicinity.

That the American troops in France were becoming well seasoned fighters was shown on July 1, 1918, when they captured the village of Vaux, and the Bois de la Roche west of Château-Thierry. Details of this interesting operation will be found in another place.

After a day of quiet on the rest of the front, French forces operating in the neighborhood of Autrèches, northwest of Soissons, made a drive at the German lines, and gained nearly half

War St. 7—U

a mile of territory. A second attack delivered later in the same region between Autrèches and Moulin-sous-Toutevent gave them more ground. In these drives the French captured more than 1,000 prisoners.

The Australian troops, who had always shown a fondness for giving the Germans surprise parties, carried out another on July 4, 1918, when advancing on a four-mile front they gained territory a mile and a half deep, including the village of Hamel and the trench system beyond it south of the Somme. In this dashing advance over 1,500 Germans were captured.

The Australians went over the top about 3 o'clock in the morning. The British artillery in this region was very strong and quite smothered the Germans' guns, which were late in getting under way.

The Germans had four divisions on this front holding the ground south of Vaux-sur-Somme, garrisoning the village of Hamel and Vaire Wood and the trench system on the other side of Hamel.

The advance of the Australians was facilitated by a squadron of tanks which led the way. Heavy smoke screens hid the moving forts from the German antitank guns. Behind these lumbering monsters came the infantry in open lines, following closely the barrage as it moved slowly forward ahead of them.

The first stages of the Australian advance were made through semidarkness, but by the time they had reached the German lines light from a pale sky was sifting through the fog and there was fair visibility.

Three or four British tanks came to grief, but their casualties were small, since by this time the Australians were masters of the situation as the Germans were tumbling out of their trenches and dugouts and surrendering in batches.

Over the battle field the British aviators were flying back and forth, dipping down now and again to drop bombs on the German positions. The village of Hamel next received their attention and though mostly in ruins, the flyers, using their bombs freely, started many fires in the place, and the German garrison must have had an uncomfortable time of it.

After the British guns had further crushed resistance, Hamel was rushed by the Australians and taken with the loss of only a few men. In Vaire and Hamel Woods, where many German machine guns were stationed and which were strongly held by considerable forces, the Australians made record time in "mopping them up." In less than two hours after they went over the top they had completed the job, eliminating a salient in the British line and gaining much valuable territory.

The German guns in this region did not get really into action until the fight was over, when they began to shell the new Allied positions. In the evening they launched three counterattacks on the wings and center of the Australian lines, but were not pressed with spirit and failed.

In honor of American Independence Day the little French villages close to the firing line displayed the tricolor and American flags. Some of the latter were of home manufacture and lacking in essential details, but they symbolized the friendly feeling of the French toward the great republic.

In proportion as the Germans ceased to press the offensive the French increased their raids on the German lines, capturing positions and points of observation which, apart from their present importance, were valuable assets for the future.

The German command claimed to have taken 15,000 prisoners when the offensive of June 9, 1918, was arrested. Since that date the French and their American comrades had captured about 10,000 Germans in raids and minor operations and had regained quite as much territory as the hordes of General von Hutier had overrun. In the week closing July 6, 1918, the French alone had taken over 4,000 prisoners. All the irregularities in the French line across the Oise to the Marne at Château-Thierry had moreover been straightened out and the defenses strengthened and powerfully organized against future attacks.

On July 6, 1918, the Australians who had carried out such a brilliant attack on the German lines south of the Somme on the Fourth of July began another push in the same sector.

The Germans had been so badly battered in the previous encounter that they had not attempted to retaliate, but had established some advanced posts in no-man's-land which the Australians thought it wise to wipe out. It was known that an epidemic of Spanish influenza was raging among the German troops in this sector, which accounted in a measure for the very poor showing they made. That their morale was shaken may be illustrated by the following incident: After one of the German outposts was under rifle and grenade fire for some time a British soldier went out to see the effect of the damage done. Almost immediately a German officer and twelve men came tumbling out of a dugout and surrendered to him, and the proud Tommy led back his baker's dozen of captives to the British lines.

The Australians in this push on the 6th advanced their line by about 400 yards over a front of about a mile beyond Hamel, which rounded out the gains made in this sector on July 4, 1918.

The Germans continued inactive as far as military operations were concerned, but back of their lines vast preparations were under way, as noted by the Allies' observers, and it was evident that a new offensive would not long be delayed.

Meanwhile the French continued to make gains daily. On July 8, 1918, southwest of Soissons, General Pétain's men broke the German line on a two-mile front in the outskirts of Retz Forest, in the region of Longpont. In this push the French gained three-fourths of a mile, occupying Chavigny Farm and the ridges and heights to the north and south of the farm. In this operation the French captured nearly 400 Germans, of whom four were officers.

A new stroke against the enemy was delivered by the French on the following day when they attacked west of Antheuil between Montdidier and the River Oise on a front of two and a half miles, piercing it to a depth of more than a mile at some points, and making prisoners of 450 men, including fourteen officers. Later the Germans attempted to counterattack in this sector, but it was pressed with vigor and they were thrown back on their own lines.

Up in Flanders there was violent shelling of the British roads around the Scherpenberg, which was the outer bastion of the Allies' defense. Farther to the south the Australians had ad-

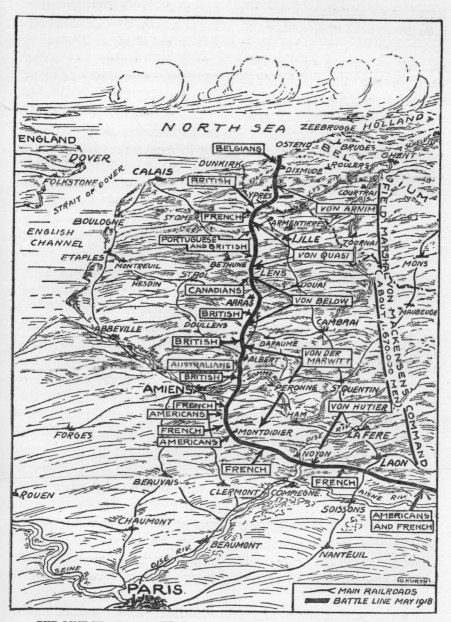

THE LINE-UP AT THE GREAT GERMAN OFFENSIVE, MARCH-JUNE, 1918

vanced their line beyond the German outpost positions near Morris on a 1,200-yard front.

Near the Aisne the French infantry broke the Germans' defenses at several points north of Chavigny Farm. They took possession of the quarries on the east, pushed forward to the outskirts of Longpont, and penetrated the northern section of Corcy. This town was captured on the following day (July 11, 1918), together with the railway station and the château to the south of the place, an important observation point.

The Germans were evidently too much occupied with preparations for a new offensive to trouble themselves with minor operations, as for several days they had only attempted a few feeble attacks that failed in every instance.

In the course of July 12, 1918, the French delivered two hard blows against the German lines that are deserving of record. The most important was struck in Picardy when General Pétain's troops, advancing on a three-mile front north of Mailly-Raineval, broke into the German front to the depth of a mile and a quarter. The village of Castel on the Avre River and important positions south of the village were occupied by the victors, who captured over 500 prisoners of all ranks.

The second blow was delivered in the area southwest of Soissons, where the French had been "nibbling away" for some days with satisfactory results. Here they captured the village of Longpont, a continuation of their advance north of Chavigny Farm and east of Faverolles.

On July 14, 1918, the national fête day of the French Republic, the British and American troops joined heartily in the celebration, and little flags of the Allies fluttered among the ruins and on every building all along the fighting front.

It was a dull day, with gray skies and mist and rain, but the weather could not dampen the enthusiasm of the participants in the fête. It is possible that the weather, however, had something to do with the movements of the Germans, who had probably intended to launch their offensive on the French national holiday, but for the storm. So the attack they had been preparing against the Allies was made early in the morning of the following day.

CHAPTER XL

THE NEW GERMAN DRIVE AROUND RHEIMS—
THE NEW BATTLE OF THE MARNE—THE
ALLIES LAUNCH A GREAT OFFENSIVE
MOVEMENT

IT was shortly after midnight on June 15, 1918, while in some parts of the fighting front British, French, and Americans were still feting the national holiday, that the German guns from the Marne near Château-Thierry heralded the new offensive. Soon along a front of sixty miles, extending to the Argonne, the German artillery was thundering. Men who had seen fighting since the war began describe the artillery preparation for the drive as beyond anything the Germans had attempted up to that time on the French front. Not only were the Allies' lines front and back shelled, but behind the lines to a distance of twenty and thirty miles.

About daybreak the German infantry attacked. East and west of Rheims a large number of tanks assisted the advance. The French had already anticipated the drive and were fully prepared. On the whole front east of Rheims they held up the German hordes for five hours. It was only in the neighborhood of the Souain Road and Prunay that the Germans made any notable advance. Here on a narrow front they succeeded in penetrating for about one and a half miles.

The most important achievement in the morning of the first day was the crossing of the Marne of 15,000 German troops, and an advance of a mile beyond on a ten-mile front.

East of Rheims, and east and west of Château-Thierry, American troops received the full force of the German blows in those sectors. The success of our soldiers in stemming the German advance is described in detail in another place.

In the first day's fighting the Germans employed fifty-six or fifty-seven divisions of their best troops, fourteen on either side of Rheims in the front line, and as many in the second line.

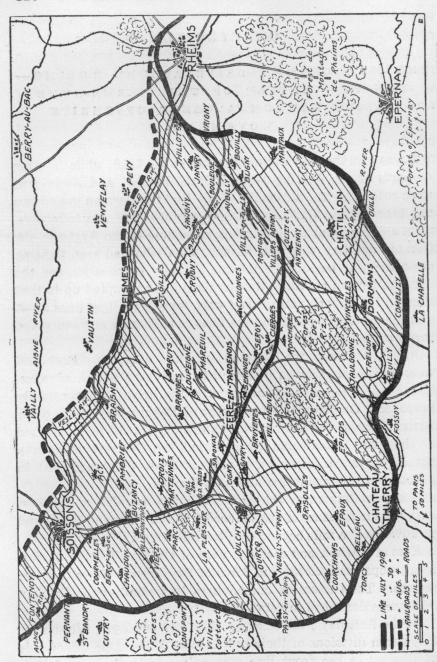

THE ALLIED COUNTEROFFENSIVE ON THE MARNE. THE SHADED PART SHOWS THE GAINS OF THE ALLIES

General von Einem commanded in Champagne, Fritz von Below around Rheims, and General von Boehm on the Marne.

By noon the Germans had begun to throw bridges across the Marne where the river makes a salient northward with the point at Jaulgonne. Three times the American guns shattered the pontoons that the Germans were trying to throw across the river, but the fourth time they succeeded in bridging the stream and made an advance of about two miles, the Americans falling back to the base of the salient made by the river.

Comparative quiet reigned on the fighting fronts during the night following the offensive. The only explanation of the Germans' failure to push on must be attributed to their fear of failure. They had not achieved the success they hoped for in the first onrush and their losses had been far heavier than they anticipated.

From early dawn until dark on the second day of the German offensive (July 16, 1918) the battle raged with unabated fury from Château-Thierry to the Argonne. Southwest of Rheims the Germans started a heavy drive, which they hoped would enable them to reach Epernay, by pushing forward to St. Agnan, La Chapelle and Monthodon. Here they were attacked in force by French and American troops and driven out of the villages of St. Agnan and La Chapelle and from the heights to the north dominating the Marne Valley at this point.

Where the battle front crossed the Marne south of Chatillon intense fighting took place for the possession of Mareuil-le-Pont on the southern bank of the river. General Pétain's troops were heavily reenforced by Americans at this point, but the Germans were in overwhelming numbers, and the Allies were forced to fall back fighting every foot of the way to positions two miles southeast along the river toward Epernay. Later in the day the Germans occupied Chatillon, which marked some progress in the carrying out of their plan to flank Rheims from the west.

Prunay, about five miles southeast of Rheims, was won by the Germans from the French by a strong thrust. The French intrenched themselves on the southern bank of the Vesle River and the enemy was unable to make any further advance in this sector.

West of Rheims the Germans attacked in very considerable strength at two places, by way of the Marne railway and in the region south of Dormans. In this region they succeeded in throwing six bridges across the Marne, between Reuilly and Dormans, but at no point on this twenty-five-mile front did they succeed in penetrating more than four miles into the French positions.

At the close of the second day of the offensive the Germans, according to their official report, claimed to have taken only 13,000 prisoners, a small number indeed considering the large forces they had employed in the advance. In the fighting around Prunay, where the struggle was especially intense, they used up 65 per cent. of their effectives and were forced to bring up reserves into the battle area, which they had been holding back for later attacks.

The third day of the offensive (July 17, 1918) the fighting continued along the whole front and ends, under rainy skies, and occasional showers. The German gains in territory were unimportant except to the southwest of Rheims, where they made an advance of about a mile and a half. East and west of the martyred city most of their attacks were broken up, and the whole Champagne line remained intact.

In the morning, Germans in a determined thrust broke through at Oeuilly on the Marne and captured Montvoisin, seven miles west of Epernay. In the regions west of this they were heavily reenforced by fresh troops, but were unable to make any advance against the magnificent defense of the French forces, who held them firmly on the southern outskirts of Bouquigny and Chataignières. North of St. Agnan the Germans were better favored by fortune, for they succeeded in penetrating La Bourdonnerie. Here the French had the cooperation of American troops and the enemy was held in check.

A decisive blow was struck by the Allies in the morning of July 18, 1918. The mighty counterattack was launched without any preliminary artillery preparation, and proved to be a complete surprise to the enemy. The drive was made on the twenty-eight-mile front from the Aisne to the Marne and in the course of the advance more than twenty villages were captured and the Allies' lines were pushed to within a mile of Soissons.

The ground regained at its extreme width was about six and a half miles in the region to the south of Soissons. The attacking troops drove forward as far east as the little river Crise, an advance especially important, because it gave the Allies possession of high ground that dominated the German supply lines to the city.

To the west of Soissons, American troops carried out successful operations against the enemy, capturing over 4,000 prisoners, 30 guns, and much war material. Farther south on the same side of the German salient the Americans cooperating with French forces captured the town of Vierzy and made an advance of three miles to the east of it.

North of the River Ourcq the Germans fought with desperate and stubborn energy, but they were more than outmatched by the French, who broke down their resistance and drove forward into the western outskirts of Chouy and Neuilly-St. Front, and on to Belleau Wood, an average depth of advance of about three miles.

The magnitude of the French and American effort will be appreciated when it is understood that they had achieved more in this operation than the Germans had accomplished in their hard drive on both sides of Rheims. In six hours French and Americans working together had advanced double the distance it had taken the Germans three days to cover.

South of the Marne, the French lost some ground, but nowhere else could the Germans make gains, while several of their attacks broke down with appalling losses. Montvoisin, which the enemy had captured on the previous day, was recovered by the French. Chêne-la-Réine was also occupied to the west, and what was even more important, the heights west of these villages overlooking the Marne. Other victories of importance were won by the French north of the Marne, where they captured the forest known as Bois du Rois and the village of Venteuil.

French and American forces continued their advance on July 19 between the Aisne and the Marne, gaining ground of about two miles at some points. Since the drive of the Allies began 17,000 Germans had been captured and 360 guns.

In a desperate attempt to stem the tide of the advance, the Germans had brought great numbers of fresh troops into the fighting area. The plateau southwest of Soissons in the Crise River region, which the Germans lost on the previous day, was the scene of an intense and bitterly fought struggle. Despite the Germans' determined efforts to regain the plateau, the Allies firmly held their positions, and in the afternoon began a further advance.

To the south the Germans were driven from the plateau northwest of Bonnes, but not before they had fought with determined resistance that was deserving of better fortune. Progress was also made by the Allies southwest of Rheims, where the French and Italians fought together.

The British, who had so far been spared in the recent German offensive, had a small victory to their credit on the same day (July 19, 1918) that the French, Americans, and Italians were pushing back the enemy all along the front. Meteren, a valuable observation point in the Bailleul sector, was captured by Scottish and Australian troops. Four hundred Germans were taken and a number of machine guns.

Heavy fighting was resumed late in the afternoon of July 19, 1918, along the Aisne-Marne front. The French were fighting uphill, but the Germans could not keep them back, and were slowly pushed out of their strongest positions in this region.

The large numbers of fresh troops thrown into the battle to support the crown prince made it necessary for the French to fight every foot of the way. On a twenty-eight-mile front the average advance of the Allies was only one mile, and they fought hard from noon on July 19, 1918, to 9 o'clock on the following morning to accomplish this.

The Germans, violently attacked on their right flank and south of the Marne, were forced to retreat and recross the river. The whole southern bank of the Marne was now in French possession.

In the three days' fighting the Allies had captured over 20,000 prisoners and over 400 guns.

On the following morning the Allies resumed the offensive, forcing the Germans to give way gradually on both sides of the deep pocket of which Rheims and Soissons mark the edges. In this pocket the Germans suffered heavy casualties from the long-range guns and airplane bombers of the Allies.

Château-Thierry was occupied by French and American troops on July 21, 1918, the Germans evacuating the place under strong pressure. In their withdrawal from that pivot point on the Marne salient they were closely followed by the Allies' forces, who, cooperating with troops at Vaux and to the northward, swept the Germans back for miles, and beyond the highway to Soissons.

Farther north and almost reaching to Soissons, French and American forces drove on to the Soissons-Château-Thierry highway at Hartennes, and gaining the railway under the Allied guns, threatened Oulchy. As a result of these operations the entire front was straightened out and a gain was made of over seven miles of territory.

On the east side of the salient, between Rheims and the Marne, French and British troops fighting shoulder to shoulder were driving back the Germans, who, opposing a strong resistance, and supported by reserves, were unable to stem the Allies' advance. In the course of the fighting in this sector the French and British occupied the village of Bouilly.

The heavy artillery of the Allies continued on July 21, 1918, to hammer German positions in the districts north of the Marne. Indian scouts who were with Pershing in Mexico were active in gathering information in the river region.

In all sections of the line, from Soissons to Rheims, the hard struggle continued with undiminished intensity. Although the Germans maintained a desperate resistance at the bottom of the Marne salient, it was evident that they would be forced soon to make a wide retreat. This was indicated by the great concentration of German troops at the top of the salient which could only mean that they were making preparations to retire to a new line.

The entire Château-Thierry-Soissons highway from the Ourcq south was now occupied by the Allies. Epieds was captured and territory gained northeast of Mont St. Père, and east of La Croix, and Griselles. Near the last place named the Germans gained some slight temporary advantage, but it had no effect on the continued advance the Allies were making.

Having cleared the Germans out of the district south of the Marne, the Allies were busy constructing bridges and getting troops and supplies across the river. On July 22, 1918, the enemy were trying to keep a hold on the river bank extending from Mont St. Père to east of Reuilly. In the face of a furious fire the French succeeded in getting two strong bodies of troops across the stream at Mezy and Courcelles, who at once started the construction of footbridges while under the grilling fire of the German guns.

The Allies continued to make progress in the Soissons-Rheims salient on July 23, 1918, although the Germans with the support of fresh troops developed stubborn resistance. The most important operation of the day was the advance of the French forces on both sides of the Ourcq southward toward Fère-en-Tardenois, the great German supply center. North of the river General Pétain's troops occupied Montgru on the bank of the stream and two other towns.

South of the Ourcq the Allies were even more successful in gaining ground. Here the French and Americans, cooperating, drove the Germans back nearly a mile beyond the Château-Thierry-Soissons road. Meanwhile, in the Montdidier sector, Foch struck a hard blow at the enemy and achieved a brilliant success. The French troops, attacking on a four-mile front north of Montdidier, made a forward drive of two miles, capturing Mailly-Raineval, Savillers, and Aulvillers. The heights commanding the Avre River were also won, and over 1,500 Germans were captured.

At other points, notably east and northeast of Château-Thierry, at the bottom of the great salient, the French troops, ably assisted by American forces, gained ground. Along almost the entire line between the Ourcq and the Marne German resistance was broken by the resistless onward sweep of the Franco-American forces.

During the night of July 23-24, 1918, the Germans delivered a terrific counterattack in the neighborhood of Epieds, where they were opposed by American troops. The Germans succeeded after a hard fight in recapturing the village, and another in the neighborhood, but they were unable to hold their gains. On the following day the Americans drove them out of these villages and pushed on beyond Courpoil, more than a mile to the northeast.

North of this fighting area French troops had penetrated as far as Brecy, while to the southeast French and American troops drove forward through the woods on a wide front beyond Preloup on the Marne. The advance of the Allies at several points was about two miles.

The Germans had nearly half a million troops concentrated in the Marne salient. Attacked on three sides by British, French, and American forces, their position was extremely perilous. To continue resistance in a position so threatened might appear to be an act of madness, yet it was a maxim of Napoleon's that, where forces are about equal, the inside fighters have the advantage over an adversary in concentric formation.

The Allies continued to bend in the salient, the French and Americans on the west, and the French and British on the east. The most important point held by the Germans, and the Allies' main objective, was Fère-en-Tardenois, the junction of several roads, and a chief distributing point.

This nerve center of the German front, subjected to constant cross fire from French and American guns, was fast becoming untenable. Indeed there was no corner of the salient where the Germans were not constantly harried by the artillery of the Allies.

The most important gain made by the Franco-American forces on July 25, 1918, was below the Ourcq River. In the course of this advance the Allies captured Hill 141 southeast of Armentières, and the village of Coincy on the south, and pushing ahead in a northeasterly direction they occupied most of Tournelle Wood, which is only three miles from Fère-en-Tardenois. Farther to the south an advance was made as far as the forest of Fère and to the general line of Beuvardes-Charmel. Ground was also gained north of Dormans on the Meuse.

As a result of these advances the Allies had taken about forty miles of territory from the Germans, and had acquired almost a straight line running southeast from Armentières to Vincelles on the Marne.

In the sector west of Rheims, British and French troops had advanced to Guex and Mery-Premecy, which meant a push of two miles in the direction of Fismes, and the narrowing of the mouth of the salient to that extent.

Ten divisions of reserves had been rushed to the aid of the German crown prince, drawn from the army of Prince Rupprecht of Bavaria in the course of the week's fighting, but the new forces were unable to stay the victorious advance of the Allies.

As the result of the last week's operations the whole situation on the western front was transformed. The Germans had used up sixty-five divisions on the Champagne front and all of the crown prince's reserves. They had only about thirty divisions left belonging to Prince Rupprecht's Army to draw on.

The Germans were certainly in an awkward situation, but it was no worse than that which confronted the British Army in the Ypres salient before the capture of Messines Ridge. The Ypres salient was about five miles wide, and five miles deep, and the German guns commanded it. The German salient was at this time about twenty miles wide by twenty deep, and the artillery of the Allies could sweep every corner of it.

From documents captured from the Germans, it was learned that on the day after the Allies assumed the offensive a retirement was ordered to a line either along the Avre or the Vesle Rivers. These orders were subsequently canceled, because an orderly retreat could not be made in such a pinched salient, so the Germans had been commanded to maintain their positions as long as possible.

Unable to further withstand the tremendous pressure of the Allies' armies, the Germans began a retreat along the whole front north of the Marne late in the morning of July 27, 1918. They relinquished the strong grip they had held on the north bank of the river, which extended from Vincelles nearly ten miles east to Reuil, and also fell back on both flanks.

It was the purpose of the Germans to reach the Ourcq, on a line reaching from Fère-en-Tardenois to the northern top of the De Riz forest which lies before Charmel.

In the course of the day the French, British, and American troops, pressing hard on the heels of the German rear guards, had reached the line of Bruyères, Villeneuve-sur-Fère, and Courment, all within a few miles of the great German supply center of Fère-en-Tardenois, which was now so hemmed in that its evacuation must soon follow. The advance of the Allies in a northeasterly direction from Château-Thierry had now reached ten miles. Since the beginning of the counteroffensive 30,000 German prisoners were taken.

The Allies continued their triumphant progress on July 28, 1918. The Germans in the Soissons-Rheims salient were forced to accelerate the speed of their retirement northward, closely followed by tanks, cavalry, and infantry patrols of the Allies.

French cavalry, supported by some infantry elements, had reached in the morning of July 28, 1918, the district south of Villers-sur-Fère, a little over a mile from Fère-en-Tardenois and Sergy.

The success of the Allies along the whole front was now complete and about half of the pocket in which the enemy had been cornered was retaken.

The Germans were retiring as swiftly as they could, but their losses were tremendous, as French and American troops harried them on the center, and French and British were dealing hammer blows on both of their flanks. While the cavalry were hard at it, the tanks had pushed their way in among the retreating forces, where they did effective work. The Allies' aviators meanwhile, flying a few hundred feet overhead, were machine-gunning columns on the march and bombarding German batteries.

In the Soissons area the Germans had massed a large number of heavy guns on the heights around Juvigny and Chavigny, and from these points they bombarded the western wing as far south as Oulchy-le-Château. Yet the Allies in the Oulchy region continued to make progress, though facing some of the finest German divisions, and the concentrated fire of a vast number of machine guns.

On the eastern wing the Allies were gradually gaining control of the whole road leading from Dormans to Rheims. The Germans had assembled on this side a strong array of artillery near St. Thierry, which served to protect their left flank, and which delayed, though it could not stop, the Allies' advance.

The German retreat, it should be noted, was conducted in an orderly manner and was in no sense a rout. The method of retirement employed at this time, and which the Germans indeed adopted on other occasions, was as follows: One company withdraws from every two on the first line; the remaining troops redouble their fire to give the impression that the line is still strongly held. Out of each remaining company two sections are then taken out, leaving but one section in the line. When this last section is ordered to withdraw, a few men are left behind to occupy small posts well furnished with machine guns and these keep up a vigorous fire to protect the retreat. The few men left behind for this work seldom escape death or capture, but they are sometimes able to regain their own lines.

The retreat continued on July 29, 1918, with the Allies in close pursuit. The Germans had brought more heavy guns into play and succeeded in slowing up the advance, though they could not stop it. In the course of twenty-four hours the Allies had pushed their lines forward from two to three miles on a twenty-mile front. The Germans had been forced to abandon the line of the Ourcq and proposed to fall back to a line beyond the Vesle between Soissons and Rheims.

One of the most important operations at this time was the French drive east and northeast, from the neighborhood of Oulchy-le-Château, at the salient in the German line, which opened the way for the advance of the Allies to Fère-en-Tardenois and beyond. Grand Rozoy and the heights to the north of it were occupied and also Cugny, which stands one mile east of Oulchy. Farther north of Grand Rozoy the troops of General Pétain were pushing forward to capture the hills that dominated a wide area north and south.   In these operations the French captured nearly 500 Germans.

The fighting around Sergy on the north bank of the Ourcq was of a specially violent character, the place changing hands no less than nine times in twenty-four hours.   Here, where the Americans had only the assistance from the French of a few armored cars, they fought practically "on their own" with distinction and bravery.   (Details of their achievements in this struggle are noted in another place.)

To the east, and just north of the Ourcq, the Allies won possession of the villages of Vallée and Givray.   Toward Soissons a hard fight was in progress for the possession of Buzancy.   It had twice been won by the Allies and then the Germans captured it. New Scottish troops, aided by a few British columns, attacked the town and it was won for the Allies.

After defeating the Prussian Guards and Bavarians, the American forces made an advance of two miles beyond Sergy on July 30, 1918.   The German resistance to the Allies' thrusts now became increasingly vigorous.   Along almost the entire front to the east they launched fierce counterattacks, but only succeeded in gaining a little ground near St. Euphraise to the southwest of Rheims.

The main advance of the Allies on the westerly side of the front was near Grand Rozoy, where the French were pushing north to the crest of the plateau between the Vesle and the Ourcq.

The intense struggle which had continued without pause for two weeks on the Marne battle front now showed signs of slackening.   The only fighting worthy of note took place in the Fère region, on the front held by American troops around Seringes and Sergy.   Here the Germans made a hard fight during the night and morning of July 30-31, 1918, to dislodge the forces of General Pershing, but were badly beaten.   (Details of the struggle are described on another page.)

The hope of the Germans that the Allies were in a state of exhaustion, and that the offensive had broken down for the present, was rudely shattered on the first of August, 1918.   On this date the Allies attacked on a ten-mile front from Buzancy to Fère-en-

Tardenois and Seringes. They drove forward nearly two miles at one point, and carried important heights, including Hill 205 north of Grand Rozoy, which resulted in wiping out the angle of the battle line east of Oulchy.

Where the Allies marked their greatest advance was in the region northwest of Fère-en-Tardenois. The villages of Cramoiselle and Cramaille were occupied, as well as Bordeux to the north, and Servenay to the northeast. As a result of this thrust the victors captured 600 prisoners. In the course of the operations from July 15 to July 31, 1918, the Allies had taken 34,400 Germans.

These successful operations on the Buzancy-Fère front, carried out by French forces with the support of British units at the north, linked up the gains made by the Americans on the previous day and night in the area east and southeast of Seringes.

Farther to the east in the Ville-en-Tardenois region, on the left flank of the fast decreasing German salient, French forces, after an especially murderous and close struggle, drove the enemy out of the village of Romigny and occupied the place.

Apart from the important gains in territory made by the Allies in the two weeks' offensive operations, the result of the victories was to shake the belief of the German army in their own invincibility. They had failed in their objectives, first in the thrust toward Rheims, and afterward in their efforts to hold out against a counterassault. Twice they had made determined and exhaustive attempts with large forces of men to stem the advance of the Allies, and had failed in each instance. They had employed their best troops, who fought with courage and daring and with reckless disregard for life, but were unable to build a barrier that the Allies could not shatter. It was not believed by the Allied High Command that the morale of the German fighters had been seriously sapped by their forced retreat, but the news would drift back to Germany in soldiers' letters and in other ways, creating a feeling in the Empire that their army was not equal to its task, and a consequent loss of faith in the flamboyant promises of victory proclaimed by Hindenburg and Ludendorff.

PART IX—THE UNITED STATES AS A BELLIGERENT

CHAPTER XLI

FORCE TO THE UTMOST

ONLY the sword could impose peace. The kaiser said it. His mouthpieces, Count von Hertling and Count Czernin, said it, by way of buttressing much verbal camouflage conveying that their peoples would like peace by gentler means—that is, by the Allies yielding. Lloyd-George said it without camouflage. But it was left to President Wilson to say it with finality. Despairing of drawing from the Central Powers any lucid declaration to show that they were honorable opponents with whom honorable enemies could negotiate, he swept aside German chicanery by leaving no loophole open for the determination of the war by any other means than the sword. Germany had slammed the door of peace in her own face.

Hark the kaiser, accepting an address in Hamburg, in February, 1918, on the conclusion of peace with the Ukraine:

"He who will not accept peace, but on the contrary declines, pouring out the blood of his own and of our people, must be forced to have peace. We desire to live in friendship with neighboring peoples, but the victory of German arms must first be recognized. Our troops under the great Hindenburg will continue to win it. Then peace will come."

The dissembling ministers of Germany and Austria, in essaying public debates with President Wilson, tried to build a fabric of peace on a foundation of sand. In their utterances they

339

"played up" to one another. Their outgivings suggested a vaudeville act in which one player provides cues for the witticisms of the other. Thus, Count Czernin, dense to the Allied scorn of the deceits of his partner, Count von Hertling, announced that Austria, too, agreed that President Wilson's four points provided a suitable basis on which to begin negotiating a general peace. More than that, he complacently viewed President Wilson's address as actually offering an olive branch to Austria:

"He (President Wilson)," he told the Vienna City Council, "thinks, however, that Vienna presents more favorable soil for sowing the seeds of a general peace. He has perhaps said to himself that the Austro-Hungarian Monarchy has the good fortune to have a monarch who genuinely and honorably desires a general peace, but that this monarch will never be guilty of a breach of faith; that he will never make a shameful peace, and that behind this monarch stand 55,000,000 souls.

"I imagine that Mr. Wilson says to himself that this closely knit mass of people represents a force which is not to be disregarded and that this honorable and firm will to peace with which the monarch is imbued and which binds him to the peoples of both states is capable of carrying a great idea in the service of which Mr. Wilson has also placed himself."

No one believed, outside the countries of the Central Powers, that Austria-Hungary was blessed with a monarch who would "never be guilty of a breach of faith," who would "never make a shameful peace," and who ruled over a "closely knit mass of people." In the same breath he said:

"Whatever may happen, we shall not sacrifice German interests any more than Germany will desert us. Loyalty on the Danube is not less than German loyalty."

Here was the real Austria speaking, and her spirit was made more manifest when Count Czernin proceeded to defend the political crime of thrusting peace upon Russia by invasion:

"The first breach in the determination of our enemies to war has been driven by the peace negotiations with Russia. That was a break-through by the idea of peace.

"It is a symptom of childish dilettantism to overlook the close relationship of the various peace signatures with each other. The constellation of enemy powers in the east was like a net. When one mesh was cut through the remaining meshes loosened of their own accord."

Austria plainly wanted peace, but by negotiation, since it was dawning upon the Teutonic powers that they could never effect a peace by force of arms. Wouldn't President Wilson kindly open negotiations without delay? But Germany and Austria must be left with the whole vast east under their control. Apparently Count Czernin was willfully blind to the fact that the terms of peace forced upon Russia and Rumania had closed all avenues of peace in the countries of the Allies.

President Wilson cleared the air. Peace conversations in the world arena with the German chancellor and the Austrian foreign minister had reached a hopeless stage of sterility. They spoke smooth words; their military leaders committed rapacious deeds that made their words an object-lesson in studied irony. On April 6, 1918, the anniversary of America's entrance into the war, the President took occasion to bring about a very decided turning point in the diplomacy of the war. It was a world-stirring declaration, made at Baltimore to inaugurate the campaign for the Third Liberty Loan, and told the Teutonic powers that their arduous and ever-recurrent peace propaganda had killed itself.

" . . . I have sought to learn from those who spoke for Germany," he said, "whether it was justice or dominion and the execution of their own will upon the other nations of the world that the German leaders were seeking. They have answered— answered in unmistakable terms. They have avowed that it was not justice, but dominion and the unhindered execution of their own will. The avowal has not come from Germany's statesmen. It has come from her military leaders, who are her real rulers. . . .

"We cannot mistake what they have done—in Russia, in Finland, in the Ukraine, in Rumania. The real test of their justice and fair play has come. From this we may judge the rest. . . .

"Their purpose is, undoubtedly, to make all the Slavic peoples, all the free and ambitious nations of the Baltic Peninsula, all the lands that Turkey has dominated and misruled, subject to their will and ambition, and build upon that dominion an empire of force upon which they fancy that they can then erect an empire of gain and commercial supremacy—an empire as hostile to the Americas as to the Europe which it will overawe—an empire which will ultimately master Persia, India, and the peoples of the Far East. . . .

"That program once carried out, America and all who care or dare to stand with her must arm and prepare themselves to contest the mastery of the world—a mastery in which the rights of common men, the rights of women and of all who are weak, must for the time being be trodden underfoot and disregarded and the old, age-long struggle for freedom and right begin again at its beginning. Everything that America has lived for and loved and grown great to vindicate and bring to a glorious realization will have fallen in utter ruin and the gates of mercy once more pitilessly shut upon mankind!

"The thing is preposterous and impossible; and yet is not that what the whole course and action of the German armies has meant wherever they have moved? I do not wish, even in this moment of utter disillusionment, to judge harshly or unrighteously. I judge only what the German arms have accomplished with unpitying thoroughness throughout every fair region they have touched.

"What, then, are we to do? For myself, I am ready, ready still, ready even now, to discuss a fair and just and honest peace at any time that it is sincerely purposed—a peace in which the strong and the weak shall fare alike. But the answer, when I proposed such a peace, came from the German commanders in Russia and I cannot mistake the meaning of the answer.

"I accept the challenge. I know that you accept it. All the world shall know that you can accept it. . . .

"Germany has once more said that force, and force alone, shall decide whether justice and peace shall reign in the affairs of men, whether right as America conceives it or dominion as she conceives it shall determine the destinies of mankind. There is, therefore, but one response possible from us:

"Force, force to the utmost, force without stint or limit, the righteous and triumphant force which shall make right the law of the world and cast every selfish dominion down in the dust!"

Germany only recognized physical force; no other force counted. President Wilson, in countering, set at its true measure the might of the United States, joined with the might of the other active belligerents, Great Britain, France, and Italy.

CHAPTER XLII

THE AMERICAN LEGIONS

WHEN the German spring offensive of 1918 came and hewed a great dent in the western front, the cry went up from the Allied capitals for American aid. "Hurry!" entreated Lloyd-George. "Hurry!" came the echo from Paris. Then, almost like an answering echo, was heard the tramp of American legions on the soil of France. Week after week, through the spring and summer, United States troops spread their columns fanwise from their ports of debarkation, until their multiplying presence was felt, where not seen, along the entire fighting line from the Belgian coast to the Swiss frontier.

Another army had preceded them, armed with picks and shovels, trowels and axes. It was an army of tool chests, building gear and rails. More than one western port of France, slumbering in its ancient ways, had to be transformed, to give proper entrance to the shiploads of soldiers from the New World, with their mountainous equipment, and new roads had to be cut through France to convey them to the front. One regiment was of foresters, with knocked-down sawmills, who went into the woods of France to cut down trees and shape them into timbers for building large docks. Another corps of advance guards were the American engineers, later organized into five regiments and nineteen battalions, all engaged in railroad construction and operation to facilitate the movement of American troops. So with new and spacious gateways, which transformed the restricted port facilities of the French coast towns, and with huge warehouses, ordnance depots and barracks neighboring the new docks, the American troops found an ingress on French soil and accommodation for themselves and their leviathan equipment in keeping with the vast scheme of warfare that represented American belligerency.

From the French ports ran a double line of railroad which was extended by American army engineers to the battle front. The use of these preexisting lines for American troops called for the additional construction of hundreds of miles of trackage for yards, sidings, and switches. Thus was called into being the United States Military Railroad in France. It started from the seaport terminals, with their new docks verdant with the rawness of fresh-cut timber, with their tipples and cranes and wharf houses and warehouses, and spread over a mass of tracks that meandered and forked into division yards, curved on to divergent lines or connected with light railways at the fighting front some 600 miles distant.

With new ports and new railroad systems virtually constructed for their passage, the American troops moved to their allotted places at the front under conditions that gave their journey an uncommon éclat. They were sorely needed, for one thing, and, for another, preexisting port and transit facilities did not suffice to bear them to their destination. A new path had to be blazed for the armed entrée of the New World into the Old World.

The gateways widened as each shipload grew in numbers and frequency. The beginning of the overseas movement was slow; the United States stumbled through weary-dragging months before its awakened militancy got into its stride in spanning the ocean. In May, 1917, the month following the American declaration of war, only 1,718 officers and men landed; in June, 12,261; July, 12,988; August, 18,323; September, 32,523; October, 38,259; November, 23,016; December, 48,840. The beginning of

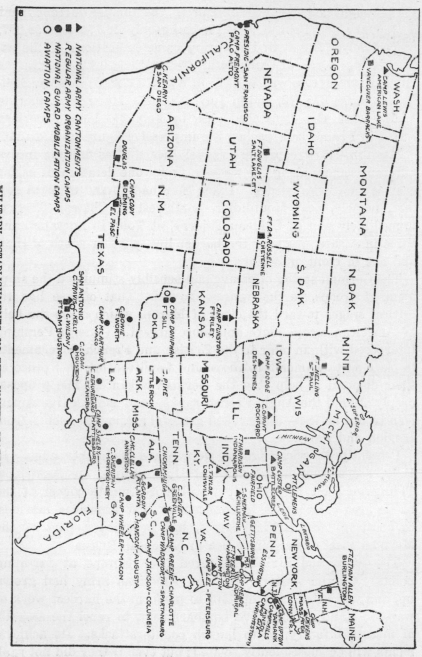

MILITARY ESTABLISHMENTS IN THE UNITED STATES

1918 brought no perceptible expansion, the number of troops sent in January and February, 1918, being only 46,776 and 48,027, respectively. But with the spring came indications of the accumulating force of American preparations. In March the number sent across was 83,811; in April, 117,212; in May, 244,-345; in June, 276,372, and in July, 300,000. Marines numbering 14,644 were also dispatched. So by July 31, 1918, American forces in France had reached the impressive figure of 1,319,115.

Meantime the troops were vaguely heard of as fighting in five different sectors along the western front, one detachment as far east as the Swiss border. Later they had spread to eight sectors, namely, near Montdidier, northwest of Château-Thierry, immediately east of Château-Thierry, at Toul, in Lorraine, and three in Alsace, one near the border line, another south of that, and one in front of Belfort.

The German spring offensive had sensibly stimulated the shipment of troops, as the figures showed. That offense had its critical stages toward the close of March, which made the help of American troops more and more urgent. General Pershing interposed with an offer to the British and French Governments to place all the American troops and facilities then in France at their disposal to help stay the German advance. The proposal deeply stirred the Anglo-French ranks—and the inactive American troops no less—and evoked grateful acknowledgments from London and Paris.

Presently American troops were heard of further afield—in Italy, for service under General Diaz against the Austrians. Tidings of their presence at a still more remote corner of the battle area came in the announcement that American marines, cooperating with British forces, had occupied a part of the Murman coast of the White Sea in European Russia.

The Stars and Stripes fluttered over Europe at far-flung points. On the western front an American army had grown up, and was rated as competent to perform the hardest work of war—to stand an intensive bombardment, to repel the assaults of massed infantry, or to launch counterattacks. Its achievements will be subsequently related; but even if they did not rank

in numbers with those of the British and French, the mere
presence of American soldiers at the forefront of one of the
world's greatest battles stood out as a transcendent historical
event. The forces of the New World had appeared to save
liberty in Europe. They were there to establish a reorganization of the world on the American plan—not for the glory of the
Stars and Stripes, but for a vindication of the ideas which the
flag represented.

CHAPTER XLIII

RAIDING THE NEW FOE

AMERICAN activities had hitherto been confined to what became known as the original American front, facing Lorraine
beyond St. Mihiel. This was apparently an irregular line, in
the vicinity of the Rhine-Marne canal, and fronting Nancy,
Luneville, Toul, and other towns whose existence became known
by General Pershing's reports.

It was their "breaking in" ground. American troops there
obtained an intimate acquaintance with modern warfare. The
numerous trench raids that marked their operations apparently
had no strategical relations to the movements on the battle line
elsewhere, nor even disclosed any local tactical object. Americans and Germans seemed merely to be watching each other
with lynx eyes, each on the alert to catch the other napping and
steal a march for the glory of the achievement.

The casualties in these skirmishes were usually slight, and a
few prisoners now and then would fall to one or the other side.
But few raids took place without losses, which gradually became impressive as the engagements increased in frequency and
scope. A trench raid is a trivial thing, with an inconsequential
outcome when it has any outcome at all; but repeated daily, the
casualties such raids produce, added to the fatalities resulting
from random artillery fire, assume the dimensions of those of
an extensive battle. They do not stand out as distinctive oper-

ations; proceeding upon established methods, there was a general sameness in their repetition, and they only became noticeable for the outstanding incidents that were bound to arise in each undertaking.

An early attack by the Germans was made behind a dense fog after daybreak, through which came a violent artillery barrage as a forerunner. The fog was of a density that blotted out everything but the nearest enemy positions. Through it enemy projectiles exploded on three sides of an American listening post just outside the wire, within forty-five feet of an enemy listening post. In a few minutes hundreds of high-explosive shells had dropped round the post and the surrounding ground, cutting off the men there. American artillery replied; but all traces of German dead and wounded were removed by the time the Americans had emerged from their dugouts after their barrage was raised.

The Germans followed their sortie against the listening post by a heavy bombardment of the American lines a few days later. American guns responded, shell for shell, wrecking several of the enemy's dugouts, and badly damaging some of his first-line positions. They were caved in by the American 75's, and the Germans spent several days in repairing them and patching up gaps in the barbed wire before the wrecked trenches could be reoccupied. A number of the men who were wounded slightly by shell splinters were treated in the lines with their first-aid packets and insisted on remaining at their posts until the fight was finished.

The enemy's next artillery exercise was a concentrated fire on one of the American positions with the object of obliterating it. Americans guns at once punished the German batteries with a retaliatory fire of double force, and then swept the enemy lines with a vicious barrage. Whereupon the German guns ceased firing.

The enemy presently resorted to the use of gas to harass the American positions. Aimed at a wood, a rain of shells, largely composed of gas and high explosives, came from the German minenwerfers. They burst in the air, the high explosives detonating when they came in contact with the earth, and broke into fragments among a number of men before they could adjust their masks. Other troops were overcome by the fumes while asleep in their dugouts. The fumes lingered in the gassed area long after the shells had exploded, filling shell holes and other depressions, and incapacitating men who ventured to work in the vicinity. But the American guns exacted swift retribution. They leveled a heavy fire on the German minenwerfers, and in half an hour had razed the position. Timbers were thrown high in the air, and explosions, probably of enemy ammunition, testified to American marksmanship. The ground about the German batteries was churned upside down, and there was no doubt of the fate of any German soldiers who were on the spot.

The beginning of March, 1918, saw the first pitched battle between Americans and Germans in the St. Mihiel salient north of Toul. The enemy started it by a morning raid in a driving wet snow, preceded by heavy gunfire, intermixed with poison gas. The latter was discharged on the trenches in a generous hail of shells, the Germans evidently thinking that this second cloud of gas would daunt the American troops after their previous foretaste. The Americans were not daunted; their masks quickly covered them, and few troops were affected.

The woods behind the salient were shot to pieces by the German fire. As soon as the barrage was raised on the trenches to the right of the salient, some 300 Germans swept forward under the protection of their fire. They jumped into what was left of the trenches, expecting to make a haul of prisoners; but they found the Americans ready for them.

A fierce hand-to-hand fight followed in front of wire entanglements and in shell holes. Meantime American barrage fire swept no-man's-land, catching many running Germans who had turned tail from fighting at close quarters.

The Germans were thrown back, leaving ten dead in the American trenches. Two were officers, entangled in the wire. The ground was littered with enemy hand grenades, boxes of explosives for destroying dugouts, and incendiary bombs the enemy had no opportunity of using. The enemy had paid dearly for his enterprise, but the Americans also suffered in proportion. Berlin claimed that twelve had been captured.

They had cut the American wire with caution, making no noise, but the sentry was watching their performance all the time, and let them proceed until he was sure of routing them.

Another American patrol experienced, for the first time, a German attack of liquid fire. Enemy troops were about to throw flame projectors into the American trenches when an American patrol near by opened fire on them. The Germans fled precipitately, pursued by the Americans, and dropped four projectors, two of which were flaming. All the projectors had been punctured by American shots.

The foregoing series of engagements shows that in every case the Germans were the aggressors. The Americans, in fact, were merely holding the Lorraine sector without aspiring to take the field until they were better acquainted with trench warfare. The Germans, believing they had green troops before them, were accordingly venturesome, and disposed to put them on their mettle, which they accordingly did, only to find that the supposedly raw American troops were no longer raw. The Germans themselves had contributed to ridding them of any greenness with which they credited them. The Americans had occupied the Lorraine sector as substitutes for the French, and the Germans were accordingly eager to know the quality of their new antagonists. Hence these series of raids made on the American front. Soon the tables were to be turned by the Americans conducting raids of their own.

CHAPTER XLIV

AMERICA OVER THE TOP

THE first direct attack on the German lines made by American forces in the Lorraine sector took place on the night of March 9, 1918, with the cooperation of the French. Two raids were made. The troops engaged were ordered to cut off the two ends of a salient in the German line, flatten out the salient by artillery fire, enter the trenches, bomb the dugouts, sweep the trenches generally, and return.

Intense artillery fire, lasting four hours, leveled the German positions before the Franco-American troops advanced. They were divided into two forces, with small French detachments flanking each, and went forward at midnight behind a creeping barrage, each on a front of six hundred yards. Starting simultaneously, one advanced northwest of the salient, the other to the northeast. On the German first lines being reached, the barrage was lifted so as to box in the enemy positions at both points.

The troops dropped into the trenches, expecting a hand-to-hand fight, but found that the Germans had fled. Continuing, they reached the second German line six hundred yards farther on while American machine guns fired on each flank of the two parties to check flanking operations by the enemy.

The yield in prisoners was poor, the Germans having decamped. One French flanking party found two wounded Germans. The Americans found none. But they blew up a number of excellent concrete dugouts and returned with large quantities of material and valuable papers. While they were in the vacated German lines, enemy artillery began a vigorous counterbarrage, but it was quickly silenced by gas shells hurled by American heavy and light guns.

The raid was followed by a second on another part of the line, undertaken without the aid of the French. A preliminary bombardment swept the Germans' front trenches, tearing gaps in their barbed-wire entanglements, and wrought other destruction. The German batteries came into action, but accomplished nothing to halt the American progress. Entering the German trenches behind one side of a "box" barrage, which moved forward in front of them, they found numerous Germans hiding in the dugouts. Hand-to-hand fighting followed, the Americans using their automatic pistols and rifles. They penetrated 300 yards of the enemy line, going beyond their objective. More fighting developed, but the Germans were not equal to the assault and fled, leaving a number of dead and wounded in their trenches. The Americans fought so fast in effecting their object that the army doctors who accompanied them had little to do. They returned to their own lines without being impeded by a single German shell, and without fatalities. It was all over so quickly that the German batteries had no chance to get into real action. It was just a fifteen-minute adventure undertaken by way of feeling their way in testing their capacity to give the Germans a taste of their own medicine.

Following these engagements, the actual locality of which was not disclosed, American forces were reported to be very active in aggressive operations in the neighborhood of Luneville, a town east of the Toul sector. This information revealed an extension of the American positions in Lorraine and an augmentation of forces that made the new sector one of the most active on the front. It appeared that the two simultaneous raids mentioned took place in this vicinity, northwest and northeast of Badonviller. The trenches evacuated by the Germans were occupied by the Americans, who consolidated them with their own lines. This forward movement, though a small one, marked the first permanent advance by the American army in France, and enabled the Americans and French to operate from higher ground than heretofore. The Germans made only feeble attempts to retake the position, and each time were repulsed. The parapets were turned toward the enemy, dugout entrances were changed, and new dugouts built to protect the troops. An exploring patrol examined the trenches, proceeding laterally until they established contact with the enemy. They came upon snipers' posts, listening posts, and nests from which machine guns had been firing into the American lines. These ambushes of the enemy were turned over to the tender mercies of the American batteries, which wiped them out. The positions of the Germans were made so uncomfortable at various points that they tried to regain their lost foothold by connecting shell holes. Their guns pounded the new American positions with heavy shells, some of the twelve-inch type, without affecting the Franco-American consolidation.

A German battery of mine throwers, one of which had made a direct hit on a dugout occupied by American soldiers, next received the earnest attention of American guns in the Luneville sector. The battery had been causing considerable trouble. It was finally located, and upon it high-explosive shells were concentrated. It was blown up.

More German trenches in the Luneville sector were destroyed. The enemy vacated them. When a patrol, without assistance from the artillery, crossed no-man's-land, they found the first and second positions wiped out. The patrol obtained further information and returned without casualties, the Germans apparently not daring to molest them. The indications behind the German lines were that they saw the need of constructing stronger earthworks to withstand the American fire. A patrol ascertained that the enemy had constructed trenches built of concrete half way up the side, and was using rock crushers and concrete mixers for building a number of "pill-boxes" opposite the American front.

Meantime the foe gave renewed attention to the Toul sector. One new form of attack came from a German aeroplane, which dropped rubber balls filled with liquefied "mustard" gas. The effect of these novel air missiles was not serious. The gas merely infuriated the troops, and when the Germans heavily attacked the American positions with shell fire, gas shells were hurled at the enemy from American batteries. Four gas attacks were launched at the Germans, whose guns were presently silenced.

The Germans later responded by concentrating a heavy gas attack on a town behind the American lines. No wind was blowing and the fumes of the "mustard" gas from the shells hung low over the lines for a long time. The batteries firing the gas shells were located and the American gunners retaliated with doses of gas twice as large as the American positions received. In fact, two towns held by the Germans were so heavily gassed that one of them, Réchicourt, north of Xivray, one of the American targets, was abandoned.

German snipers in this sector were also a constant worry to the Americans. As fast as one nest was silenced, another was found, and the task of wiping out the nuisance had to be repeated. In one instance, a group of American snipers discovered an enemy nest close by and promptly opened fire on it. The Germans replied with their rifles, and then fired about three dozen or so of grenades. Apparently the Germans had come to stay and did not intend to be chased out. One of the American 37-millimeter gun teams then got into action against the nest, and owing to its accurate fire no more Germans were seen at this particular point. The Germans were frequently presented with examples of the accuracy of the fire of these 37-millimeter guns. An enemy machine-gun emplacement which had been annoying the Americans was located and then the battery of "little fellows," as the guns were known along the front, got into action, firing rapidly. They secured a number of direct hits and destroyed the emplacement guns.

These small guns, which are about the size of a one-pounder, were easily moved from place to place even in the trenches. They also secured direct hits on the junction of communication trenches as men were passing, and into the entrance of the dugout which a number of the enemy were seen to enter and from which smoke was issuing. None of the enemy was seen to come out.

In April the Germans attempted an ambitious local operation against the Americans northwest of Toul. They planned to enter the third line positions, it was subsequently learned, and for this purpose they sent a special battalion of 800 shock troops equipped with wire, dynamite, intrenching tools and other implements for adapting trenches to their own use. The attack was preceded by a violent bombardment of the American positions, lasting three days. Hundreds of shells fell, many of them charged with gas. At sunrise on April 10 the German infantrymen signaled their batteries for a barrage, and under it they started out for the American line. They were selected from the best men of three regiments and were preceded by shock platoons. The American gunners did not wait for any rocket signal from their own side before getting into action. They immediately started a counterbarrage, which caught the advancing Germans before they could reach the American wire entanglements. The German officers sent their troops through the answering barrage, with the result that fewer than 200 of the 800 troops succeeded in making any advance. Only two reached the American line; both were captured and one died immediately after from wounds.

The fighting developed on no-man's-land. American outposts moved to the first line and with other infantrymen and machine gunners waited for those of the attackers who survived the American barrage. As the raiders neared the Americans poured a deadly fire into them, then climbed out of the trenches and engaged them with grenades and in hand-to-hand fighting. The enemy was driven back to his own lines, suffering serious casualties from American heavy machine-gun and rifle fire rained on his men as they fled. No-man's-land was strewn with German dead; several bodies hung on the barbed wire after the enemy retired; and numbers were killed by American guns before they could leave the German trenches. The fight lasted two hours in a heavy morning mist; but the American gunners found their aim despite the poor visibility.

It was a crushing defeat, and two days later the Germans, smarting under it, sought to avenge it by reorganizing the 800 shock troops, which were filled out by picked men from other units, and ordering them to take the American positions. As before a violent bombardment, accompanied by gas shells, signalized the attack. The German guns kept up a harassing fire all night, and with dawn came the infantry attack, directed against French troops who flanked the American forces on the left in the forest of Apremont. While this engagement was proceeding the Americans launched a counterattack on the German line, moving forward behind a perfect curtain fire. The enemy, driven out of his trenches, was forced to fight in the open. A deadly machine-gun and automatic-rifle fire was poured into the Germans, who offered stubborn resistance at first, but latter retreated to their second line, hotly pursued by the American troops.

After an interim the Germans resumed the attack at a point farther to the right. The American barrage fire cut them off, but the German officers drove their men through the exploding shells until a few succeeded in penetrating the American front line. A counterattack by the Americans ejected the enemy, driving him back to his positions.

The struggle lasted throughout the day, and was the first all-day battle in which the Americans had been engaged. Their loss was slight. They lost no prisoners, but gained thirty-four of the enemy. The prisoners taken belonged to six different organizations. Five were Uhlans, and all were carrying haversacks well filled, as if in preparation for a protracted stay in the American trenches, corroborating the stories told by prisoners previously taken, who said that the Germans had been ordered to penetrate the American third line at all costs.

Several deeds of individual heroism marked the engagement. In one case a young lieutenant, with three men, attacked nineteen Germans who had penetrated into one of the American trenches. The lieutenant called on the Germans to surrender. One of them raised his pistol, as if to shoot, but the lieutenant shot him through the head, upon which the others lifted their hands high in the air and yelled "Kamerad." The lieutenant marched the prisoners in to the rear and then returned to the front and resumed the command of his platoon.

Five other Americans penetrated into a German dugout where twelve of the enemy were slightly wounded. The Germans resisted surrender, but our men threw grenades into the dugout killing four of the foe. The others quickly gave themselves up.

Despite their failure, the Germans the next day continued their efforts to drive through to the American third line. A incessant artillery fire blended with gas shells prefaced two bitter attacks both of which the Americans withstood. In all, the enemy spent four days in trying to take the Apremont position.

German activities against American forces were next heard of north of St. Mihiel, where a new American sector, located on the right bank of the Meuse, south of Verdun, was disclosed. The enemy's raid had the usual characteristics. It was made by a force of 400 picked troops brought from the Russian front, who outnumbered the Americans by more than two to one. The Germans leaped from their trenches under their barrage; the Americans did likewise; and there was a hand-to-hand affray with grenade and bayonet. The upshot was a German casualty list of sixty-four dead, many wounded, and twelve prisoners, and the hurling back of the survivors to their own lines.

While these scattered local operations enlivened the various American sectors, the great German spring offensive was proceeding against the British and French well out of the established American zones. As that offensive developed in its scope, less attention was paid to the American lines east of Verdun, and save for the Seicheprey raid and the clash at Xivray, both to be presently described, the operations there were of little moment.

The usual little amenities of war went on between isolated groups of combatants, mostly local scrimmages in which not more than a dozen or twenty men participated. These took the customary form of patrol actions, clashes between scouts, the uprooting of enemy's snipers' nests and the occasional invasion of trenches by one or the other side. There were ceaseless artillery duels, accompanied by clouds of gas, and daily fatalities, not all of them due to actual warfare.

Here and there small engagements, by reason of a swinging, thoroughgoing effectiveness on the part of the bands of Americans who shared in them, stand out of the daily routine of the trench warfare. In one that took place near Bremenil, east of Luneville, in May, 1918, when a body of Germans essayed to attack the American positions, solely to take prisoners to ascertain the American strength, not a single German got back who succeeded in entering the American trenches. A gas bombardment led the attack, followed by a heavy barrage fire, under which fifty German soldiers attempted to reach the American line; nine of the fourteen raiders were killed outright, four were captured, and one died of wounds. No American was captured.

While comparative quiet reigned in the St. Mihiel, Toul, and Luneville sectors, as the summer advanced, a further extension of American sectors, eastward of these positions, running almost to the Swiss border, became revealed in General Pershing's reports. American forces were heard of at St. Dié, Mulhouse, Colmar, and near Belfort. With the main German forces busily—and unsuccessfully—engaged on other parts of the front, the Americans hereabout appear to pass uneventful days. The German forces before them, barring their occasional liquid fire, artillery outbreaks, air reconnoissances, and machine-gun activity, were disposed to let well enough alone.

By July, 1918, Americans practically occupied the whole of the Lorraine-Alsace front. Their positions gradually became disclosed and may now be stated with some particularity as follows: First, east of St. Mihiel; second, north of Luneville; third, east and a little south of Luneville or north of Badonviller; fourth, near St. Dié; fifth, just west of Gebweiler, which is just east of the battle line, and, sixth, east of Belfort, near Altkirch. Roughly speaking, these positions were about equally distant from one another and divided the entire front from St. Mihiel to the Swiss border into sections averaging about twenty-five miles each, over a front of approximately 150 miles. This became now the distinctly American front, and extended approximately one-third of the entire western front.

The United States, to all intents and purposes, had created an "Eastern front" of her own in taking over the southeastern portion of what was known as the western front. Here General Pershing's legions could drive directly into Germany by the shortest route with the least cost in men and material, and with the least delay.

CHAPTER XLV

AT SEICHEPREY AND XIVRAY

THE Germans had reached the conclusion that the Americans must be taught a lesson. The latter were making a disquieting impression elsewhere on the western front in cooperating with Anglo-French forces who were resisting the German advance. Moreover, the Americans in their own sectors showed an unseemly enterprise and eagerness to meet the kaiser's hosts at close quarters, and even to hold them in small esteem. Besides, the people at home must be persuaded that the hordes of untrained and raw Americans who were spreading along the western front were negligible and despised factors as belligerents, and the best way to drive this conclusion home to the German people was to give the Americans a sound thrashing. Such a disciplinary measure, the German mind reasoned, would also have the effect of discouraging the Americans from continuing to come to the rescue of their sorely pressed Allies.

The American sector running eastward of the famous salient of St. Mihiel was chosen as the location of the castigation. In this sector lay the village of Seicheprey among rolling hills, overlooking a winding valley that runs to the northeast. The German positions were on high ground, commanding the Allied trenches, and directly opposite them, behind the American line, Seicheprey nestled on the southwestern slope of a steep hill some 900 feet high. On the right, the hill was approachable on a gradual incline, the greater part of which is covered by a small rectangular grove called the Wood of Remières. Here the American line joined the French.

The front of the attack made by the Germans ran something under two miles from Seicheprey to the Remières Wood. Their object appeared to be threefold, apart from the ultimate aim to discourage the Americans and convince the German people that the United States was a poor antagonist. One was to test the American strength and determine whether the Americans, still unseasoned, as measured by the hardened condition of the other Allied troops, after their four years of war, would brave heavy shell fire, followed by strong infantry attacks. The second was to widen the base of the St. Mihiel salient, which was too narrow to hold with security. The third was to drive a wedge between the American and French lines.

The assault came at sunrise on April 20. An all-night bombardment, which sent a deluge of shells, many of them of poison gas, into the American positions, preceded it. A German barrage was launched; the Americans met it by a counterbarrage. In short, the regulation artillery curtains were swept across the battle zone, under which the opposing forces tried conclusions.

On a front extending for a mile and three-quarters the enemy sent a force of 3,000 men, preceded by picked storm troops, who advanced in three columns. They had been specially trained for the operation and greatly outnumbered the resisting Americans; they carried rations and intrenching tools, indicating that the aim was to occupy the American trenches—if taken—for a long period. On the left and in the center the assault was repelled, but on the right the assailants succeeded in occupying Remières Wood, whose eastern edge was a short distance behind the American line. The Germans pursued their customary tactics of "infiltration," that is, of gradual progress in small groups, supported by quick-firers along the line of entry made in the Allied position with the object of taking the American center in the rear. Protected by trees and favored by the character of the terrain, the Germans were so far successful that by night they had reached the crest of the hill flanked by Remières Wood, and delivered a heavy attack on Seicheprey.

The Germans carried the village, but only after furious hand-to-hand fighting. They entered it in the belief that the Americans had gone, and with good reason, since liquid fire, gas, and other devices of frightfulness had been used to clear the village. But some Americans had remained, and they attacked the Germans with hand grenades, killing many of them. The Americans only fell back when they were greatly outnumbered, after making a stubborn defense. German airmen poured machine-gun fire upon them; but the antiaircraft batteries came into play and American airmen took the air, bringing down two of the enemy planes and dispersing the others. Before retiring the Americans fought for every inch of the way, yielding slowly, and pouring a deadly machine-gun, rifle, and automatic fire into the advancing enemy.

The Germans were not permitted to hold either Seicheprey or the Remières Wood. Without a moment's delay the Americans and French organized a counterattack and drove them out of the village.

It was found that the retreating Germans had set traps there in the form of boxes containing high explosives to which they had attached wires stretched across the streets. Some of the advancing troops stepped on the wire, causing explosions and the traps had to be removed. Before dawn of the next day the Franco-American forces had not only recovered the village but forced the enemy back to the hilltop above it.

The battle circled about the brow and slope of the hill on which Seicheprey stood and the wood of Remières at its foot. The Germans returned to the charge with forces estimated at three battalions, led by storm troops. Two hours' hard fighting followed. Finally, the Americans, supported, as before by the French from an adjoining sector, now drove the Germans down the slope into Remières Wood, already held by the foe, and fought them among the trees all the morning. Toward noon the Allies swept forward irresistibly and retook the wood completely. Fighting stubbornly, the Germans were pushed back beyond the wood's eastern fringe to their own trenches, where they endeavored to maintain themselves. But a new Franco-American advance, combined with pressure from the flank, forced them to retreat, and by evening they had retired to the original starting point, and the American line was completely reestablished.

It was the first time the Germans had met the Americans in serious fighting on a scale which removed the engagement from the category of small skirmishes in local operations, and apart from the ultimate result, which was a defeat for the Germans, they learned something of the quality of Americans, both as massed and individual fighters.

North of Seicheprey an American detachment was separated into small groups and was cut off from the company to which it belonged throughout the entire fight. Behind the Americans and on their left flank were German units, but they could have retired on the right. They decided to fight, which they did notwithstanding the incessant enemy bombardment and rifle fire. Numerous hand-to-hand combats were fought in the course of this long struggle, from which the Americans found themselves obliged to retire toward nightfall, but only after destroying their machine guns.

In Seicheprey a squad of Americans found several cases of grenades, with which they made a determined fight, holding out the entire day on the northern extremity of the village. They refused to surrender when summoned to do so, and at the end of the fighting only nine out of the original twenty-three were left. A cook surprised by the Germans, and half stunned by a blow from a grenade, seized a rifle and continued firing until he fell dead.

Toward evening a hospital which had been established in Seicheprey was blown up, along with the doctors and ambulance men. The chief surgeon of the American regiment engaged hurried to the spot with French and American ambulance cars. The rescue party passed through a severe barrage fire, but eventually reached the village, where they tended to the wounded for many hours under a heavy enemy fire.

The American losses were never clearly known. They were estimated at 200. The Germans claimed 183 prisoners, which would leave only seventeen dead and wounded on the American estimate. The scope of the battle showed that the American losses in dead and wounded were much more than that, hence the number of prisoners the Germans claimed was discredited.

As to the German casualties, a German prisoner put them at 600 killed, wounded and missing, of these, more than 300 German dead were found in the American trenches and in no-man's-land. The defeat of the Germans was sufficiently proved by the omission of the German official bulletins and the German press to mention the successful counterattack.

The Xivray affair (June 16, 1918) in the Toul sector furnished another example of American alertness and vigor in an emergency. Xivray was originally behind the German lines, but they had been penetrated by the Americans, and the town was in American hands. As was the case in other engagements, German prisoners betrayed that the enemy's purpose in raiding the town was to carry off as many Americans as possible with a view to extracting information from them. The enemy's design, as thus revealed, was to send a large party without preparatory artillery fire. They were to take up a position near the American barbed wire, and send a signal rocket for a box barrage to cover Xivray and the approaching communication trenches, while heavy artillery bombarded the villages in the rear.

The American fire apparently precipitated a violent bombardment. It came at 3 o'clock in the morning and was directed at the American first line before Xivray, the American batteries, and at villages far in the rear. An Associated Press correspondent thus described what follows:

"Six hundred men advanced to the attack in no less than a dozen different columns, led by 200 picked Bavarian storming troops. They came up on the right flank, on the left, and on the center under cover of smoke, making a dark night still darker. They crept up the ravines and slipped through the hollows. The sharp ears of sentries alone prevented a total surprise.

"Their guns laid down a heavy box barrage that prevented the reenforcing of the front line. One platoon, led by Lieutenant Doan, got through the first curtain of fire. Doan even went through the second with some volunteers, but that was all the help that could be sent to the 225 men that were holding the line attacked. They were only one to three, but they fought in a way to surprise and dismay the 600 Germans.

"One machine gun section in the village was reduced to two men—Monfort Wyckoff and John Flynn. Their gun jammed and Flynn kept the Germans off with his revolver while Wyckoff got the quick-firer going again. They held their ground to the end. Two other men, unable to get a sight at the Germans from their trench, climbed the parapet and stood there erect, firing their automatics from the shoulder.

"Two companies of infantry, without dugouts to shelter them, held their ground on the right of the position through a heavy artillery preparation and kept the enemy from bringing up re-enforcements throughout the fight. Meanwhile, in the center at Xivray and on the left, the machine gunners did the rest.

"The enemy's plan, according to prisoners, was to force the village, destroy the defense works, make the place untenable, and take prisoners. The effort was well organized and might have succeeded but for the work of the quick-firers.

"The Germans had lost a third of their 600 men when growing daylight impaired the effectiveness of their smoke screen, and they began to retire. The fifty-odd unwounded Americans left out of 225 went over the top after them.

"Two hundred is a conservative estimate of the German losses, for our men buried forty-seven of them on the field, and there were more corpses in the tall grass facing the position out of reach. Thus the Germans lost nearly as many men as they had facing them during the fight."

CHAPTER XLVI

ON THE CHEMIN-DES-DAMES

AS early as February, 1918, American batteries were heard on the French lines east of Rheims, where American gunners were apparently under training by the French before going into action on their own front. An opportunity came to them to show their quality when the French determined to suppress a German salient which dipped into the French position between Tahure and Butte du Mesnil, in the Champagne. It was a difficult operation owing to the nature of the ground, which formed a basin-like depression, into which the Germans could pour the fire of their concentrated guns from the surrounding heights.

Artillery did the main work. American gunners took part in a six-hour bombardment of the salient on a front of a mile, and so thoroughly were the German defenses demolished that it took the French assaulting troops only an hour to gain all the objectives in view. Afterward the American gunners, with their French comrades, extended their range, developing an effective barrage to prevent counterattacks on the newly won ground. "American batteries gave very effective support," said the French communiqué in reporting this successful raid.

About the same time American units appeared on the Aisne fighting front in the vicinity of the famous Chemin-des-Dames. They had been detailed there for training purposes; but their location was not revealed by General Pershing until the Germans themselves knew of their presence. They had been there weeks before their presence became known. Suddenly ordered from their billets, they entrained to the railhead, and passed through mile after mile of shell-scarred, desolate ground and through several great piles of stones and débris which once were villages but now had not a single house standing. They took up their positions without a hitch to the music of roaring guns, both friendly and hostile, their flashes stabbing the blackness of the night, first here and then there, as far as the eye could see.

Many of them were quartered in quarries twenty feet underground, one quarry having room for sheltering 3,000 men. Other recesses beneath the surface occupied by them were partly natural in formation and improved through blasting operations by the Germans, who occupied them for three years. But most of the American troops were above ground, having established themselves in trenches and dugouts which they had cleaned, strengthened, and improved and protected by barbed-wire entanglements.

The cave dwellers' chief barracks was seventy-two feet underground. This cave ran in long galleries with cement ceilings, and was lighted by electricity, acetylene lamps, and oil lanterns. The troops slept on low, double-tiered wooden bunks provided with straw. Here the troops usually remained from four to six days each, a company being assigned to a certain portion of the cavern. Being new to active field service, they were not permitted to roam about at will, lest they be lost, nor to leave the cavern at all except on duty, lest they be detected by enemy airmen.

The appearance of Americans on this sector was greeted by the Germans with a sign reading: "Welcome, Yankees." It was promptly riddled with bullets till it looked like a sieve.

The French and Americans responded to this little pleasantry by an attack on the German lines at Chevregny on February 23, 1918. The French organized a little raid on the German lines, aided by twenty-six picked Americans, and rehearsed the operation the day before. An hour's barrage at dawn brought the Americans moving forward eagerly with their French comrades. They moved so fast, indeed, that they came within thirty yards of the dropping shells on reaching the enemy lines. It was the first time American troops had essayed an attack under such a curtain of fire, and their ardor actually took them beyond their objectives.

In the German trenches officers were making the rounds after morning relief when the Americans and French burst in. The Germans rushed to shelter in a dugout roofed with rails and sandbags; but this refuge was immediately shattered by a French shell.

Deprived of this cover, the Germans scattered about the trench. The entire party at this point was captured after some hand-to-hand fighting. Other shelters and communicating trenches were cleared without yielding any prisoners. A German counterbarrage caught the raiders and their captives on returning across no-man's-land, wounding five Germans and six Frenchmen, but no Americans.

The Germans directed a strong retaliatory assault against this sector a few days later. Its repulse revealed that the Americans were in sufficient force to hold a considerable portion of the front line. Three companies of trained shock troops were sent to take the American trenches under a heavy German barrage.

American soldiers starting out to storm Cantigny, on the Picardy front. They were aided by French tanks. The attack, which took place on May 21, 1918, was entirely successful

American artillery responded with a like curtain of fire as soon as the German barrage was raised, and American machine guns sent streams of bullets into the advancing enemy. The fighting was brisk for about an hour; but the accurate machine-gun and rifle fire from the American front lines, coupled with the perfect American barrage, which prevented reenforcements from coming up, forced the Germans to withdraw after sustaining heavy casualties and without having set foot in the American trenches.

After the attack a patrol was found to be missing. A platoon set out into no-man's-land to find them in a rain of machine-gun bullets. The German fire was too heavy, and they returned without finding any trace of the missing men. It was assumed that the latter had been too venturesome and were captured.

CHAPTER XLVII

BEFORE AMIENS

THE Allies' resistance to Germany's spring offensive of 1918, which aimed to reach the Channel ports and Paris, at first revealed no indication that American forces were taking part in the defense. The sweep of her first advance, begun on March 21, 1918, extended from the vicinity of Arras, on the north, to La Fère, on the south. The latter town was near a great bend then in the western line around the wood of St. Gobain, a short distance northwest of the Chemin-des-Dames, where, as shown in the previous chapter, Americans were stationed. Hence the German attack swept within fighting distance of American arms.

The United States was in sufficient strength along the western front to make it certain that General Pershing would not let Great Britain and France bear the sole burden of meeting the German advance. But for some days the share of the American forces in the fighting was veiled in mystery. Berlin finally shed a little daylight on the subject. In its official communiqués of

War St. 7—X

March 24 and 25, 1918, it alluded to American reserves having been thrown back on Chauny, which is eight miles west of La Fère. These bulletins contained the following passages:

"The British Third and Fourth Armies and portions of Franco-American reserves who had been brought up were beaten, and on the line of Bapaume-Bouchavesnes and behind the Somme, between Péronne and Ham, as well as at Chauny, were repulsed with the heaviest of losses.

"The corps of Generals von Webern and von Conte, and the troops of General von Geyl, after a fierce battle, crossed the Crozat Canal.

"French, English, and American regiments which had been brought up from the southwest for a counterattack were thrown back on Chauny in a southwesterly direction."

The next day General Pershing threw further light on the mystery in a message to the War Department:

"Reference to the German communiqués of the 24th and 25th regarding American troops: Two regiments of railway engineers are with the British armies involved in this battle. Three companies of engineers were working in the areas mentioned in the communiqué in the vicinity of the Crozat Canal."

Thereby hung a tale similar to that which recorded the part American engineers took at Cambrai, as told in the previous volume. By true Teutonic indirection, the German "Vorwärts," in commenting on the battle in the area named, indicated that the American share in it was not negligible:

"Attacks of combined Allied forces against the pivot of the German attacking front near La Fère were particularly heavy. These counterattacks did not find us unprepared. It testifies to the superior foresight of the German command that these attacks, in which American troops certainly participated only symbolically, were not only beaten off, but were thrown back on the Oise Canal by an energetic blow."

These allusions were foretokens that something unusual was taking place. The staid official language of General Pershing, in a communication to the War Department, thus described what had happened:

"Certain units of United States Engineers, serving with a British army battalion, March 21 and April 3, 1918, while under shell fire, carried out destruction of material dumps at Chaulnes, fell back with British forces to Moreuil, where the commands laid out trench work, then proceeded to Demuin, and were assigned a sector of the defensive line, which was constructed and manned by them, thence moved to a position on the line near War-fusee-Abancourt and extending to north side of Bois de Toil-lauw. The commands started for this position on March 27, 1918, and occupied it until April 3, 1918, during this time the commanding officer of a unit of United States Engineers being in command of the subsector occupied by his troops. This command was in more or less continuous action during its stay in this position. On April 3, 1918, the command was ordered to fall back to Abbeville."

General Rawlinson, commanding the British forces engaged in this battle, acknowledged the services performed by American engineers in a letter to the colonel commanding a United States engineer regiment.

"I fully realize," he wrote, "that it has been largely due to your assistance that the enemy is checked. . . . . I consider your work in the line to be greatly enhanced by the fact that for six weeks previous to taking your place in the front line your men had been working at such a high pressure erecting a heavy bridge over the Somme. My best congratulations and warm thanks to you all."

It appeared that a gap had to be stopped in the bending line through which the Germans otherwise would have streamed. Amiens lay before their advancing hosts, and the way was open. The critical moment came on the afternoon of Tuesday, March 26, 1918. It was imperative that more troops should be thrown into the British line to arrest the German onrush. Reenforcements were on the way, but could not arrive in time.

A dashing British officer, Brigadier General Carey, hastily improvised a scratch force of every available element within reach. American engineers were among them, and they were eagerly drawn into the fray. By telephone, messenger, and flag signals,

General Carey assembled a little army from behind the lines which included labor battalions, cooks, and orderlies, sturdy middle-aged men, of various occupations, electricians, signalers, members of an infantry training school, machine gunners hurriedly armed with rifles, engineers, and fifty cavalrymen for scouting. He also improvised a staff as he proceeded, "officers learning the ground," as one onlooker described it, "by having to defend it and every man from enlisted man to brigadier jumping at each job as it came along."

Early in the German advance, British reports had mentioned "Americans fighting shoulder to shoulder with the French and British." No American force was then identified as in the fight, and not until several days after did Pershing begin to send reenforcements to the Allies. The Americans referred to so mysteriously were part of that strangely mixed force that Carey drummed up from the void. These engineers at Carey's call picked up rifles and merged themselves in his motley corps without orders from anybody. They had been called from their work, which was constructing and operating field railways and building bridges.

The beginning of their exploits was due to three companies of an American engineer regiment being caught in the early bombardment. Ordered to fall back, one of the companies, which had been consolidated with the British Royal Engineers, was delegated to the task of guaranteeing the destruction of the engineers' dump referred to by General Pershing, which it had been decided to abandon. This detachment destroyed all the material, made a rapid retreat, caught up with the larger group, and immediately resumed work, laying out trenches. These operations lasted from March 22 to 27, 1918. As the German attack became more intense, the engineers joined up with the mixed force General Carey had assembled.

Then followed a week's brilliant defense of the road to Amiens. Led by General Carey, this assorted force, numbering 1,500 men, plunged into the swirling battle line, where they were strung over a front of 1,200 yards, against which hordes of Germans were thrown.

"It seems almost inconceivable," wrote a correspondent, "that these defenders, brave unto death though they were, could have been able to hold that long sector, but they held. The enemy advanced in force and hurled themselves time and time again against the line in this region, but they found no weak spot. This composite force stood as gallantly and as well as their comrades to the right and to the left. They clung on for many hours until the regulars came up."

What happened at Cambrai had been repeated before Amiens. American engineers, facing an emergency, had thrown their tools aside and taken up arms. They were not many; but, nevertheless, history will never record the battle of Picardy without including the story of how Carey's men acquitted themselves, nor omit the fact that Americans were in the fray.

Afterward American troops in strong force took up positions on the active fighting front in Picardy with the French and British. General Pershing's first reenforcements occupied a sector east of Amiens on a rolling terrain. The artillery was first on the line, entering on a dark night reddened by the continuous flashes of friendly and hostile guns. Under a fire at times heavy, the American gunners took up the positions of the French batteries and set about digging in. When the infantry moved in, the firing was just as intense. In some places the troops, after passing through villages, were raked with shrapnel. In several instances they found the trenches shallow; in other cases there were no trenches at all. The positions were soon improved and the shell holes connected. The American lines generally ran about 200 to 400 yards apart with the high ground about evenly divided about them.

The American troops were there to stay. The pack on each man's back as he entered the firing line was loaded with paraphernalia that pointed to permanency so far as such a condition obtains in warfare. Each carried a blanket, with a pair of shoes tied on either side of it. Among other articles carried were two pairs of socks, a suit of underwear, a towel, soap, toilet articles, two days' emergency rations of four packages of hard bread, and a can of corned beef, whatever trinkets he had, a deck of cards, a set of dice, and photographs and letters especially cherished by him. In addition he carried canteen, rifle, bayonet, 160 rounds of ammunition, a shovel, pick, and a wire cutter (or bolo).

A French communiqué, in reporting a violent bombardment of French-American positions on April 24, 1918, specifically located the American sector as "south of the Somme and on the Avre."

The opposing lines ran north and south, with the enemy between the Americans and the rising sun. Between the rear American echelons extended the main road between Amiens and Beauvais. Amiens, the German objective, lay thirty-five kilometers away on the American left. Beauvais was about the same distance away on the American right and two hours distant by train from Paris. The Americans were between the Germans and the sea.

On April 3, 1918, this American line was violently attacked by the Germans near Villers-Bretonneux—the first occasion that brought fully equipped American troops in force into the swing of the continuing Picardy battle. It was an afternoon bombardment, beginning at 5 o'clock, and lasted for two hours. The German guns were directed especially against the Americans, who were supported on the north and south by the French. The intensity of the enemy's fire slacked about 7 o'clock, whereupon the German commander sent forward three battalions of infantry. The Americans met them and a violent struggle ensued. There was hand-to-hand fighting all along the line, as a result of which the enemy was thrust back, his dead and wounded lying on the ground in all directions. Five prisoners remained in American hands. The American losses were severe, but so were the enemy's. The French were full of praise for the manner in which the Americans acquitted themselves under trying circumstances, especially in view of the fact that they were fighting at one of the most difficult points on the battle front.

An interlude of comparative quiet set in, if such a term can be used when there were daily artillery firing and patrolling. The Americans, settling in their positions, became stronger; they appeared to be better intrenched than the Germans, who were continually harassed, day and night. The enemy was wastefully lavish in the use of gas, some of it liquefied, in glass bottles which were hurled through the air apparently by means of a spring. On bursting they liberated heavy, white fumes that caused nausea, sneezing, and coughing, but did not otherwise harm the Americans. These missiles, thrown without any detonation, were a variant on the avalanche of "mustard" gas shells the Germans periodically showered. They appeared to be disconcerted by the unmoved bearing of the Americans before the gas assaults; instead of retreating from the clouds of fumes, the Americans countered by sending gas of twofold strength into the enemy's lines. In fact, the Americans always greeted every exhibition of German fire by returning it two to one. Their positions became daily more firmly established and those of the Germans more difficult to retain.

Higher up, northwest of these positions in Picardy, American troops had established positions in union with the British forces under Sir Douglas Haig. Thus "American fronts" by the middle of May, 1918, interposed along the entire western line from the North Sea to the Swiss border. Their distribution between French and British sectors placed fresh troops where they were needed and afforded scope for invaluable training in modern warfare to both officers and men that they could obtain in no other way. Those in Picardy were not long in proving that they were equal to their experienced Anglo-French comrades in arms in the task they had set themselves.

CHAPTER XLVIII

CANTIGNY

FORETOKENS of a movement against Cantigny came in the middle of May, 1918, when a searching American artillery fire exploded a huge German ammunition dump at that place and set a number of fires blazing behind the German lines in Montdidier. Near the latter town the Germans later drove a wedge

into the American line in a retaliatory attack and stayed there
for four hours. The American counterthrust hurled them back;
the troops not only drove them across no-man's-land, but followed them into their own second line and made a haul of prisoners. The Germans suffered heavily in the fighting, which was
of a hand-to-hand nature at times. The bravery of the Americans may be illustrated by the case of a private whose arm was
blown off. Dazed, he kept on fighting, and did not know he had
been injured until a comrade came to his aid.

This attack, like those made on the Lorraine front, was an
attempt to push back new troops with the object of creating a
feeling that they formed a weak link in the defending chain. The
next day, however, the weak link stretched beyond its own line
and essayed an assault on Cantigny. The action, May 28, 1918,
took place while huge German forces elsewhere were in the
swing of a drive southward through the Allied lines between
Noyon and Rheims, on a forty-mile front, and had overrrun the
Chemin-des-Dames—throwing back the American forces there
—and crossed the Aisne.

The Cantigny exploit did not bulk large in the great battle
that raged from Ypres to Rheims; but it showed that, put on
their mettle, the new troops were first-class fighting men and a
match for the Germans. Amiens, in the neighborhood of which the
enemy already had had a foretaste of American valor, was only
twenty miles away to the northwest. To the American right the
Germans were forging their way to the Marne and creating the
celebrated salient between Soissons and Rheims. Away to the
left the British and French had just checked the second phase
of the German advance between Ypres and Arras. Cantigny
brought a little consolation to the Allies, though only a counter-
diversion of small account, in the midst of the sweeping German
onslaught.

Just west of the village the Germans held a salient, which the
Americans determined to flatten out. An advance, on a front of
a mile and a quarter, was thereupon organized, involving the
employment of a considerable force, and undertaken under the
eye of veteran French officers, who made safeguarding disposi-

tions of their own forces to reenforce the Americans if necessary.

The customary artillery fire, augmented by French gunners, signalized the attack, which began early in the morning. Aided by French tanks, the Americans advanced through a mist and made the required distance of 600 yards in ten minutes under machine-gun fire. The tanks found their path easy, the American guns having already prepared the way. In fact, their fire smothered the Germans, whose resistance was so slight that the Americans proceeded to penetrate their positions to a depth of nearly a mile.

A strong unit of flame throwers and engineers aided the Americans. Moving barrages preceded the infantry advance, which followed with clockwork precision. There was some hand-to-hand fighting in the streets, but the hard-hitting Americans, wielding grenade and bayonet, managed to clear the enemy out of the village in three quarters of an hour. A number of Germans had taken refuge in a large tunnel and a number of caves, which formed part of the village fortifications, and the Americans had to hurl grenades like baseballs into these shelters in order to oust them. The Germans entombed in dugouts near by readily trooped out and surrendered when they saw the futility of resistance. In short, the garrison at Cantigny was soon accounted for; the men were either all captured or killed at a slight cost to the Americans. It was found that the Germans had honeycombed the village with outposts and machine-gun emplacements.

The Americans had obtained high ground commanding a section of plateaulike country. In straightening the salient they acquired territory the length of their two-kilometer advance, as well as Cantigny, and brought their line well east of the village.

The Germans attempted several counterattacks, persisting in them for three days. They were met by hurricanes of fire. Waves of German infantrymen were stopped dead or thrown back, leaving many of their number killed or wounded on the ground. There were night bombardments, air bombing, and even tank attacks in addition to fruitless advances of troops. Foot soldiers and tanks alike recoiled before the stone-wall resistance offered by the Americans, who did not budge an inch from the position they occupied on taking Cantigny. On the contrary, in face of continuous attempts to expel them, they consolidated their position, and finally came a quiet day, telling that the Germans had abandoned their efforts to retake the village. The attack and counterattacks yielded 242 prisoners to the Americans.

Berlin, recording the engagement on May 29, 1918, merely said:

"West of Montdidier the enemy during a local advance penetrated into Cantigny yesterday."

General Pershing found occasion to comment thus on this announcement in his report to the War Department:

"Attention is drawn to the fact that the German official communiqué of May 29, afternoon, in reporting the capture of Cantigny avoids mention of the fact that the operation was conducted by American troops. Recent marked endeavors of the Germans to discount the fighting qualities of our forces indicate that the enemy feared the moral effect of such admission in Germany."

CHAPTER XLIX

AROUND CHATEAU-THIERRY

MEANTIME, some distance to the left of this American sector at Cantigny, the German thrust between Noyon and Rheims had cut across the Aisne, took a westward turn and enveloped Soissons, proceeded south to the Marne between Château-Thierry and Dormans on a six-mile front, and swung a couple of miles along the Marne beyond Dormans. Their advance having progressed thus far, the Germans on the Marne and on the west of the salient they had formed in the Allied line found themselves facing another American army.

The narrative of American operations in France thus turns from recording local exploits such as that at Cantigny and the trench adventures that marked the inconsequential warfare along the American sectors east of St. Mihiel. It becomes merged in the story of major operations, with the Americans in the thick of a great battle, fighting shoulder to shoulder with the French on their left, and joined on their right by more French, aided by British and Italian troops. American forces in great numbers became a big factor in arresting the southward sweep of the Germans across the Marne, and in checking a plunge westward, both operations aiming at a triumphant march on Paris. Just as the Americans had aided in stopping the Germans from reaching Amiens, a pivotal point in the British lines, so did they save Paris. At the tail end of the third phase of his descent on the French capital via the Marne, the German was slowly beginning to realize that the despised Americans had become a leading factor in the war.

There was an imperative call for American aid to reenforce the French along the Marne and on the western side of the salient. They were rushed from distant training areas, or from the quiet sectors in Lorraine and Alsace or from the American positions round Cantigny and Montdidier and about Amiens on the British front, and once on the scene they immediately plunged into action to check the German drive. How one American unit hastened to fill the breach and stem the Teutonic tide was described by Junius B. Wood as typical of the expedition with which other detachments moved into the battle zone:

"One evening at 7 o'clock orders came over the long-distance telephone from headquarters to move. At 10 o'clock the same night camions were rumbling up, and after all the men had found places, started toward the fateful Marne. Before daylight they had crossed a goodly part of France and reached the reserve areas. The camions started back, while soldiers and officers stretched out along the roadside to snatch a few hours of sleep. The next night they marched into the support positions. A few more hours of sleep, and they went directly into the battle. In less than twelve hours telephone wires were strung and communication established in their territory. Every part of the organization from commanding officers to privates were working perfectly. Supplies were coming up over the roads in the rear. Ambulances were carrying back the wounded, while the trucks which had carried up ammunition with which to sow the seeds of death returned to aid refugees and thus helping to save the living.

"Along the Paris road the dust hung like a fog over the companies marching forward to take their turn at fighting and other companies returning for a few hours of sleep. Out of the brown clouds dashed staff motor cars and ambulances disregarding all speed laws. Trains of trucks passed the horse-drawn batteries moving into position. Flashes and war-splitting crashes came from batteries put in position just far enough off the roads to avoid the traffic. Men were cooking beside the guns, and others, oblivious to the suffocating dust, were sleeping in the midst of the noise and turmoil. All moved according to a well-ordered system.

"While the guns were barking under the shade trees at the roadside stolid ox teams with carts loaded with household possessions were moving to the rear. It seemed as if the guns with their muzzles pointing the other way were holding back the invaders until those fleeing fugitives should again reach safety. Other batteries were hastily unlimbered in fields and orchards where plows and harrows had been abandoned only a few hours previously by the peaceful peasants."

The Americans entered the line in the midst of a battle which raged over a hilly country and which shifted back and forth like a maelstrom. Crops were growing and there were no prepared trenches. The first unit on the scene was a machine-gun battalion, which rode on trucks throughout the night of Friday, May 30, 1918, and arrived the next morning, going into position to guard the bridges across the Marne at Château-Thierry. Another unit arrived on Sunday morning. June 2, 1918, and before 4 o'clock the same afternoon had been in three fights, in one of which it drove the Germans back two kilometers on a front of four kilometers.

The beginning of June, 1918, in fact, which marked the entrance of the Americans into the battle line of the Soissons-

Marne-Rheims salient, found them in the thick of the conflict almost before they had breathing time to dig in.

The Germans at once locked horns with them at Neuilly, Château-Thierry, and Jaulgonne. When the Americans appeared near the first-named place, the Germans were trying to enter Neuilly Wood. They had succeeded in entering the village of Neuilly-la-Poterie near by and found the adjacent woods, occupied by the French and Americans, a stumblingblock to their advance. The American machine gunners mowed down the advancing enemy battalions and later supported the French infantry in a counterattack which forced the enemy to retire beyond the northern edge of the wood. On June 31, 1918, the Germans made another attempt to drive the Americans out. They concentrated large forces and advanced in massed formation. Again they were met by a rain of machine-gun fire, which smothered a similar hail of bullets the Germans had shed on the Americans from hastily erected machine-gun positions on the skirts of the wood. The Americans advanced before the Germans reached their line, engaged them at close quarters with the bayonet, broke their formations and sent them fleeing in confusion to the ruined village beyond the wood whence they had come.

While these attacks were under way American and French troops on the Marne near Jaulgonne, east of Château-Thierry, were engaged in repelling a battalion of Germans who had forced a passage of the river at that point. In a sharp combat, marked by the fierceness of their machine-gun fire, the French and Americans, fighting side by side, almost wiped out the German forces which reached the southern bank of the Marne. Most of the survivors were rounded up in small groups and captured. They numbered a hundred. A second German attack was launched later with shock troops, who also gained a footing on the southern bank, but again their stay was not long. The footbridge on which they crossed was swept by American machine-gun fire, and rushes of American infantry forced the enemy back.

The most notable of these preliminary contacts the Germans had with the Americans on the southern arc of the salient was at Château-Thierry. The battalion of American machine gunners already mentioned, which had been posted on May 31, 1918, to guard the river bridges at that town, found the Germans already in the northern outskirts. The town lies on both sides of the Marne, which is there spanned by a big bridge. A little to the northward a canal runs parallel to the river and is crossed by a smaller bridge. The Germans had made their way into the northern part of the town through a gap they had driven in the Allied lines to the left, and began to stream through the streets toward the bridge, intending to establish themselves firmly on the southern bank and capture the town.

They reckoned without the American machine gunners, who had been suddenly thrown into Château-Thierry with French colonial troops. The Americans immediately took over the defense of the river bank, especially the approaches to the bridge. They began operations by poking the muzzles of their weapons through broken walls, bushes, and holes knocked in the sides of the houses. The guns were skillfully hidden and the Germans were unable to locate them. The latter wavered under the American fire, their advance was brought to a standstill, and a counterattack by the French colonials drove them from the town. As usual the Germans attempted a counterassault. The next night, June 1, 1918, taking advantage of the darkness, they stole toward the large bridge, in which direction they penetrated through the western suburbs to the banks of the Marne. In order to mask their movements, they made use of smoke bombs, which made the aim of the machine guns very difficult. At the same time the town underwent an extremely violent bombardment. A surprise, however, was in store for them. They were already crossing the bridge, evidently believing themselves masters of both banks, when a thunderous explosion blew the center of the bridge and a number of Germans with it into the river. Those who reached the southern bank were immediately captured. Holding the south end of the bridge, the Americans covered the withdrawal of troops across the bridge before its destruction, and although under severe fire themselves, kept all the approaches to the bank under a rain of bullets, which nullified all the subsequent efforts of the enemy to cross the river. Every attempt of the Germans to elude the vigilance of the Americans resulted in disaster to them. The upshot was that the Germans abandoned the occupation of the northern part of Château-Thierry, which American machine guns made untenable, and it became a part of no-man's-land. The Americans altogether made a brilliant defense of the town. A French staff officer described it as one of the finest feats of the war. There was little left of the town itself. It was shot to pieces and became a pile of bricks and stones.

CHAPTER L

A DRIVE BY THE MARINES

AMERICAN operations in the salient now took a more active turn to the northwest of Château-Thierry in the vicinity of Neuilly, where the Germans had already clashed with their new antagonists. There the Americans were linked with the French on a line that rested on Neuilly-la-Poterie, and ran through Champillon, Lucy-le-Bocage, and to the south of Triangle, and then meandered in an irregular course to Château-Thierry. From this line came a forward movement on June 6, 1918, directed east of Neuilly toward Torcy, Belleau, and Bouresches. The next day the line stood south of the village of Torcy, south of the village of Belleau, with the wood of Belleau partly in American possession, and through Bouresches, then south to the highway east of Thiolet, and thence to Château-Thierry. This advance represented an extension of the American line over a front of about six miles to a depth of nearly two and a half miles.

The brunt of the fighting was borne by United States Marines. It was a sustained action, extending for thirty-six hours. It held the center of the war stage; on no other part of the fighting fronts were there any measurable activities that produced like successes against German arms. The movement, which aimed to drive the German lines farther back from their Paris objective also had its significance in that its second stage was directed by American commanders and undertaken solely by American troops. Most of the fighting by Americans on the western front had been carried out under French commanders. The American units detailed to the Somme, for example, reported to the French command, who assigned them with French soldiers where they were most needed. The commander of the unit to which the marines belonged wanted full control of his own sector in the Château-Thierry region. The request was granted, and the result showed that an American unit, acting on its own initiative, could acquit itself equal to the best-trained German unit.

The first assault on the enemy lines was made at dawn, when the American marines swept forward, with the French attacking on their left, and gained over a mile on a four-mile front. By 8 o'clock they had gained all their first objectives and held all the important high ground northwest of Château-Thierry. They captured 100 prisoners, among them thirty-five mounted Uhlans, and ten machine guns.

The enemy had augmented his line recently, the Americans having pressed him so hard that he was forced to throw three new divisions of his best troops into the breach. Against them the Americans advanced in a solid phalanx, singing and whistling "Yankee Doodle," and cheering. No barrage preceded them, although there had been some advance artillery preparations. On certain parts of the line the resistance was weak; but in other instances our marines ran into German machine-gun nests which, in some cases, succeeded in inflicting considerable casualties. But they did not stop the Americans. Marines with hand grenades and rifles charged the machine guns, wiping out the nests, and in one instance capturing a gun and its crew.

From the new line gained by the first attack, a second American advance was made at five in the evening, and by night it reached Torcy and Bouresches. The next morning, June 7, 1918, the Americans were holding Torcy in the face of repeated counterattacks and pushing back the Germans through the streets of Bouresches. Torcy was not part of the American objective,

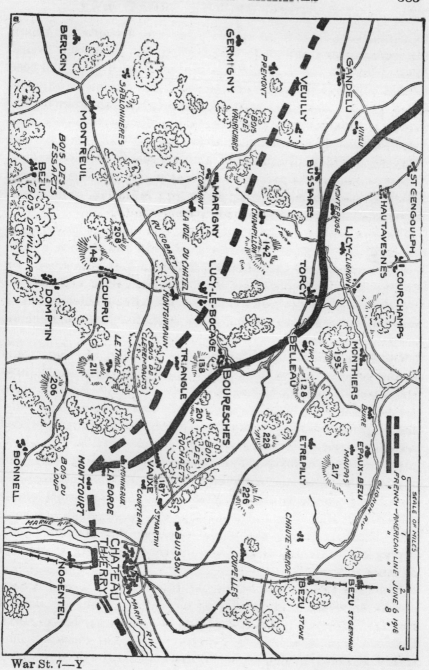

but the eager marines swept into the village by their own momentum.

The hardest fighting took place in the wood of Belleau, to the east of Torcy and between that village and Bouresches.

The wood of Belleau into which the marines penetrated with such ardor proved a hornets' nest. It was ambushed with machine guns, which hampered the American advance and caused many casualties. There were about twenty of them in the plateau formed by the wood. The Americans vainly tried to demolish them by rifles, mortars, and hand grenades. Finally, despite the streams of bullets, they surrounded the plateau, cut off the Germans in it, and went ahead, capturing a hill beyond the wood and inflicting heavy losses on the Germans as they withdrew.

The tireless and undaunted marines then moved on Bouresches. It was a night attack, marked by volleys of machine-gun fire which they poured into the enemy stationed in the village. Bayonets were freely used whenever the Germans attempted to make a stand in the streets. The path of the Americans was not easy. They drove the Germans out in the face of heavy artillery fire, including gas shells, but several times they were balked by machine guns operated by Germans from house roofs. At last a lieutenant, with what was left of a platoon, penetrated into the town under heavy German fire and cleared it of infantry. He held it for thirty minutes, until two companies of Americans came to his aid. They spent an hour routing out the German machine gunners with rifles and hand grenades, when the ammunition began to run low. A runner was dispatched for supplies and another lieutenant hastened to the rescue with a truck load of ammunition. On the road to Bouresches he was the target of a heavy fire from Germans who had hidden behind the advancing Americans; but he succeeded in getting the truck into the town and distributing the sorely needed ammunition.

The American position created by the capture of Bouresches ran from that village to Le Thiolet and guarded the highway from Château-Thierry to Paris. On June 8, 1918, the Germans vainly attacked this position. They also tried to retake Bouresches without success. They could not advance beyond the railroad tracks to the north of the town, where they had intrenched themselves after being driven out by the marines.

The Germans started a night bombardment on the position, to which the Americans did not respond until the enemy's movements revealed that an attack on Le Thiolet was intended. A heavy American barrage was thereupon laid down, which cut the communications of the attacking force and hampered its reenforcements. The Americans were in shallow trenches, hastily prepared, but well equipped with machine guns, which poured a concentrated fire on the enemy when he advanced within 600 yards. Under that fire he continued for 200 yards and then stopped. Undismayed by this repulse, the enemy sent another body of troops to attack the American positions south of the highway, where, on the edge of a wood, the Americans had posted many machine guns. The gunners allowed the Germans to advance a certain distance and then rained their fire upon them. More than a hundred German dead covered one small field swept by the American bullets. The enemy was halted and driven back by a rush of Americans from their trenches in the face of a hail of bullets showered upon them from behind the German lines. This rear fire marked both the attack and repulse, but did not deter the Americans.

It now came the turn of the marines occupying Bouresches to beat off a German attack aiming at its recapture. The trio of counterassaults appeared to have been designed so that the third should be the grand finale, or a culminating surprise for the Americans. The latter were alert, having been forewarned, and were reenforced by a number of machine guns. These they placed on the top of the embankment along which the railroad track ran. The slaughter of the Germans was ruthless when they ventured to cross the track. None returned who got past the embankment; they were either killed or captured. The attack was repeated, but each attempt to retake Bouresches failed.

The Americans with their machine guns paid the Germans back in their own coin. One of the chief obstacles to the Americans' progress was the German fire from such guns. Bouresches when taken was found dotted with positions for them in strong locations and they had to be demolished by mortars. The Germans appeared to rely more on their machine guns to arrest the American advance than on any other weapon of offense. When not fixed in locations they were portable, being mounted on carriages and pushed along by their operators. The Germans also used a light field mortar, mounted on a two-wheel truck, in the same way.

The three days' fighting produced the usual crop of striking incidents. One marine who was taking back a prisoner ran into two German officers and ten men. He fought them single-handed with his rifle and bayonet, killed both the officers and wounded seven of the men. Another sergeant was about to take a prisoner when the German threw himself on the ground and discharged his revolver at the American after calling "comrade," the sergeant shot him, as he did four others who also had surrendered, but refused to put up their hands. In Torcy twenty-five Americans engaged and drove out 200 Germans, and then withdrew to the main line on the outskirts of the town. A corporal in a company of marines, all of whose officers, including the sergeants, had been killed or wounded, took the command and led his men to their objective.

The élan of the Americans in the whole adventure was expressed by a private who was among the first to rush into Torcy:

"I never saw such wonderful spirit. Not one of our fellows hesitated in the face of the rain of the machine-gun fire, which it seemed impossible to get through. Every German seemed to have a machine gun. They fought like wild cats, but the Americans were too much for them."

CHAPTER LI

BELLEAU WOOD

THERE was a dangerous bulge in the new American line formed by Belleau Wood. In their advance the Americans had been unable to take this forested little stronghold perched on a hill among rocks, and had swept past it, after capturing a near-by elevation, and rushed on to Bouresches. The wood concealed ambushes of German infantry and machine guns, which were a thorn in the side of the Americans on the outskirts. They had made several raids in the wood, expelling groups of Germans here and there; but the next day the enemy would reappear and pour a harassing fire on the American lines. Notwithstanding searching shelling from American guns, the Germans seemed to retain a firm hold.

A German attack on June 8, 1918, to oust the Americans from the positions they held on the borders of the wood precipitated an energetic counterassault to clear the enemy completely out. The Americans had already matured plans for riddling the entire woody plateau with a deluge of shells. This artillery scheme was carried out on mathematical lines, the area of the wood being marked off into checkerboard squares, a square to each battery. Every part of the wood therefore had established targets for the American gunners to play upon. The artillery preparation lasted all of Sunday and Monday, June 9 and 10, 1918. It was the most expansive exhibition of ordnance in action that the Americans had undertaken. The wood was raked with more than 5,000 high explosive and gas shells. At 3 o'clock on Monday morning the marines, who had been in conflict with the Germans in their attack of Saturday, proceeded to advance into the wood and penetrated it for two-thirds of a mile on a 66-yard front.

The operations were tersely reported by General Pershing to the War Department as follows:

"June 11.—Northwest of Château-Thierry we were again successful in advancing our positions in the Belleau Wood. We captured 250 prisoners, of whom three were officers, and considerable material, including a number of machine guns and trench mortars."

"June 13—Yesterday afternoon our troops northwest of Château-Thierry captured the last of the German positions in the Belleau Wood, taking fifty prisoners and a number of machine guns and trench mortars, in addition to those taken on the preceding day."

The Germans now became a menace on the borders of the wood, where they impinged on a number of awkward pockets or little salients. The Americans in the wood enjoyed no sinecure, but were engaged in continuous skirmishes against groups of the enemy. One small pocket the Germans found too untenable under American fire on the northern side of the wood and hastily vacated it on June 19, 1918, enabling the Americans to advance five-eighths of a mile without resistance. A short and sharp artillery fire on the position presaged an infantry attack, which the Germans elected not to face. They carried their material with them in their retreat, and the Americans, therefore, did not take any machine guns nor prisoners. On the morning of June 21, 1918, the Americans straightened their line further on the northern and eastern side by a series of small but effective attacks. They rushed the positions held by the enemy without the customary artillery opening. The Germans for the most part fired a few shots and retired. Members of one post alone held their ground, only to be annihilated. To the east a thin line of American skirmishers obtained the objective in view there by, merely firing as they advanced.

Still the borders of the wood were not clear of the Germans. On June 23, 1918, the Americans directed their attention to the northwestern corner, where the Germans held positions that appeared impregnable. The Americans, in a night attack, started a heavy barrage, after which they went forward and drove out the Germans. The operation lasted only half an hour.

Another engagement that took place in the same quarter on the same day was more extensive in scope though local in object. It resulted in the Americans advancing their lines a distance of

200 to 400 yards on a front of one kilometer, routing the Germans out of several hidden gun nests, and the capture of five machine guns. The fighting was marked by certain features, described by Edwin L. James:

"This fight, which lasted four hours, was not accompanied by artillery or gas fire, and was mostly close hand fighting, the kind which Americans most prefer. It was a fight such as seldom occurs in this war, where usually trench positions are so well defined that barrages can be laid safely by both sides down to a matter of inches.

"Germans and Americans got so mixed up in the north end of the Bois de Belleau that neither side risked using artillery for fear of killing its own men.

"The Americans began to advance at 6 o'clock in broad daylight. In the extreme north wood the Germans had been able to establish some machine guns, which were firing against us. Our men advanced against these positions and discovered that to the north of the wood the Germans had established a strong line position."

As to the ubiquitous machine guns, the Americans found that the Germans had organized such posts with great ingenuity:

"At one point the nature of the terrain prevented machine guns on the ground from commanding the surrounding area. Here a dead German gunner was found seated in the crotch of a tree, his hand still resting on a machine gun slung from a pulley and carefully counterbalanced down so that it could be pointed in every direction. This German stayed at his post until an American shot him.

"Another machine gun was found on a cleverly concealed platform in a tree, while in another tree a one-pounder was mounted until we put it out of commission.

"Preceding the advance of our infantry, American artillery had put down a heavy bombardment of German positions in the woods, but large trees impaired the effectiveness of the shells."

The retention by the Germans of positions abutting on the wood had been reduced to a single point on the north. This remaining menace was subjected to a dashing attack by the Americans on the night of June 25, 1918. In their various forays they had cleared the enemy out of the wood several days ago; but the discovery was made that under cover of darkness the Germans had planted machine guns behind huge bowlders, in sunken road-ways, in shell holes, and in trees in a narrow area on the edge of the wood. It was most difficult to reach them in these positions, and some fierce hand-to-hand fighting occurred in the clearing process.

The attack involved an artillery bombardment lasting thirteen hours. Only a small strip of underbrush, behind which the Ger-mans had raised their defensive works, remained to be cleared; but the importance of the American advance was not to be meas-ured by the extent of territory taken. Though it only amounted to some 500 yards, it gave them possession of virtually all of Belleau Wood, and enabled them to dominate the ridge beyond, held by the Germans, besides straightening their lines for more effective resistance to counterattacks as well as for offensive op-erations. Over twenty machine guns were captured, with a num-ber of automatic rifles, small arms and ammunition, and 311 prisoners.

It was a surprise attack, in which the American artillery played a brilliant part, throwing the whole German line in con-fusion and making it such an inferno that prisoners said they were glad to get out of it alive. In advancing, the Americans went one way and the German officers tried to force their men forward the other way. One prisoner was shot in the leg by his own officer because he hesitated confusedly between the Ameri-can guns and bayonets and the pistols in the hands of the Ger-man officers.

An American private, who was in the first line of the advance, gave this glimpse of the operation:

"We took up a position in the open wood; there were no trenches. The Germans opened a heavy fire and shells fell around us like rain. We charged over the rocky hill, our fellows laughing and yelling a war whoop. We then came upon a wheat field and crossed in the face of a withering shell and machine-gun fire, and drove back the Germans at the point of the bayonet."

Interposing between the attacks around Belleau Wood were skirmishes for the possession of Bouresches. This town, being only a mile or so to the south of the wood, constituted a menace to the Americans if retaken by the Germans, and consequently the latter made several determined efforts to regain it. Two hours after the Americans made their first attack on Belleau Wood on June 10, 1918, the Germans launched heavy forces against the Americans holding Bouresches. A dark and cloudy night aided their preparations for the rush, but the Americans, expecting an assault, had the northern side of the town lined with machine guns, and had artillery trained on the railroad embankment over which the Germans had to come. When, at 5 o'clock, the Germans came they met a terrific machine-gun fire, while a heavy barrage behind the attacking party, and gradually lowered on it, not only cut off reenforcements, but killed many in it.

Two fresh divisions were thrown against the American center. Trusting to the deep woods northeast of the village and the twisted spur of a hill to conceal them, the leading divisions advanced in mass formation. They, however, were observed from the Bois de Belleau and were brought under a destructive hail of shrapnel before they could deploy. The fire was so severe that the attack was disorganized and no progress could be made for some time.

When the Germans did succeed in penetrating the defenses, they were met with such enthusiasm in cold steel that their only choice was death or surrender.

Another violent attack on the town came on the morning of June 13, 1918. The Germans succeeded in entering the town after raking the American positions by a furious bombardment. The Americans promptly darted out of their shelters and engaged the invaders in a hand-to-hand conflict, in which the latter were all killed or captured.

A moonlight sortie across the Marne east of Château-Thierry provided a diversion for the American forces at that point while the marines were busy on the Belleau-Bouresches line. Once over the river, they established contact with hostile forces, killed a considerable number, and brought back prisoners, mainly from

Landwehr units. The following description of the raid was furnished by an Associated Press correspondent:

"Heavy clouds obscured the moon and a light drizzle had just begun to fall when the two parties of Americans embarked in small boats and rowed across the river from two points of the wooded bank. They crossed without detection. One party entered the woodside held by the Germans and penetrated cautiously under the dripping trees for a few hundred feet.

"A break in the clouds suddenly let the moonlight through, and the Americans saw Germans near by. The Americans immediately opened fire from a little rise in the ground, and the Germans threw themselves flat. Rifles cracked, and then the automatics got into action. Those of the enemy who remained alive were taken prisoners. Twelve enemy dead were counted before the patrol made its way back to the boats and rowed to its own side of the river.

"The other patrol met another enemy party, apparently sentries, going on guard. Several of the Germans were killed or wounded and one was taken prisoner."

A previous diversion at midnight was directed at a wood, also to the east of Château-Thierry. Aerial photographs had revealed a host of enemy troops and much material concealed there, and upon them the American guns poured an avalanche of projectiles, sending 1,200 shells of all calibers into one small area in ten minutes. To the west of the town, a fight occurred round a commanding hill whose northern, or unimportant side, was held by the Germans. The latter sent forces around both sides and over the top to expel the American and French troops, who held the crest and the other flanks of the hill, without gaining an advantage.

CHAPTER LII

THEIR PRESENCE FELT

THE exploits of American forces during the month of June, 1918, in the Château-Thierry region of the Soissons-Rheims salient had a significance of their own, which was not lost on their admiring Allies, nor on their German foes. A new combatant, stripped and eager for action, had plunged into tasks which would have taxed the hardened and more experienced troops of France and Great Britain. Though confined to a small area, the American achievements were sufficiently notable to prove that the Americans had speedily become the equals of any other warriors on the fighting fronts. In the numerous fights centering on Belleau Wood their captures of Germans reached 1,000. A number of them belonged to the crack Fifth German Guard Division, which includes the Queen Elizabeth Regiment. There had been 1,200 Germans in the wood. With the exception of the prisoners nearly all the rest were slain. The guard division named was regarded as one of the kaiser's best body of fighters; but the Americans were surprised to find their morale very low and that they were no match for American vigor and audacity.

At the beginning of June, 1918, American troops stepped into a seven-mile sector northwest of Château-Thierry and stopped the Germans, at the very tip of their salient, from getting any nearer to Paris. More than that, on a front of ten kilometers they hurled almost constant blows, which advanced their line from two to four kilometers, all the way inflicting heavy losses on the enemy, and taking some 1,500 prisoners. Of eleven distinct engagements the Americans won ten. They kept eleven picked German divisions occupied, which might otherwise have been used with telling effect elsewhere. There was no doubt at all that the quality of the American fighters had proved a source of considerable concern to the German High Command. An oft-repeated canard current in France was to the effect that the Germans did not wish to punish the Americans by sending their best troops against them, preferring not to arouse the American spirit. Nevertheless, the kaiser had sent his most famous battalions to try conclusions with the Americans, and they had been beaten. Learning of the Americans' presence on the Marne, two crack German divisions, the Fifth Guard and the Twenty-eighth, which had been ordered elsewhere, were suddenly swung south to face the Americans. Their arrival caused some wonderment among the French and American officers. The Americans were a feared foe. A captured German officer said these two divisions were on their way to the rear for a four weeks' rest, to take part in another offensive, when suddenly they were ordered to the front northwest of Château-Thierry, "in order to prevent at all costs the Americans from being able to achieve success."

The examination of other prisoners, from the Twenty-eighth German Division, elicited information which formed the subject of a French army report.

"American assistance," this report observed, "which was underestimated in Germany, because they doubted its value and its opportunity, worries the German High Command more than it will admit. The officers themselves recognize that among other causes it is the principal reason for which Germany hastens to try to end the war and impose peace.

"In addition, the prisoners did not conceal their great surprise at the training and quickness that the Americans have shown against them, nor for the good work accomplished by the artillery, which for three days engaged them, cutting off all food supplies and all reenforcements and causing them very heavy losses—practically all of the officers and twenty-five of the men were killed or wounded in a single infantry company and twelve in a machine-gun section, of which the full quota was seventeen men."

Testimony of a similar tenor was found in a letter taken from the dead body of a German killed in Belleau Wood. It was written to his home people and dated June 21, 1918.

"We are now in the battle front," it said, "and canteens dare not come to us on account of the enemy, for the Americans are bombarding villages fifteen kilometers behind the present front with long-range guns, and you will know that canteen outfits and others who are lying in reserve do not venture very far, for it is not pleasant to 'eat cherries' with Americans. The reason for that is that they have not yet had much experience. American divisions are still too fiery.

"We will also show the Americans how good we are, for day before yesterday we bombarded them heavily with our gas. This had caused them already great losses, for they are not yet sufficiently experienced with gas bombardment. About 100 of us are lying around here.

"We have one corner of the wood and the Americans have the other corner. That is not nice, for all of a sudden he rushes forward and one does not know it beforehand. Therefore one must shoot at every little noise, for one cannot trust them."

In the fighting round Château-Thierry a number of drafted men were thrown into action to replace other units of the established army forces. The latter were men of the regular army, the marine corps, and the old national guard. All these had previous training under arms; and many had been in actual combat in the Philippines, Haiti, Nicaragua, at Vera Cruz, or on the trek into Mexico after Villa. But the drafted men had had no such hardening prior to going into cantonments, where the training, although severe and thorough, was not acquired under conditions of actual warfare with an enemy at hand. The drafted men of the new national army nevertheless went under fire before the kaiser's picked hosts, not as raw recruits, but capable soldiers of mettle and valor. They were more undisciplined, owing to the easy nature of American life, than the young men of other nations; yet they readily accustomed themselves to discipline. They were unfamiliar with war, because of their country's immunity from its terrors; yet they were equal to the emergency when it came.

The exploits of the marine corps in their swing from the original American position to the Torcy-Bouresches-Château-Thierry line stand out in strong relief. The massed efficiency of the rest of the American forces was not the less conspicuous be-

cause of the marines' achievements. That the latter acquired a
certain prominence was perhaps due to the fact that their daring
and resourcefulness was never without an element of the picturesque. They were stationed at the point nearest to Paris to protect it; but they did not wait to be attacked. They chose to take
their offensive, which continued on their own initiative, advancing beyond the object in view, and gained ground against determined opposition. Their bravery was tempered by judgment,
and their steady progress and small losses showed that it was
not marred by recklessness.

CHAPTER LIII

VAUX AND HAMEL

JULY, 1918, was a red-letter month in the annals of American
belligerency on the European battle field. Events of historic
moment, in which American soldiers, fighting shoulder to
shoulder with the French, were irresistible protagonists,
crowded one upon another. They had got into their stride; they
were seasoned and in the pink of condition; no German heroics
could withstand them.

As a sort of prelude to their memorable participation in General Foch's offensive stroke of July 18, 1918, the American
troops undertook a little offensive of their own to the west of
Château-Thierry, and accomplished their object with devastating results to the enemy.

The investment and capture of Belleau Wood to the northwest
had completed a chain of operations designed to secure the
American positions. But there remained an awkward loop or
sag which it was deemed desirable to remove. Its straightening
involved the occupation of a little village called Vaux, with its
tap on the main railroad line into Château-Thierry, the capture
of a knoblike crest of ground designated as Hill 192, on the edge
of Clerembauts Wood, and also the routing of Germans from a

sizable cluster of trees, midway between the two other points and known as the Bois de la Roche. The front of the attack was about two and a half miles, stretching from the village of Triangle, then north to the Bois Clerembauts, across the Paris road, and running south of Vaux. Vaux was an important objective, being considered vital to the Germans for holding Château-Thierry.

The Americans went over Vaux and established themselves just beyond the northern edge of the village, taking in the same rush the hills just to the west of Vaux. This eliminated the German wedge almost completely, the only remaining portion being at the wood of Clerembauts, where the Germans were in a pocket.

A merciless, methodical artillery fire was leveled at the German positions on the morning of July 1, 1918. American guns, big and little, hurled torrents of high explosive and gas shells on the village with a deadly accuracy of aim. By noon Vaux was on fire. Every house had been hit at least once. A shell would fall on some little habitation, a cloud of yellow smoke would arise, and the house was no more. The American guns continued to belch all day with an unemotional, matter-of-fact regularity from the depths of a score of leafy woods.

In the evening the infantry advanced. They swept through the enemy lines and, had their object been to continue the advance, they could have done so with the greatest ease, as virtually everything before them had been cleared.

"The advance started at 6 o'clock, and at 6.25 the first of our men entered the village of Vaux. By 6.40 they had gone through the wood, gaining all their objectives. Our stormy petrels took Vaux in clean-up style. Squads were ready with their hand grenades to clear the cellars, but many of these had been closed by our fire, and the Germans had been buried in them. From others the Germans came out and surrendered. In some there was difficulty, and in that case our men threw in hand grenades in great numbers. Generally, if there were any Germans left, they surrendered.

"Four hours after the men went over the top American telephone lines were working from Vaux back to our headquarters. By 7.30 our ambulances were running into the wrecked village.

"A wounded German brought in about 10 o'clock said that in the morning there had been 4,000 Germans in the village, but after the barrage started some had been withdrawn, leaving only those who could be sheltered in sixty-eight caves in the village. He said the cave in which he took refuge was wrecked by an American shell and that he lay wounded for six hours until the Americans came in."

For adroitness, dispatch, thoroughness, and sustained team-work, the attack on Vaux was an undoubted triumph for American arms, though a small one. Each man moved to the particular post in the town to which he had been assigned to perform his allotted task. None failed, and the operation was completed with systematic smoothness; as though in a twinkling, it was all over.

With Vaux and the Bois de la Roche in their hands, the Americans took their machine guns to the edge of the wood, expecting a counterattack. It duly came, the Germans launching a fresh regiment upon the lost positions; but an hour later all was calm—the regiment was no more. A second counterattack broke in the small hours of July 3, 1918, accompanied by a heavy bombardment. The enemy lost heavily without regaining a foot of the ground won by the Americans. The Germans advanced in close formation from their trenches without being checked. In some cases they were allowed to approach close to the American line. Then the American gunners, from their hidden nests, mowed down the enemy ranks with showers of bullets.

Later came a fight for the possession of a hill known as 204, situated between Vaux and the Bois de la Roche. The Germans held it and the French, in essaying the task of wresting it from them, invited American detachments to lend a hand. The hill stood just outside the American sector and commanded Château-Thierry. Volunteers were many; most of them were new arrivals who had never faced the Germans. Practically none had been under fire. They were waiting their chance, some swimming in the Marne, others catching baseball, when the call came, and the response was five times the number needed.

A group of thirty Americans joined the French; they were pitted against hidden machine guns, camouflaged rapid-fire nests,

American soldiers near a barricade in the Rue du Pont, Chateau-Thierry. The Germans were driven from the town in the First Battle of the Marne, 1914, and again in the Second Battle of the Marne, 1918

gas shells, and the deafening roar of a heavy barrage. They were shot at by snipers hiding in trees, they were shot at by big and little cannon with a roar that deafened them; but they went ahead with the French veterans. They took machine-gun posts, they took trench positions. But the German resistance was too strong, due in part to their new device of fighting in ambush from the tops of high trees, where they escaped shells exploding on the ground, and obtained a good vantage point for pouring shot downward on the attackers below.

Elsewhere on the western front American forces, linked with the British lines, aided a body of Australians to attack Hamel. It was an early morning advance, extending one and a half miles on a four-mile front, including the village of Hamel and the trench system beyond it, south of the Somme.

It was the first time Americans had fought with the British. They comprised only a few companies fighting as platoons among the Australians; but upon them rested the honor of the United States in the adventure. The date, moreover, was July 4, 1918.

"You are going in with the Australians," their officers told them, "and these lads always deliver the goods. We expect you to do the same. We shall be very disappointed if you do not fulfill the hopes and belief we have in you."

The Americans listened with a light in their eyes. They went in, with "Lusitania!" as their battle cry, celebrating the Fourth of July with "astonishing ardor, discipline and strength," the Australian officers said. If the Americans had any fault at all, the Australians commented, it was overeagerness to advance; they could hardly be restrained from going too rapidly behind the wide belt of the British shell fire as the barrage rolled forward.

The Hamel episode projected as a reminder that American forces were clinching with the foe on other parts of the front as well as on the Marne. But it was on the latter battle ground that the eyes of the world were presently drawn. There the American army swung into its greatest stride at this stage of the war.

War St. 7—Z

CHAPTER LIV

ACROSS THE MARNE AND BACK

OFFICIALLY Germany had refused to recognize the growing weight of American belligerency. If she could evade alluding to American forces specifically in reporting events on the battle field, she did so. "The enemy," to be sure, covered a multitude of enemies—more than half the world—so why designate which one, and why designate the one now most feared, of whose mounting strength it was not expedient to enlighten the beguiled people at home?

The pretense could no longer be sustained after her abortive drive against the eastern and southern flanks of the Soissons-Rheims salient on July 14, 1918. There was a reason. Germany might ignore the presence of American detachments operating with the French or British and be airily blind to the activities of American patrols along the Lorraine or Alsace fronts. They were merely "the enemy." But in making this plunge to widen the salient by way of encircling Rheims and cutting another way to Paris she crashed into an obstacle that compelled recognition. It was the First American Army Corps, numbering some 250,000 men, under the command of Major General Hunter Liggett. If Americans, in her self-deceiving view, had before been as needles in a haystack, here they had become the haystack itself, and it was all needles!

The American army skirted the southern arc of the salient, eastward along the Marne somewhere beyond Jaulgonne, westward through Château-Thierry to Torcy, where it joined the French. Germany's first operation was to make a feint of attacking the American lines northwest of Château-Thierry by way of screening her major operation, which was to break through the American barrier guarding the Marne. The assault was especially violent in the Vaux area, which was enveloped in a heavy barrage following the usual bombardment of high explosives and gas. Under the barrage storming parties attacked the village.

The system of infiltration by groups was followed and some of the groups succeeded in penetrating one of the American outposts on the northeast. The Americans swarmed out and poured a withering rifle and machine-gun fire on the assailants, and counterattacked on the latter's right, where the penetration had taken place. It was a direct and flanking fire, held in reserve until the foe had approached the American front-line trenches, from which the troops had withdrawn. Its effect was to demoralize the attackers, who retired in disorder.

The counterattack brought the American lines 750 yards ahead and yielded a number of prisoners, whose capture was due to a barrage laid by the American artillery, which cut off the enemy's retreat.

The attack had an immediate sequel in the evacuation by the Germans of Hill 204, upon an advance by the Americans up its west side. The Germans had paid much to hold this hill, resisting many assaults, notably the one described in the last chapter, and now they chose to vacate it rather than defend the hill further. Their tenure of all this area was to be very brief, and perhaps they knew it.

Soon after the Vaux demonstration, the Germans attacked the American and French positions all along the Marne. Ordered to break through the Americans holding the line south of the Marne, and reach a line running eleven kilometers south of Jaulgonne, running through Montigny, they crossed the Marne under the protection of a severe bombardment, and pushed ahead three kilometers to a line through Crezancy.

The grand advance was signalized by a long-distance bombardment of towns in the rear of the American lines. Heavy shells from German naval guns fell in regions far behind the actual battle area, some reaching points twenty to thirty miles distant. It was mainly a night display, marked by a constant hurtling of projectiles from ten- and fifteen-inch naval guns, and canopied the whole countryside with a blaze of light. The German purpose was to batter towns and communication lines beyond the defense line and to harass the movement of supplies and reenforcements.

The Marne curls to a salient northward at Jaulgonne, and the peak of this bend provided the first crossing for the Germans. Descending upon this point in great force, they succeeded in crossing the river in the face of a destructive fire from American machine gunners and infantry, who fought and died where they stood. The salient could not be held, being exposed to fire from three sides. Westward of it toward Château-Thierry, and eastward toward and beyond Dormans, the German advance likewise could not be stayed, and there was a general withdrawal of American forces along the river bank.

The Germans succeeded in crossing at ten points between Château-Thierry and Dormans. They threw many pontoon bridges over to bear their troops. Shoals of canvas boats were also brought into requisition. These proved more serviceable than the bridges, the laying of which was repeatedly thwarted by American fire. Protected by the heavy bombardment, the boats managed to carry the members of the kaiser's famed Tenth Guard Division, twenty to each boat; but very few of them got back.

American guns foiled their passage three times. Machine gunners clung to their posts on the river bank here and there till the last moment. They poured deadly streams of bullets into the enemy, and only withdrew when their guns were so hot that they could not be fired. One group happened to be in a place where the Germans were anxious to erect a bridge, but their efforts were fruitless. The American bullets piled up the German dead on the opposite side of the river every time the enemy started to cross.

South of Jaulgonne the enemy crossed the Marne on six pontoon bridges, hurriedly thrown over the stream, and masses of infantry swarmed forward. The artillery constantly had the bridges under the heaviest fire, and at least two direct hits were made, two of the bridges being blown up. The task of preventing German swarm, despite these checks, proved too great, and the Americans fell back to the base of the salient made by the river.

Once on the southern bank of the Marne, the German masses, augmented by numbers of machine gunners, proceeded to force the Americans farther back toward Condé. They had succeeded in landing a force estimated at 15,000 men in the river sector abandoned by the Americans. This force promptly started to fight its way south, having a point about nine miles distant as its objective. The Americans and French held up this advance to such an extent that two hours after the time set by the enemy for reaching his objective, he was still far away from it. The Germans specially suffered heavy losses in the woods forming the triangle from Fossoy to Mézy and Crezancy. There the Americans were overwhelmed by such large numbers that the line could not hold; but nevertheless they refused to retreat where they could possibly hold a place in the woods. This sent the German advance sweeping over large numbers of nests which sheltered ten, five, or two Americans, and sometimes one, who held on while the Germans passed by and then opened fire on them.

It was manifest that the advance could not be allowed to continue. The enemy by noon had driven forward over two miles on a front of about three and a half miles south of the Marne through the American positions; but he got no farther. Even while fighting in the open continued, the Americans organized a counterattack in the region of Condé, below Fossoy, about the time the German advance had apparently eliminated the salient. There, because of their heavy losses, they seemed content to stand, and there they remained for four hours. Meantime American reenforcements came up. Light artillery was hurried into position. It concentrated a heavy fire at short range, and when this fire ceased, the augmented American infantry dashed from cover. Machine gunners moved forward, and, lying on the ground, poured a stream of bullets into the enemy. The fierceness of the fire brought the Germans up short. They would not face the steel, and, retiring, hesitatingly at first, finally broke and fell back.

Points that had fallen to the Germans—Fossoy, La Chapelle, St. Agnan, Bois de Condé, Crezancy, and Mézy—were recovered with French aid. By 4 o'clock in the afternoon the Germans had been driven to the railroad track skirting the south bank of the Marne. There they took up positions; but there was no pause for them. The American gunners got the range of the landing places, where the Germans had stretched cables by which they hauled boats across the swollen stream, and there was no retreat in the way they had come. The Americans pursued them behind the railroad embankment. Slowly the gray-coats were forced back. Some of them swam the Marne to safety, but their number was few. Many of them were drowned in the river. The Americans in front were on open ground, making the best use of whatever shelter offered. German forces were on the hills on the opposite side of the river, showering high explosives and gas shells upon them, but the Americans went forward, nevertheless, with gas masks adjusted, and crawling at times for a considerable distance on all fours. In this way they advanced bit by bit, and when they came within range close enough they drove the enemy back.

The Germans retained some precarious positions south of the Marne; but they were completely swept back across the river between Château-Thierry and Jaulgonne. They were driven where they were before the advance began. They vented their wrath the next morning by sending thousands of high explosive and noxious gas shells into the American lines. They had set out to swing their line northeast of Château-Thierry; but it still swung northwest, and presently it was to swing much farther back.

The American losses were serious, as was to be expected in the most important action in which the Americans had yet engaged. In return, however, they exacted a toll from the Germans that made their losses seem light. It was estimated that they killed, wounded, or captured 20,000 of the enemy. Hundreds of the latter were slain while retreating across the Marne. One battalion of the 6th German Grenadiers, according to prisoners, was annihilated in the woods, and of the other battalion only one company survived. The south bank of the Marne was lined with German dead, while in the woods south of Mézy, through which the Germans advanced and retreated, 5,000 enemy dead lay, some bodies three and four deep where they had dared, in close formation, the American machine guns.

There were sporadic counterattacks, which were readily repulsed by the Americans and French. The lines wavered back and forth, and then came a sudden shift of the pivot of the entire German action in the Soissons-Rheims salient. The Marne was no longer an object to be gained, but rather a danger to flee from.

CHAPTER LV

FORWARD WITH FOCH

AMERICAN forces mingled with French troops on all sides of the German salient when General Foch struck its western side. In proportion to the combined number of French, British and Italian troops, they were not many. For that reason their achievements stood out with greater distinction; inferiority of numbers made their exploits conspicuous. They were with the French south of Soissons, on the southwest corner of the salient, west of Château-Thierry, along the Marne east of that town, and east of Rheims, the latter outside the salient proper. They were thus in the full swing of the Foch counteroffensive which finally was to crumble the salient to extinction and bring them along its top at the Vesle River.

No clearly defined picture can be drawn of their share in this advance. Their operations blended too intimately with the French movements. Here and there the situation in certain areas disclosed Americans to be acting on their own initiative. But in the main it was a Franco-American operation. The movements of each were interdependent. The advance of both progressed with the uniformity of a curved chain dragged from each end along a highway. There were dents and wrigglings in the chain at times; but it moved on.

The advance lent a significance to the earlier operations of the Americans northwest of Château-Thierry, when they straightened their line by extending it to the outskirts of Torcy, capturing Belleau Wood, Bouresches and Vaux. From this line, along a front of forty kilometers to Soissons, the attack was made at 4.45 on the morning of July 18, 1918. The perspective is too long for its development to be described with clearness. Only glimpses can be obtained of the American participation at points where there were eyewitnesses.

What was clear was that in their initial effort the Americans carried all before them. By the late afternoon they had proceeded so fast that cavalry was thrown into action. By night American headquarters—a movable fixture that day—were well inside territory held by the Germans in the morning. The line, in short, before the day was over, had advanced at varying depths, the most being ten kilometers, or a little over six miles, and the day's captures by the Americans embraced a number of towns, over 4,000 prisoners, fifty cannon, thousands of machine guns, vast quantities of munitions and stores, and airplanes.

Foch's counterattack apparently did not at first contemplate an assault on the southern arc of the salient formed by the Marne. But his success in breaking into the western flank evidently encouraged him to extend his operations to the south. Here American energies came into full play. Early in the day on July 19, 1918, the Germans had premonitions of what was to happen, and hastily prepared to withdraw from the positions they had retained on the south bank. The previous day they had been clinging in small numbers to the crook of the river near Jaulgonne, but southeast of that place, on to Oeuilly, thousands held positions won in their advance across the river, as already described. Hereabout, along the Dormans line, they were eight kilometers south of the Marne. Between Château-Thierry and Jaulgonne they had failed to hold the southern bank and had to retreat. So from these points the ground was in the hands of the Americans and French for offensive purposes, and they set about attacking the German positions early on July 19, 1918, on the west, south, and also east of Dormans. They signalized the attack with short but intense artillery work, putting down a barrage along the river bank, to prevent the Germans from retreating without paying a heavy price for having ventured so far south.

"The advance proceeded well from the start," wrote one onlooker. "By 4 o'clock the Germans were as far east as six kilometers west of Dormans. South of Dormans the enemy, with his retreat cut off, made a determined but vain stand.

"By 6 o'clock detachments of Americans and French reached the river bank in one place, and soon after a message was flashed to all the armies that the Germans had been put back across the Marne.

"The German artillery gave the men very poor support, and the chief fighting on their part was done with machine guns. The reason of the lack of German artillery work is explained in a report of American aviators that the Germans were busy all yesterday afternoon drawing back their guns from the heights north of the river.

"While we were pushing north from Château-Thierry to Dormans the French, with the Americans on their left, attacked the region of Oeuilly, gaining that place and pushing the enemy back on Chatillon, north of the river."

A further clearance was made by the Americans northwest of Château-Thierry. One of their lines ran round Hill 204, which the Germans had just evacuated, after holding it for five weeks. In Franco-American hands the hill swung the line more to the east in the track of the general advance. The movement in this direction caused the withdrawal of German forces holding the northern part of Château-Thierry. On July 21, 1918, the whole city was occupied by the French and Americans. Strong positions were established on the north of the river, bridges were thrown across, guns were brought up, and heavy firing was directed over the river to prevent German bombers from interfering with Franco-American troops crossing over. Jaulgonne was presently occupied by American troops.

When the Americans crossed the Marne they discovered that the Germans sought to deceive the Allied air bombers, who were seeking out bridges and boats along the river and otherwise preventing the Germans from crossing the stream.

The Americans found submerged boats and floats, held down by rocks, but so arranged that they could be made accessible for use by the Germans in short order for crossing. In some instances these floats spanned the river and were held by cables, and it required only a short time to float them.

The Germans did not get a chance to use their impromptu bridges, but the French and Americans made use of the floats when they came in pursuit of the enemy.

There was now a general advance from the north of the Marne, hitherto securely held by the Germans. Some fifteen kilometers north of Château-Thierry, behind a series of hills forming an almost continuous ridge, the Germans had established artillery positions, and on the hill itself their infantry waited, prepared for a stand, with machine guns. The French and Americans advanced, their backs at last to the Marne, despite the artillery fire from the hill to cover the slow retreat of the Germans. The latter continued their backward movement with sullen and stubborn rear-guard actions, leaving numbers of machine-gun nests in the path of the Franco-American movement. At times the Americans encountered the stiffest resistance, which took the form of counterattacks rather than defensive retreats. A village in this sector being reduced by the American guns, as its occupation by the Germans was imminent, the enemy was thus forced into the open, where heavy punishment was inflicted. The fighting was so fierce as almost to rob it of the suggestion that it was a rear-guard action. Nevertheless, during the intense struggle the work of moving stores was under way. With a minimum artillery fire on both sides the Americans advanced their skirmish line over yellow wheat fields, dotted with poppies, and through clumps of wood. It was Indian fighting, modernized by machine-gun work. Fighting in open order in this way brought the American line by July 22, 1918, to more than ten kilometers north of Château-Thierry, and beyond Bezu-St. Germain.

CHAPTER LVI

FIGHTING THROUGH FORESTS

NOW came a bitter struggle for the possession of Epieds and Trugny, to the east and southeast of Bezu-St. Germain. Below Trugny lay Barbillon Wood, also an objective of the attackers. The Germans viciously defended these points. A give-and-take battle raged round the two towns all day on July 23, 1918; but in the region of Barbillon Wood the Germans fell back, burning depots and ammunition and supply dumps, and evacuating many farms which had been strongly fortified for defense. The fighting extended still farther east in front of Jaulgonne and Charteves. The American progress here was made in the face of most obstinate resistance by the Germans, who fought every foot. Even when making steps backward, they endeavored to render the American progress costly by leaving behind German machine gunners cleverly concealed in nests. These gunners were not told that the main body was withdrawing, and were left at the mercy of the advance. Several of them when captured expressed unfeigned surprise when told that their comrades had withdrawn.

Châtelet Forest was another stumblingblock. Several sallies into these woods having proved abortive, the French swung round to the north, and the Americans to the south. Machine guns and American light artillery played on the woods, and the Germans were finally uprooted from their main ambushes there. It was one of the positions the Germans had chosen for the stand after their withdrawal from the Marne.

The terrain was mostly woody in the area above the Marne where the Franco-American line had reached. The fighting was therefore pursued in the midst of concealed antagonists. In the forest of Barbillon the Germans had a machine gun screened every ten yards of their front. Their hidden artillery impeded American reenforcements. The attackers had to beat their way into the woods, encountering rocky ledges that formed excellent nests for enemy machine guns. The German positions were excellent for defensive fighting; but with the slow but sure closing in of their western flank, and a like movement proceeding east of them, the woods would become traps if they retained them. They did not retain them. They merely fought spitefully to impede the Franco-American progress and safeguard the retreat of their main forces out of the dangerous Marne pocket.

They desperately clung to the region of Epieds and Trugny. At this point German infantry, which had been pushed back, were thrust forward again to check the Franco-American advance from the southwest toward Fère-en-Tardenois.

"The Germans," reported Reuter's correspondent with the American troops, "fought well and checked the advance for some thirty-six hours, and three times wrested the village of Epieds from their determined American opponents. In the meantime the village grew constantly smaller under the ceaseless bombardment from both sides and finally disappeared, not even a large pile of bricks being left behind.

"When the village disappeared the Germans were in possession. The Americans, tired of the ceaseless ebb and flow of the fighting there, had taken the slopes on either flank and forced the Germans to make their final massed attack into the ruins of the village.

"Meanwhile the Allied guns had been brought up beyond the crest of the hill, and as soon as the Germans took possession of the village they concentrated a terrific fire upon it until the place smoked with its own red dust as though on fire. When the guns ceased firing there were no Germans left to capture, or even to bury.

"At the edge of the wood beyond Trugny the German machine guns, stationed ten yards apart, held up the advance a little longer. Making a feint frontal attack, however, the Americans crept, Indian fashion, around the flanks and captured all the guns.

"Afterward the pace of the advance quickened. All the high ground north of Epieds was taken and the line carried beyond Courpoil."

A series of like local actions brought the Franco-American line by July 25, 1918, well beyond the foregoing points and into the region of the Fère and Riz forests, where the Germans had retreated from Epieds. They were dense woods of poplar and oak rising amid thick underbrush. Hidden among the clustered foliage, German machine gunners desperately contended for every inch of ground before surrendering it. They vainly tried to hold the French and Americans in the southern part of the Riz forest with the object of saving huge supplies gathered there. An examination of the woods afterward showed hundreds of tons of ammunition for big German guns, piled six feet high in rows a hundred yards long for some distances. This ammunition had been stored there to be used in the advance on Paris.

By a flanking movement above the forest of Fère the Americans carried the village of Beuvardes, making their line run from that point through the northern part of Fère forest to Le Charmel and through the Riz forest southeast to above Dormans. Le Charmel, which lies on the Jaulgonne road, with a wooded hill on each side, changed hands twice before taken by the Americans. The Germans had strong machine gun positions both in the village and on the hills. Their fire raked the Americans when they charged the village and compelled them to retire. Later, assisted by comrades from the two forests, the Americans overcame the Germans, who withdrew from Le Charmel slowly and stubbornly.

By July 27, 1918, the Franco-American forces had driven the Germans almost entirely out of the wooded area they had been so obstinately defending. The pressure was constantly maintained toward the road junction of Fère-en-Tardenois, the Franco-American objective, and thither the pursuers progressed through the remainder of the dense woods and over rain-soaked fields and hills on their outskirts.

In the course of this forest fighting the troops were warned to watch for Germans wearing American or French uniforms, a device they had successfully practiced. Rushing across an open place in the forest when German nests had been discovered, a German, speaking perfect English, called to American machine gunners:

"Don't shoot. There are Americans in that thicket."

The Americans were at the edge of the forest, firing into a wood opposite. They ceased when the detachment appeared. The detachment entered a forest to the right of the Americans, and in a few minutes a hail of machine-gun bullets came from that direction. The Americans realized that they had been duped, and turned their machine guns upon the impostors.

On July 28, 1918, the Americans were on the south bank of the Ourcq. This river, intended by the Germans to be a halting line, but which they could not hold, marked a notable point in the American progress from the banks of the Marne. Foch's forward movement from the west and southwest had been proceeding simultaneously and now became merged along this river into the movement up from the south.

American participation from the west had been less conspicuous; but American troops left their mark, whatever their zone of operations, and in this area they made their presence painfully felt south of Soissons. At the beginning of the western advance, east of Vierzy and northeast of Chaudon, they encountered the pick of the German shock troops after fighting for thirty hours. The result was that the youthful Americans, meeting the kaiser's best, who were fresh and in the pink of condition, themselves essayed the task of becoming shock troops. They had reached their objectives, a varying number of miles eastward, and were consolidating their positions when the shock came. Against one American unit two German shock divisions were hurled; against another came the famous Prussian Guards. The Germans had machine guns mounted on wheels and rolled them to the edge of the woods where the fighting occurred. These guns shot explosive bullets at the Americans. Shock troops came to close grips with shock troops—and the Franco-American advance was not only sustained but extended.

CHAPTER LVII

SERGY AND SERINGES

THE next striking feature of American participation in the squeezing of the Germans out of the Soissons-Marne-Rheims salient was the crossing of the Ourcq and the taking of Sergy and Seringes just beyond that river. The Germans had meant to make a stand on the north bank of the Ourcq and hold the Americans on the south bank while their main withdrawal was effected to the Vesle; but the charge of the Americans over the river balked this plan. The fighting thus shifted to the north side, where the Germans, reenforced by two divisions of Bavarian Guards, settled down to resist the Americans to the utmost. Although heavily assailed, the Americans replied in kind, especially in and out of Sergy, three miles southeast of Fère-en-Tardenois. The Germans bent all their strength toward forcing a recrossing of the Ourcq. The Americans held their ground, and it was the Germans who finally had to yield, but only after vicious and bitter fighting.

The Americans began their attack on Sergy early on the morning of Saturday, July 27, 1918. By night they had been driven back some distance, but on Sunday morning, when they resumed their advance under cover of their artillery—a few pieces going forward with their advanced line—they proceeded almost unchecked to the river, crossed the river and entered the town. The Germans used gas; but the Americans had long ago had their baptism of gas fumes and knew how to utilize their masks and avoid the ravines through which the gas filtered. When the town was occupied there was some street fighting, which the Germans abandoned by retiring to higher ground beyond. On Monday morning, July 29, 1918, came a counter-attack by the Fourth Prussian Guard Division, which had arrived only a few hours before from their training ground in Lorraine. A conflict then ensued which ebbed and flowed constantly, the town changing hands nine times before it was won.

The Americans immediately advanced two miles, again defeating the Prussian Guards and Bavarians, though the latter succeeded in winning Cierges, southeast of Sergy, and holding it for a spell. By the night of July 30, 1918, the Americans were well to the north of Sergy, on long slopes approaching heavy woods beyond Nesle, a town directly east of Seringes-et-Nesle, for which the Germans fought bitterly.

As a preliminary to the attack on Seringes, a strongly fortified position, Meury Farm, had to be taken, as from the farm the Seringes defenses could be outflanked and approached by a less steep ascent than by a direct attack. In this group of farm buildings the Germans had, on their withdrawal, left behind a strong force of machine gunners and infantry, which set up a strong defense.

"The Americans," ran one account, "moved forward through the yellow wheat fields, which were sprayed and torn by bullets. But they advanced as though on a drill ground.

"The American guns laid down a heavy artillery fire, but notwithstanding this many Germans remained when it came to hand-to-hand fighting. The Germans stuck to their guns, and the Americans rushed them and killed the gunners at their post.

"It was a little battle, without mercy, and typical of similar engagements along the whole line. The Prussian Guards and Bavarians everywhere fought in accordance with their training, discipline, and traditions, but were outwitted and outfought.

"To the north of the farm, up the long slopes leading to the woods, the Americans encountered the fiercest exhibition of Germany's war science. The Germans laid down a barrage which, it was said, was as heavy as had ever been employed. The American guns replied as heavily.

"On through the barrage the Americans went into the German positions, attacking fiercely the machine-gun and infantry detachments. The barrage died away, the Germans leaving the work of resistance to the men they had failed to protect with their heavy guns.

"The Germans were decimated and the Americans held their new line, just east of the forest. Not many prisoners were taken, but here and there a few were rounded up and brought in. One sergeant contributed fourteen. He attacked eighteen Germans who had become separated from their command, killing four of them and capturing the others. Heavy execution was done by the Americans. Eight captured Guards said that they were all that remained of a company of eighty-six."

The way was now open for the assault on Seringes, which the enemy held in great strength. The village was also protected by machine-gun nests on either side. "The attack," wrote Reuter's correspondent, "was an almost incredible affair for the coolness with which it was carried out and for the mere fact that it could be done under such conditions." The village changed hands five times. After its first capture by the Americans on Monday, July 29, 1918, the Germans forbore returning with the usual infantry counterattack, but kept up a constant artillery and machine-gun fire. This attempt to drive the Americans out continued all the next day. Toward evening the Germans, evidently thinking that the spirit of the defenders was weakening under such withering fire, emerged from the Nesle forest to retake the village.

"The Americans," said Reuter's correspondent, "after three days of to-and-fro fighting through villages, had learned subtlety and were determined to have a real fight to a finish. They consequently pretended to withdraw as though retiring from Seringes. Some of them did withdraw, but others remained in the houses and other points of vantage, and the Germans crept down from the high ground convinced they had their opponents beaten. Additional German troops came pouring in until the town was occupied as it never had been before.

"But as the new occupants began to organize their defenses they found that bullets appeared to be coming in from three sides of the village, and it was not long before they discovered that the Americans, while withdrawing from the front of the town, had commenced an encircling movement on both sides, thus forming a ring almost completely around it.

"The Americans used machine guns, rifles, and pistols, and employed both the bayonet and the rifle butt with great effective-

ness. The fighting in the streets was savage, but of comparatively brief duration.

"The Prussian Guard had voted not to surrender, and their
opponents were just as anxious to see the thing through. It
became an affair of small arms, but the Americans proved to be
better shots, and slowly picked off men here and there.

"Then the Americans began to advance, and slowly their encircling ring closed about the village. As the ring drew closer
and the defenders saw their doom approaching, they redoubled
their fire; but still the Americans came on unfalteringly, like a
storm, or the unavoidable stroke of fate.

"When the Americans reached the precincts of the village
their fire ceased, and with one wild yell they closed with the foe.
The fierce uproar suddenly gave place to a strange silence as
man grappled with man. Only the clash of steel on steel and the
groans of the stricken could be heard.

"The issue was never in doubt for an instant. At this kind
of fighting the American is more than equal to any Prussian
Guardsman, and in a little more than ten minutes all was over.
Except for a few German prisoners, every German in the village
had breathed his last. Such was the final capture of Seringes."

The Americans awaited the coming of other Germans, but they
came not. So the French and Americans moved on beyond the
village, straightening out the line from that point to Cierges
by bringing their heavy artillery to bear on mile after mile of
barbed wire which the Germans had placed through the hills,
forests, and other open places.

The Americans reached Fismes, on the Vesle River, on August
2, 1918, the Germans retreating before them. They had advanced
about forty kilometers in fifteen days, fourteen kilometers having been gained in the last two days of their pursuit. On July
18, 1918, they were intrenched only about Château-Thierry to
Belleau; now they were in the heart of the German salient
which, thanks largely to American aid, was a salient no more

PART X — RUSSIA

CHAPTER LVIII

THE PEACE WITHOUT TREATY

THROUGHOUT the first ten days of February, 1918, the world waited impatiently and anxiously for a final conclusion to the peace conference between the representatives of Russia and the Central Powers, at Brest-Litovsk. Trotzky was still the central figure. Meanwhile the Bolsheviki leaders were straining every effort to spread their propaganda throughout the civilian populations of the Central Powers, as well as among the soldiers on the eastern front. Rumors of strikes in Germany inclined even those who had previously been skeptical to believe that the Bolsheviki method might yet gain a great victory for the cause of the democratic nations.

Ukrainia, as already noted, had declared itself an independent nation, with a republican form of government, professedly socialistic in tendency, with Vinitchenko as President. As a matter of fact, however, the Rada, or Ukrainian legislative assembly, was almost completely in the hands of the landowners who, naturally, were bitterly opposed to Bolshevikism and its program of land nationalization. Against them had risen the Bolsheviki elements of Ukrainia, supported by the Petrograd Bolsheviki. The conflict between the two factions had created a state of civil war. The landowners' Rada had sent delegates to the peace conference, and at first the Petrograd delegation, under the chairmanship of Trotzky, had raised no objection against the Teutons recognizing them as the proper representatives of Ukrainia. But during the last days of January, 1918, came reports of the mili-

417

tary success of the Ukrainian Bolsheviki, even that they had captured Odessa and Kiev, and then Trotzky contended that the Ukrainians at Brest-Litovsk no longer truly represented their constituency. The Germans, however, had forestalled him by quickly recognizing Ukrainian independence under the Rada.

The German policy was obvious. By recognizing the conservative Rada, they created a split among the Russian delegates as a whole. Furthermore, they realized that the Ukrainian landowners feared the Bolsheviki domestic program far more than they feared German domination, and in whatever treaty they entered into would offer large concessions in return for German military aid against Bolsheviki domination. Thus the Central Powers suddenly found an ally in the Ukrainian Republic. It also gave them a moral pretext for their attitude toward the provinces under dispute: Courland and Lithuania, and parts of Livonia and Esthonia and what had formerly been Russian Poland, whose populations, the Germans contended, had already declared themselves for German suzerainty.

The session of the Brest-Litovsk peace conference which was held on February 9, 1918, was the one at which both sides concluded their arguments and worked up to the climax of the following day. That same day the Teutonic delegates had signed a treaty of peace with the Ukrainian delegates.

"We have officially informed you," said Trotzky, "that the Ukrainian Rada was deposed, yet the negotiations with a nonexistent government have been continued. We proposed to the Austro-Hungarian delegation that a special committee should be sent to Kiev, in order to verify our contention that the Kiev Rada no longer exists and that further negotiations with its delegation would have no value. We were told that this would be done and that the delegates of the Central Powers would not sign a peace treaty until the return of the investigating commission. Now we are told that the signing of the peace treaty could no longer be postponed. . . . Such conduct arouses doubts of the sincerity of the Central Powers. . . . The conduct of the other side, so far as this question is concerned, gives us the impression that they are endeavoring to make the situation impossible for us. We cannot consider any treaty binding to the Russian Federal Republic which is not signed by our delegation."

The main point of difference, however, remained the same as before: the refusal of the Central Powers to withdraw from what had been Russian territory, in order to allow the populations to decide for themselves what their governments should be. This was the ultimatum of the Germans, as worded by Von Kühlmann: "Russia must agree to the following territorial changes which will enter into force after the ratification of the peace treaty. The regions between the frontiers of Germany and Austria-Hungary and the indicated line will not be in the future a dependency of Russia. As a result of their former adhesion to the Russian Empire no obligations will bind them to Russia. The future destiny of these regions will be settled in agreement with the peoples concerned, namely, on the basis of those agreements which have been concluded between them and Germany and Austria-Hungary."

In the afternoon the conference was adjourned that the delegates might consult among themselves. The last and climaxial session was held on the following day, the 10th, when Trotzky, after a hot denunciation of German imperialism, declared that Russia would never agree to the German terms and would refuse to sign any treaty on such a basis. At the same time he declared that Russia would not fight any longer and would withdraw from the war. This decision was approved at Petrograd and an order for the demobilization of the Russian armies had been sent out.

This unprecedented conclusion rather nonplused the German delegates and deeply displeased them. Kühlmann was of the opinion, however, that Russia could not end her participation in the war in this fashion; that peace could only be brought about by a special treaty, in the absence of which the state of war would automatically be resumed at the termination of the armistice, which had only been arranged for the purpose of arranging a peace by understanding. The fact that one of the parties concerned was demobilizing its forces would not change the situation. The Russian version of the session, as given out officially from Petrograd, was as follows:

"Yesterday, at the session of the All-Russian Central Executive Committee of the Councils, the president of the peace delegation, Trotzky, reported on the course and results of the negotiations at Brest-Litovsk. Not only the representatives of those political parties constituting the Government majority, but the representatives of the opposition groups as well, recognized the fact that the decision taken by the Council of the People's Commissaries was the only correct one and the course which could be taken with dignity. The speakers of the majority and the opposition put forward the question as to whether there was the possibility of a resumption of German hostilities against Russia. Nearly all were of the opinion that such an offensive was extremely unlikely, but all uttered warning against too optimistic an attitude in this regard, because the war party elements in Germany might force the German Government to such a course. In the opinion of all the speakers it would be the duty of all Russian citizens, in such a case, to defend the interests of the revolution. All were of the opinion, however, that the masses of Germany and Austria-Hungary would not allow a resumption of hostilities against the Russian socialists, because such a course would be too obviously a raid for plunder. The People's Commissary for Foreign Affairs concluded this report with the statement that Russia is withdrawing from the war not only in appearance, but in reality. It is canceling all agreements with its former allies, and reserves perfect freedom of action for itself in the future. At the conclusion of the session a resolution was passed approving the action of the delegation to the Brest-Litovsk Conference."

The first general news of peace with Russia caused public rejoicing in Germany and Austria-Hungary, but when the details became known the German and Austrian papers showed the bitter disappointment which prevailed.

Meanwhile, the Ukrainians were further playing into the hands of the Central Powers, spurred on by the domestic situation. Said the "Cologne Gazette," for February 17, 1918:

"Our bread peace with the Ukraine is threatened. Fighting between the Bolsheviki and the Rada already has brought the Rada government into such peril that it has been transferred from Kiev to Zhitomir, and the suburbs of Kiev are already in the hands of the Bolsheviki. . . . The Bolsheviki are rushing troops to reenforce the anti-Rada forces. . . . Further fighting is to be expected, of serious significance to us."

The true significance of the pact between the Ukrainian landlords and the Germans became still more obvious on February 17, 1918, when an appeal "to the German people" was published. In this document the bourgeois character of the Rada Government was indignantly denied and socialistic principles were proclaimed. The Bolsheviki were bitterly denounced and accused of possessing nothing more than a desire for conquest and pillage. Having thus prepared the German mind for its reception, the appeal is delivered in the final paragraph, in the following words:

"In this hard struggle for existence we look around for help. We are firmly convinced that the peaceful and order-loving German people will not remain indifferent when it learns of our distress. The German Army, standing on the flank of our northern enemy, has the power to help us and, by its intervention, to protect the northern frontiers against further invasion by the enemy. This is what we have to say in this dark hour, and we feel confident that our voice will be heard."

Such was the moral pretext of the Central Powers for a further invasion of Russia. In return for the protection of their private property, the landowners constituting the Rada Government were willing to accept German domination and to send all surplus foodstuffs across the frontier.

Germany gave ample warning of her intention to continue active hostilities at the expiration of the armistice at noon on February 18, 1918. It was officially announced that this decision had been taken at a conference of all the German war chiefs and political leaders, attended also by the emperor. Austria-Hungary, however, took a very much more moderate stand and showed strong disinclination to renew the war. The Vienna papers were practically unanimous in their opinion that Austria had no further business in Russia, since there was no longer a common frontier, and with Ukrainia there was a definite peace treaty. On February 18, 1918, it was officially announced from Vienna that "an agreement has been reached between Germany and Austria-Hungary whereby, in the event of military action being necessary, the German troops will be confined to the frontier of Great Russia, and the Austrians to the Ukraine only."

CHAPTER LIX

THE GERMANS RENEW HOSTILITIES WITH RUSSIA

AT 2 o'clock in the afternoon of the 18th, just two hours after the armistice had expired, German troops began pouring across the Dvina Bridge. The disorganized Russians fled before them, allowing the Germans to occupy Dvinsk unopposed. Up and down the whole eastern front the German lines began a simultaneous movement eastward, the immediate object being the occupation of the territory coveted by Germany, the moral pretext being that Germany desired to rescue the oppressed population from the anarchy of Bolsheviki rule. Farther south an advance was also made into Ukrainia, but there it was on the invitation of the Ukrainians themselves, according to the Germans.

The news of the German advance acted on the Petrograd authorities like an electric shock, awakening them from their delusions. There was something of panic in the haste with which the Council of People's Commissaries, the body corresponding to the Cabinet of other governments, assembled for conference the moment the news reached the capital. Throughout the whole night they remained in session, in hot argument over the question of capitulation or resistance.

On this vital issue the two leading figures of the Bolsheviki Government split; Lenine was in favor of unconditional surrender to the German demands, while Trotzky declared himself for continued resistance. Had he remained of this mind he might have changed the course of events, but before the question was put to vote, he swung over to Lenine, and the Council decided in favor of surrender, but only by one vote.

Early next morning the Council issued a proclamation, to the effect that "under the present circumstances the Council of the People's Commissaries regards itself as forced formally to declare its willingness to sign a peace upon the conditions which had been dictated by the delegations of the Quadruple Alliance at Brest-Litovsk. Later in the day Ensign Krylenko, the commander in chief, issued a general order to his armed forces in which they were enjoined to attempt to parley with all forces of armed Germans they might encounter and persuade them to desist from advancing farther into Russian territory, but in case these attempts failed, then a determined resistance should be made.

The decision of Petrograd to capitulate had been communicated to German headquarters by wireless. Late in the afternoon the German commander, General Hoffmann, replied to the effect that the message had been received, but since a wireless message could not bear signatures, without which no communication could be regarded as official, he requested the Petrograd authorities to forward the same message in written form, properly signed, to German headquarters at Dvinsk. A courier was immediately sent with an authentic copy of the Russian capitulation to Dvinsk.

The Germans, however, were in no hurry to respond. The German soldiers continued their eastward advance day by day, practically unopposed, gathering in some 10,000 prisoners and vast quantities of arms, heavy guns, ammunition and other war material. By February 21 German forces had arrived seventy miles northeast of Riga, and Esthonia was completely occupied.

By this time it began to dawn on the Bolsheviki leaders in Petrograd that the Germans meant to occupy all the territory they desired before they would reopen negotiations. On February 22, 1918, a proclamation was promulgated, in the following terms:

"We agreed to sign peace terms at the cost of enormous concessions in order to save the country from final exhaustion and the ruin of the revolution. Once more the German working class, in this threatening hour, has shown itself insufficiently determined to stay the strong criminal hand of its own militarism. We had no other choice than to accept the conditions of German imperialism until a revolution changes or cancels them. The German Government is not in a hurry to reply to us, evidently aiming to seize as many important positions in our territory as possible. The enemy has occupied Dvinsk, Werder, and Lutsk, and is continuing to strangle by hunger the most important centers of the revolution. Even now we are firmly convinced that the German working class will rise against the attempts of the ruling class to stifle the revolution, but we cannot predict with certainty when this will occur. . . . The Commissaries call on all loyal councils and army organizations to use all efforts to recreate the army. Perverted elements of hooligans, marauders and cowards should be expelled from the ranks, and, in the event of resistance, be wiped out of existence. The bourgeoisie, who under Kerensky and the Czar evaded the burden of war and profited from its misfortunes, must be made to fulfill their duties by the most decisive and merciless measures. . . . The German generals desire to establish their own order in Petrograd and Kiev. The republic is in the gravest danger. The duty of Russian workingmen and peasants is defense to the death of the republic against the masses of bourgeoisie and imperialists of Germany. German militarism wishes to smother the working classes and the Ukrainian masses, to give back the land to the landowners, factories and workshops to the bankers, and power to a monarchy."

Finally the Germans condescended to open negotiations with the Russians once more. On February 23, 1918, Foreign Secretary von Kühlmann opened up communication with Petrograd, offering to arrange a new peace conference. The terms could not now, of course, be so generous as were those offered at Brest-Litovsk, the negotiations must be concluded within forty-eight hours and ratified within two weeks.

As outlined by Von Kühlmann, the new conditions were: Livonia and Esthonia immediately to be cleared of Russian troops; this territory to be policed by the Germans until such a time as these countries should establish governments of their own. An immediate peace between northern Russia and the Ukrainians. Ukrainia and Finland to be evacuated by all Russian forces. A complete demobilization of the Russian armies, including the newly organized Red Guards. Russian warships in the Black Sea, the Baltic and the Arctic to be interned in Russian harbors, warships of the Entente Powers to undergo similar treatment. Merchant navigation of the Black Sea to be renewed. The Russo-German commercial treaty of 1914 to be enforced again. And all revolutionary propaganda among German soldiers and civilians to be stopped immediately and absolutely.

During the entire night of the day on which this communication was received the Council was in conference, adjourning now and then to allow party caucuses. At first there was a strong feeling in favor of resistance, especially among the members of the opposition. Premier Lenine's influence was thrown strongly in favor of peace and an unconditional acceptance of the terms which the enemy offered.

In the early morning of Sunday, the 24th, the Central Executive Committee decided to accept the German terms, by a vote of 112 against 84. The German Government was then informed that a Russian representative would leave immediately for Dvinsk, carrying with him the official acceptance of the German terms. A new peace delegation was elected to attend the coming conference, for both Trotzky and Joffe, who had been the leaders of the first commission, refused to serve again. Meanwhile a request had been made to the German military commander that another armistice be declared, to last until the conclusion of the peace negotiations. But this request the Germans flatly refused, and the German armies continued their advance eastward.

This policy on the part of the Germans, to continue military aggression to the last moment, finally roused a fighting spirit among the Bolsheviki organizations. Under the supervision of the Petrograd Soviet extensive preparations were made to renew armed resistance. Recruits to the Red Guard regiments were enlisted and armed with feverish haste and hurried out to the front, to take the place of the fleeing regulars, who were completely useless and demoralized. Fully 100,000 joined the Red

Guard detachments, among them being many officers of the old army who, without sympathizing with Bolsheviki principles, joined them from pure patriotism.

The results of these exertions were soon made manifest on the fighting front, for now came reports indicating that the Germans were obliged to fight desperately to make any headway. On February 26, 1918, the Russians made so determined a resistance at and near Pskov that the Germans were temporarily driven back and halted for several days, until they could bring up their heavy ordnance.

On March 3, 1918, the Germans announced that they had ceased hostilities, the Russian delegation to Brest-Litovsk, where the second conference was held, having signed the peace treaty. They then reported the capture of 6,800 officers, 57,000 men, 2,400 cannon, 5,000 machine guns, 800 locomotives, and large quantities of other war material. The territory overrun was all that part of Russia lying west of a line drawn from Narva, on the Gulf of Finland, due south to Kiev, including Russian Poland, Lithuania, Esthonia, Livonia, and the outlying islands in the Gulf of Finland. By refusing to sign a treaty of peace at the first conference the Russians lost territories amounting to almost one-quarter of Russia in Europe, inhabited by about a third of the total population. By the new treaty the Russians lost Finland, Poland, Ukrainia, Lithuania, Esthonia, Livonia, Courland, and a portion of Transcaucasia, southeast of the Black Sea.

CHAPTER LX

THE PEACE TREATY THAT WAS SIGNED

THE Russian delegates at the second peace conference had signed practically blindfolded. Gradually the German terms were given out to the world. Probably nothing during the war, except the sinking of the *Lusitania*, had so contributed to turning sympathy in neutral countries away from Germany as the conditions which were forced on Russia. The following summary gives the outstanding features of the treaty of peace which still exists between Russia and the Central Powers:

An end to all propaganda among the soldiers and civil populations of the Central Powers. Russia to relinquish all claims to the territory occupied and held by the Germans, the fate of these countries to be decided by Germany. Russia must evacuate the Anatolian provinces taken from Turkey, as well as the districts of Kars, Erivan and Batum. Russia must demobilize all her armies. All Russian warships to be interned in Russian harbors until a general peace has been declared. Russia must conclude an immediate peace with the Ukrainian Republic and recognize the treaty of peace between Ukrainia and the Central Powers. All revolutionary propaganda in Ukrainia must cease. Finland and the Aland Islands must be evacuated by all Russian armed forces, both military and naval. A general exchange of prisoners of war is to be begun at once.

The document presenting these terms had yet to be ratified by the highest ruling powers in Russia, and, according to the German demands, within two weeks. Trotzky, hitherto the dominating figure of the Bolsheviki party, was apparently opposed to the acceptance of the treaty and refused to be a delegate to the final peace conference, as already noted. For this reason he also resigned as Foreign Minister, declaring that he could not agree with the point of view of Lenine, and was succeeded by Tchitcherin. Trotzky was now made chairman of the newly created government of Petrograd, known as the Petrograd Labor Commune, which was responsible "for the safeguarding of revolutionary order and defending the city from the enemy."

The treaty was presented for ratification to a Pan-Soviet Congress, held in Moscow on March 14-16, 1918, the Soviet Government being by this time established in Moscow. The Congress consisted of 1,164 delegates, the majority being soldiers, sailors, and workingmen, with Bolshevist constituencies in the industrial centers, the peasants being represented in a much smaller proportion. Of the total number 732 delegates were declared partisans of Lenine; thirty-eight were Socialist Revolutionists, with more moderate tendencies than the Bolsheviki.

Again Lenine strongly advocated for peace at any price, contending, as before, that it would be only a matter of time until the working classes of the whole world would overthrow their capitalist and imperial masters and come to the rescue of the Russian proletariat. The treaty was finally ratified by a vote of 704 against 261. Two Bolshevist commissaries, Debenko and Kolantai, and four Socialist Revolutionaries, Steinberg, Kalagaiev, Karelin and Broshian, resigned their posts in the cabinet when the result was announced.

At the congress the following telegram from President Wilson was read, at the opening session:

"May I not take advantage of the meeting of the Congress of the Soviets to express the sincere sympathy which the people of the United States feel for the Russian people at this moment when the German power has been thrust in to interrupt and turn back the whole struggle for freedom and substitute the wishes of Germany for the purpose of the people of Russia? Although the Government of the United States is, unhappily, not now in a position to render the direct and effective aid it would wish to render, I beg to assure the people of Russia through the Congress that it will avail itself of every opportunity to secure for Russia once more complete sovereignty and independence in her own affairs and full restoration to her great rôle in the life of Europe and the modern world.

"The whole heart of the people of the United States is with the people of Russia in the attempt to free themselves forever from autocratic government and become the masters of their own life."

The following day the Congress adopted the following reply to President Wilson's message of sympathy:

"The Congress expresses its gratitude to the American people, above all to the laboring and exploited classes of the United States, for the sympathy expressed to the Russian people by President Wilson through the Congress of Soviets in the days of severe trials. The Russian Socialistic Federative Republic of

Soviets takes advantage of President Wilson's communication to express to all peoples perishing and suffering from the horrors of imperialistic war its warm sympathy and firm belief that the happy time is not far distant when the laboring classes of all countries will throw off the yoke of capitalism and will establish a socialistic state of society, which alone is capable of securing just and lasting peace as well as the culture and well-being of all laboring people."

CHAPTER LXI

CONTINUED GERMAN AGGRESSION

ON the day the Russian delegates to Brest-Litovsk had signed the peace treaty the Germans had announced an end to military activities on the eastern front, and until the treaty had been ratified they did indeed refrain from further aggression. It was even reported that practically all the German forces on the Russian front had been removed to the western front and those few that remained would be insufficient to carry on any further operations, even against the disorganized Russians. But after the middle of March reports of military operations began to appear again, the pretext of the Germans being that they were "establishing order" along the new frontier and were merely suppressing irresponsible bands.

The Teuton advance was most pronounced in Ukrainia, where the legal authorities were ostensibly cooperating with the invaders. Apparently the forces employed in the conquest of this territory were largely the Slavic contingents of the Austrian Army, supported by the so-called Ukrainian troops, regiments recruited from the Ukrainians which had formerly been units of the Russian Army and were now loyal to the Rada. German officers were in the higher commands, so that the operations were entirely in the interests of the German Government.

Thus, by the end of the third week in March the Teutons had overrun all of Ukrainia west of the Dnieper and were in possession of the chief center, Kiev, as well as the important cities of Zhitomir, Nikolaiev, and the chief seaport of southern Russia, Odessa. Bolsheviki Red Guards succeeded in driving the invaders out of Odessa some days later, but it was again captured on the arrival of Austrian reenforcements. Over two thousand ships and great quantities of war material were seized. According to some reports, even the Rada became alarmed and protested at continuous invasion, but no heed was taken of the request.

Up in northern Russia there was also continued aggression. An advance on Petrograd was begun, but when the Soviet Government became established in Moscow, the Germans switched off in that direction, especially from the direction of Ukrainia, whose borders with Russia proper were crossed for a considerable distance, to within 150 miles of Moscow.

The peace treaty provided for the ceding to the Central Powers of the Transcaucasian provinces, already mentioned. But here the people had organized a constituent assembly of their own, which now refused to recognize this provision of the treaty. Meeting in Tiflis, the assembly declared for a defensive war, and independence was declared. In the middle of April the Armenian National Council, in an official protest addressed to the German Government, said:

"Following upon the withdrawal of the Russian troops Turkish forces have invaded the undefended country and are not only killing off the Turkish Armenians, but all the Russians as well. In spite of the terms of the peace treaty, which recognizes the right of self-determination for these Caucasian regions, the Turkish Army is advancing toward Kars and Ardahan, destroying the country and killing the Christian inhabitants. The responsibility for the future destiny of the Armenians lies entirely with Germany, because it was Germany's insistence which resulted in the withdrawal of the Russian troops from the Armenian regions, and at the moment it rests with Germany to prevent the habitual excesses of the Turkish troops, increased by revengefulness and anger."

In Russia, the Bolshevist leaders had actually betrayed their country to the Germans. In Finland, it was the conservative element that welcomed the Teutons. Hatred of Russia and fear of the excesses committed by the extreme Socialists had made the Finns strongly pro-German. For the Socialists were not only a numerous element in Finland, but were well organized in the Labor party. In January, 1918, these radicals, corresponding to the Bolsheviki in Russia, rose in armed revolt and seized Helsingfors, driving the members of the Government north, where it established its headquarters at Vasa, under the leadership of M. Svinhufvud. The Socialists organized a government of their own in the old capital, the head of their cabinet being Kullervo Manner. Thus was begun the civil strife with the conservative White Guards on the one hand and the Socialist Red Guards on the other, the former receiving German support, the latter being backed by the moral and a great deal of material support from the Soviet Government of Russia. The Germans occupied the Aland Islands, March 2, 1918, and in April took Helsingfors and Viborg, cooperating with the Finnish White Guards. At the end of April, Finland was practically controlled by Germany. Meantime the Germans were organizing the conquered provinces taken from Russia.

The continued aggression of the German forces aroused a very bitter spirit among the Russians. Even Lenine openly declared that the peace was only for the purpose of reorganizing the war. Trotzky, who at least outwardly opposed the acceptance of the treaty, came to the fore again. He declared for the organization of an army of half a million men on the regular disciplined basis. On April 2, 1918, Podvoisky, assistant commissary of war, announced that Russia would establish an army of 1,500,000 men, in which the elective principle would be more limited, and some of the leaders openly advocated conscription. On April 10, 1918, Trotzky was again admitted into the cabinet as minister of war.

Meanwhile there were strong indications that a more conciliatory attitude would be adopted toward the "capitalistic" governments of the Allies, who had been denounced as only a little less hostile to Russia than Germany. Tchitcherin, the foreign minister, made the statement that "Russia's relations toward the Entente are unchanged."

CHAPTER LXII

JAPANESE TAKE ACTION IN THE EAST

THE Allied Governments, naturally, including that of the United States, refused to recognize the treaty of peace which Germany and Austria had imposed on the helpless Russians. It was their recognition of the helplessness of the Russians which caused them to realize the fact that Germany might still further force them into a position which would be detrimental to the Allied cause; that, in a sense, the Russians were not responsible and that therefore it might become necessary to take certain measures which would prevent their falling too far under Teuton control, or permitting Russia to become a vast storehouse and granary for the Central Powers, which might exploit and develop Russian resources to further Austrian and German ends. Now that Russia was not even nominally hostile to Germany, she became a potential auxiliary instead of a menace to the military success of the Central Powers.

Just before the collapse of Russia, brought to a climax by the rise into power of the Bolsheviki, large stores of military supplies from Japan and the United States had been accumulating at the Vladivostok terminus of the Siberian Railroad. It was only natural to assume that it would be Germany's great desire to obtain possession of these stores. What quickened anticipation of this possibility was the rumor that large numbers of Austrian and German prisoners had been armed in Siberia and were gathering along the line of the Siberian Railroad. Both Lenine and Trotzky denied this report most vigorously and invited the Allies to send representatives into Siberia to investigate. This was done, notably by the United States, and the reports of the investigators seemed to indicate that there had been no foundation to the rumors.

Nevertheless, the danger remained and action became necessary. Japanese intervention in the East now became a lively subject of discussion in the Allied countries. On April 5, 1918, two companies of Japanese marines were put ashore in Vladivostok, the immediate pretext being some disorders ashore, in which a Japanese subject had been killed. The local soviet reported that the Japanese had taken this action on their own initiative, without consulting the diplomatic representatives of any other of the Allied countries. But a later report indicated that the British had also landed marines, and on the following day the Japanese put ashore another small landing party. The Japanese naval commander, Admiral Kato, issued a proclamation in which he assumed personal responsibility for the landing of forces, and stated that it had absolutely no political significance, the object being merely to protect Japanese lives and property until the local authorities could guarantee law and order themselves. The local governing bodies, however, protested vigorously.

The news of the landing produced keen excitement in Moscow and was construed as the beginning of Japanese intervention in Russian domestic affairs. On the following day, April 6, 1918, the Soviet Government issued a statement in which it declared that the murder of the Japanese subject was part of a prearranged plan and that "the Japanese have started a campaign against the Soviet Republic." Two days later Premier Lenine said, in a public speech:

"It is possible that, within a short time, perhaps even within a few days, we shall be compelled to declare war against Japan."

Two days later it was reported that Russia had requested the German Government to permit postponement of that provision of the peace treaty which demanded the demobilization of the Russian military forces, on account of the possible need of defensive military action against the Japanese.

On April 16, 1918, Mr. Francis, American ambassador to Russia, issued the following statement:

"The Soviet Government and the Soviet press are giving too much importance to the landing of these marines, which has no political significance, but merely was a police precaution taken by the Japanese admiral on his own responsibility for the protection of Japanese life and property in Vladivostok, and the Japanese admiral, Kato, so informed the American admiral,

Knight, and the American consul, Caldwell, in Vladivostok. My impression is that the landing of the British marines was pursuant to the request of the British consul for the protection of the British consulate and British subjects in Vladivostok, which he anticipated would possibly be jeopardized by the unrest which might result from the Japanese landing. The American consul did not ask protection from the American cruiser in Vladivostok Harbor, and consequently no American marines were landed. This, together with the fact that the French consul at Vladivostok made no request for protection from the British, American, or Japanese cruisers in the harbor, unquestionably demonstrates that the landing of Allied troops is not a concerted action between the Allies."

The fears of the Soviet Government were not completely allayed, however, for they began to remove the stocks of war material westward, with the result that on April 20 the Japanese landed still more marines to reenforce those already on guard ashore.

On April 26, 1918, Tchitcherin, the foreign minister of the Soviet Government, informed the representatives of the United States, Great Britain, and France that his Government desired the recall of their consuls stationed at Vladivostok on account of their participation in counter-revolutionary plots. He also asked them to set forth their attitudes toward the Soviet Government. An official report of the demand for the removal of John K. Caldwell, the American consul at Vladivostok, was received by the American State Department on May 6, 1918, from Ambassador Francis. The State Department replied that it had no definite information on which to base such charges and refused to remove the consul. These charges were largely in relation to the counter-revolutionary movement which had been instigated by General Seminov, who had established himself in the Transbaikal and had gathered around him a number of former officers in the Russian army of high rank and who were now inspired, either by a hope that a monarchial form of government might be reestablished, or at least that a less radical form of government than that of the Bolsheviki might take its place.

Here were gathered also many civilian enemies of the Bolsheviki, with the same hope of overthrowing them by military force.

During the middle of April, 1918, hostilities were reopened by General Kornilov against the Soviet forces, but his campaign from the Cossack country in the south met with disaster in its incipiency, and Kornilov was himself badly wounded.

It was also stated that General Dutov, another anti-Bolshevist Cossack leader, was captured by the Bolshevist troops, and that Seminov, the leader of the anti-Soviet forces in Siberia, was killed.

Meanwhile the Germans were continuing their aggressive operations, largely through Ukrainia, where they were almost completely in possession of the country. The German Government was evidently keenly disappointed in its hopes of obtaining food supplies from this region.

If the demanded food supplies were to be had, it was obvious that stronger measures must be resorted to. In the latter part of April it was announced officially by the Washington State Department that the Ukrainian Rada was to be dissolved by the Teuton military commander in Kiev and another government established in its place.

The pretext came with the "arrest" on April 24, 1918, of a prominent pro-German banker by an organization calling itself the Committee of Ukrainian Safety. The German Vice Chancellor, Von Payer, said before the Main Committee of the Reichstag that this secret society had as its object the expulsion of the Germans from the country, which it proposed to accomplish by means of the old terrorist methods employed in the earlier days of the autocracy. Among the members of the organization were many men of public prominence, and it was said that its central executive committee had been meeting in the residence of the minister of war. The German ambassador had demanded an investigation, but the Rada would not, or could not, take action.

Within forty-eight hours the commander in chief of the Teuton forces in Ukrainia, General von Eichhorn, proclaimed a state of "enhanced protection," tantamount to martial law.

On April 28, 1918, while the Rada was in session, the doors to the assembly chamber were suddenly thrown open by German soldiers and a number of the members of the assembly were seized, among them being the minister of war. When the president of the Rada protested against the outrage, he was struck by a soldier and thrown to the floor.

On the following day a convention of wealthy peasants and landed gentry, who were holding a convention in the city, proclaimed itself the government of the land, declared the Rada non-existent, and proclaimed General Skoropadsky, a strong pro-German and a reactionary, hetman of Ukrainia, thus giving him practically dictatorial powers, subject to German approval. The German Government hastened to recognize the new governing power.

A German tool from the beginning, the Rada had nevertheless failed to satisfy the German demands because of its democratic form, which enabled an honest minority within its composition to block the pro-German majority. With the autocratic powers of the new dictator at their disposal, the Germans now hoped to accomplish their ends more effectively, for now they could place the responsibility squarely on him.

In their drive for food supplies, however, the Teutons were not disposed to confine themselves to the boundaries of Ukrainia. They still continued their military expeditions into the territories of the Soviet Government.

In the early part of June, 1918, the Germans made an advance into the Roslav region, in the Province of Kursk, taking Roventki. On May 10, 1918, they began an eastward advance, sixty miles wide, between Valuyki and Zhukovo. On that date they captured Rostov on the Don, an economic center of great importance, but held it only overnight, as the next day they were driven back by the Russian Red Guards. Finally, however, during this period, but on a date not mentioned in the dispatches, Sebastopol was captured, very little resistance being offered on this occasion. Here the majority of the ships constituting the Russian Black Sea fleet were captured, but, according to a German report, it was found that the ships were in a deplorable condition; only the battleship *Volga* and the cruiser *Pamyat Mercuria* were in serviceable condition. The rest of the fleet consisted of the battleship *Rostislav*, the cruiser *Potemkine*, and a number of torpedo boats and submarines and twenty transports. The protected motor-boat flotilla had already been seized at Odessa, as had been the new war vessels still lying on the slips in the shipyards. The latter consisted of a dreadnought of 23,000 tons, two protected cruisers of 7,600 tons, and two unprotected cruisers.

CHAPTER LXIII

GERMAN POLICY OF AGGRESSION

THE White Guards of Finland, having triumphed over the Socialistic Red Guards, with the active assistance of German intervention now began to show a disposition to widen Finnish territory in truly Prussian fashion. Already in May Finnish and German troops had begun operations in the direction of the Murman Coast, the main object undoubtedly being to seize the railway from the interior of Russia to the Arctic ports of Alexandrovsk and Archangel, where large supplies of war material were stored. It was stated that a small force of English and French marines had been landed here and were cooperating with the Bolshevist Red Guards in defending this territory against Teutonic invasion; that the war council attached to the local Murman Soviet consisted of one Russian, an Englishman, and a Frenchman. At any rate, the German Government made the landing of Allied troops at Alexandrovsk the pretext for a strong protest to the Soviet Government. In the early part of June, 1918, the Finnish Government, in response to communications from the French and English Governments, informed its ambassador in Stockholm that Finland had no desire to take possession of the Murman Railroad, but it could not undertake to forego its ambition to annex Russian Carelia. Apart from the small number of Russian immigrants in Carelia, the note said, the population was entirely Finnish and had preserved its national character during a century of oppression.

"Heretofore it has been impossible for the Finnish Government," the note continued, "to support these national desires, but the Finnish Government feels that it cannot for all time disregard its duty to liberate Carelia from the Bolshevist bands, of Russian and Finnish origin, which are terrorizing the peaceful population. Intervention may become necessary for purely defensive reasons, since the Bolshevist bands are threatening devastation to the territories on the Finnish border. Many attempts at invasion have already been repulsed. . . . Many pathetic appeals have been received from the Carelians to help them place in order their administrative and economic life where Russian methods have made all civilizing work impossible."

The German policy, obviously, where actual conquest was not practical, was the dismemberment of the former Russian Empire. Every encouragement was given to the separatist tendency. As an instance, the German Government was reported to have inquired of the local Crimean authorities concerning the nationalization of their flag, which the Soviet Government naturally interpreted as an indication of the German desire to separate the Taurida Republic from the Russian Federative Republic.

The annexation of Bessarabia to Rumania was another German intrigue to diminish the territory of the Russians. According to a Rumanian report on April 9, 1918, the National Assembly of Bessarabia had voted for annexation to Rumania, by a vote of 86 against 3. The Rumanian Premier had then proclaimed the union to be "definitive and indissoluble," and a delegation was sent to Jassy to present the homage of the people of Bessarabia to the Rumanian king. This action was taken at the suggestion of Germany, that Rumania might partly compensate herself for the loss of territory to Austria-Hungary and Bulgaria, according to the conditions of the peace she had signed with the Central Powers. Previously, in March, Russia and Rumania had agreed that Bessarabia was to be evacuated by Rumanian troops, whence they had gone to establish "law and order" at the request of the population, or, more accurately, the landed gentry, who desired them as a protection against Bolshevism. Local militia was to take the place of the Rumanian troops of occupation, while military garrisons were to be occupied by Russian troops. Russia undertook to leave Rumania the surplus of Bessarabian grain remaining after the population and the Russian troops had been provided for. All these arrangements were now revoked through German intrigues.

On the other hand, the captured provinces of Esthonia and Livonia were given a comparatively free hand by the Germans, the understanding being that they should remain in the Russian Federative Republic, if their populations so desired. Yet here Germany endeavored to accomplish by propaganda what she did not choose to attain by armed force.

In March, 1918, the Lithuanians had organized a provisional government, which immediately demanded recognition of Germany.

On May 5, 1918, the British Government granted an informal recognition to the Esthonian Provisional Government, and, as stated by Mr. Balfour, reaffirmed a "readiness to grant provisional recognition to the Esthonian National Council as a de facto independent body until the peace conference, when the future status of Esthonia ought to be settled as far as possible in accordance with the wishes of the population."

CHAPTER LXIV

GERMANY'S APPEAL TO CLASS HATREDS

A SURVEY of the geographical position of the Murman Peninsula and its harbors will show at a glance the strategic and economic importance of this region and explain the keen desire of the Germans to obtain a foothold here. The Murman Coast is that section of the Arctic shore stretching from the frontier of Russia with Norway, at the mouth of the Voryema River; to Cape Svyatov, on the White Sea, a distance of about 250 miles.

On the west the coast is a succession of precipitous cliffs and bluffs, pierced by a number of deep inlets, of fiords, several of which are excellent harbors for large ships. An inward sweep of the Gulf Stream washes the shore, keeping it free of ice the year around, though the White Sea, to the southward, is icebound six months of the year.

On this account it was long ago planned to connect this ice-free piece of coast with the interior of Russia by means of a railroad, but the project never went beyond paper until the beginning of the present war, when it suddenly assumed unusual importance. It was realized that practically all other Russian ports would be closed to commerce, but that the Murman Coast could still be reached by an open sea route. In the winter after the outbreak of hostilities the construction of the railroad to Kola was begun and completed by the fall of the following year, 1916. The railroad, which is about 800 miles in length, runs from Petrozavodsk to the little port of Kem, on the White Sea. Here it follows the coast to Kandalaska, also on the White Sea, whence it crosses the Kola Peninsula to the Port of Kola. This terminal port can be reached by ship from England quicker than Petrograd, while the route from New York is twenty-four hours shorter than from New York to Libau.

While this railroad remains in Russian hands, Russia has an open trade route with the outside world. Possession of this railroad would give the Germans control of this open doorway and so increase the strength of their economic grip on Russia. Furthermore, it would prove an invaluable base for submarine warfare.

As already stated, the Finnish-German forces began operations in this direction in April, and the Allies immediately landed a small force of marines to support the Red Guard defense of this important region. In June, 1918, the Finns and Germans resumed their advance on the railroad, heading for the important stations of Kem and Kandalaska. According to one report, the Germans had completed a railroad to Kem, along which they proposed to transport some 40,000 troops, stationed at Viborg. Lenine was disposed to make concessions at this point to the Germans. The local population, which is largely Russian, was violently opposed to German invasion.   On July 7, 1918, it was reported that the people of the Murman Coast had risen against the Soviet Government, declared themselves independent, and appealed to the Allies for protection.

French, English, and American forces were immediately landed, in spite of the strong protest of the Moscow Government.   As a matter of record, before landing, the British commander of the landing forces had requested permission of the Soviet Government, which had been immediately granted by Trotzky, minister of war.   The protest which followed was therefore compelled by German pressure, which was applied so strongly that the Soviet Government made a show of mobilizing a special army for transportation to the Murman Coast.

After the landing of the American forces, in the early part of July, 1918, the Allied troops advanced on Kem and occupied that port, then continued on toward Toroki, the Bolshevist forces there withdrawing to Nirok.   By the end of July, 1918, the whole Murman Coast had been occupied by the Allied troops, the German-Finnish forces, amounting to about a division, being too far south to offer any opposition.   According to one dispatch General Gurko, one of the chief commanders of the Russian troops in the days before the revolution, had been placed in command of the Murman Coast army.   It was also said that an appeal had been made for the support of the local population, which was being given with hearty enthusiasm.

The grip which Germany had taken on Finland was indicated when even so strong a reactionary as General Mannerheim, commander of the Finnish White Guards, resigned early in July, 1918, and left the country for Stockholm.   Here he stated publicly that Finland had practically become a territory of the German Empire and would remain so unless expelled by force.   He added that he was waiting for the opportune moment to rally the patriotic Finns against the Germans.   Said Hugo Haase, leader of the German minority Socialists, in a speech in the Reichstag:

"The list of those sentenced to death in Finland contains the names of a former premier and fifty Socialists, members of Parliament, some of whom have already been shot.   Owing to the number of daily executions in the town of Sveaborg that place has been renamed 'Golgotha.' "

The Finnish Constitutional Committee, by a vote of 16 against 15, has decided on a monarchial form of government, and the new constitution is being drafted accordingly.

CHAPTER LXV

ASSASSINATION OF THE GERMAN AMBASSADOR

THE policy of Lenine, as has already been noted, was one of protesting acquiescence to German outrage and demands; he snarled and assumed indignation, but complied. But this attitude was not by any means participated in by all the radicals. Even Trotzky, it will be remembered, had resigned his post as foreign minister because he had been unable to agree with Lenine on this point.

It was among that ultraradical group, the Socialist Revolutionists, that bitterness against Germany glowed hottest, so hot that its members, though having much in sympathy with the Bolsheviki, split away from them on the peace policy. Kerensky himself had been of this school of politics. In the early days of the autocracy, before the war, it had been this group which had carried on those terrorist activities which had given the Russian Revolution so bad a name among the conservatives of all countries.

Again they resolved to resort to these methods. On July 6, 1918, General Count von Mirbach, the German ambassador to Moscow, was assassinated by members of the Socialist Revolutionist Party.

Among others of the prominent Socialist Revolutionary leaders who were said to have been seized for this crime were Tseretelli, Chernov, Skobelev, and Savinkov, all of whom had been members of the Kerensky Cabinet. On July 12, 1918, it was reported that

Chernov was marching on Moscow at the head of an army of peasants.

Contrary to general belief in the Allied countries, Germany was inclined to hold the Lenine Government blameless of the murder of Count von Mirbach, for on July 10, 1918, the Berlin Government announced that it did not intend to hold the Soviet responsible. "The German Government and the nation," the dispatch added, "hope that the Russian Government and people will succeed in nipping the present revolutionary agitation in the bud." In a speech on July 11, 1918, Von Hertling, after having laid the blame to the intrigues of the Allies, said:

"We do not want fresh war with Russia. The present Russian Government wants peace and needs peace, and we are giving it support in this peaceful disposition and aim. On the other hand, it is true that political currents of very varied tendencies are circulating in Russia—movements having the most diverse aims, including the monarchist movement of the Constitutional Democrats and the movement of the Socialist Revolutionaries. We will not commit ourselves to any political countercurrent, but are giving careful attention to the course Russia is steering."

Apparently the personality of Von Mirbach had also something to do with his assassination, for as an intriguer he was reported to be absolutely without conscience. After his death the Constitutional Democrats made an official statement to the effect that he had called to him representatives of their party and, while professing to be upholding the Lenine Government, promised them German aid in overthrowing the Bolsheviki under certain conditions. Germany, he told them, desired a more conservative government in Russia, and if the Constitutional Democrats would be willing to establish a monarchy, under German influence, then they might expect a substantial revision of the Brest-Litovsk peace treaty, to the advantage of Russia. This offer the Constitutional Democrats had indignantly refused.

Not alone in Great Russia was it that the bitter hatred of the Germans was breaking out into flames. In the middle of June, 1918, it was reported from Kiev that the peasants were breaking out into local disorders and attacking the soldiers who were protecting the wheat-gathering expeditions. A dispatch dated in June, 1918, indicated that these disorders had taken on a more general and better organized aspect; that 40,000 peasants were assembled in an army and were entering the streets of the capital, where they were attacking the garrison and exploding artillery munitions. Later dispatches indicated that the revolt had spread into the Poltava and Chernigov districts, and ten days later the number of armed and officered insurgents was said to number 200,000. At the village of Krinichki, in the province of Ekaterinoslav, the peasants attacked the Germans in big force and a pitched battle took place, the Germans being driven back with a loss of over 1,000 men. In response to a call from the German commander in Kiev it was reported that Germany was obliged to send over a quarter of a million men to reenforce the German and Austrian forces in Ukrainia.

CHAPTER LXVI

THE MARCH OF THE CZECHO-SLOVAKS THROUGH SIBERIA

BY far the most picturesque of the events occurring in Russia during June and July, 1918, was the so-called Czecho-Slovak movement.

In the earlier periods of the war, but especially after the first revolution, in March, 1917, great numbers of Czechs, or Bohemians, and Slovaks, in the Austrian Army, had surrendered to the Russians voluntarily, on account of their hatred of Austria. The Bohemians and Slovaks are Slavs by race, so closely allied racially to the Russians that they are able to converse together with little difficulty. Whole regiments of them had come over to the Russians, en masse, and were enrolled as special regiments in the Russian Army.

Shortly before the Brest-Litovsk Peace Conference the French Government requested the Lenine Cabinet to equip and send on their way for the western front these Slavic soldiers of the Russian Army. This request was granted by the Soviet Government, and the Czechs and Slovaks, said to number 100,000, were allowed to retain their arms and entrain for France, via the Siberian Railroad.

At this time the Czecho-Slovak troops were decidedly not opposed to the Bolsheviki; on the contrary, most of them were known to be Socialists, and their sympathies were inclined to be in favor of all radical Russians. Upon hearing that this large body of soldiers was to leave Russia for the western front, Germany, naturally, raised a strong protest after the signing of the peace treaty. By this time the Czecho-Slovaks were en route on Siberian territory.

As to the cause of the friction which arose between them and the Soviet Government forces, there are two versions. One side contends that German pressure forced the Bolsheviki to endeavor to disarm the Czecho-Slovaks and intern them again. This effort was violently resisted and led to open hostilities.

The Bolsheviki affirm that the request of the French Government was not made in good faith; that behind it was an intrigue whose object was to make of the Czecho-Slovaks an armed force which should be the nucleus of an uprising against the Soviet in Russia. At an opportune moment the Czecho-Slovaks were to attack the Red Guards, hoping to rally around them all the anti-Bolsheviki forces in Russia, and so cause an overthrow of the Soviet.

Whatever the truth may be, open hostilities began on May 26, 1918, when Czecho-Slovak forces began operations in the Volga district and in Siberia simultaneously. Early in June, 1918, they had taken possession of a considerable stretch of territory in the Volga district, including several important towns. At about the same time some thousands of them, arriving at the terminus of the railroad, in Vladivostok, precipitated an uprising there and took possession of the city. On June 9 and 10, 1918, they occupied Samara and advanced to Ufa, in the Urals, where they were able to seize the railroads by which European Russia obtained its food supplies from Siberia. By the middle of June, 1918, they were in control of the southern section of the Trans-Siberian Railroad, from Samara to Chelyabinsk, the northern branch from Chelyabinsk to Ekaterinburg, and the main line on the east of Novonikolaiefsk. Some weeks later they held the railroad from Chelyabinsk, in the Ural Mountains, to Krasnoyarsk, a distance of 1,300 miles, as well as its eastern terminus, while scattered units of the Czecho-Slovak army stretched clear across Siberia.

On June 30, 1918, a pitched battle was fought with the Red Guards at the important city of Irkutsk, in Siberia, from which the local Bolshevist soviet was ousted. On the same day the last of the Bolsheviki were driven out of Vladivostok, the fighting being so severe that the Japanese and English warships in the harbor were obliged to land marines to protect the Allied consulates. Having established themselves in Vladivostok, the Czecho-Slovaks advanced into the Amur region and took Nikolaiefsky, on the Amur River, besides a number of other towns. By the middle of July, 1918, most of the Trans-Siberian Railroad was in the hands of the Czecho-Slovaks.

Meanwhile the Czecho-Slovaks in the Volga region were also engaged in heavy fighting with the Soviet troops. On July 9, 1918, the Soviet Government announced that it had delivered a heavy defeat to the Czecho-Slovaks at Bugulma, the enemy fleeing in the direction of Samara. Another dispatch stated that Muraviev, the commander of a large force of Soviet troops, suddenly decided to go over to the enemy and march with them on Moscow. When his soldiers refused to obey him, he committed suicide.

The commander in chief of the Czecho-Slovak forces in Russia is the Russian General Dieterichs, who was chief of staff under Dukhonin, after the fall of Kerensky. In a statement addressed to the American representative of the Finnish People's Republic, the Czech Socialist Federation of the United States insisted that the Czecho-Slovak movement in Russia was in no way connected with counter-revolutionary intrigues tending toward a re-establishment of the autocracy, or of a constitutional monarchy, the great majority of the Czecho-Slovaks being themselves Socialists. Professor Masaryk, representing the movement in Washington, says:

Admiral Knight's flagship, the old cruiser "Brooklyn" of Spanish-American War fame, is lying in the harbor of Vladivostok, to coöperate with the American and other Allied troops who have landed in Russia. Behind the "Brooklyn" is the British cruiser "Suffolk"

"Our army is struggling against the external foe. We are the guests of our brothers in Russia and we will not interfere in their internal affairs."

On July 10, 1918, a new, autonomous Siberian Government was proclaimed, with headquarters at Novonikolaiefsk, on the River Ob. The new government, while anti-Bolshevist, is radical in character and is based on universal suffrage and a constituent assembly representing all classes of the population.

On the same date, July 10, 1918, General Horvath, vice president of the Chinese Eastern Railroad, proclaimed himself military dictator of another government of Siberia. He established his headquarters at Harbin.

CHAPTER LXVII

EXECUTION OF EX-CZAR NICHOLA'

SINCE the latter part of June, 1918, there had been frequent rumors to the effect that ex-Czar Nicholas had been executed. The first of these stated that he had been killed by Red Guards at Ekaterinburg. This dispatch was denied officially, but was followed by another report that the ex-Czar had been tried and executed by the Bolsheviki at the city of the same name. This report was confirmed apparently by advices reaching the Washington State Department.

The next report was what purported to be an intercepted wireless message from the Soviet Foreign Minister Tchitcherin, in which it was stated that Nicholas was dead. Still another report had it that he had been bayoneted by Red Guards while being taken from Ekaterinburg to Perm.

On July 20 an official statement was issued from Moscow which stated definitely that the one-time autocrat of Russia had been shot on July 16, 1918.

The most prominent issue regarding Russian affairs which has been before the public of the United States and the other

War St. 7—CC

Allied countries during the past month or more has been the question of extending assistance to Russia in reestablishing herself as a free, independent nation, with the power to resist German aggression; whether this should be done through active military intervention from the east, or whether it should be confined to economic and financial aid. On this point there has been a wide division of opinion, not only in this country, but among Russians as well.

The Bolsheviki, naturally, are strongly opposed to any military aid, which they would interpret as an attempt on the part of the capitalists of the Allied countries to suppress the socialistic state which they claim to have erected on Russian soil.

The membership of the Great Russian Cooperative Movement, expressing its views through its leaders and its official organs, is also opposed to military intervention, having small faith in the benevolent intentions of the Japanese Government. The cooperators, however, realize the danger from German economic contι and have been fighting it with intensive effort. The Narodnι Bank and the Consumers' Union, in Moscow, have opened offices in London and New York, and have opened a campaign for British and American aid in their efforts to stem the German economic invasion. The contention of their representatives is that the cooperative movement of Russia is a weapon which could be used by the Allied countries to great advantage, and should be aided in an extension of credit and loans of capital, with which their cooperative industrial system might be developed to such dimensions as to form an invincible bulwark against the flood of German capital flowing into Russia.

So far as reports from Russia indicated, the Russians in favor of military intervention by the Allies were largely among the conservative elements, represented by the Constitutional Democrats, and among those comparatively moderate radicals represented by Kerensky and Konovalov. The first group are largely of the professional classes and the so-called bourgeoisie who have not been able to bring themselves to prefer German dominance to even the disorders of Bolshevikism. Among the second group are many of the old-time revolutionists, such as

Tchaikovsky, Prince Kropotkin, Kathcrine Breshkovskaya, Vladimir Bourtsev and Maria Spiradonova. These latter are, most of them, of the old Social Revolutionary Party.

On July 31, 1918, the New York "Times" published the following Washington dispatch:

"Negotiations between the Entente Powers, Japan, and the United States regarding the extension of aid to the Czecho-Slovaks in Siberia and Russia have advanced another step. Information sought by the Japanese Government upon certain points of the American proposal looking to a definition of the aims and scope of any joint action now has been furnished by the State Department. This places the whole subject again before the Japanese Foreign Office at Tokio, which must determine whether the American proposal is now in a sufficiently concrete form to warrant the inauguration of a policy of action. . . . Meanwhile, from unofficial sources, comes news that in anticipation of a satisfactory conclusion of the negotiations, Japan and the Entente Allies are perfecting their arrangements for the organization of whatever military force may be necessary for the execution of the joint agreement. Because of their proximity to Siberia, Japan and China have been foremost in this work, with a full understanding and cooperation between the military commanders, though for strategic reasons the exact extent and nature of these preparations cannot be disclosed. It is generally realized, however, that upon these two countries will lie the burden of providing the greater part of any military force that may be employed. To preserve the international character of the enterprise France and Great Britain are preparing contingents. Both of them will draw on their near-by colonies."

By the end of July, 1918, it was practically certain that the United States Government had consented to participate in a limited military expedition into Russia, by way of Siberia, not for the purpose of conquest or interference in the internal affairs of the Russian Republic, but to create a nucleus about which all the anti-German forces of Russia might rally for the reestablishment of an eastern front against Germany.

PART XI — AUSTRO-ITALIAN CAMPAIGN

CHAPTER LXVIII

ITALY REVIVES

AFTER the few local engagements which, during the last few days of January, 1918, resulted in some slight Italian gains and a corresponding improvement of the Italian positions in some sectors, comparatively little of importance happened during the first half of February, 1918. On the first of that month the Italians succeeded in advancing their lines to the head of the Melago Valley, while an attempt on the part of the Austro-Hungarian forces to reach the Italian lines by means of a drive against the Italian position on Monte di Val Bella failed.

Artillery fire was the extent of military operations on February 2 and 3, 1918, being restricted on the first of these two days to the Asiago Plateau and the front east of the Brenta, but spreading on the next day along the entire front.

During the next few days the outstanding feature was increased aerial activity on both sides. On February 4, 5, 6, and 7, 1918, Italian and British airplanes made repeated successful attacks against the Austrian positions and a number of Austrian aviation grounds. On the other hand the Austrians bombed repeatedly Venice, Mestre, Treviso, Calviano, and Bassano. On some of these days there were also artillery duels and outpost actions, although the weather seriously interfered with military operations almost along the entire front.

Lively artillery duels and concentrations of fire in the Val Brenta and in the Mt. Melago and Mt. Asolone areas occurred during February 8, 1918. Austrian patrols attempting a surprise attack against some Italian troops were repulsed by hand-grenade fire. Between the Posina and the Astico, east of Lake Garda, and along the coast, Italian reconnoitering parties effectively harassed the Austrian outposts. During the evening two infantry attacks in force were attempted by the Austrians south of Daone, west of Lake Garda, but failed under the heavy fire of the Italian advanced posts.

Along the whole front fighting activity was confined on February 9, 1918, to artillery actions, more intense and frequent in the eastern sector of the Asiago Plateau and in the area west of Mt. Grappa.

On February 10, 1918, very violent concentrations of fire and offensive thrusts of infantry were repeatedly carried out by the Austrians to the east and west of Val Frenzela, at the eastern end of the Sette Comuni, or Asiago Plateau.

At the new Italian positions of Mt. Val Bella and Col del Rosso, four and a half miles east of Asiago, Austrian attacks were promptly frustrated by the very effective fire of the Italian batteries. Farther to the east, on the southern slopes of Mt. Sasso Rosso, seven miles northeast of Asiago, Austrian detachments made various attempts to reach, under the protection of fire, some advanced trenches in front of the Italian lines, which had been evacuated, but they did not succeed, owing to the deadly Italian barrage fire.

On February 13, 1918, it was semiofficially announced that the British part of the battle line on the Italian front had been lengthened considerably east of the Montello ridge along the Piave and extended then some miles east of Nervesa.

Opposite the Montello, on February 15, 1918, British reconnoitering parties crossed the Piave and reached the Austrian lines. There were the usual artillery actions in the plains; one of the Italian patrols, starting from the bridgehead of Capo Sile (northeast corner of Venetian lagoons), surprised an Austrian post, killed or put to flight its garrison, and returned without losses, bringing back the captured arms.

Lively artillery actions took place in February 16, 1918, to the west of Lake Garda, to the east of the Brenta, and on the

Middle Piave. Allied batteries carried out effective concentrations of fire on Austrian movements east of Val Frenzela and on the back slopes of Col della Berretta, two miles east of Brenta. In the Val Lagarina, east of Lake Garda and south of Canove on the Asiago Plateau, Austrian reconnoissance parties were repulsed by rifle fire.

Between the Posina and the Astico Italian patrols, on February 16, 1918, displayed increased activity, and small caliber batteries harassed with frequent bursts of fire Austrian movements in the basin of Laghi. On the Asiago Plateau Allied artillery fired on Austrian troops marching along the Galmarara Valley, and carried out concentrations of fire on the sector Val Frenzela-Val Brenta; the Austrians repeatedly shelled Italian positions on the eastern edge. Between the Brenta and the Piave there was a reciprocal cannonade at the salient of Mt. Solarolo. Allied patrols carried out effective harassing actions against the Austrian advanced posts at Grave di Papadofoli. Along the coast region the Austrians intensified the artillery fire at different points, and pushed various patrols toward Cortellazzo, at the mouth of the Piave. They were, however, driven back by the hand-grenade fire of the sailors who garrisoned the bridgehead.

Again on February 18, 1918, artillery activities greatly increased, especially toward the eastern edge of the Asiago Plateau, and occasionally in the Val Giudicaria, west of Lake Garda, in the Posina-Astico sector, east of Lake Garda, on the front of Mt. Tomba, west of the Piave, and to the south of Ponte della Priula, on the Piave.

Italian batteries opened a sudden fire in strong Austrian parties in the Galmarara and Seren valleys and dispersed them. French batteries carried out effective concentration fire along their sector of the front. British patrols, having forded the Piave, raided the Austrian advanced trenches.

During the next few days aerial activity became especially marked. Austrian aviation grounds were bombed successfully by British and Italian squadrons. Austrian airplanes, too, were more active. Padua, Vicenza, Mestre, and Venice were bombed

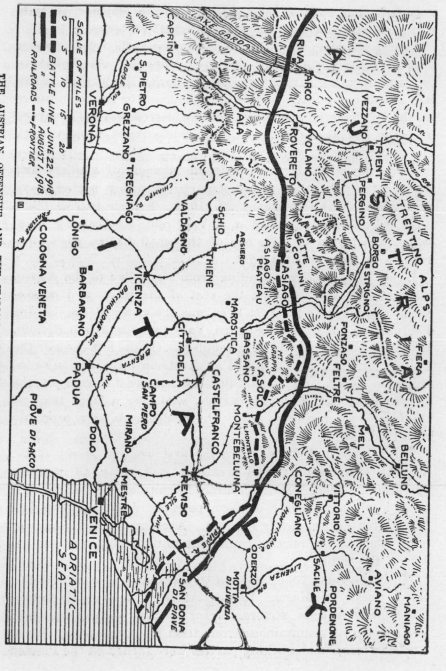

THE AUSTRIAN OFFENSIVE AND THE ITALIAN COUNTEROFFENSIVE, JUNE-AUGUST, 1918

repeatedly and suffered considerable material damage, in spite of the efficient work of Italian antiaircraft batteries.

During February 21, 1918, the Austrians shelled with greater frequency the southeastern slopes of Montello. At the Grave Austrian scouting parties were driven back. An English patrol had an encounter with an important group of the Austrian forces on the left bank of the Piave. Italian patrols having advanced as far as the islet of Folina in the Middle Piave, brought back two machine guns.

Along the whole front a moderate struggle of artillery and lively activity by Italian and Austrian scouting parties were maintained during February 22, 1918. British patrols made a few prisoners. At the bottom of Val Brenta an Austrian force, which was trying to seize one of the small Italian posts, was repulsed after a spirited fight.

Lively reciprocal cannonading from the Adige to the Astico, moderate fire actions along the rest of the front, and intense aerial activity over the first lines was the order of the day for February 23, 1918. At Lagoscuro, Val Camonica, and at Rivalta, Brenta, Austrian patrols were repulsed. On the left bank of the Piave a British patrol attacked an Austrian force, causing considerable losses. At Capo Sile, the northeast corner of the Venetian lagoons, Austrian parties, who over a large tract of the front were trying to attack the bridgehead, were promptly dispersed.

The balance of February and the first week of March, 1918, brought extraordinary bad weather, restricting all military operations. There were, of course, in spite of the weather the usual local engagements between patrols. Aerial activity had to be given up practically entirely. Artillery activity, too, was more moderate, increasing from time to time along various sectors of the front.

Much the same conditions continued during the second and third weeks of March, 1918. Artillery activity increased occasionally in some sectors, as for instance during March 8, 1918, along the mountainous front from the Adige to the Piave. Austrian troops and working parties were shelled on the Plateau of Tonezza, at the Assa-Astico confluence, and at the head line of Val Frenzela. Counterattacks were carried out by the Austrian artillery with more liveliness in the southern region of the Montello, but showed less activity along the rest of the front.

More or less unsuccessful air raids were made by Austrian planes against Naples and Venice on March 10, 1918. Reconnoissance combats were daily occurrences at many points of the front. Artillery duels of varying extent and violence, too, were reported every day, without, however, causing material changes on either side.

Much the same conditions continued during the last week of March, 1918. There were frequent local engagements between patrols and other small units at many points along the entire front.

The conclusion of peace with Russia, of course, was an important factor in the further development of affairs in the Austro-Italian theater of war. Large bodies of troops, formerly employed on the Austro-Russian front, became available for the Austro-Italian front. As early as March 28, 1918, it was reported that forty Austro-Hungarian divisions had been transferred from the eastern to the Italian front.

However, there were no immediate developments of any importance. Throughout a great part of April, 1918, the weather was very bad. Again there were daily actions between patrols and reconnoissance detachments. Artillery activity at times became very powerful, suffering on the whole, however, from the inability of the air service to function at its best on account of the bad weather.

During May, 1918, too, there was little change, though fighting increased in violence and frequency. The Italians gained some local successes, notably the capture on May 9, 1918, of a strongly organized Austrian position on the 6,000 feet high Monte Corno in the Vallarsa, southeast of Rovereto; advances in the region of Capo Sile, the northeast corner of the Venetian lagoons on May 20 and 21, 1918, and again during the night of May 26 and 27, 1918; and the capture on May 25 to 27, 1918, by Alpini of a number of strongly fortified Austrian positions, located at a great height in the Tonale region, some twenty miles south of the southeast corner of Switzerland.

During the first half of June, 1918, the same kind of spasmodic fighting was the order of the day. If there was any change as compared with the previous months, it consisted of a slight tendency on the part of the Austrians to be more aggressive. Indeed, toward the middle of the month this tendency increased considerably and, as a result, rumors began to be heard of an approaching new Austrian offensive.

Before long the storm broke. On June 15, 1918, the Austrians launched their new offensive on a front of about 100 miles, from the Asiago Plateau to the mouth of the Piave. For a few days it seemed as if they might be successful. On June 16, 1918, they succeeded in crossing the Piave at a number of points near Nervesa, Fagare, and Musile, ten, eight, and fifteen miles respectively north, northeast, and east of Treviso. On that day the Italians also were forced to give way at the Sette Comuni Plateau, and immediately to the east in the region of Monte Asolone and Monte Grappa. Later, however, they were able to reestablish their lines.

On June 17, 1918, the Austrians were checked by Italian and British troops in the mountains east of the Sette Comuni, but were able to extend their gains at the other end of the front, west and south of Musile, where they succeeded in capturing Capo Sile.

Still less successful were they on the next day, June 18, 1918; again they were repulsed at the eastern end of the Asiago Plateau, and an attempt to cross the Piave at still another point, between Maserada and Cardelu, about three miles northwest of Fagare, resulted in enormous losses.

The Italian resistance grew stronger now day by day. It was helped considerably by heavy rains which created flood conditions at many points along the Piave. All attempts of the Austrians to gain new crossings were repulsed with heavy losses to their troops. By June 20, 1918, it became clear that the Italians had regained the initiative and were attacking furi-

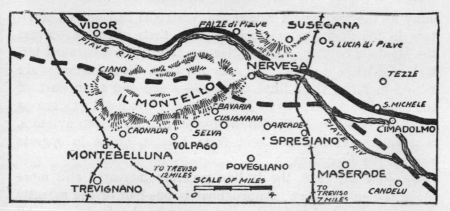

THE "MONTELLO" WHERE THE AUSTRIAN OFFENSIVE BROKE DOWN

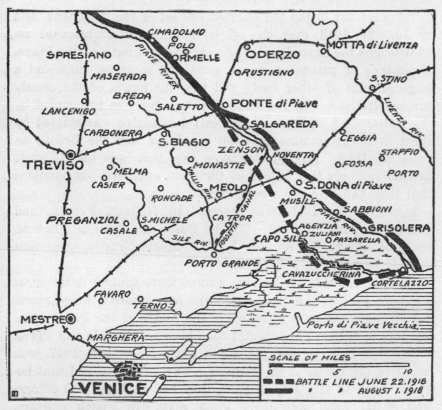

AUSTRO-ITALIAN OPERATIONS ON THE LOWER PIAVE RIVER

ously at the few points where the Austrians had gained territory in the first two or three days of their offensive. From
the Montello heights, west of Nervesa, the battle continued bitterly and without pause. On June 20, 1918, the Austrians were
forced to retire their lines on the Montello and from part of
the Capo Sile sector. British, French, and Czecho-Slovak troops
were of great help to the Italian forces, and American aviators,
who had hurriedly been sent from France, began to operate
against the Austrians.

On June 21, 1918, the Italian pressure increased still more
along the entire front. Approximately one-half of the recently
gained ground had to be given up again by the Austrians. All
efforts to counterattack were promptly repelled.

The next day began the hurried retreat of the Austrians, and
by June 24, 1918, even the official Austrian announcement acknowledged the evacuation of the entire right bank of the Piave.
Thousands of prisoners, many guns and machine guns and a
large amount of other booty fell into the hands of the closely
pressed Italians. On the same day Nervesa was reoccupied by
the Italians. A strong and successful offensive was started by
them in the mountains between the Piave and the Brenta on
June 25, 1918. Day by day now the Austrians had to yield
ground, not only that gained by their last offensive, but positions
that they had held for a considerable time.

Monte di Val Bella was stormed by Italians, French, and
British on June 30, 1918. Col del Rosso and the Col d'Echele,
south of Asiago, fell on July 1, 1918, Monte Grappa, somewhat
farther east, on July 2, 1918.

On July 4, 1918, the Italians gained more ground in the most
southern part of the front, near the sea, where a long-drawn-
out struggle had been going on in the region of the Piave delta.
By July 6, 1918, all the coastal zone between the Sile and Piave,
stubbornly held by the Austrians since November, 1917, was
again in the hands of the Italians. The latter claimed that between June 15 and July 6, 1918, they had captured 523 officers
and 23,911 men, sixty-three guns, sixty-five trench mortars,
1,234 machine guns, and a vast amount of material.

During the balance of July, 1918, there was not a great deal more fighting on the Italian front. On July 8, 1918, the Italians extended their lines in the Monte Grappa and Col Caprile regions. Austrian attacks against the Cornone slopes on July 13, 1918, were promptly repulsed. The French gained some ground by a surprise attack near Bertigo and Zocchi, and on July 20, 1918, the Italians recaptured Monte Stabel and reoccupied Corno di Caverto. From then on the fighting on the Italian front simmered down again to local engagements between opposing patrols and reconnoissance detachments and to artillery and aeroplane duels.

PART XII—THE WAR ON THE SEA

CHAPTER LXIX

NAVAL WARFARE

THE submarine blockade was continued by the Germans during the six-months' period, February 1 to August 1, 1918, but with considerably smaller results. Figures, as in the past, were difficult to compile, and as the war progressed this difficulty increased. However, the British Admiralty officially announced that during the eleven months—March, 1917, to January, 1918, inclusive—a total of 1,239 British ships had been sunk by mines or torpedoes, an average of 112.6 ships per month and an average of 25.1 ships per week. Beginning with February, 1918, losses became very much smaller, partly on account of the greater number of submarines sunk or captured by the Allies, and partly on account of the ever-increasing efficiency of the submarine-chasing and convoy services.

In April, 1918, the British Admiralty discontinued its weekly report of merchant ships destroyed by mines or torpedoes, and substituted a monthly report in terms of tonnage. The following figures are taken from the official British reports and show the steadily decreasing success of submarine warfare:

Period 1917	British	Allied and neutral	Total
January	193,045	216,787	409,832
February	343,486	231,370	574,856
March	375,309	259,376	634,685
Quarter	911,840	707,533	1,619,373

Period 1917	British	Allied and neutral	Total
April	555,056	338,821	893,877
May	374,419	255,917	630,336
June	432,395	280,326	712,721
Quarter	1,361,870	875,064	2,236,934
July	383,430	192,519	575,949
August	360,296	189,067	549,363
September	209,212	159,949	369,161
Quarter	952,938	541,535	1,494,473
October	289,973	197,364	487,337
November	196,560	136,883	333,443
December	296,356	155,707	452,063
Quarter	782,889	489,954	1,272,843
1918			
January	217,270	136,187	353,457
February	254,303	134,119	388,422
March	216,003	165,628	381,631
Quarter	687,576	435,934	1,123,510
April	226,108	85,348	311,456
May	224,735	130,959	355,694
June	161,062	114,567	275,629
Quarter	611,905	330,874	942,779

On February 5, 1918, the British liner *Tuscania* (Captain
J. L. Henderson), serving as a transport for American troops,
was sunk by a submarine off the coast of Ireland. The *Tuscania*
carried 2,177 U. S. soldiers of whom 117 were officers, 2 civilians,
2 naval ratings, and a crew of 16 officers and 181 men. She
was a steel twin-screw steamer of 14,384 tons, built at Glas-
gow in 1914 for the Anchor Line and had a speed of 17½ knots.
212 U. S. soldiers lost their lives. Though hit without any

warning and during the night, the troops reached their boat stations without panic and in splendid order. Unfortunately some of the lifeboats capsized, a fact which was responsible for some of the losses. Others died later in hospitals from shock and exposure; while still others had fallen victims to the explosion caused by the two torpedoes. The survivors were landed in Ireland and Scotland, where those of the bodies which were recovered found a last resting place. British destroyers were instrumental in saving many lives and also immediately gave chase to the submarine which, it is believed, was sunk by depth bombs.

Spanish losses became very heavy. On February 9, 1918, the *Sebastian* was sunk in her way to New York; the *Mar Caspio* went to the bottom on February 23; the *Neguri* on February 26; the *Sardinero* on February 27; and a grain ship, chartered to the Swiss Government, on March 2, 1918.

On February 26, 1918, the British steamer *Glenart Castle,* serving as a hospital ship, was sunk in Bristol Channel. Fortunately she had no patients on board; she carried a crew of 120, 54 members of the R. A. M. C. and 8 female nurses, of whom 153 were reported as missing. This was the second attack on the boat, the first one having been made on March 1, 1918, in the channel. She was then full of wounded from France, all of whom were saved while the vessel itself was taken to harbor and repaired. The *Glenart Castle* was formerly known as the *Galician* and was previous to the war owned by the Union Castle Company. She was the seventh British hospital ship torpedoed at night and without warning.

During February, 1918, too, the British S. S. *Minnetonka* of 13,528 tons was sunk in the Mediterranean. Previous to the war she had been a well-known passenger liner of the Atlantic Transport Line, running between New York and London.

Another large steamer which became the prey of submarine warfare was the *Celtic,* torpedoed off the Irish coast on April 1, 1918. However, she succeeded in reaching port in safety.

Spanish ships were continued to be sunk and on April 11, 1918, it was announced that Germany had begun a submarine

It was on April 23, 1918, that the British cruiser "Vindictive" defended the operation of sinking two old cruisers filled with cement to block the submarine base at Zeebrugge. On May 10 the battered "Vindictive" herself was sunk to close the base at Ostend

blockade of Spanish ports as a result of a commercial treaty signed between Spain and the United States.

On the same day Uruguay asked the German Government, through the Swiss minister at Berlin, whether Germany considered that a state of war existed between the two countries. The inquiry was the result of the capture by a submarine of a Uruguayan military commission bound for France.

One of the largest German submarines appeared, on April 10, 1918, in the port of Monrovia, the capital of Liberia, on the west coast of Africa, after having seized the day before the small armed Liberian vessel *President Grant*. The crew were taken prisoners and the boat sunk. Liberia, it will be remembered, had declared war against Germany on August 4, 1917. The German commander dispatched by the Liberian crew an ultimatum to the Liberian Government, in which he threatened that, failing the dismantling of the wireless stations and the closing of the French cable, the town of Monrovia would be bombarded. The stations were accordingly closed, as the capital was under the fire of the German guns, but later the U-boat commander insisted upon their being destroyed. This the Liberian Government refused to do, and the German submarine thereupon bombarded Monrovia for over an hour, destroyed the stations, and inflicted some casualties. Fortunately for the town a steamer appeared at that moment. The submarine gave chase and did not return again.

The most important American losses in April, 1918, were the S. S. *Lake Moor*, manned by naval reserves and sunk in European waters on April 11, 1918, with a loss of 5 officers and 39 men; the *Florence H.*, wrecked by an internal explosion while at anchor in a French port, with a loss of 29.

Neutral shipping continued to be a heavy loser. The Norwegian Government, for instance, announced that from the beginning of the war to the end of April, 1918, Norway's losses had reached the total of 755 vessels, aggregating 1,115,519 tons, and accompanied by the loss of 1,006 seamen, while 700 more out of additional 53 ships were missing.

War St. 7—DD

On the other hand it was announced that during April, 1918, 12 German submarines had been captured or sunk in European waters by American and British destroyers.

On May 3, 1918, the Old Dominion liner *Tyler* was sunk off the coast of France with a loss of 11 men, including 5 naval gunners.

Another British S. S. serving as transport for U. S. troops, the *Moldavia*, was torpedoed and sunk on May 23, 1918, 56 U. S. soldiers being reported as "unaccounted for." Two British transports, the *Ansonia* and *Leasowe Castle*, were sunk on May 26, 1918, with losses of 40 and 101 lives respectively.

While returning to the United States the U. S. transport *President Lincoln*, formerly a Hamburg-American liner, was sunk in the naval war zone on May 31, 1918, with a loss of 4 officers and 23 men.

In the meantime some German submarines put in their appearance off the coast of the U. S. They began their operations on May 25, 1918, and maintained them with varying success and at varying distances from the coast until well into August, 1918. As a result the following boats were sunk up to June 20, 1918:

Jacob H. Haskell, schooner, 1,362 tons.

Isabel B. Wiley, schooner, 611 tons.

Hattie Dunn, schooner, 365 tons.

Edward H. Cole, schooner, 1,791 tons, subsequently raised and saved.

Herbert L. Pratt, tank steamer, 7,200 tons.

Carolina, passenger steamer, 5,093 tons.

Winneconne, freighter, 1,869 tons.

Hauppauge, auxiliary schooner, 1,500 tons.

Edna, schooner, 325 tons, subsequently towed in.

Texel, steamship, 3,210 tons.

Samuel M. Hathaway, schooner, 1,038 tons.

Samuel C. Mengel, schooner, 700 tons, unconfirmed.

Edward Baird, schooner, 279 tons.

Eidsvold, Norwegian steamship, 1,570 tons.

Harpathean, British steamship, 4,588 tons.

Vinland, Norwegian steamship, 1,143 tons.

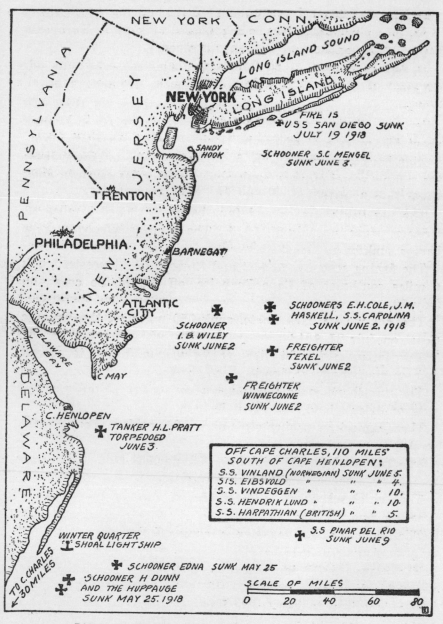

RAIDS OF GERMAN SUBMARINES ON UNITED STATES
SHIPPING ON THE ATLANTIC COAST

Desauss, schooner, 500 tons.

Pinar del Rio, steamship, 2,504 tons.

Vindeggen, Norwegian steamship, 2,632 tons.

Henrik Lund, Norwegian steamship, 4,322 tons.

Later victims were, according to the New York "Times":

The Norwegian freighter *Augvald,* sunk June 23, 1918, 125 miles east of Cape Race; the British transport *Dwinsk,* sunk about 550 miles east of Sandy Hook, June 24, 1918; the Norwegian bark *Manx King,* July 6, 1918; 300 miles off Cape Race; the sailing vessel *Marosa,* sunk about 1,200 miles east of Sandy Hook July 8, 1918.

The tug *Perth Amboy* and four barges attacked 3 miles off Orleans, Mass., on July 21, 1918. The tug was burned and the barges sunk by gunfire.

The fishing schooner *Robert* and *Richard* of Gloucester, sunk 6 miles southeast of Cape Porpoise, off the Maine coast, on July 22, 1918.

The Portuguese bark *Porto,* sunk 550 miles off the Atlantic Coast on July 27, 1918.

The Japanese freight steamer *Tokuyama Maru,* torpedoed and sunk off the Nova Scotia coast on August 1, 1918.

The British schooner *Dornfontein,* set on fire 25 miles southwest of Brier Island on August 2, 1918.

Three American fishing schooners off the Nova Scotia coast on August 3, 1918.

The Diamond Shoals Lightship 71, anchored off Cape Hatteras, N. C., shelled and sunk on August 6, 1918.

The British schooner *Gladys M. Hollett,* sunk off the Canadian coast on August 5, 1918.

The American steamer *Merak,* sunk off the North Carolina coast on August 6, 1918.

The Standard Oil tank steamer *Luz Blanca,* sunk 40 miles west of Halifax on August 5, 1918.

The American tanker *O. B. Jennings,* sunk off the Virginia coast.

The American schooner *Stanley L. Seaman,* sunk on August 5, 1918, when 110 miles east of Cape Hatteras.

Nine American fishing schooners sunk on August 3, 1918, off George's Bank, 60 miles from Nantucket Island.

The Norwegian freighter *Sommerstad*, 3,875 gross tons, torpedoed and sunk 25 miles southeast by east of Fire Island on August 12, 1918.

The British steamship *Penistone*, 4,139 gross tons, torpedoed on August 11, 1918, about 100 miles east of Nantucket.

The Swedish steamship *Sydland*, 3,031 gross tons, bombed and sunk on August 8, 1918, about 100 miles southeast of Nantucket.

The American oil tanker *Frederick R. Kellogg*, 7,127 gross tonnage, torpedoed 10 miles off Barnegat, N. J., sank in 4 minutes; 7 men killed by the explosion.

The five-masted American schooner *Dorothy Barrett*, 2,088 gross tonnage, sunk with a cargo of coal 20 miles from Cape May, N. J., August 14, 1918.

It was announced in the U. S. Senate that 28 submarines had been sunk by the American Navy between January 1 and June 15, 1918.

Norway continued to be a severe loser. Twenty of her ships were sunk in May, 1918, causing a loss of 31 lives, and 14 more in July, 1918, with a loss of 55 sailors.

On June 27, 1918, another hospital ship was sunk when the Canadian S. S. *Llandovery Castle* went down off the British coast. Two hundred and thirty-four persons were reported missing.

Another former Hamburg-American liner, the *Cincinnati*, renamed the *Covington*, and serving as a U. S. transport, was sunk while returning to the U. S. Six of her crew lost their lives.

On July 14, 1918, the French transport *Djemnah* was sunk in the Mediterranean with a loss of 442 lives. The well-known former Cunard liner *Carpathia*, remembered especially for her services to the survivors of the ill-fated *Titanic* and the *Volturno*, was sent to the bottom off the west coast of Ireland on July 17, 1918. Three days later the White Star liner *Justicia* was sunk off the north Irish coast after a fight with a submarine lasting 24 hours.

Losses, not resulting from naval actions, to the naval forces
of the various belligerents, as far as they became known, were
comparatively small. Germany, besides her losses of submarines, lost some destroyers and mine sweepers. Austria, in
May, 1918, lost the battleship *Wien*. England lost some destroyers, torpedo boats, and mine sweepers. Seven British submarines, caught in Russian waters by the collapse of Russia, were
sunk by their own crews off Helsingfors between April 3 and 8,
1918, upon the approach of German naval forces and transports. The Japanese battleship *Kawachi,* of 21,420 tons and
20 knots, blew up on July 12, 1918, while at anchor in Tokuyama Bay, and sank with a loss of over 500 officers and men.
The U. S. armored cruiser *San Diego* was sunk off Fire Island,
N. Y., on July 19, 1918, by a mine apparently having been laid
by one of the German submarines then operating in American
waters.

On February 24, 1918, the German Government announced
that the auxiliary cruiser *Wolf* had returned to the Austrian
harbor Pola, after a 15 months' cruise in the Atlantic, Pacific,
and Indian Oceans. Claims as to the number and tonnage of
ships sunk by the *Wolf* as made by the German authorities
differed widely from the losses compiled by the British authorities, the former amounting to 35 ships of 210,000 tons, the latter
to 17 ships of about 40,000 tons. One of the boats attacked
by the raider, the Spanish S. S. *Igatz Mendi*, was captured, and,
after a prize crew had been sent aboard, took over the passengers and crews of half a dozen ships which had been sunk.
Attempting to return to a German port, she stranded on February 25, 1918, off the Danish coast. Passengers and members
of the crews with civil status were sent to their various homes,
while the German prize crew and some British military men
were interned.

A number of minor naval engagements were fought between
small units of the belligerents' naval forces.

A swift raid was made by a flotilla of large German torpedo-
boat destroyers early in the morning of February 15, 1918, on
British patrol forces in the Dover Straits. One trawler and 7

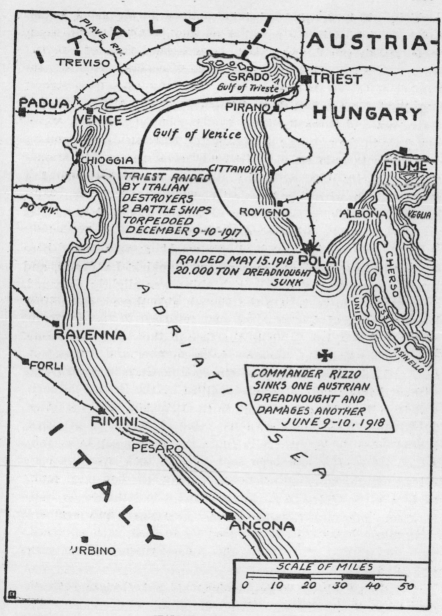

TRIEST RAIDED
BY ITALIAN
DESTROYERS
2 BATTLE SHIPS
TORPEDOED
DECEMBER 9-10-1917

RAIDED MAY 15.1918
20.000 TON DREADNOUGHT
SUNK

COMMANDER RIZZO
SINKS ONE AUSTRIAN
DREADNOUGHT AND
DAMAGES ANOTHER
JUNE 9-10, 1918

SCALE OF MILES
0   10   20   30   40   50

ITALIAN NAVAL EXPLOITS

drifters, which were occupied in hunting a submarine, which had been sighted in the patrol, were sunk. After having sunk these vessels the German destroyers returned rapidly to the north before any of the Allied forces could engage them. A large number of the crews of the vessels sunk lost their lives.

A light Franco-British division, composed of three French destroyers and three British ships, joined battle in the North Sea early in the morning of March 21, 1918, with a detachment of German torpedo vessels of the "A" type, two of which were sunk. Shortly afterward, the same light division fought a second action with five big destroyers which had been bombarding Dunkirk. One German destroyer was sunk, and it is probable that two other enemy destroyers were lost.

From information received, it would appear that three flotillas had been ordered to bombard Dunkirk, La Panne, and Bray Dunes. One of the British ships was slightly damaged, and returned to port. On the French side there were neither killed nor wounded.

British boats, belonging to the Grand Fleet, made an excursion into the Kattegat, the strait between Sweden and Denmark, on April 15, 1918, sinking 10 German trawlers and returning without having suffered any casualties.

British light forces operating in the Helgoland Bight on April 20, 1918, obtained touch with German light forces, who retired behind mine fields. A few shots were exchanged at extreme range and one German destroyer was observed to have been hit.

Early in the morning of April 23, 1918, British naval forces made a successful attack against Ostend and Zeebrugge, both of them important German submarine bases. The raid was undertaken under the command of Vice Admiral Roger Keyes, commanding at Dover French destroyers cooperating with the British forces. There were six obsolete cruisers which took part in the attack—*Brilliant, Sirius, Intrepid, Iphigenia, Thetis,* and *Vindictive.* The first five were filled with concrete, and were to be sunk in the channels and entrances to the ports if that could possibly be managed. *Vindictive,* working with two auxiliary craft, ferryboats well known on the Mersey, *Daffodil* and *Iris*, carried storming and demolition parties to the head of the mole at Zeebrugge. *Vindictive* was specially fitted with brows for landing the storming parties and armed specially for the operation with batteries of Stokes mortars, flame throwers, &c. The men employed on the blockships and in the storming and demolition parties were bluejackets and Royal Marines, picked from a very large number of volunteers from the Grand Fleet.

There were light covering forces belonging to the Dover command, and Harwich forces, under Admiral Tyrwhitt, covered the operation in the north.

A force of monitors, together with a large number of motor launches, coastal motor boats, which, as is known, are small, fast craft, carrying a minimum crew of six, and other small craft took part in the operation.

It was a particularly intricate operation, which had to be worked strictly to time-table and involved very delicate navigation on a hostile coast without lights and largely under unknown navigational conditions, which have developed since the war, with the added danger of unknown mine fields. One of the essentials to success was a high development of the scientific use of smoke or fog—it is more fog than smoke—for which certain conditions of force and direction of wind were necessary, so as to protect the operation from batteries which could have flanked it.

The general plan of operation was as follows:—After an hour of intense bombardment of Zeebrugge by the monitors, *Vindictive*, with the auxiliaries *Iris* and *Daffodil*, were to run alongside the head of the mole, attacking with gunfire as they approached; storming parties and demolition parties were to be landed. Meantime three blockships, assisted by the coastal motor boats and launches, were to make for the entrance to the canal and to be run aground and blown up. Two old and valueless submarines were to run against the pile work connecting the masonry portion of the mole with the shore, and, being filled with explosives, were to be blown up, destroying the pile-work connection.

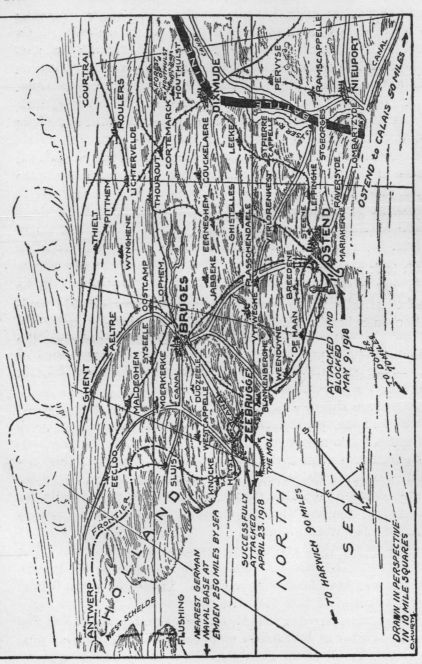

BRITISH NAVAL ATTACKS ON THE GERMAN BASES OF ZEEBRUGGE AND OSTEND

At Ostend the operation was simpler. Two of the blockships were to be run aground and blown up at the entrance to the port. The difficulties of this part of the undertaking were considerably increased by mist and rain, with corresponding low visibility and consequent absence of effective aerial cooperation.

At Zeebrugge, of the three blockships two attained their objective and were sunk and blown up in the entrance of the canal. The third one grounded in the passage in. One of the old submarines succeeded in obtaining its objective and was blown up to the destruction of the piling of the approach to the mole. Storming parties from *Vindictive, Iris*, and *Daffodil* attacked under extremely heavy fire, and fought with the greatest possible gallantry, maintaining their position alongside the mole for an hour, causing much damage to the enemy and inflicting considerable losses upon him. The objectives for the storming and demolition parties were (1) the German forces holding it, (2) the battery upon it, (3) the destroyer and submarine depots upon it, (4) the large seaplane base upon it. The three vessels, *Vindictive, Iris,* and *Daffodil*, after reembarking their landing parties, withdrew. This attack was primarily intended to engage the attention of the garrison on the mole, thereby allowing the blockships to enter the harbor.

At Ostend the wind prevented the effective use of the smoke screen and the two blockships had to be run ashore and blown up without attaining their objective. The British loss in vessels was small: one destroyer and two motor launches. But fire from German guns wrought heavy havoc in the ranks of the British seamen: nineteen officers and 170 men were killed; two officers and fourteen men were missing, and twenty-nine officers and 354 men were wounded.

On May 10, 1918, the Ostend operation was completed. The old cruiser *Vindictive* was sunk at the entrance to the harbor, after having been filled with concrete. The losses of the British forces engaged in this operation were small.

It was later reported that twenty-one German destroyers and a large number of submarines were penned in the Bruges Canal docks as a result of the naval operations against Zeebrugge.

Engagements, without leading to any results, occurred on April 23, 1918, between five Austrian and two British destroyers.

Early in May, 1918, reports about a mutiny in the Austrian navy, which was said to have taken place some months before, seemed to be correct. The mutiny, it was claimed, began at Pola, but spread quickly to Cattaro. It was among arsenal workmen that the rising, according to the London "Times," began at Pola. They demanded the cessation of various disciplinary measures and punishments inflicted both in vessels and ashore. The movement soon spread to the ships in harbor; the crews left their posts and thronged the decks shouting, hurrahing, and acting as they pleased. The officers were powerless, but there seems to have been no fighting between them and the men. The naval authorities parleyed with the men for a week, and finally all the sailors' and workmen's demands were granted.

At Cattaro the mutiny took a more serious turn. Six cruisers and several destroyers hoisted the red flag. The German and Magyar elements in some of the ships held aloof, and there were encounters between them and the mutineers, the guns of one cruiser being turned on another and some mutineers being killed. However, the mutineers got the upper hand after three days and became masters of the port.

Negotiations were eventually opened on an equal footing between the admiral and the mutineers, and finally the latter consented to surrender their vessels on receiving written guarantees that no action would be taken against any man, and that a number of grievances would be settled. The Cattaro fleet then returned under the Austrian flag, after being eight days in open revolt.

PART XIII—THE WAR IN THE AIR

CHAPTER LXX

BOMBING AND RECONNOISSANCE

THE importance of aerial operations, great as it had been since the beginning of the war, gradually increased in a way which even the most sanguine believer in the possibilities of flying machines would have hesitated to prophesy. This was due to a great extent to the remarkable advance that had been made on all sides as a result of experience in respect to the mechanical development of airplanes. But an even greater factor, perhaps, was the development of the technique of flying, which, step by step, progressed to a point that fell little short of the miraculous. Especially wonderful appears the development of squadron flying. So well trained had become the intrepid airmen that evolutions which a short time ago aroused the admiration of the whole world when carried out by individual planes and flyers were now successfully undertaken by large groups, each plane cooperating with the most wonderful precision and daring with every other unit.

Although the business of scouting, observation, and direction of artillery operations still formed an important part of the flying service, new duties had been delegated to the airmen. In ever-increasing squadrons, mass attacks against hostile forces, both in the air and on the ground, were being carried out as effectively as formerly by bodies of cavalry and infantry. Even part of the work, formerly executed exclusively by the artillery, now had become a regular feature of the flying arm of the various armies. Large air squadrons were laying down with their machine guns barrage fire which had as deadly and accurate results on advancing bodies of infantry as had previously been achieved only by heavy artillery.

Aerial activity by now had become as regular a part of military operations on every front as any other form of warfare. The most important events of the war in the air, of course, occurred on the most important of the many theaters of war, the western front. Fairly regular reports, however, are available only for the British air forces.

During the first week of February, 1918, the weather interfered a great deal with flying, but in spite of that hardly a day passed without some bombing expedition being undertaken by British airplanes. On February 9, 1918, several successful reconnoissances were carried out by British machines in spite of low clouds, mist, and high winds. German batteries were engaged effectively by our artillery with observation from the air, and nearly one ton of bombs was dropped on various targets. In air fighting, one German machine was driven down out of control. One British machine, too, was lost.

On the night of February 9-10, 1918, British night bombing machines carried out a successful raid into Germany, although the weather was by no means good. Nearly a ton of bombs was dropped with very good results on the important railway junction and sidings at Courcelles-les-Metz, southeast of Metz. One of the British bombing machines failed to return.

On February 11, 1918, mist, high winds, and low clouds again made weather conditions unfavorable for flying. Little work was possible with the artillery, but British aeroplanes carried out several successful reconnoissances, and dropped over a ton of bombs on various targets behind the German lines. No fighting took place. Another successful raid into German territory was made, however. The objective this time was the town of Offenburg, about twelve miles southeast of Strassburg and about forty miles from the French frontier.

On February 16, 1918, fighting machines on both sides were most active, and frequent attacks were made by the Germans on British bombing, photographic, and artillery machines. Fourteen German machines were brought down, and seven others were driven down out of control. British antiaircraft guns shot down two other German machines, one of them being a large bombing machine, which carried four men. This latter machine fell inside of the British lines and its four occupants were taken prisoners. Another German aeroplane, making the 17th accounted for during the day, in addition to those driven down out of control, landed near one of the British aerodromes, and its occupants were also taken prisoners. Five British aeroplanes were reported missing.

During the night of February 16-17, 1918, British machines dropped 400 bombs on German aerodromes in the neighborhood of Ghent, Tournai, and Laon. The railway station and sidings at Conflans—fifteen miles **west of** Metz—were also successfully bombed from a low height, **bursts** being observed in the sidings.

The weather was again fine and very favorable to aerial actions on February 17, 1918. Bombing, which had been carried out incessantly throughout the previous thirty-six hours, was continued, and over six tons of bombs were dropped by British machines on various targets, including German aerodromes in the neighborhood of Tournai and Lille, a large ammunition dump near Courtrai, and numerous billets. Ten German aeroplanes were brought down and six others were driven down out of control. Three British machines failed to return.

On the night of February 17-18, 1918, further bombing raids were carried out against German aerodromes south of Ghent and west of Tournai as well as against many of the German billets.

Another most successful raid was carried out on the railway station and sidings at Conflans (west of Metz). A ton of bombs was dropped.

On February 18, 1918, bombing squadrons raided the barracks and railway station at Treves, on the Moselle, and the steel works and railway station at Thionville. The raid was carried out in broad daylight, and excellent results were obtained. Although German antiaircraft gunfire was again considerable and accurate, all the British machines returned safely.

During that day continuous fighting took place, resulting in eleven German machines being brought down and six others driven down out of control. Two British machines were lost.

Following on the successful daylight raids on February 18, 1918, against Treves and Thionville, British night flying squadrons went out after dark and again attacked these towns from a low height with equally good results. German aircraft and antiaircraft guns were very active during both raids, and one of the British machines failed to return.

On February 19, 1918, another raid in broad daylight, making the third within thirty-six hours, was carried out against Trèves. On this occasion well over a ton of bombs were dropped on the objective. Eleven bursts were observed on the railway station and six on buildings in close proximity to it. Three good fires were started.

During the next day the weather prohibited extensive aerial activities. But it improved again on February 21, 1918, and British aeroplanes were able to accomplish a full day's work in the air.

Many successful reconnoissances, in the course of which photographs were taken, were carried out. The usual work in conjunction with the artillery continued all day, good visibility enabling excellent results to be obtained.

More than 300 bombs were dropped on German billets and on railway sidings at Courtrai, Ledeghem, and southeast of Douai.

In air fighting, seven German machines were brought down and two others driven down out of control. Three British machines were reported missing.

During the night of February 21-22, 1918, British aeroplanes dropped a total of 678 bombs on various targets. Three hundred bombs were dropped on an aerodrome southeast of Le Cateau used by the German night bombing squadrons. Nineteen direct hits were observed on hangars. The remaining bombs were dropped on German aerodromes in the neighborhood of Ghent and Tournai, and on billets. One of the British machines failed to return.

On February 24, 1918, in spite of bad weather, British aeroplanes carried out one or two reconnoissances and observed for the artillery. Bombs were dropped on various targets, including German billets, transports, and working parties. Two British machines were reported missing.

After dark, British night flying squadrons dropped over 200 bombs on German aerodromes near Courtrai and on billets northeast of St. Quentin.

On February 25, 1918, low clouds and a very strong wind prevented work in the air during the day. After dark, the sky cleared, though a very strong westerly wind continued.

British night bombing squadrons displayed great activity, dropping a total of over 1,200 bombs in the course of the night. The targets chiefly attacked were the aerodromes south of Ghent and west of Tournai used by the German night flying machines, and other aerodromes in the neighborhood of Courtrai.

German billets round Douai and east of St. Quentin were also heavily bombed, over 350 bombs being dropped in the latter area. All the British machines returned.

The weather was fine on February 26, 1918, but a very strong west wind greatly favored the German machines in air fighting.

British aeroplanes carried out several long-distance reconnoissances and took many photographs of aerodromes and railway communications in the back areas, in addition to photographs of German trench lines.

Other British machines working with the artillery were busy all day, and good visibility enabled good results to be obtained.

Four tons of bombs were dropped on the large railway sidings at Courtrai, the railway junction midway between Douai and Valenciennes, two German aerodromes north of Douai, and billets.

Fighting in the air was severe, and many combats took place between the German scouts and British reconnoissance, bombing, and fighting machines.

One German aeroplane was forced to land behind the British lines by one of our scouts. Twelve other German machines

War St. 7—EE

were brought down, and one was driven down out of control. Another machine was brought down by antiaircraft gunfire. Eight British machines failed to return.

During the night of February 26-27, 1918, over half a ton of bombs were dropped on barracks and railway stations at Treves, four bursts being observed in furnaces in the gas works and eight in the railway station. On the same night nearly one and a half tons of bombs were dropped on a German aerodrome near Metz, good bursts being observed in the hangars and hutments. One German machine was encountered close to the aerodrome and brought down. All the British machines returned safely, though fire from antiaircraft guns and machine guns was considerable.

British aeroplanes took advantage of the few fine intervals on February 28, 1918, to carry out work in conjunction with the artillery and also to drop bombs on two of the German ammunition dumps south of Lille, as well as on railway sidings at Courtrai and Deynze (southwest of Ghent). One British machine was lost. After dark British machines again took the air in the intervals between hailstorms. Four tons of bombs were dropped on a large German aerodrome midway between Tournai and Mons, and on billets in the neighborhood of Douai.

Great aerial activity prevailed on March 8, 1918. Work in conjunction with the artillery, reconnoissances, photography, and bombing was carried out incessantly by the British aeroplanes. Over 400 bombs were dropped on German ammunition dumps and sidings at Menin, Busigny, and Guise, east of St. Quentin, in spite of the most determined attacks made by the German scouts against the British bombing machines. In air fighting, twelve German aeroplanes were brought down and ten others were driven down out of control. Another machine was shot down by antiaircraft gunfire. Three British aeroplanes were lost. After dark, the greater part of the front was enveloped in mist, but in one sector British night flying machines dropped twenty-four heavy bombs and forty-eight lighter bombs on the ammunition dump and railway sidings at Fresnoy, northeast of St. Quentin.

At midday on March 9, 1918, the railway sidings and factories at Mainz, at the junction of the rivers Rhine and Main, in Germany, about 130 miles northeast of Nancy, were bombed by British aeroplanes with good results. Well over a ton of bombs were dropped, and bursts were seen on and around the barracks, on the railway sidings, and on a factory. A large fire was started. All the British machines returned. Six hundred bombs were dropped by other British machines on German ammunition dumps, billets, and aerodromes, and on an important railway center northeast of St. Quentin. In particular, a most successful attack was carried out at a low height by a large number of British machines against three hostile aerodromes. Bombs were dropped from an average height of 400 feet, and at each of the aerodromes direct hits were obtained on hangars and on machines in the open. While returning from this attack the British pilots flew at a height of 100 feet, firing on favorable targets on the ground with their machine guns and causing casualties and much confusion among the Germans. In one case a horse transport on the road was engaged, with the result that some of the wagons were upset into the ditch. In another horses in an orchard were stampeded. A company of German infantry was scattered in all directions and a group of officers on horseback dispersed. The fighting in the air was heavy. Ten German machines were brought down and ten others driven down out of control. A German observation balloon was also destroyed. Two of the British machines failed to return.

On March 10, 1918, Germany was again bombed by British aeroplanes in broad daylight. On this occasion the Daimler Motor Works at Stuttgart were attacked, and over one and a quarter tons of bombs were dropped. Stuttgart is about 136 miles east of Nancy. Several bursts were observed on the railway station, where a stationary train was hit and set on fire. Three bursts were seen on the munition factory southeast of the town, and other bursts on the Daimler works and on buildings round them. German machines made a weak attempt to attack the formation over the objective, but withdrew on being attacked. All the British machines returned except one, which evidently had engine trouble and went down under control just before recrossing the lines on the homeward journey.

During the same day the thick haze rendered work in conjunction with the artillery almost impossible. Several reconnoissances, however, were carried out, and over 400 bombs were dropped. Among other targets, Menin, Roulers, Ledeghem, Cambrai, and Solesmes railway stations were bombed by British machines. Three German observation balloons were destroyed, and five German machines were brought down in air fighting, in addition to seven others driven down out of control. One low-flying German machine was shot down by British infantry. Four British aeroplanes were lost.

Another fine day on March 11, 1918, enabled the British aeroplanes to continue their activity. Visibility, however, was again poor and prevented work with the artillery from achieving much success. Over 500 bombs were dropped, the chief target being the large sidings and ammunition depots at Aulnoye, southeast of Maubeuge, and ammunition depots south of Valenciennes, southeast of Cambrai, and south of Douai. As the result of air fighting ten German machines were brought down and seven others were driven down out of control. In addition a German observation balloon was attacked, and brought down in flames. Two British machines were lost. After dark most of the British night bombing machines were again prevented from leaving the ground by mist, but on the southern portion of the front, where the night was clear, 200 bombs were dropped on a German ammunition dump and railway sidings northeast of St. Quentin. The Germans also dropped a few bombs during the night, but lost a four-seater machine, which landed in the lines. The occupants were taken prisoners.

On March 12, 1918, another daylight raid into Germany, making the third within four days, was carried out by British aeroplanes. On this occasion the factories and station and the barracks at Coblenz, at the junction of the Rhine and the Moselle, 135 miles north-northeast of Nancy and about fifty miles southeast of Cologne, were attacked. Over a ton of bombs were dropped, and bursts were seen on all the objectives, causing two fires. A hit obtained upon a building in the southwest corner of the town created a very large explosion. A few German machines were encountered, but all the British machines returned safely.

During the night of March 11-12, 1918, in addition to the raids already reported, over three tons of bombs were dropped on Bruges docks.

On March 12, 1918, a distinct improvement in visibility enabled more work to be done in conjunction with the artillery than had been possible during the last few days. Many reconnoissances also were carried out and photographs were taken. Bombing was continued with even greater vigor than on previous days. Over thirteen and a half tons of bombs were dropped on various targets, which included the railway sidings at Mons and at Bavai, midway between Valenciennes and Maubeuge, on large ammunition depots northeast of St. Quentin, and south of Douai, and on billets east of Lens. In the course of the fighting, which was continuous throughout the day, fourteen German machines were brought down, and eight others were driven down out of control. One hostile observation balloon was also destroyed. Six British aeroplanes were bagged by the Germans.

During the night of March 12-13, 1918, seven tons of bombs were dropped on German billets between Lille and Cambrai. On the afternoon of March 13, 1918, British squadrons attacked the munition works and barracks at Freiburg, in Germany. All machines reached their objectives, and nearly a ton of bombs was dropped. They were seen to burst on the railway station and round the power station. Just after the British pilots had released their bombs their formation was attacked by a large number of German machines. A fierce fight ensued, which lasted until all the German machines had been forced to withdraw. Three of the British machines failed to return.

On March 16, 1918, further military objectives in Germany were attacked by British aeroplanes. Fourteen heavy and ten lighter bombs were dropped on the barracks, munition factories, and railway station of Zweibrücken, in the Rhine Palatinate. Bursts were seen on the barracks and all round the railway station.   The formation was attacked by German scouts and engaged by antiaircraft guns, but all machines returned.

Still another raid into Germany was made on the next day, March 17, 1918.   The barracks and railway station at Kaiserslautern, likewise in the Rhine Palatinate, were attacked with good results.   Direct hits were observed on the railway station and a large fire was caused.   The formation was attacked by a large number of German machines, which were driven off.   All the British machines returned.

During that day the German billets, which had been bombed continually for the last twenty-four hours, were again heavily attacked.   A total of thirteen tons of bombs were dropped, the objectives including two German aerodromes and three large ammunition dumps, in addition to billets.   At one of the aerodromes a hangar was completely burned, and a Gotha machine which was in the act of rising from the ground was seen to crash.

The fighting was intense during the morning, but became slightly less vigorous during the afternoon.   Sixteen German machines were brought down and seven others were driven down out of control.   Six British machines were reported missing.   After dark the German rest billets were again attacked, bombs being dropped until just after midnight, when a thick mist developed.

The atmosphere was again clear on March 18, 1918, and favored the cooperation of the aeroplanes and artillery.   Several long-distance reconnoissances were successfully completed, and many photographs were taken.   Nine tons of bombs were dropped on German rest billets and ammunition dumps and also on Busigny railway station and two German aerodromes. Fighting in the air was exceedingly intense, encounters taking place between large formations of British and German machines. Nineteen German aeroplanes were brought down and nine driven down out of control.   Twelve British machines failed to return.

British bombing machines also attacked military objectives at Mannheim, on the Rhine, dropping over a ton of bombs with excellent results.   These aeroplanes were attacked by two German formations.

Following a successful daylight raid on Mannheim, other objectives in Germany were attacked during the night. Half a ton of bombs were dropped on the railway stations at Cologne, where a fire was started. Over a ton was distributed between Luxemburg railway station, where a fire was started, and Courcelles railway station, east of Metz. Two tons of bombs were dropped on Metz railway station. Direct hits were obtained on a bridge southeast of the town and on a stationary train, which was set on fire. A large fire was started on this occasion also. Other machines dropped a ton of bombs on Thionville railway station, where a moving train was derailed.

On March 25, 1918, British aeroplanes were employed almost entirely at combing the enemy's troops and transports massed in the areas behind the battle front and in attacking them with machine-gun fire from a low height. A total of twenty-two tons of bombs were dropped in this work and over 100,000 rounds were fired from machine guns. A certain amount of fighting in the air took place, but it was less intense than on the previous day. Thirteen German machines were brought down and ten were driven down out of control. Eight British machines were reported missing. During the night British night flying aeroplanes continued to bomb and to attack with machine-gun fire German troops in their forward areas and their transports on the roads leading to the front.

Thirty tons of bombs were dropped, and hundreds of thousands of rounds of ammunition were fired into the German ranks. While this fighting was maintained throughout the day, British infantry aeroplanes kept watch along the front and reported the changes in the situation as they occurred. Twenty German machines were brought down in air fighting, and two other German aeroplanes were shot down by antiaircraft guns. Twelve British aeroplanes were reported missing.

During the night British night flying squadrons kept up a continuous attack upon the German troops in Bapaume, Cambrai, and Péronne. Twenty-five thousand rounds were fired by them, and twenty-four tons of bombs were dropped on important centers of the battle front. In addition, four tons of bombs were dropped on Valenciennes railway station, through which the German troop trains were passing on their way to the front.

On March 27, 1918, low flying was again carried out by large bodies of British aeroplanes, while infantry machines continued the work of reporting the position of the British battle line. Over thirty tons of bombs were dropped and a quarter of a million rounds of ammunition were fired from a height that insured accuracy on different targets. Several casualties were inflicted on the Germans and the bringing up of their troops and ammunition was delayed. Twenty-four German machines were brought down in air fighting, and seven others were driven down out of control. Two observation balloons were also destroyed.

Nineteen British machines failed to return, though a proportion of these were known to have landed on their side of the line. Very heavy fire directed against the British machines from the ground accounted for the greater portion of the casualties.

During the night the bombing of Bapaume, Bray, and Péronne was continued with the utmost vigor. Over a thousand bombs were dropped, and thousands of rounds of ammunition were fired at good targets, which were plentiful and easy to see in the moonlight. Sablon station at Metz was bombed. Well over a ton of bombs were dropped; good bursts were seen on the sidings and alongside the railway.

On March 28, 1918, British machines carried out a successful raid on the station at Luxemburg. Twenty-one heavy bombs were dropped, and several were seen to burst on the objectives.

On March 28, 1918, British aeroplanes carried on their attacks with bombs and machine-gun fire on German troops on the battle front. The majority of these attacks took place south of the Somme, in which area large concentrations of German troops were constantly reported. The work was continued till dark in spite of bombs being dropped, and nearly a quarter of a million rounds of ammunition being fired. Nine German machines were brought down and five others driven down out of control. In addition, two machines were shot down by fire from the ground. Twelve British machines were reported missing.

During the morning of March 29, 1918, low clouds and rain greatly interfered with flying, but, in spite of the weather, valuable work was again accomplished by the British aeroplanes. Some of these were concentrated upon the battle front south of the Somme, where observers had previously reported large German columns. A good deal of fighting took place, the German low-flying machines being particularly active in this area. Nine German aeroplanes were brought down and two others were driven down out of control. Two British machines were lost. During the night over twelve tons of bombs were dropped on Bapaume and on roads in the vicinity, and also on roads and villages east of Arras. Direct hits were obtained on dumps and transports and on the railway line.

After midday on March 30, 1918, the weather completely broke, but, in spite of driving rain, British pilots continued to take part in the battle south of the Somme, and dropped bombs and used their machine guns until a late hour. There was heavy fighting in the air between British low-flying machines and those of the Germans. Twelve of the latter were brought down and three others were driven down out of control. One German balloon was destroyed, and two German aeroplanes were shot down by antiaircraft guns. Five British planes failed to return.

On March 31, 1918, British observation balloons and aeroplanes were active, the good visibility enabling the former to carry out useful work in conjunction with the artillery. The activity of the aeroplanes was chiefly centered south of the Somme. A close watch was kept on German movements in this area, and a large column of their troops or transports seen was bombed and engaged with machine-gun fire.

Very little fighting took place in the air. Two German machines were brought down and one other was driven down out of control. Four British machines were reported missing. Night flying was not possible till after midnight owing to low clouds. From midnight until dawn British bombing machines were constantly at work. Twenty-four tons of bombs were dropped on the railway stations at Douai, Cambrai, Bapaume, Rosières, and Thourout, and on the docks at Bruges. Troops and transports in the neighborhood of Bapaume and Chaulnes were also attacked with bombs and machine-gun fire.

This completed the work of the British flying corps on the western front for March, 1918. A remarkable record had been made, 383 German machines having been destroyed or captured and 207 driven down out of control, while only 155 British machines had been reported missing. The French, too, had been notably active during March, having captured or destroyed 115 German machines.

PRONOUNCING VOCABULARY

Pronunciation of Geographical Names Occurring in this Work

Aachen (or Aix-la-Chapelle) ah'ken
Aalst (or Alost) alst
Ablain ab-lan'
Ablainzeville ab-lanz-veel'
Abu Zenaima aboo' zay-ny'ma
Achi Baba achee baba
Achiet-le-Grand ashyay'-la-grong'
Adige adee'ghay (Austrian)
    adee'jay (Italian)
Aerschot ahr-scot'
Agincourt a-zhan-koor'; Eng. aj'in-
    kort
Agordo agor'doh
Ahrweiler ar'wi-ler
Aidin i-deen'
Aiguizy ay-gwee-zee'
Ailly-sur-Noye ah-yee'-sur-nwa'
Aisle ale
Aisne ane
Aix ex
Aix-la-Chapelle ex-la-shapell'
Aix-Noulette ex-noolet'
Akabah akah'ba
Akhtunski Pass akhtoon'sky
Albert al-bair'
Aldershot awl'dershot
Alexinatz alexee'nats
Allenstein al'en-shtine'
Alost alost'
Alsace German "elsass"
Alsatian alsay'shen
Alt-Aux alt-owts'
Altigny at-in-yee'
Altkirch alt'kirk
Ambleny om-ble-nee'
Amiens ah'mee-en
Ampezzo am-pet'so
Ancerville anser'vee
Ancre (river) an'kr
Andrechy andreshee'
Anizy an-ea-sy'
Annopol anno'pol
Antheuil an-tuh'eel
Apremont apr'mong

Arco ar'ko
Ardahan ardahan'
Ardennes arden'
Argonne argonn'
Arleux ar-luh'
Arlon ar-lon'
Armentières armangtyare'
Arras arass'
Artois ar-twa'
Arusha arro'sha
Asiago azeeah'go
Asiero az-yer'o
Asma Dere dai'ray
Asnieres ass-nee-air'
Asolo a'zo-lo
Assobam assobahm'
Atakpame a'tak-pah'may
Ath-Waremme at-war-em'
Attigny a-tee-nyee'
Aube (river) ob
Aubenton o-ban-ton'
Aubercourt obey-coor'
Auberive oh-breev'
Aubers oh-bear'
Aubigny o-be-nyee'
Aubilly o-bee-yee'
Auchy o-she'
Audenarde (or Oudenarde) ou-de-
    nar'de
Auerstadt our'statt
Augustijnow avgoostee'noff
Augustovo avgoost'ava
Aulnoye ohl-nwa'
Auronzo ou-ront'so
Autreches oh-tresh'
Aveluy av-lwee'
Avesnes a-vayn'
Aviano a-vyah'no
Avlona avlo'na
Avre avr
Avricourt a-vree-koor'
Ayette ah-yet'
Ayun Monsa a'yoon
Azannes az-an'

Azerbaijan azerbyjan'
Azizi azee'zee

Babina Glava ba'beena gla'va
Baccarat bak-a-rah'
Badia bah-de'a
Badonviller bah-don-vee-yay'
Baghche bag'cheh
Bailleul bah-yul'
Bailly bah-yee'
Baku ba-koo'
Bâle (or Basel) bahl
Banais ba-nice'
Bapaume ba-pom'
Baranovitchy barano'vichy
Baraque de l'Epine barrack del
  epeen'
Barbarano bar-ba-rah'no
Barchon Fort barshong'
Bar-le-Duc bar'-le-dük'
Barr bahr
Basancourt bazancoor'
Basel (or Bâle) bah'zel
Basozches ba-zosh'
Bassano bas-sah'noh
Bassée, La la ba-say
Bastogne bas-ton'y
Batum batoom'
Bavai bav-eye'
Bazar Siak syak
Beaumont bo-mon'
Beauséjour boh-sezhoor'
Beauvais bo-vay'
Beauvraignes bo-vrain'
Bedzin bedzeen'
Belfort bel-for'
Belgrade bel-grad'
Bellewaarde Wood belleh-ar'deh
Belloy bell-wah'
Belluno bel-loo'no
Berchem - Sainte - Agathe ber'shen-
  sant-agaht'
Beresina berrezee'na
Bereza beray'zah
Bergen-op-Zoom zome
Berjan ber-jan'
Berlaimont ber-le-mon'
Berry-au-Bac o-bac'
Bertincourt ber-tan-koor'
Bertrix ber-treece'
Besançon be-zan-son'
Bethany bettah'nee
Bethune bettune'
Beuthen boi-ten

Beuvraignes bövrain'
Bezzecea betsek'ka
Biecz beeyets'
Bielostok byai-lo'stok
Bienvillers bee-an-veeyay'
Biercza be-yertsa
Bijeljina be-yel-yee'na
Bir Mabeiuk ma-bay'yook
Bitburg beet'boork
Bitolia bee-tol'ya
Bitsch bitsch
Bixschoote bix-sko'teh
Blamont blamong'
Blankenberghe ber'gay
Blaques blahk
Blerancourt bler-an-coor'
Bligny blin-yee'
Blonie blo-nee'
Bober bobr
Boche French slang for a German
  "Square-head"; "Thick-head"
Bochina bokh'nya
Boesinghe boo-sing'er
Bohain bo-an'
Bois Bolante bwa bolant'
Bois d'Ailly bwa dah'yee
Bois de Forges forzh'
Bois de Mont-Mare mong-mar'
Bois-des-Loges bwah-day-lozh'
Bois-le-Peetre pater
Boisleux bwah-luh'
Bolimow bolee'moff
Bologna bolon'ya
Boloto bolo'toh
Bonaberi bonnabay'ree
Bonnay bon-ay'
Bordeaux bordoh'
Boshdarevatz bozhdaray'vats
Bosphorus (or Bosporus) bos'po-rus
Bosut boss'oet
Botoshani bo-to-shan'y
Bouchain boo-shan'
Boudonville boodong-vee'
Bouillon boo-yon'
Boulogne boo-lon'y; Eng. boo-lon'
Bouresches boo-resh'
Bouvines boo-veen'
Boves bov
Bozanne boz-an'
Brabant-le-roi bra-ban'-le-rwah'
Braila bra-e'la
Braine-le-Comte bra'-le-kont'
Braisne brain
Bramont bramong'

Branjevo branyay'vo
Braunsberg brouns'berk
Braye brah-ee'
Bray-sur-Seine bray'-sür'-san'
Brazincourt brazangcoor'
Brecy bre-see'
Breganze bray-gant'say
Breisgau brice'gow
Brescia bres'chiah
Brest-Litovsk brest'-lye-tofsk'
Breza bray'za
Bribano bri-bah-noh
Briey bree-ay'
Brimont brecmong'
Brindisi brindee'zee
Brodjanska Glavitza brudyans'ska-gla'veetsa
Brouillet broo-yay'
Bruges brüzh
Brusa (or Brussa) broo'sa
Bruyeres bru-yair'
Brzezany bzhe-zah'nee
Brzostek bzhos'tek
Bucquoy bu-kwah'
Buczacz boo-sass'
Bug (river) boog
Bukharest (or Bucharest) boo-ka-rest'
Bukowina booko-vee'na
Burano boo-rah'no
Burnhaupt boorn'howpt
Bussieres buss-yair'
Butaniyeh bootanee'yay

Caestre ça-est'
Calais callay'
Cambrai cambray'
Cambrin com-bran'
Camisano ka-me-zah'no
Camp de Mailly may'yee
Canteleux cantlŏ
Cantigny kon-tee-nyee'
Caorle ka-or'leh
Caprino ka-pre'no
Carency caran'see
Carignan car-i-nyan'
Carlepont kar-le-pohng'
Carole ka-ro'lay
Carvin car-van'
Casarsa caz-ar'sah
Castelfranco kas-tel-fran'ko
Cateau, Le le ka-to'
Cattaro cat'taro
Cavalese ka-va-lay'zay

Cavarzere ka-var'dzay-ray
Cernavoda (or Tchernavoda) cherna-vo'da
Cettinje setteen'yay
Challerange shal-e-ronzh'
Châlons - sur - Marne sha-lon'-sur'-marn'
Chalon-sur-Saône sha-lon'-sur'-son'
Chambley shom-blay'
Chambrettes shom-bret'
Chamery sha-mer-ee'
Champagne-Pouilleuse pooee-yös'
Champigny shan-pee-nyee'
Champlat-Bligny shon-pla-blinyee'
Chantilly shon-tee-yee'
Chapelle St. Roch shapell' St. Rosh
Charleroi sharl-rwa'
Charleville sharl-vcell
Charmel shar-mel'
Châteauroux sha-to-roo'
Château-Thierry shatto'tee-err'y
Châtel sha-tel'
Chatelet shatlay'
Chatillon - sur - Marne sha-te-yon'-sur'-marn'
Chaudfontaine sho-fonten'
Chaulnes shown
Chaumont sho-mon'
Chauny sho-nee
Chemin-des-Dames shman-day-dam'
Cherbourg sher-boor'
Chevrincourt shev-ran-coor'
Chezy-sur-Marne che-zee-sur-marn'
Chimay shee-may'
Chiny she-nee'
Chioggia kyod'ja
Chipres sheepr
Chocimierz khotsimyerts
Chodorow khodo'roff
Cholm kholm
Choruk kho'rook
Chotin khotin
Chyrow khee'rov
Cierges see-erzh'
Ciezkovice - Walastow ches'kovitz-valas'tov
Cilicia selish'ya
Ciney see-nay'
Cirey see-ray'
Cittadella cheet-ta-del'la
Cittanuova chit-ta-nu-oh'va
Cividale chivvy-dah'ler
Civy-Salsogne see-vee-sal-sun'ye
Clary kla-ree'

Clermont clare-mohng'
Coblenz ko'blents
Codroipo ko-dro'ee-po
Coeuvre cuv
Col de Bonhomme bonnom'
Cologne ko-lohn'
Combles kon'bl
Combres com'ber
Comines commeen'
Commercy ko-mer-see'
Compiègne comp-yen'
Condé kon-day'
Conegliano ko-nal-yah'no
Conflans kon-flan'
Conselve kon-sel'vay
Constanta (or Kustendje) kon-
  stan'tsa
Corbie cor-bee'
Cortina kor-tee'na
Coucy koo-see'
Coucy-le-Chateau coossee'le-shatto'
Coulommiers coolomeer'
Coulonges coo-lonzh'
Courcelles koor-sell'
Courmont coor-mong'
Courpoil coor-pwol'
Courrieres coo-ree-air'
Courtrai coortray'
Couvrelles coovrell'
Cracow (or Krakow) krah'ko
Crajova (or Craiova) kra-yo'va
Craonne kra-on'
Crécy (or Cressy) kray-se'; Eng.
  kres'i
Crécy-sur-Serre kray-se'-sur'-sair'
Creil cray-eel'
Crepy cre-pee'
Crimea kri-me'a
Crise kreez
Croiselles crwah-sell'
Croix Ricard krwah-rik-ahr'
Ctesiphon tay'zee-fon
Cuinchy canshee
Cutry ku-tree'
Cuvilly cu-vee-yee'
Cuxhaven cooks-hah'fen
Czarkowa tsar'kova
Czenstochowa chen-sto-ko'va
Czernovicz tser'novits

Dammartin dan-mar-tan'
Damvillers dan-vee-yay'
Daniele da-nyay'lay
Dannemarie dan-mah-ree'

Danzig (or Dantzic) dan'tsik
Dardanelles dar-da-nelz'
Daume dome
Debreczen debrets'en
Dedeagatch day-day-ah-gatch'
Delatyn (pass) de-lah'tin
Dembica dembits'a
Demir Kapu cap'poo
Denain de-nan'
Dendermonde (or Termonde) den-
  der-mon'de
Diarbekr (or Diarbekir) de-ar-bek'r
Diedenhofen (or Thionville) de'-
  den-hof-en
Dieppe dee-ep'
Dieuze dee-uhz'
Dijon dee-zhon'
Dinant deenang'
Dixmude dixmoo'deh
Djakova jak'ova
Djamschato jamshah'toh
Dnieper (river) ne'per
Dniester (river) nees'ter
Dommary Barancourt barancoor'
Dommiers dom-ee-ay'
Dompaire don-pair'
Domremy dong-ray-mee'
Donaueschingen doh'now-esh'ingen
Dormans dor-mongse'
Douai doo-ay
Douaumont do-oh-mohng'
Doullens doo-lan'
Dravigny dra-vi-nyee'
Driegrachten dree'grakhten
Drina River dree'na
Drocourt dro-coor'
Droghitchin dro-ghit'chin
Drohobycz dro-ho'bich
Dubiecko doo-be-ets'ko
Dubno doob'no
Dubovitza doo-bo-veet'sa
Dubowoje doobovo'yay
Duffel düf-fell
Dukla Pass dook'la
Dulcigno dool-cheen'yo
Dunajec River doo'nayets
Dunquerque dun-kerke'
Dun-sur-meuse dun'-sür'-muhz'
Durazzo doorat'so

Ecaffaut ekaffo'
Ecurie ay-curee'
Eecloo ay-klo'
Eghezee eggav-zay'

Elabe   ellah'bay
Epagny   ay-pa-nyee'
Epehy   ep-hee'
Epernay   a-per-nay'
Epieds   e-pyay'
Epinal   epee-nahl'
Epine de Vedegrange   epeen'de-vaid-grahnj'
Epirus   e-pi'rus
Eregli   er-e-gle'
Erivan   eri-vahn'
Ermenonville   veel'
Erzerum   erts-room'
Erzingan   er-zin-gan'
Estaires   es-tair'
Esti   es'tee
Estrees St. Denis   esstray-san-denee'
Etain   a-tan'
Etampes   ai-tonp'
Etchmiadzin   etch-mya-zeen'
Euphrates (river)   u-fra'teez
Evegnee Fort   ev-en-yea'
Eydtkuhnen   eit-koo'nen
Eylau   eye-low

Faverolles   fav-rull'
Feltre   fell'treh
Fère Champenoise   fair shampnwahz'
Fère - en - Tardenois   fair'-an'-tardnwah'
Fère, La   la fair'
Ferfay   fer-fahee'
Ferme-des-Loges   ferm-day-luzh'
Ferté - Gaucher, La   la fer-tay'-goshay'
Ferté-sous-Jouarre, La   la fer-tay'-soo'-zhoo-ar'
Festubert   fest-u-bair'
Filipkowu   ko'voo
Fismes   feem
Fiume   fee-oo'meh
Flanders   flan'ders
Fleurbaix   flörbay'
Fleury   flur-ee'
Flirey   flir-ee'
Fontainebleau   fone-tan-blow'
Fontenoy   fone-te-nwah'
Fonzaso   fon-tsah'zo
Forest of Compiègne   compe-en'
Fort Belfort   beh-for'
Fort Besançon   bay-zang-sson
Fort Breedonck   bray-donk'
Fort Broeckem   broo'kem

Fort of Boncelles   bong-sell'
Fort Carnot   carno'
Fort Douaumont   doo-omong
Fort Emines   emmeen'
Fort of Loncin   long-san'
Fort Maizeret   maze-ray
Fortress Osowic   vits
Fort Stabroek   stabrook
Fort Yeni Kale   kah'ler
Fort Zwyndrecht   zwine'drekt
Foucaucourt   foo-koh-coor'
Fouquescourt   fook-es-coor'
Fourmies   foor-mee'
Framerville   fram-ay-veel'
Franvilliers   fran-vee-yay'
Fresnes   frane
Fresnes-en-Woëvre   fren'-an'-vo-ev'r
Fresnoy   fren-wah'
Fromentieres   fro-mong-teeair'
Fruges   früzh
Furnes   fürns

Gaba Tepe   teh-peh
Galatz   ga'lats
Galicia   galish'yeh
Gallipoli   gallip'poli
Garbunovka   garboonof'ka
Gargnano   gar-nyah'no
Gehweiler   geb'wi-ler
Gembloux   zhom-bloo'
Gemona   ja-mo'na
Genappe   zhe-nap'
Gerardmer   zhair-ar-mare'
Gerbéviller   zhair-bay-vee-yay'
Gerechamp   ger-shong' (G hard)
Gimors   zhee-morse'
Gironville   zhee-ron-veel'
Givenchy   zhivon-shee
Givet   zhe-vay'
Gleiwitz   gley'vits
Gnesen   g'nay'zen
Gorizia, Italian; Austrian, Görz, or Göritz
Gorlice   Gorleet'sa
Gouzeaucourt   goo-zo-coor' (G hard)
Grabiowiec   grabyo'vyets
Gradisca   gra-dees'ka
Grado   grah'do
Grafenstafel   grah'fens-tah'fel
Gravelotte   grahv'lot
Gricourt   gri-coor' (G hard)
Grivillers   gri-veeyay'
Grootfontein   grote'fontane
Grybow   gree-boff'

Guillaucourt gee-oh-coor' (G hard)
Guiscard gees-kar'
Guise gheeze
Gumbinnen goom-bin'en

Haelen hah'len
Haftdewan dewan'
Hailles ah-yeel'
Haisnes aynes
Hal hal
Halicz ha'litch
Hamel am-el'
Hangard ang-aar'
Harbonnieres ar-bon-yair'
Hartennes ar-ten'
Hartmannsweilerkopf vilerkopf
Hasselt has'selt
Hautebraye oat-brah-yee'
Haute Chevauches ote-shevoshe'
Hautmont o-mon'
Hazebrouck has-brook'
Hebuterne ebu-tern'
Heldhoek helt'hook
Helgoland (or Heligoland) hel'go-lant
Hericourt ayr-i-coor'
Herzegovina vee'na
Hesdin hes-deen'
Hinges anzh
Hirson eer-son'
Horodenka ho-ro-den'ka
Houdain oo-dan'
Hulluch hoollookh
Huy hoi

Inovolodz eenov'olodge
Isonzo eez-on'zoh
Issy les Molineaux issee-lay-mo-leeno'
Ivangorod eevango'rod

Jamboli (or Yamboli) yam'bo-le
Jaroslav (or Jaroslau) ya-ros'laf
Jasiolda River yashold'a
Jassy (or Yassy) yas'e
Jaulgonne zhohl-gun'
Jazarzew ya'zar-zef
Jena yay'na
Jonchery zhon-she-ree'
Juniville zhü-ne-veel'

Kaisarieh (or Kaisariyeh) ki-sa-re'ye
Kaiserslautern key's... low-tern

Kalisz kalish
Kaluszin ka-loosh'in
Karun River karoon'
Katchanik katcha'nik
Keetmanshoop kate-mans-hope
Kekkau kek-cow
Keltsy (or Kielce) kyel'tsi
Kholm kolm
Khorassan san'
Khotin ko'tyen
Kiao-Chau kee-ah-o-chow'
Kief (or Kiev) kee'yef
Kielce Hills kyel'tse
Kishinef (or Kishinev) ke-she-nyef'
Kniashevatz knya-zhevatz
Kolomea ko-lo-may'a
Königsberg kö'niks-berk
Koprikeui koy
Korelitchy korell'itchy
Kovel ko'vel-y
Koziany kotsee-ah'ny
Koziowa kotsee-o'va
Kragujevatz goo'ye-vats
Krakow (or Cracow krah'ko
Kremenchug (or Krementchug) krem'en-chook
Kremnitz krem'nits
Kreuznach kroits'nahk
Kuczurmik koot'soormik
Kum Kale koom-kah'leh
Kuprikeui see Koprikeui
Kur or Kura (river) koor; koo'ra
Kurische Haff koo'risheh
Kurschany koorsha'nee
Kurumum kooromoon
Kustendje (or Constanta) kus-ten'je

La Bassée bassay'
La Cour de Soupir coor-de-soopee'
La Fère fair
La Fère-Champenoise la fair'-shan-pe-nwahz'
Le Ferté Gaucher go-shay'
La Ferte Milon lafert-meelohng'
La Ferté-sous-Jouarre la fer-tay'-soo'-zhoo'-ar'
La Fontaine-aux-Charmes fonten-o-sharm
Lagny lan-yee'
Landrecies lan-dres-see'
Langres lan'gr
Languion lan-ge-on'
Laon lauv

Lassigny lass-in-yce'
Latisana la-te-sah'na
Laventie la-vong-tce'
Laversine la-ver-seen'
Le Cateau catto'
Le Catelet le cat-lay'
Le Chatelet luh-shat-lay'
Le Chesne luh-shane'
Le Mesnil mez-neel'
Le Nouvion luh-noo-veeohng'
Le Ployron le-plwah-rohng'
Le Quesnoy le ka-nwah'
Le Thillot lu-teo yoh'
Le Thiolet le-tee-olay'
Legnago la-nyah'go
Lemberg (or (Lwów) lem'berk
Lendmara lend-mah'ra
Lens lans
Les Esparges lays es-parzh'
Leuze lez
Levico la'vee-ko
Liancourt le-an-koor'
Liart lee-ahr'
Libau lee'bou
Liège lee-ezh'
Lierre le-air'
Ligny len-yee'
Ligny - en - Barrois len-yee'-an'-ba-
    rwah'
Lille (or Lisle) leel
Livenza (river) le-vent'sah
Locon lo-kohng'
Locre loke'
Lodz (or Lódz) lodz; looj
Lomza lom'zha
Longarone lon-gah-ro'nay
Longwy lon-vee'
Loos lohs
Lorraine (or Lothringen) lo-rain'
Losnitza lozh-nee'tsa
Lothringen (or Lorraine) lot'ring-en
Lötzen löt'sen
Louvain loovang'
Lublin (or Lyublin) lyoo'blyen
Ludihorecza loodihor'etcha
Lunéville lü-nay-veel'
Lutzy or Lutsk) lootsk
Luxemburg loox'em-boork
Lwów (or Lemberg) lvoof
Lys (river) lees

Maastricht mahs'strickt
Magyars mad'yars
Mährisch-Ostrau may'rish-os'trou
    War St. 7—FF

Main de Massiges man-duh-
    masseezh'
Mainz (or Mayence) meynts
Maisons-Alfort ma-zon'-zal-for'
Maizieres may-zeeair'
Malamocco ma-la-mok'ko
Malines maleen'
Malmedy mal-muh-dee'
Mannheim man'hime
Mantua man'tu-a
Marche marsh
Marcoing mar-kwan'
Marienburg ma-ro'en-boork
Marqueglise mark-ai-gleese'
Marquivillers mar key-vee-yay'
Marseilles mar-say-yee'
Massevaux mas-vo'
Massiges masseezh'
Massil mass-eel'
Matigny ma-tin-yee'
Maubeuge ma-bözh'
Maupertuis mo-per-twee'
Mayence (or Mainz) ma-yans'
Meaux mo
Meduno med-u'no
Melicocq mel-ee-cuk'
Melincourt melan-coor'
Melun me-lun'
Memel may'mell
Mendawi men-da'wee
Menin muh-nan'
Merville mer-veel'
Messancy me-san-see'
Messines messeen'
Mestre mes'tray
Meuniere men-ec-air'
Meurthe mört
Meuse Valley möz'
Mézières mez-yare'
Mezo-Laborcz laborts'
Mezzo-Lombardo met'so-lom-bar'do
Miedzyrzets mezheretch'ye
Miraumont meeromong'
Mirecourt meer-koor'
Mitau (Russ.) meeta'va
Mitrovicza (or Mitrovitz) me-tro-
    vet'sa
Mlawa mla'va
Mocziska mot-chees'ka
Moggio mod'jo
Mohileff mo-ghee-leff'
Mojkovac mozh'kovats
Moldava (river) mol-dah'va
Molsheim mols'hime

Monastir mon-as-teer'
Monastryzek monastree'zhek
Monfalcone mon-fal-co'neh
Mons mons
Montagnana mon-ta-nyah'nah
Montcornet mohng-cor-nay'
Montcourt mohng-coor'
Montdidier mon-dee-dyay'
Montebelluna mon-teh-bell-u'na
Montfaucon mon-fo-kong'
Monthureux mon-tü-ruh'
Montmédy mon-may-dee'
Montmirail mongmee-rye'
Montreuil mon-truhy'
Morbeeque mor-bek'
Moreuil mo-ruh'y
Morisel mor-ee-sel'
Morlancourt mor-lan-coor'
Moronvillers morongveeyay'
Moselle mo-zell'
Mount Croce cro'cheh
Mt. Lovcen lof'chen
Mount Turchenkeui koy'
Mount Viatrovka vyatrof'ka
Mourmelon moor-melohng'
Mouvaux moo-vo'
Mouzon moo-zohng'
Moyenmoutier mwa-yan-moo-tyay'
Muchavka moo-chaf-ka
Muizon mwi-zohng'
Mulchy mul-shee'
Mülhausen mül-hou'zen
Mulhouse mül-hooz'
Munkacs moon-katsh'
Münster mün'ster
Mush moosh

Nagy Polena nady
Nakhitchevan na-ke-che-van'
Nampoel nam-poh-el'
Namur nammür'
Nancois nong-swa'
Nancy nan-see'; Eng. nan'si
Narew or Narev (river) nah'ref
Nesle nail
Neufchâteau nuh-sha-to'
Neuilly-sur-Marne nu-ye'-sur'-marn'
Neu Sandek noi-zan'dek
Neutitschein noi'tit-shin
Neuve Chapelle nuv-sha-pel'
Nida River nee'da
Niemen River nee'men
Nieuport neev'port
Nikolaief nyee-ko-lah'yef

Nîmes (or Nismes) neem
Nivelles nee-vell'
Nizankowice nee-zan'ko-vits
Nogent no-zhan'
Nomeny no-me-nee'
Norrent-Fontes nor-rong-fohnt'
Nouvron noo-vrong'
Novogeorgievsk no-vo-ge-or'ge-yefsk
Novo Radowsk ra'dofsk
Novy-Sacz satch
Noyon nwa-yong'

Oderzo o-dert'so
Oikovice o-ee-ko'vits
Oise wahz'
Old Zuczka Tsootch'ka
Olizy ul-ee-zee'
Olmütz ol'mütz
Opoczno opoch'no
Orchies or-shee'
Orsova or'shova
Ostiglia os-teel'ya
Ostrog os-trok'
Ostrow os'trof
Oudenarde ou-de-nar'deh
Oulchy ool-shee'
Ourcq oork'
Ourthe oort'

Padua pad'u-a
Pagny pan-yee'
Pagny-sur-Meuse pan-yee'-sür-muhz
Paliseul pal-ee-sull'
Palmanova pal-ma-no'va
Pancsova pantch'ova
Parenzo pa-renz'oh
Pas de Calais pa-de-callay'
Passchendaele pass'ken-dah-lay
Pellestrina pel-les-tree'na
Perarolo pay-rah-roh'lo
Péronne pay-ron'
Pervyse per-vie'zeh
Peschiera pa-sky-ay'ra
Petrokov (or Piotrków) pye-tro-kof'
Philippeville fe-lep-veel
Piacenza pya-chent'sa
Piave (river) pyah'va
Picardy pee-car-dee'
Pierrefitte pyair-feet'
Pierrefonds pyair-fon'
Pierrepont peeair-pohng'
Pietro pye'tro
Pieve di Cadore pyeh'vay de kah-do'ray

Pilaskowice pilasko'vits
Pilisca pee-leets'a
Pilwiszki pill-vish'ki
Pinczow pinchoff
Pion pee-ohng'
Piotrkow pyotter-koff
Piove pyo'vay
Pirano peer-ah'noh
Ploegsteert ploog'stairt
Podgorze pod-goo'zheh
Poelcapelle pool-capel'leh
Poissy pwa-see'
Poitiers pwa-tyay'
Poix pwah
Pomme-Py pom-pee'
Pont-à-Mousson pon'-ta'-moo-son'
Pont Arcy pohng-ar-see'
Pontebba pon-teb'ba
Pontoise pon-twahz'
Pont Ste. Maxence pon' sant'-ma-sans'
Pordenone por-da-no'nay
Portogruaro por'to-groo-ah'ro
Pouillon pooee-yong'
Pozieres poz-ceair'
Pozzachio pod-zak'kio
Prague prahg'
Predazzo pra-dat'so
Primolano proe-mo-lah'no
Pripet pree'pet
Prisrend pree'zrent
Proszowicz prosh-o'vitz
Provins pro-van'
Proyart prwah-yar'
Pruszkow proosh'koff
Pruth (river) proot
Przasnysz pshas'nish
Przeczyca pzho-sheet'sa
Przemysl pzhay'misl
Puisieux pwis-yuh'
Pultusk pool'toosk
Pusterthal Railway poos'ter-tahl

Quatre-Bras ka-tr'-brah'
Quennevières ken-vyare'
Quesnoy, Le le kay-nwah'
Quinchy kanshee'

Radom rah'dom
Radzivilov rad-zee'vee-lof'
Rajac rah'yats
Ramillies ra-me-yee'
Ramscappelle rams-ca-pel'leh
Raon-l'Etape ran'-la-tap'

Rastenburg ras'ten-boork
Raucourt ro-koor'
Rawa ra'va
Rawa-Ruska ra'va-roos'ka
Reillon ray-eeyong'
Remiremont ruh-meer-mon'
Ressons-sur-Matz ressohng'-sur-mats
Rethel re-tel'
Rheims ranz'
Ribecourt reeb-koor'
Ribemont reeb-mon'
Riga ree'ga
Rochefort rosh-for'
Roclincourt roclan-coor'
Rocroy ro-krwah'
Roermond roor'mohnt
Roisel rwah-zel'
Roisieres rwaz-eeair'
Romilly ro-mi-yee'
Roubaix roo-bay'
Rouen roo-ong'
Rougemont roozh-mohng'
Roulens roo-longse'
Roulers roo-lay'
Roverbella ro-ver-bel'la
Roveredo ro-va-ray'do
Rovigo ro-vee'go
Roye Rwah'
Rozoy-sur-Serre ro-zwa'-sür'-sair'
Rue d'Ouvert doovair'
Rue du Marais marray'
Rzezow zheshoff

Saar (river) zar
Saar-Albe sar-al'beh
Saarbrücken zar-brük'en
Sacile sa-chee'lay
Sadowa-Wisznia sado'va-vish'nya
Saghandere sa-gan-day'reh
Sailly sah-yee'
Saint-Amand san-ta-man'
Saint-Denis san'-de-nee'
Saint Dié san-dee-eh'
Saint-Hilaire santil-lair'
Saint Hubert san-tü-bair'
Saint-Omer san-to-mair'
Saint-Quentin san'-kan-tan'
Saint-Souplet soo-play'
Saint-Trond san'-tron'
St. Dizier san dee-zee-ay'
St. Eloi ell-wa'
St. Goar san go-ar'
St. Gobain san-go-ban'

St. Just-en-Chaussee san-zhost-en-shossay'
St. Laurent san-lorong'
St. Maur san more'
St. Menehould main-ool'
St. Mihiel mee-yel'
St. Pol san-pul
St. Simon san-see-mohng'
St. Stefano san-stef-ah'no
St. Valery san val-er-ee'
St. Venant san-venong'
St. Vito san-vee'to
St. Wendel san ven'del
S. Bonifacio san-bonif-a'chio
S. Giorgio san geor'gio
S. Martino san-mar-tee'no
Salins sal-an'
Salò sa-lo'
Saloniki sa-lo-ni'ki
Salvore sall-vo'reh
Sambre (river) san'br
Santa Maria san'ta ma-ree'ah
Sarajevo sarra-yay'vo
Sarrebourg sarr-boorg'
Sarreguemines sar'-guh-meen'
Save River sah-veh
Saverne sa-vern'
Savieres sah-vee-yair'
Scheldt skelt
Schio skee'o
Schirmeck sher'meek
Schlettstadt shlet'staht
Schoorbakke shore-bak'keh
Scutari (or Skutari) skoo'ta-re
Sedan se-dan'
Seicheprey saish-pray'
Senlis sen-lee'
Seres ser'es
Sereth (river) say-ret'
Sergy ser-zhee'
Seringes ser-anzh'
Sézanne sa-zan'
Siedlce (or Syedlets) shel'tse
Siegen zee'gen
Signy l'Abbaye seen-ye' la-bay'
Sinob (or Sinope) se-nob'
Sinope (or Sinob) si-no'pe
Sissonne see-son'
Sivas see-vas'
Skierniewice skyer'nee-vits
Skoplje (or Usküp) skop'lye
Sofia (or Sophia) so'fee-a; so-fee'a
Soissons swa-son'
Sokolof (or Sokolow) so'ko-lof'

Soldau zol'dow
Solesmes so-laim'
Somme (river, department) som
Souain soon-ang'
Souchez soo-shay'
Steenwoorde steen'wurde
Stettin shte-teen'
Stralsund shtrahl'zoont
Strassburg stras'boork
Stryj stree
Strypa stree'pa
Suippes sweep
Suwalki Province soo'valkee
Swinemünde svee-ne-mün'de
Syedlets (or Siedlce) syed'lyets
Szaki shak'ee
Szcezerzyny shtchet'ser-tseenee

Tabriz ta-breez'
Tagliamento tal-ya-men'toh
Tarcento tar-chen'to
Tarnopol tar-no'pol-y
Tarnoviec tar-no-viets
Tarnow tar'noof
Tchernavoda (or Cernavoda) cher-na-vo'da
Telepovee telepoft'seh
Tepe teh'peh
Termonde (or Dendermonde) ter-mond'
Thann tann'
Thiaucourt tee-o-coor'
Thielt teelt
Thiene tye'nay
Thionville (or Diedenhofen) tyon-veel'
Thuin tu-an'
Tilicz Pass tillish
Tilloy til-wah'
Tintigny tan-tin-yee'
Tirlemont teer-le-mohng'
Tolmezzo tol-met'so
Tomaszow toh-mash'off
Tongres ton'gr
Toul tool
Tourcoing toor-kwang'
Tournai toor-nay'
Toutencourt toot-on-coor'
Tracy trah-see'
Tregnano tray-nyah'no
Trélon tray-lon'
Tresnes tren
Treviso tray-vee'zo
Trier: German for Trèves

Trieste (or Triest) tree-est'
Trou Bricot troo-briko'
Troyes troo-wah'

Udine oo'dee-na
Umago oom-ah'go
Urmiah (or Urmia, Urumiah) oor-mee'a
Usküb (or Usküb, Skoplje) üs-küp'
Ustanov oos-ta'noff
Uzsok ootsok

Valenclennes va-lan-syen'
Valjevo (or Valyevo) val'yay-vo
Varennes va-renn
Vauclerc vo-clair'
Vaudelicourt vodc-li-coor'
Vauquois voh-kwa'
Vaux vo
Veldhoek felt'hook
Venezia (or Venice) vay-net'sya
Venice (or Venezia) ven'is
Venzone ven-zoh'neh
Verdun ver-dun'
Vereczke veresh'keh
Verlorenhoek ferlo'ren-hook
Verona ve-ro'na; It. vay-ro'na
Versailles ver-sah'y; Eng. ver-sailz'
Verviers ver-vi-ay'
Vervins ver-van'
Vicenza vee-chent'sa
Vieux Berquin vyu-ber-kan'
Villafranca veel-la-fran'ka
Ville-en-Tardenois veel-an-tar-duh-nwah'
Ville-en-tourbe veel-ong-toorb'
Villeneuve veel-nuv'
Villers-Bretonneux veeyay-bre-ton-nuh'
Villers-Cotterets veeyay'-cutray'
Villers-la-Ville ve-lair'-la'-veel'
Vimy vee-mee'
Vincelles van-sell'
Violaine vee-olain'
Visé ve-zay'
Visnyvtszyk vis-nift-sheek

Vistula (or Weichsel) vis'tu-la
Vitry - en - Artois vee-tree'-an'-ar-twah'
Vitry-le-François vee-tree'-le-fran-swah'
Vittorio vit-ohr'yoh
Vlamertinghe fla'mer-tin-gay
Volga vol'ga; Russ. vol'ga
Volhynia vol-in'i-a
Volovco volof'tso
Volta vol'ta
Voormezeele vor-mez-eele'
Vosges vohzh'
Vouziers vooz-yea
Vysztyt Lake visktit

Waerloos var'lohs
Warta (or Warthe) var'te
Wassigny va-se-nye'
Wavre vav'r
Weichsel (or Vistula) vike'sel
Weissenburg weis'en-boork
Wieliczka vee'lish-ka
Windhoek vind'hook
Woevre wo-ayvr'
Wola - Szydlowieca vola - sheed - lo-veets'a
Würzburg würts-boork
Wyszkow Pass vish'koff
Wytschaete vite-shah'teh

Yassy (or Jassy) yas'e
Ypres cep'r
Yser ee'zer
Yvoire e-vwar'

Zabern tsah'bern
Zaleszczyki za-lesh-chik'ee
Zamosk (or Zamosc) za'moshch
Zamszysko zam'shees-ko
Zandvoord zant'fort
Zeebrugge zay'broog-geh
Zell zell
Zittau tsit'ou
Zloczów zlo'choof
Zweibrücken zwi'brück-en

INDEX

Administration, criticisms of, 118

Aerial warfare, 260-268

Air, mastery of, by Allies, 312

Aisne, American troops along, 365

Aisne area, German wedge in, 312

Aisne, French attack north of, 47

Aisne, French offensive of October, 1917, 48

Allied counteroffensive, beginning of, 328

Allied opinion of American troops, 393

Allied Powers' attitude toward Pope's proposals, 99

Allied prisoners in May offensive, 310

Allied War Conference, results of, 80

Alsace, French operations in, 56

Alsace, operations in January, 1918, 74

America at Allied War Conference, 77

American army, scope of operations, 81

American artillery near Rheims, 364

American coast, German submarines along, 464

American cooperation with Australians, 399

American cooperation with French, 405

American declaration of war with Austria-Hungary, 105

American engineers at Chauny, 368

American engineers, deeds of, at Cambrai, 94

American expeditionary force in France, 83

American fishing schooners, sinking of, by submarines, 467

American force in the great offensive, 377

American forces in France, 351

American forces on Murman coast, 441

American front, extent of, 373

American front, winter conditions on, 96

American Independence Day, celebration of, by Allies, 321

American losses on sea, 463

American participation in Siberia, 449

American prisoners first taken by Germans, 88

American reenforcement of Allies, 371

American soldiers first killed in battle, 91

American successes at Jaulgonne, 327

American successes at Seicheprey, 360

American successes at Xivray, 364

American successes west of Soissons, 329

American troops, Allied opinion of, 393

American troops, first engagement of, 86

American troops in Italy, 346

American troops, training of, in France, 84, 85

American troops, urgent need of, 82

Amiens, April offensive against, 289

Amiens, German threats against, 274

Amiens-Paris railway, German efforts to capture, 289

Anglo-French forces in Italy, 207

Ansonia, British transport, sinking of, 464

Arabia, campaigns in, 238-240

Arras, operations around, in March, 1918, 281

Artillery, American, work of, at Belleau Wood, 390

Asiago sector, operations in, 213

Australians at Polygon Wood, 40

Australians, defeat Germans at Morlancourt, 304-306

Australians in Flanders, 36

Australian troops, successes of, 320

Austria-Hungary, American declaration of war with, 105

Austrian attitude toward peace, 110

Austrian defense of Russian invasion, 340

Austrian prisoners taken by Italians, 189

Austrian reply to Pope Benedict, 101

Austrian retreat in Italy, 458

Austro-German offensive in Italy, 200-213

Aviators, American, training of, 120

Aviators, French and British, work of, around Lens, 21

Bagdad, operations around, 242

Bailleul, capture of, by Germans, 295

Baker, Secretary, criticism of, 114

Baker, Secretary, statement of performances by, 115

Bapaume, German attacks against, in March, 1918, 280

Bavarian troops, capture of British trenches by, 73

Belgium, British air raids in, 75

Belleau Wood, American marines in, 381, 384

Belleau Wood, description of fighting in, 388

Belleau Wood, German assaults against, 387

Below, General Fritz von, attacks Rheims salient, 317, 379

Below, General Otto von, commanding German seventh army, 273

Bessarabia, annexation to Rumania, 438

Böhm, General, facing French third army, 274

Boehm, General von, commanding German troops on the Marne, 327

Bolsheviki, emergence of, 135

Bolsheviki leaders, characteristics of, 147-153

Bolsheviki negotiations with Germany, 155

Bolsheviki propaganda, attempt to spread, 417

Bolshevist revolution, 142

Bombing raids in Germany, 477

Bouresches, capture of, by American marines, 384

Bouresches, German attempts to retake, 391

Bourlon Wood, British withdrawal from, 67

Bourlon Wood, fighting in, 62

Brest-Litovsk conference, renewal of, 418

Brest-Litovsk negotiations, result of, 420

Brest-Litovsk, peace negotiations at, 163

Brilliant, sunk to block the harbor of Zeebrugge, 470

British assault at Ypres in October, 43

British center, withdrawal of, 293

British counterattacks at Merville, 318

British operation in Flanders in 1917, 30

British successes between Ancre and Somme Rivers, 304

Bullecourt, German operations around, 72

Byng, General Sir Julian, commanding British third army, 273

Cadorna, General, preparations of, 201

Cadorna, General, superseded by Diaz, 209

Cambrai area, German gains in, 66

Cambrai, deeds of American engineers at, 94

Cambrai, fighting around, in March, 1918, 276

Cambrai, operations around, 60

Cambrai salient, German assaults against, 285

Camp conditions, investigation into, 117

Canadians, capture of Passchendaele by, 55

Canadian successes around Lens, 23

Canadian troops at Lens, 10

Cantigny, capture of, by Americans, 374

Carey, General, closes gap before Amiens, 369-371

Carpathia, sinking of, 467

Cattaro, naval mutiny at, 474
Champagne, French activities in, 34
Château-Thierry, American defense of, 380
Château-Thierry, Americans at, 378
Château-Thierry, evacuation of, by Germans, 381
Château-Thierry, German advance upon, 308
Chemin-des-Dames, German assault upon, 307
Chemin-des-Dames, German retreat from, 54
Coal famine in United States, 101
Coblenz, British air raids on, 482
Commodity prices, rise of, 125
Concrete blockhouses, German system fails, 37
Conflans, bombing of, by British airplanes, 477
Congress, war appropriations by, 111
Congressional investigation into camp conditions, 117
Constituent assembly, dissolution of, 183
Cossacks, rebellion of, 160
Council of the Russian Republic, 141
Courtrai, British air raids upon, 479
Czecho-Slovaks in Siberia, 444
Czernin, Count, address on Wilson's peace aims, 109

Daimler motor works, British air raids on, 481
Dead Man Hill, capture of, by France, 26
Democratic Congress in Petrograd, 140
Destroyers, employment of, 120
Diaz, General Armando, American troops under, 346
Diaz, General Armando, Italian commander in chief, 209
Dieterichs, General, 446
Dixmude, German attacks upon, 270
Drafted men, first engagement of, 395
Dukhonin, General, murder of, 160

East Africa, conquest of, 244
Einem, General von, commanding German troops in Champagne, 327

Embargo on neutral exports, 128
Engineers, American, at Chauny, 368
Engineers, American, deeds of, at Cambrai, 94
Epieds, American struggle for, 409
Explosive capsules used by Germans, 14

Fère-en-Tardenois-Buzancy line, fighting along, 338
Finland, agitation for separate Government, 140
Finland, attitude toward the Germans, 401
Finland, German operations in, 431
Finland, relations with Russia, 183
Finnish Government, aims of, 431
First American army corps, 400
Fishing schooners, American, sinking of, by submarines, 467
Fismes, American arrival at, 416
"Flaming bullets," use of, by Germans, 38
Flanders, Franco-British offensive, 9
Flanders, general British offensive in, 46
Flanders, German raids in, March, 1918, 272
Foch, General Ferdinand, appointment as generalissimo, 283
Foch, General Ferdinand, begins counteroffensive, 405
Foch, General Ferdinand, success in counteroffensive, 406
Food administration, campaign of, 127
Food as a war factor, 124
Food control, governmental, 125
Food exports to neutral countries, 128
Food substitutes, 126
Fourteen articles for peace, 106
Franco-British offensive in Flanders, 9
French advance in Flanders in October, 1917, 51
French attack north of the Aisne, 47
French counterattack at St. Quentin, 16
French offensive at Verdun, renewal of, 28
Fresnoy, British air raids upon, 480

Garfield, Harry A., Federal fuel administrator, 131

George, Lloyd, statement in relation to peace, 103

German activities in February, 1918, 269

German advance in Russia, 422

German aggressions in Russia, 429-431

German artillery operations around Cambrai, 71

German assault against American troops, 366

German assaults on American lines, 356

German assaults on the Meuse, 39

German attack in Flanders, 37

German attacks against Americans in Lorraine, 347

German casualties at Seicheprey, 362

German cities bombed by British aviators, 476

German comments on American troops, 89

German counterattacks in Bourlon Wood, 63

German defeat by Americans in Lorraine, 355

German defense, changes in, 21

German defense, weakness of, 44

German destroyers, raid of, 468

German discussion of Wilson's fourteen articles, 106

German evasion of American strength, 400

German loss in great offensive, 303

German losses in October offensive, 44

German losses in retreat across the Marne, 404

German March offensive, results of, 286

German March offensive, second phase of, 284

German offensive around Cambrai, 69

German offensive, checking of, 288

German offensive in Flanders, March, 1918, 273

German offensive, renewal of, 306

German opinion of American troops, 394

German peace terms, acceptance of, by Russia, 425

German prisoners, 330

German prisoners in great British offensive, 62

German prisoners taken at Ypres, 41

German prisoners taken by the French in October offensive, 53

German reenforcements from Russia, 282

German reply to Pope Benedict, 100

German repulse at Lens, 12

German repulse by Americans at Jaulgonae, 379

German retreat, beginning of, 330

German retreat, continuation of, 336

German retreat from Château-Thierry, 381

German retreat to Ourcq River, 335

German reverses west of the Oise, 315

German ships seized by America, 123

German strength at Verdun, 42

German strength in great March offensive, 275

German strength in third offensive, 325

German strength on Franco-British front in November, 1917, 70

German strength on western front in January, 1918, 76

German terms of peace with Russia, 176-179

German third offensive, beginning of, 325

German troops from Russia, 76

German troops in Russia, 422

Germans, hatred of, in Russia, 443

Germans in American uniforms, 411

Gough, General Sir Hubert, commanding British fifth army, 273

Glenart Castle, sinking of, 462

Gouzeaucourt, capture of, by Germans, 65

Governmental control of railroads, 133

Greece, conditions in, 247

Guynemer, George, death of, 39

Haig, Field Marshal, attacks east of Ypres, 35, 40

Haig, Field Marshal, strikes at Ypres, 43

Haig, Field Marshal, begins offensive on Flanders front, 46
Hamel, capture of, by Australians, 321
Hangard, fighting around, 296
Havrincourt, capture of, by British, 60
Hedjaz, revolt in, 240-242
Hertling, Count von, address before Reichstag, 106
Hill 204, capture of, by Americans, 401
Hill 304, capture of, by French, 28
Hindenburg line, British offensive against, 58
Hoover, Herbert C., 125
Horne, General Sir Henry, commanding British first army, 273
Horvath, General, 447
House, Edward M., at Allied War Conference, 77
Humbert, General, commanding French third army, 274
Hutier, General von, 321

Indian scouts, with Pershing on the Marne, 331
Industries, closing of, to conserve coal, 131
"Infiltration" of troops, employment of, 401
Inter-Allied Naval Council, 81
Intrepid, sunk to block the harbor of Zeebrugge, 470
Iphigenia, sunk to block the harbor of Zeebrugge, 470
Irkutsk, capture of, by Allies, 446
Italian offensive, 456
Italian offensive in August, 1917, 188
Italian successes, 192
Italy, American troops in, 346
Italy, Austrian retreat in, 458
Italy, Austro-German offensive in, 200-213
Italy, revival of military strength, 450

Japan, action of, in Siberia, 432
Jerusalem, capture of, 223-232

Kaiser William on Ukraine peace, 339
Kaledine, General, 139
Kato, Admiral, Japan, proclamation of, 433

Kattegat, British naval raid on, 470
Kawachi, Japanese battleship, sinking of, 468
Kerensky, beginning of downfall, 137
Kerensky, efforts to revive Russian army, 134
Kerensky, flight from Petrograd, 146
Keyes, Vice Admiral, commanding raids at Zeebrugge and Ostend, 470
Kornilov, General, rebellion against Soviets, 435
Kornilov, General, rebellion of, 137
Kornilov, General, speech of, 136

La Bassée Canal, German attacks against, 290
Lake Moor, sinking of, 463
Lancashire troops, performances of, 58
Langemarck, capture of, by Allies, 19
Lansdowne, Marquis of, efforts toward peace, 101
Lenine, declaration on peace, 154
Lenine, Nikolai, 148-155
Lens, British success at, 13
Lens, Canadian successes at, 32
Lens, result of German bombardment of, 18
Liberty Loan, second, 112-113
Liggett, General Hunter, commands first army corps, 400
Liquid fire, employment of, against Americans, 350
Livonia, German attitude toward, 439
Loos, British bombardment of, 17
Lorraine, American operations in, 347
Lorraine, American successes in, 351
Lorraine front, occupation of, by Americans, 358
Ludendorff, General, plans new German offensive, 305
Luneville, American operations around, 352
Lys region, fighting in, 297

McAdoo, Wm. G., appointed Director General of Railroads, 131
Machine gunners, German, in Epieds Forest, 411
Mainz, British air raids upon, 481
Malmaison Plateau, capture of, by French, 48

Marine Corps, exploits of, 395
Marines, American, success in Belleau Wood, 384
Marne, American sortie across, 391
Marne, crossing of, by Americans, 407
Marne, crossing of, by Germans, 327, 402
Marne, French counterattack on, 406
Marne, German advance along, 310
Marne, new battle of the, 325
Marne, recrossing of, by Germans, 404
Marne salient, German strength in, 333
Marwitz, General von der, commanding German second army, 273
Massed formation, employment of, by Germans, 65
Matz, French retreat along, 313
Menin, British air raids upon, 480
Messines Ridge, attempts of Germans to capture, 293
Meuse, French lines on, 30
Milne, General G. F., commanding British troops in the Balkans, 245-246
Minnetonka, steamship, sinking of, 462
Mirbach, General Count von, assassination of, 442
Moldavia, transport, sinking of, 464
Montdidier, French successes at, 1918, 314
Montdidier, German successes around, in June, 1918, 312
Montdidier, operations around, in March, 1918, 283
Monte di Val Bella, capture of, 458
Monte Santo, capture of, 187
Mont Kemmel, assault against, by Germans, 300
Moreuil, operations around, 287
Murman coast, American forces on, 441
Murman Peninsula, German desire to seize, 439

National army, training of, 116
Naval Conference, Inter-Allied, 81
Naval engagements, 468
Navy, expansion of, 119

Neutral countries and food exports, 128
Neutral shipping, submarine destruction of, 463
Neutral vessels in American ports, 128
Neuve Eglise, capture of, by Germans, 294
Nicholas II, murder of, 447
Nieuport sector, artillery operations in, 75
Norwegian marine, losses of, by submarines, 463

O. B. Jennings, sinking of, 466
Oise, operations along, 308
Ostend Harbor, blocking of, 473
Ourcq, French and American successes along, 332

Palestine, campaign in, 214-238
Passchendaele-Gheluvelt Ridge, capture of, by British, 43
Peace efforts of Pope Benedict, 97
Peace move of Bolsheviki, 153
Peace negotiations of Bolsheviki and Germany, 156, 157
Péronne, operations around, in March offensive, 278
Pershing, General John J., announces Americans in the trenches, 85
Pershing, General, message of, to War Department, 368, 369
Pershing, General, offers American troops to Foch, 346
Pershing, General, report of, on Belleau Wood, 387
Pershing, General, report of, on Cantigny, 376
Petain, General, reputation of, 284
Petain, General, receives American reenforcements, 327
Petain, General, troops of, in Picardy, 324
Petrograd Council, reaction in, 139
Piave, Italian halt at, 208, 209
Picardy battle, American operations in, 372
Poison gas, employment of, by British, 35
Pope Benedict, efforts at peace, 97
Pope Benedict, reply of Wilson to, 99

Portuguese troops, performances of, 291

President Grant, sinking of, 463

President Lincoln, sinking of, 464

Prices, increase in, 125

Prisoners, Allied, in great German offensive, 277

Prussian Guards, defeat of, by Americans, 412

Railroads, American condition of, 133

Railway construction, American, in France, 344

Rawlinson, General, praises American engineers, 369

Remières Wood, capture of, by Americans, 361

Rheims, attacks of Germans around, 57

Rheims, German attack upon, 317

Roye, capture of, 280

Rumania, conditions in, 250-252

Russia, German advance in, 436

Russia, German peace with, 420

Russia, National Conference in, 135

Russia, refusal of Central Powers to withdraw from, 419

Russia, result of collapse of, on German forces, 76

Russian constituent assembly, failure of, 168

Russian counter-revolution, attempt at, 165-168

Russian Grand Dukes, arrest of, 137

Russian hatred of Germans, 443

Russian peace terms with Germany, 424

Russian peace treaty, divisions of, 426

Russian peace treaty, ratification of, 428

Russian state documents, secret, publication of, 158

Russian surrender to Germany, 423

Russian territory taken by Germans, 426

Saarbrücken, British air raids on, 50

St. Gobain Forest, German assault against, 76

St. Mihiel salient, American operations in, 349

San Diego, American cruiser, sinking of, 468

Sarrail, General, commanding Allied troops in the Balkans, 245, 246

Scherpenberg, assaults of Germans against, 302

Second Liberty Loan, 112, 113

Seicheprey, American losses at, 362

Seicheprey, attack on Americans at, 359

Seicheprey region, fighting in, 318

Sergy, capture of, by Americans, 413

Sergy, fighting around, 337

Seringes, capture of, by Americans, 414

Shipping Board, performances of, 122

Shipping, investigation of, 121

Siberia, American attitude to Japanese intervention in, 433

Siberia, American participation in, 449

Siberian Government proclaimed, 447

Skoropadsky, Hetman of Ukrainia, 436

Sneezing powder, use of, by Germans, 305

Soissons, French successes around, 322

Soissons, operations around, 311

Soissons-Rheims salient, Allied progress in, 332

Somme, British retreat from, 285

Sophia, Queen of Greece, intrigues of, 248

Soviets, President Wilson's message to, 428

Spanish losses at sea, 462

Stuttgart, British air raids on, 481

Submarine blockade, results of, 460

Submarines destroyed by U. S. naval vessels, 467

Submarines, German operations of, 253-256

Supreme war council, 81

"Tanks," employment of, by British, 59

Tanks, first employment of, by Germans, 298

Thetis, sunk to block the harbor of Zeebrugge, 470

Third French army, operations of, 274

Titles, abolition of, in Russia, 169

Tonale region, operations in, 456

Torcy, capture of, by Americans, 382

Toul sector, American operations in, 353, 354

Trench fighting, first American experience in, 88

Trentino, operations along, 191

Treves, bombing of, by British airplanes, 477

Trotzky, Leon, beginning of power, 141, 142

Trotzky, Leon, career of, 152

Trotzky, Leon, denunciation of German imperialism, 419

Trugny, American struggle for, 409

Tuscania, sinking of, 461

Udine, capture of, by Austrians, 206

Ukraine, agitation for separate government, 140

Ukraine, independence of, 161

Ukrainia, conditions in, 185

Ukrainia, German policy in, 418

Ukrainia, invasion of, by Germans, 429

Ukrainia, martial law in, 435

United States, dependence on, by Allies, 77

United States military railroad in France, 344

Vaux, capture of, by Americans, 319, 397

Vaux, German counterattacks at, 398

Verdun, French gains at, 25

Verdun, German assaults upon, 22, 23

Verdun, German attacks northwest of, 52

Villers-Bretonneux, capture of, by British, 299

Villers-Cotterets Wood, French successes in, 319

Vindictive, in raids at Zeebrugge and Ostend, 473

Vladivostok, o c c u p a t i o n o f, by Czecho-Slovaks, 446

War aims of Allies, restatement of, 102

War appropriations by Congress, 111

War Department performances, 119

Weather conditions on western front, 72

Westhoek Ridge, German assaults upon, 15

Wheat requirements of Allies, 127

Wien, Austrian battleship, sinking of, 468

Wilson, President, address of, April, 1918, 349

Wilson, President, address to Congress on peace, 103

Wilson, President, message to Russian Soviets, 428

Wilson, President, reply to Pope Benedict, 99

Wolf, German cruiser, vessels destroyed by, 468

Xivray, German attack upon, 363

Ypres, bombardment of, by Germans, 301

Ypres, British attack around, 35

Ypres, British retirement from, 297

Ypres-Commines Canal, German attacks on, 12

Ypres-Menin road, British lose ground on, 37

Ypres-Menin road, operations around, 29

Zeebrugge Harbor, blocking of, 470-473

DATE DUE